IN THE LAND OF BELIEVERS

IN THE LAND OF
BELIEVERS

An Outsider's Extraordinary
Journey into the Heart of the
Evangelical Church

Gina Welch

METROPOLITAN BOOKS
HENRY HOLT AND COMPANY
NEW YORK

Metropolitan Books
Henry Holt and Company, LLC
Publishers since 1866
175 Fifth Avenue
New York, New York 10010
www.henryholt.com

Metropolitan Books® and ⅢⅢ® are registered trademarks of
Henry Holt and Company, LLC.

This book is the true story of my involvement with Jerry Falwell's church.
Except for the names of certain public figures, I have changed the names of the church members
I met to protect their privacy.

Library of Congress Cataloging-in-Publication Data

Welch, Gina.
   In the land of believers : an outsider's extraordinary journey into the heart of the evangelical
church / Gina Welch.—1st ed.
      p. cm.
   ISBN 978-0-8050-8337-8
   1. Evangelicalism—United States.   I. Title.
   BR1642.U5W435 2009
   277.3'083—dc22   2009030677

Henry Holt books are available for special promotions and premiums.
For details contact: Director, Special Markets.

First Edition 2010
Designed by Meryl Sussman Levavi
Printed in the United States of America
1   3   5   7   9   10   8   6   4   2

For my mother

Neither do men light a candle, and put it under a

bushel, but on a candlestick;

and it giveth light unto all that are in the house.

—MATTHEW 5:15

CONTENTS

———

SALT AND LIGHT

IN THE LAND OF BELIEVERS

INTRODUCTION

—

B EYOND THE ENTRANCE COLUMNS OF JERRY FALWELL'S THOMAS
Road Baptist Church, beyond the lobby's lake of dark marble, down
past the cavernous sanctuary and The Lion and Lamb Café, deep into the
linoleum warren of offices, closets, and classrooms, I am sitting under
buzzing fluorescent lights, facing a blank dry-erase board, waiting for my
evangelism class to begin. This class is one of dozens of groups being
kicked off across church that night, with titles ranging from "Money Management" and "Wise Guys Bible Study" to "Classic Car Restoration" and
"The Biggest Loser." I wonder where the people I know from church are,
having guessed some of them might want to try the evangelism class. My
two classmates—a stout, heavy-lidded man challenging the seam strength
of his button-down and suspenders, and a toothless fellow wearing a
T-shirt on which an eagle is swooping down over the American flag—are
discussing good places to plant a new church.

"Would you go where people are out drinking beer in the street, to
the impoverished neighborhoods that need Christ," the man in suspenders asks, "or would you go where the rich people are?"

The toothless man rubs his whiskered chin. "I surely don't know.
What about Canada?"

Just as I consider picking up my things and popping into "Cake Decorating" down the hall, a bald, guided missile of a man strides into the
room and begins squeaking a pen across the dry-erase board. I know
who this man is, although I hadn't realized he would be teaching the
class. He is the lead pastor in EPIC, the church Singles Ministry, and he

frequently gives prayers during Sunday's main church service. He is a military something-or-other, and I remember that Jerry Falwell had once joked that he had "left his toupee in Iraq." He is bronzed, mid-forties, with tiny, glinting eyes and a white, bristled goatee. Embroidered in gold thread on his fleece jacket are the letters TRBC. *"100% Effective Evangelism,"* he writes, *"has moved to Dr. Falwell's conference room."* He turns to us.

"I'm Ray Fletcher," he says in a banjo twang. "We're going to go on a long walk."

IF YOU KNEW ME, you would think I had no business being in Jerry Falwell's conference room. Falwell and I weren't even in the same ideological atmosphere. Beyond our citizenship, our native tongue, and the basic biological processes of being human, we shared almost nothing. I considered him a homophobe, a fearmonger, a manipulator, and a misogynist—an alien creature from the most extreme backwater of evangelical culture.

I could probably guess what Falwell would have thought of me. I am a secular Jew raised by a single mother in Berkeley, where we took a day off school in October for Indigenous Peoples, not for Christopher Columbus. I cuss, I drink, and I am not a virgin. I have never believed in God. One day when I was in first grade, my mother received a call from my school asking her to pick me up. Out on the playground, classmates had begun shoving me when I told them there was no Santa and no God. The principal wanted me off the premises for the rest of the day.

Several years later, I was at an overnight summer camp, annoyed that counselors made me endure suppertime prayers and services on Sunday. The rituals were nondenominational, but at ten years old I had anointed myself as a hardened little atheist and I dug my claws against being drafted into religious worship, of any kind. I wrote to my father, a member of the Revolutionary Communist Party, and appealed for sympathy.

"Hello Happy Camper!" my father wrote in his reply. "Don't worry about saying grace. It probably won't ruin your appetite. Just put your hands together and mumble under your breath, THERE IS NO GOD. The world is complicated enough to figure out without always explaining things by saying some big white dude up in the clouds is responsible. Religion is really something that belongs in the museums."

What little I had learned about the evangelical Christian macrocosm always seemed that way to me—like some inscrutable artifact from a civilization long vanished. For the better part of my life I felt comfortable not understanding its mysteries. Our orbits were simply so different, so remote from one another, that I could safely forget Evangelicals existed.

When I relocated from California to Virginia for graduate school in 2002, I thought of my move as a kind of elaborate performance art project. Citified, punk-rock, atheist me, with a Billy Idol haircut and a soft spot for Dennis Kucinich, living in the Christian South. And I treated the South like a joke for a while, ironically eating barbecue in smoke-hazed roadside joints, ironically staggering through the funhouse at the state fair, ironically wearing gingham checks. I thought it was all very funny. I'd even cultivated a pretty canny impersonation of wholesome southerners, or so I thought. One night, a classmate raised in Texas and South Carolina said to me, hard fibers of irritation in her voice, "Whenever you use that accent, you make southerners sound really stupid."

So she didn't think it was funny? In all my flush-cheeked pride about being from open-minded, openhearted, open-zippered Northern California, I'd never considered that I was hermetically prejudiced against the very people I'd chosen to live among.

And the weird thing was, I was starting to like Virginia. It was a fascinating transition state: rich with the concentrated, complicated essence of the Old South but invigorated by the progressive pockets around universities and growing cities. Virginia wouldn't go for Barack Obama until six years after I'd moved there, but you could feel the tectonic plates groaning underfoot. And I liked much of the Old South essence, too: people were so nice and easygoing, so garrulous, willing to cast out a spreading quilt of narrative over the deli counter. Friendliness wasn't so bad, and neither were unpretentiousness, slow-motion summers, unpillaged antiques shops selling homemade preserves at the register, or cicadas buzzing the dark trees around a dimly lit front porch.

Acclimating to southern culture, I gradually relinquished my idiotic notion that a southern accent made people sound stupid. To my surprise, I stopped living ironically in the South and just started living there. But confronting the Christian issue was another matter.

In the years following my move, evangelical culture became ever more influential. Evangelicals were instrumental in securing George W. Bush's second term in office; there was perpetual news coverage of enormous evangelical churches; and enormous Christian universities were busy shaping leaders to shape policy. Rick Warren's evangelical mission statement, *A Purpose-Driven Life,* had sold around 25 million copies, Tim LaHaye and Jerry Jenkins had sold 65 million books in the *Left Behind* series, and 2004's *The Passion of the Christ* became the ninth-biggest box office moneymaker ever, ahead of *Jurassic Park.* How had the evangelical phenomenon grown so large so fast?

My personal experience recognizing evangelicalism's power was like something out of a science-fiction movie. I had thought I was on holiday from secular America in the quaint biodome of the South, when suddenly secular America was revealed as the biodome, limited real estate on the vast territory controlled by Christians, who were so organized. Worse, Christians seemed to want to declare an end to the secular experiment. They thought our values were debased, our entertainment vulgar, and our politics corrupt and out of touch. Cleverly, they claimed they were the revolutionaries—pointing to the mainstream war on Christmas, the dominating liberal media, the systemic persecution of the faithful—and that they were here to restore America to purity.

I nourished my fear on the fleet of books by liberals out to dissect the evangelical body politic. They warned of a generation of Christians groomed to trundle Trojan horses of ideology into media, culture, and politics. The apparent tug-of-war between Red State Christians and Blue State liberals consumed the punditry. The popular documentary *Jesus Camp* introduced a shocked audience to the indoctrination and emotional manipulation of children by a Pentecostal zealot in North Dakota. Articles on Christian wackiness on the *New York Times* website frequently shot to the top of the "Most Emailed" list and lingered there for days.

Newly alert, I vacuumed up information about Evangelicals, feeling it was necessary to educate myself about my host country. And yet the more I learned, the less I understood. My anthropological inquiries lit up only the most alarming fragments of the evangelical picture, turning up the contrast and blacking out the relatable qualities. They were shrill and prudish, they loved bad music and guns and NASCAR, told corny jokes and spoke in sound bites, were unshakably loyal to exposed liars, and their children were going to bully our children into prayer.

They were scary, all right, but they didn't seem quite real, and I hadn't seen anyone who matched that description around Virginia—

even though about a third of the state is born again. I wanted to know what my evangelical neighbors were like as people, unfiltered and off the record, not as the subjects of interviews conducted by the "liberal media." I wanted to try to take them on their own terms. Who, exactly, did they think they were? Why were they so determined to convert non-Christian America? And how were they going about it?

I decided to do something radical: I decided to go undercover at Jerry Falwell's Thomas Road Baptist Church in Lynchburg, Virginia.

Going undercover seemed like the only way to access the truth about the other side. Evangelicals were so suspicious of the "liberal mainstream media," so schooled in image management, branding, and talking points that I felt I needed to go unnoticed if I was going to get an authentic understanding. They needed to know the microphone was off. I'd do whatever it took to get the story. When I began, I thought this meant I would have to mimic the rituals, recite the songs, and ape the dialect. A long time passed before I understood that there was something serious behind the gloss, that there was meaning behind the music and minds behind the slogans.

IN THE FALL OF 2005, Thomas Road Baptist Church was preparing to move out of the humble cluster of buildings in which it had been worshipping since a twenty-two-year-old Jerry Falwell established his ministry in an old Donald Duck cola bottling plant. On Thomas Road's fiftieth anniversary—July 2, 2006—the new church was scheduled to open next door to Falwell's Liberty University in a large network of buildings formerly occupied by Ericsson Telecommunications.

On the national scene, Falwell was a star guttering out. In the twilight of the Carter presidency—a disappointment for Evangelicals who had imagined they'd have a Christian brother in the Oval Office—Falwell founded the Moral Majority, galvanized by theologian Francis Schaeffer's suggestion that evangelical Christians could be herded into a conveniently unified voting bloc. Instrumental in securing Ronald Reagan's election, the Moral Majority solidified that bloc, and Falwell rose to national prominence as a controversy-courter and a culture warrior. But in the mid-2000s, the Moral Majority had long since dissolved, and Falwell was better known for his laughable jeremiad against Teletubby Tinky Winky and his hateful ascription of blame for 9/11 to the gay community, feminists, and abortion doctors.

In spite of his reputation, he remained a force among Evangelicals and claimed to have a standing weekly telephone call with President Bush. Politicians wooing the evangelical vote still regarded appearances at Thomas Road and Liberty University as mandatory—John McCain delivered the 2006 commencement address at Liberty (despite the fact that in 2000 he had labeled Jerry Falwell an "agent of intolerance"), and Mike Huckabee, emerging victorious from wins in seven state primaries during his own presidential bid, told Jerry Falwell Jr. on a second visit to Thomas Road that he wasn't "sure we would be here had you not had the courage and convictions to stand with us."

Regionally, church membership was in the thousands and growing and Liberty University was fast becoming what the founder had hoped it would be: a Brigham Young University for Evangelicals.

These factors positioned Thomas Road at the very center of a great transition that Christian America was negotiating: becoming modern and inclusive without sacrificing bedrock ideals. Because the church itself was a repository for the phantoms of fifty years of evangelical history, and—with the new mega-sanctuary and a flourishing university—a cradle of possibilities, being down in little Lynchburg, Virginia, was like being in the engine room of a great ship, which was sprinting into the future.

THE RABBIT HOLE

THE PART OF YOU
THAT'S YOU FOREVER

—

WHEN I BEGAN AT THOMAS ROAD IN THE FALL OF 2005, I WAS more worried about telegraphing a plausibly conservative image than I was about the scruples of telegraphing at all. It wasn't that I had zero misgivings about going undercover—I did meditate on the wrongness of lying and the string of betrayals my project would likely leave behind—it was that I sort of managed to balance the whole messy moral equation on an unsteady ball bearing of cliché: *You have to break some eggs to make an omelette.* The collateral damage of going undercover, I thought, was mitigated by the possibility that the enterprise would open channels of understanding writ large between Evangelicals and the rest of us. I saw myself as an armchair anthropologist, mapping the evangelical culture; as reality TV troublemakers put it, I hadn't come to make friends.

I defended this blithe attitude vigorously to myself, and it hardened into the carapace that allowed me to arrive in Lynchburg with confidence. I never expected to outgrow it.

INITIALLY, IT DIDN'T OCCUR to me that to become a member of Thomas Road I could just start showing up at church on Sunday, get talking to people and listen to the sermons. I didn't know that no one needed to invite me and I didn't have to be a Christian. In fact, this is the way many people eventually become Christians: you go and you go and you go and then one day a new panel in your brain illuminates, lighting up the once-inscrutable Gospel message, making it gleam with instant, permanent truth. I had no idea that this is part of the purpose of Sunday morning: win the lost.

I thought I had to be the subject of some kind of targeted evangelism effort to plausibly appear at church. So after doing a little research on the Thomas Road Baptist Church website, I decided to attend an evangelism event called Scaremare. It was several steps short of full-fledged church attendance, and here, I figured, I could force the epiphany that would lead me to Sunday services.

Scaremare is a "hell house," a haunted house run by Christians capitalizing on Halloween's spook appeal to draw in secular audiences, terrorize them with slasher scenes and then offer them the opportunity to repent and get saved. There are other, more notorious Christian hell houses, designed to erase the visitor's perceived line between horror and hell, between fear and godlessness. These hell houses stage actual sin and damnation—dramatizing botched abortions using meat from butcher shops. Hell itself is often dramatized, evoked by foul odors, a heated room, and an encore performance by sinners now suffering under the cloven hooves of demons. One of the most prominent hell houses is run by Bloomfield, Colorado, pastor Keenan Roberts, who justifies the extremity this way: "Sometimes you have got to shake 'em to wake 'em."

Scaremare is the original hell house, started at Liberty University in 1972. Though it too is intended to "shake 'em awake," the enormity of its popularity in central Virginia is due to the fact that it can be enjoyed on a more basic level: the simple pleasure of being scared witless. The house opens at dusk for six nights in October, and Liberty reports around 20,000 visitors pass through each year.

I had read that in past years Liberty had staged Scaremare at horror-friendly locations like abandoned orphanages and hospitals. This year Scaremare was being held in a boarded-up brick building at the wooded edge of a soccer field. It was rumored to have been some kind of spooky abandoned tobacco storage house where someone may or may not have died at some point.

My visit to Scaremare was my second trip ever to Lynchburg. I was living two hours away, in Richmond, but before that I had lived an hour to the north in Charlottesville for three years as a graduate student and teacher. For most of that time all I knew of Lynchburg was what I had heard: it was a place with good thrift stores and lots of Jesus people. I had the opportunity to see for myself in November 2004, during the run-up to the presidential election, when I signed on to canvass for John Kerry in Lynchburg. On that trip I learned there was a dilapidated corner of town where demented-looking mutts prowled the streets uncollared and eviction notices stickered doors and windows. Almost everyone I met was going for Kerry.

This second trip was to be very different. To prepare to meet the Jesus people, I felt I had to forgo my usual tight jeans and T-shirt-with-the-neck-slashed-out and dress like somebody else. I put on boot-cut jeans and pearl earrings, a bulky sweater and a khaki jacket. I told myself I would fake it if I must, but that I would try very hard to be open to changing my life, believe the Gospel message, to be struck by the truth that Jesus died for my sins. A Charlottesville friend marveled that this was like "forcing yourself to go insane," which should have clued me in to the impossibility of plotting to believe in something I distinctly did not. But by showing up in a sort of costume—stuffing another layer of distance between myself and Christians—I was preventing the likelihood of a real awakening. I was eavesdropping, not listening.

THE NIGHT I WENT the line for Scaremare was a hardship line, the kind people wait in for something they can't live without—three and four abreast, leading away from the house under a series of canopies and through switchbacks up a hill, and then all around the soccer field. I got there at 11 p.m. and was one of the last to enter—a police officer closed the entrance gate shortly after I passed through.

A small movie screen stood in one corner of the soccer field to distract the crowd from the long wait. They were showing M. Night Shyamalan's *The Village*, to set a spooky mood, I guess. The movie was about a community of settlers living in a clearing, surrounded by a forest infested with dangerous beasts. The perimeter of their settlement is complexly booby-trapped so that any intruders will be instantly discovered. The settlers' peasant rags and stilted diction suggest that the movie is set sometime in the eighteenth century. But at the film's end, we find out that these pioneers are actually plain old late-twentieth-century Americans, so alienated by the lawlessness and vulgarity of modern life that they decide to wind back the clock, exiling themselves on a wild slab of private property, reinventing life without trade, without technology, and—most curious—without people of color.

I thought the movie was a pretty nifty metaphor for the self-segregation of evangelical Christians. I had read a theory that the modern evangelical megachurch was meant to serve as an alternative to traditional secular communities, and that the desire for such an alternative had its genesis in the legacy of the Scopes trial, which opened up a chasm between creationists and evolutionists. After Scopes, Christians began to perceive they were being ridiculed as Philistines; add to that shame confrontation with a culture increasingly permissive of the Seven Deadlies, the theory went, and it was easy to see why Evangelicals found it necessary to build higher walls.

As I fell in line behind three sweatshirted Liberty boys, the leading lady in *The Village*—on a mission through the woods to get medicine for her fiancé—was shoving a beast into a ditch.

"See, that's why I love this movie," one of the boys ahead of me in line said. "She's so dedicated. She's doing all this for her dude."

His friend, features shadowed under a white Liberty cap, noticed me smiling at this observation and asked if I was a Liberty student. I told him no, that I had gone to UVA for graduate school but now lived in Richmond.

"We killed your guys' golf team last week," said the first boy.

These boys weren't local either—they had come to Liberty from New Jersey, South Carolina, and West Virginia. Tonight was the university's night at Scaremare, they said, so I should go through with them for a discount. I was surprised: first that there were any Liberty students from the Northeast, more so that these guys—who exuded a warm, boozy odor, smoked cigarettes, and suggested I falsely present myself as one of them—were evangelical Christians.

They asked why I had come alone, so I told them a friend in Charlottesville had recommended Scaremare but didn't feel like going again. This was half true: my friend had told me about Scaremare but she had never attended and I didn't invite her along for fear she'd accidentally give me away.

"That's so awesome," the boy in the cap said. He and his friends were nodding and grinning at me intently, seemingly transfixed by my dull answer. I turned my back to watch the end of *The Village*. I wasn't nervous they were going to whip out their Bibles—I thought I was prepared for that. It was more that I was suddenly pierced with the fear that one of them was going to ask me out.

The line moved forward almost imperceptibly. One of the boys ran across the soccer field and down the hill to buy kettle corn from a food trailer. People waiting formed circles, wrapped their arms around each other, and jumped up and down for warmth. In the distance, a chainsaw rumbled every few minutes from the vicinity of the boarded-up brick building, and a glowing white tent periodically released figures into the night.

After *The Village*'s final credits rolled, a short film made by Liberty students played. It opened on a blond college kid relaxing at his desk, chatting on the phone. "It's going to be a sweet party, dude," he says into the receiver.

When the kid gets off the phone and stands up to leave for the sweet party, there is a knock at the door. He opens it to find a boy in a collared blue shirt and khakis, a soft smile curving below his dewy cheeks.

"Hey, Jesus, come on in," the kid says.

Jesus enters without saying a word.

The kid tries to urge Jesus over to the TV—"You want to play a video game?" But Jesus just stands there, looking at him.

The kid sits Jesus down on the couch and offers him a Bible as I might offer a beer, saying he'll be back later, at one or two in the morning. It seems as if they have been through this routine before.

As the kid opens the door to leave, Jesus rises from the couch and moves toward him, still silent. The kid slams the door. "I don't want you following me everywhere I go," he says, approaching Jesus. "I don't want you in every part of my life. You have to stay here." As he speaks, he backs Jesus against a wall. "Stay here!" The kid lifts Jesus' arms and begins to slowly drive imaginary nails into his hands with an imaginary hammer. "Stay here!" When he finishes crucifying Jesus on the wall of his dorm, he stalks off to his party. Jesus' head lolls on his chest. The end.

Poor Jesus. Perhaps, I thought, using his power to see into the future, Jesus knew that the boy was going to get into a fatal car accident and wanted to protect him. Perhaps he just wanted to be invited to the party, too? In any event, he seemed to have the boy's best interests in mind, which made him come across in this representation as a kind of unappreciated dad. In that way, this film seemed aimed at those who already had a relationship with Jesus—someone has to be in your life before you can undervalue him. The boy from the film knew Jesus well enough to express no surprise at finding him in the hallway outside his dorm room.

A family that had negotiated their way through the closed entrance gate noisily got in line behind me. Less wary now with other people nearby, I tried to strike up a conversation again with the Liberty boys. The one in the white cap—the rest, at this point, no longer seemed interested in talking to me—said he'd just transferred to Liberty from the Citadel. I asked if he had wanted to be in the military.

"No," he said. "The Citadel is a really good school. I didn't want to go to a party school." I nodded, and suddenly realized that I hadn't smelled booze on them at all. It was simply cologne.

The boy—Randall—pointed out that I was very tall but somehow still attractive, and he suggested we exchange information before leaving so that he could take me to his favorite steakhouse in Richmond. I told him I had a boyfriend. Randall nodded and asked me where my boyfriend was. I said that he was a musician and was working in the studio and couldn't come. "If you were my girlfriend," he said, "I wouldn't let you wait by yourself in line all night."

Then he turned around and didn't speak for a long time. Echoes of his words passed through me like sonar waves; I felt warmed and impressed by his chivalry.

The line went on and on. A cop came by and told us some people had waited for six hours that day. Up ahead, a pizza trailer collapsed its awning and drove away. The teenage girls behind me took cell phone pictures of each other for something to do. Finally, Randall asked me if I'd ever been to one of these before.

"No," I said.

He said, "At the end they try to take you in a room and talk to you about the Gospel." I nodded. "You don't need someone to talk to you about the Gospel, do you?"

I couldn't read his tone. "I don't know," I said, wondering if I could work up the nerve to get religious right there on the soccer field should he start witnessing.

"Well, don't worry," Randall said. "I'm not going to do it. There are some people who feel like they have to shove it down your throat, but I'm not like that."

Randall wasn't the arrogant jock I had assumed he would be. I liked him. And liking Randall became the windowbox for my first seeds of guilt: I hadn't been honest with him about why I was there and yes, I probably did need someone to talk to me about the Gospel.

Off to our left was the dark brick building we were waiting to enter, the tobacco house. With its windows boarded up it was sufficiently menacing.

After we paid at the ticket window we were herded into a brightly lit army tent. At the far end of the tent, Scaremare workers periodically waved groups through a heavy black curtain. After a few minutes, a person wearing a white mask and a black jheri-curled wig appeared on a television monitor in the corner of the tent, dispensing the Scaremare rules in a voice so slow it was as if his words were glued to his tongue. "Turn off your cell phone. Don't touch anything in Scaremare. Don't touch anyone in Scaremare. No smoking. If you're claustrophobic or have a heart condition, turn back now." After hours of waiting, it seemed a little late for that last slip of advice.

The Liberty boys and I were the last group of the night, passing through the curtain at 2 a.m. I wondered if I—or anyone else, for that matter—would have the energy to accept Christ at the end of the tour.

Randall held the curtain open for me. We were briefly outside again in the sting of night, stalled between the army tent and another curtain, and then we plunged through it into a corrugated steel tunnel, so pitch black I felt vertigo. Thrusting my hands in front of me, I teetered along what seemed to be planks of plywood on the floor of the tunnel. After a moment, I could hear some girls behind me, their squeals amplified by the metal walls. I thought back to the warning about claustrophobia and heart conditions and I wondered how far they were going to go to scare God into us. I mean, was I actually in danger? Would the ground drop away beneath my feet? Would I be separated from Randall, whom I suddenly felt was the only person looking out for me?

I crouched over and lurched forward, Quasimodo-style. After a minute or so of this, I emerged through another curtain into woods, where I hustled to keep up with the Liberty boys as zombies sprang from the bushes and hissed in my ear. We curved a U through the woods, the girls shrieking freely behind us, up toward the tobacco house. We passed a man maniacally swinging a chainsaw, followed a black tarp hanging along the side of the house—cringing at the roars and screams muffled by its walls—and came to the entrance to another metal tunnel. Here the floor planks were wet and canted downward so steeply I found myself wishing for cleated shoes.

Skidding along, it occurred to me that so far this haunted house was designed to deliver me into the arms of a very particular God. If at the end of our torturous little adventure I was supposed to be beaten-down, vulnerable, desperate for salvation (I was sort of feeling that way already), yearning for something to put out the fires of dread; if I was supposed to fear God's absence more than his presence, then it was unlikely I was sliding into the wrathful fist of judgment. Instead, I would be nestling in the palm of a warmer, cuddlier God—the kind who loved me and delivered touchdowns to my home team.

The tunnel dumped us out in a flagstone courtyard in front of the tobacco house, where zombies milled about a stone fountain filled with blood. We entered the house.

The first room was a yellow-lit parlor, where lifelike mannequins in nightgowns swung from nooses along one wall, and several girls in Victorian dress screamed from their seats, their hair and faces clotted with blood. A boy in a suit churned around the room, laughing menacingly, as if delighted by their pain.

Passing another room patrolled by zombies, we entered a pitch-black hallway. The hall was so narrow that as you walked you could easily run your hands along the walls to find where it turned. Nevertheless I found myself crashing face-first into plaster. The girl behind me kept slamming into me and screaming, "Who is that?" Each time I assured her, ow, it was still me, and we'd walk awhile with her hand clutching at my shoulder.

Zombies leapt out from around corners. Sometimes the floor of the hall would tilt, leaning me into the wall. I kept sensing that something was going to come down and chop off my head. In places, the hallway narrowed so much that I had to turn sideways to pass through it. I thought of suggesting that Scaremare append a warning to its orientation video that visitors better not be fat.

Finally the hall released us into a ghoulish dentist's office, where the patients looked like they'd eaten sloppy tomatoes. The dentist danced around, brandishing his glinting tools. In another hall, an open space where the lights flashed on as vertical coffins flew open, zombies sprang out for an instant before plunging back into the darkness. More gruesome scenes punctuated the twisting dark hallways: Dead Santa slumped over in a chair, a group of ghoulish construction workers in hardhats and flannel shirts wielding power saws as they careened around kicking over orange cones and sawhorses.

Another hallway delivered us to an operating room where patients were lying on the floor moaning with their guts spilled out, or sprawled across operating tables like blood-drenched overcoats. Two doctors in bloody smocks stomped around the room. One came so close to me that I turned away, cringing. He brought a glinting butcher knife up to my face.

"Why are you turning away?" he said. "What are you afraid of?"

I could see Randall pausing at the entrance to the next hallway, looking back to see if I needed him. I didn't have a heart condition, but I felt one coming on.

"Why won't you look?" the doctor screamed. Before I realized I could simply walk away, I felt he might actually touch his knife to my skin. I hurried to the next hallway without answering.

After one last strobe-lit bloody zombie scene, we came to a final, silent room, in which a boy posed as Jesus on the cross, wrists bound to the planks with wire. His feet rested on a little shelf and he was covered in drippy blood, just as the other victims of Scaremare had been. Like the Jesus in the Liberty video, his head lolled on his chest. Two women in burgundy robes knelt at his feet, weeping. The change in mood, from harrowing to solemn, was a little abrupt.

Outside at last, I felt like pulling the cold air down around me and kissing its face. Freedom!

Down a path, the three Liberty boys trudged ahead in silence, and I wondered if their subdued seriousness was a Jesus thing. I had a hard time seeing how it could have been: Jesus' cameo was so out of the tenor of the event. For me the tour had been like apple, apple, apple, spaceship. The spaceship didn't fit into the sequence, so my mind erased it.

We approached a glowing white tent. Two soap-star handsome teenagers in fleece jackets waited beside a rudimentary wooden cross stabbed into the ground.

"Did you all enjoy it?" one of them asked. This seemed like the wrong verb choice, but the Liberty boys answered yes, so I did, too. The teenagers in fleece herded us into one of the sectioned-off rooms in the large tent. There seemed to be no option to leave.

Inside, five or six people were already waiting, their expressions flat. Penitence, cynicism, exhaustion—what they felt wasn't clear. We stood on a dirt floor, in the middle of which was a lumpy mound of dirt marked by a cardboard headstone with *RIP* written on it in black Sharpie. Everyone looked blankly at either the grave or their shoes.

Finally, the family that had been behind me arrived in the tent, and they were followed by one of the teenagers from outside. He had dark brown hair, rosy cheeks, and an easy smile. He stood at the head of the grave, clasped his hands together and asked what everyone's favorite room was. Several people nominated the strobe-lit room just before Jesus' room.

"A lot of people have been saying that tonight," he said. "I'm going to have to commend those guys." He smiled and looked around, taking in each of our faces. There was a good cop–bad cop disjunction in being treated with such warmth moments after having a knife held to my face. I mean, I know that Scaremare was make-believe hell, but many of the performances—particularly the doctor's—seemed powered by something real and ferocious, which was hard to reconcile with the sweetie pie boy-next-door standing before me. What had they all been so worked up about?

"Can anyone tell me what the theme of Scaremare is?" the boy asked.

We all averted our eyes. The boy waited. "Death?" someone finally said.

The boy nodded encouragingly. "That's right: death. Because when you die, your body goes into the ground. It goes somewhere like this," he said, gesturing at the pile of dirt at his feet. "But your soul—the part of you that's you forever—doesn't go with your body. It ends up in one of two places: heaven or hell. And you can't get to heaven just by being good and doing good deeds. Even if you go to church every day and you're religious and you're a good person, you're not going to get into heaven."

Around the tent, people were blinking sleepily.

"You're only going to get into heaven if you accept Jesus Christ as your personal savior. Because God loves you. God loves all of us so much that he gave his only son, who died for our sins." The boy delivered this news with unnerving cheer, I thought, as if he'd chugged a few Red Bulls. "We are all sinners. We have all done things to sin against God." He lifted one hand up near his sightline and held the other near his chest. "God's up here and we're down here. God wants us to be with him, but we can't because we've sinned and that's brought us down here. And the wage of sin is death." He repeated this phrase several times. "The wage of sin is death."

The ominous drama of this mantra had the effect of smelling salts on me. Did he mean that we were our own murderers? And if we were not sinners, then what—we would just keep on living? Ignorant of basic Christian doctrine, I didn't yet understand that yes, this was in fact the idea: death was the musty, unwanted armoire passed down from Grandpa Adam.

The boy continued, springs of hope welling in his voice: "The only way to make up for your sins is to accept Jesus Christ into your heart." He explained to us that without Jesus we were staggering through life just as we had in the black hallways, blind and lost (and, I suppose, hurrying into the clutches of the terrible thing around the corner).

He asked us all to close our eyes and bow our heads. "If you'd like to accept Jesus tonight, repeat after me in your mind." His prayer was ad-libbed and colloquial, meandering and repetitious. He reiterated that Jesus died for our sins, and said that personally, *he* wanted to go to heaven.

As the boy spoke, I thought that if Jesus was going to go to the trouble of dying for our sins, he might be generous enough to save even the cynics. And I also thought pawning one's punishment off on Jesus was a peculiar kind of absolution. What about owning up to mistakes? What about conscience?

He asked us to keep our eyes closed and invited those who had repeated the prayer along with him to raise their hands, which it seemed was the official Scaremare survey that generated salvation data for the website. A few moments passed as the boy counted hands. Mine were at my sides. I knew I was going to have to fake it sometime, but did it have to be tonight? I was exhausted and had a long drive ahead of me and didn't want to have to spend any more time at Scaremare.

When I opened my eyes I saw that the boy had a satisfied smile on his face, as if he himself had found the prayer therapeutic. Everyone else in the tent still wore the same inscrutable expression—boredom? irritation? newfound peace?—and it was impossible to tell if anyone had been lastingly affected by the experience. The boy gave us a card with a few website addresses and phone numbers printed on it in case we wanted further guidance. Then, standing beside the headstone, he said, "If you've accepted Jesus or you're going to accept Jesus then you don't need to worry about this"—he swept his hand across the grave. "You don't have to be afraid anymore."

As I walked past the Liberty boys on my way to the parking lot, I was stirred by a desire to know more about Randall, to know if the sight of

Jesus on the cross had overcome him at the end, if he had said the prayer along with the boy. But it was very cold and very late, and I thought I might seem suspicious keeping him for an interview in the parking lot. With a spare good-night, I drove out of Lynchburg, drunk not on the Spirit but with exhaustion.

I WOKE THE NEXT morning feeling weirded out by my evangelical foray. I couldn't understand what they hoped to achieve, how anyone could be drawn to Jesus by Scaremare. Cowering through the tunnels and cringing through the shrieking I hadn't had a quiet moment to ponder the part of me that was me forever and its place in eternity. And I hadn't automatically identified with the ghouls of Scaremare—watching the construction-worker zombies lurch around didn't exactly inspire me to think, *That'll be me someday.*

But when the boy in the tent had asked me to imagine my body underground I had complied. Someday I would be a corpse, decaying under a pile of dirt like the one at our feet in the final tent. I didn't like thinking about the part of me that's me forever suffering in hell—whatever that meant exactly. The boy hadn't addressed the notion I'd held my whole life, that the part of me that's me forever just vanishes. What if that's my belief, and what if I'm okay with that?

My secular ideas, thoroughly protected by fortresses of logic, were invulnerable to the visceral theater of Scaremare. I had to find an inroad that appealed to the head instead of the gut. Someday I'd need a conversion narrative to present to Christians I met at church, and to make it sound plausible, I knew I'd need to convince myself of the plausibility of belief.

TOUCHES OF LOVE

———

BEING ONLY A MEDIOCRE ACTRESS, I FELT I WOULDN'T BE ABLE to claim convincingly that I'd experienced a spiritual awakening at Scaremare. So I went back to the Thomas Road website to figure out a different approach to the church. A mass event seemed like it had been the wrong approach; I needed something more tailored, something with a built-in opportunity to ask questions. I came across a Sunday School class called Connections, an introductory course for folks interested in joining the community. This sounded like just the right fit—maybe I'd be there with other people like me, people a little bewildered by it all.

I found myself striding toward church—the old Donald Duck bottling plant—on the first Sunday of December without any ready explanation for my arrival. I knew that many Evangelicals believe God gently directs people in their decisions (*Perhaps like the way I feel when I'm deciding what to eat?*), and so it seemed sufficiently credible that I felt something *steering* me toward Thomas Road.

The night before it hadn't occurred to me that a passable outfit might require planning—possibly the input of someone who had actually been to church—and I was left to throw something together at dawn. I had grown my short hair out to a nondescript bob, but I might have undermined my gesture at conservatism with the oddball outfit I chose to wear: a black cardigan, a knee-length, tricolor mohair skirt, brown flats, and a huge white purse. My legs were chicken-skin bare and freezing. I hadn't even brushed my hair, because, well—I didn't own a hairbrush.

And I was late. I had gone back and forth on Lynchburg's Escher-like bypasses, which afforded me the chance to remember to make a pit stop at a gas station to chip the Kerry/Edwards bumper sticker off my car with my credit card.

The church sat impressively at the crest of a steep hill on Thomas Road. A parking lot spread across half of the property, and it was full when I arrived. A handful of policemen stood in the street near the entrance, managing traffic flow and directing cars down to a second lot at the bottom of the hill. From the street, the church looked like an elementary school. Two brick structures and a big round building bracketed an outdoor flight of stairs, which led to several other buildings. People were moving with purpose in every direction—getting into their cars to leave from what I assumed were early morning prayers, shepherding children into the brick buildings, filing with their Bibles into the round structure, which I took to be the main sanctuary. As I passed it, heading for the stairs, a cursory glance at the women confirmed that black pantyhose were the preferred winter leg attire.

Connections met on the second floor of a building up the hill, where the bone-colored linoleum floors and Creamsicle-orange cinder-block walls brought back surging feelings of high school suffering. All of the doors were closed but one. I stood in the entrance. Chairs were arranged in three separate circles, and about two dozen attractive people in their early thirties sat in them, laughing and eating muffins, like something out of a continuing education brochure.

A man with a shaved head noticed me and scooted his chair back. "Can I help you?" he said, smoothing his tie. I told him I was looking for the introductory course. "Connections," he said, "it's back this way." He got up and led me down the hall to another door.

"It's closed," I said.

"They should be in there," he said, knocking, opening it for me.

Indeed, they were: a woman with a duck-butt hairdo and red ankle boots, an elderly man in a suit that fit him like a cardboard box, a cute guy about my age who appeared to have shaved without a mirror, a weary-faced woman in black with a well-worn Bible on her knees who reminded me instantly of Sissy Spacek's mother in the movie *Carrie*. Immediately to my left was a man standing at a black aluminum lectern. His silver hair was gelled vertical and he wore a navy pin-stripe suit, his tie decorated with white Jesus fish and knotted tight. He looked at me with surprise and a smile full of fine teeth. "Hello there!" he said. "Welcome!"

I sat down in an empty row of folding chairs and apologized for being so late. The man in the Jesus-fish tie, the pastor I guessed, brushed off my apologies and had the cute younger man retrieve a photocopied packet from a basket so I could fill out a personal information page.

I began to talk in incredible detail about driving and traffic, as if to spray the repellant of boredom at them. Whatever they had been discussing before I arrived, they tabled it for me. And they were looking at me with great intensity and interest. A friend later told me something she learned from a therapist: when people have something big on their mind, something they'd rather keep secret, they talk about traffic. Which is what I was doing: traffic, bypasses, parking lots! Gas prices, mileage! I was so nervous that I couldn't see into the murk of my purse to find a pen. I felt like diving inside and zipping it closed over my head. But then the young man handed me a pen, and I was forced to set my purse aside, sit still, and return the pastor's twinkling gaze.

The pastor introduced everyone: the woman with the Bible on her knees was Rhoda, a realtor, and she was the only one actually taking the Connections class with me. The young man was Reid, a Liberty student apprenticing with the pastor; the woman in red ankle boots was the pastor's wife, Lacey (she'd been married thirty-five years "*to the same man!*"); the old man next to her was Pastor Navin; and the man at the lectern was named Woody Buchanan—Pastor Woody.

Pastor Navin, his quivering hands on his knees, asked, "How ever did you find us?"

I didn't really know what he meant. I told him I'd gone to the Thomas Road website looking for an introductory course at the church and then I'd written down directions I got from Mapquest.

"Amazing," Pastor Woody said with a generous smile. "But how did you hear about our *church*?"

Oh. I said I had a friend in Charlottesville recommend it to me.

"Is it Suzanne?" he asked.

"No," I said, fear zigzagging behind my ribs. Who the hell was Suzanne? Would she know me? The sudden, obvious possibility struck me that central Virginia was too small for me to get far lying about my identity.

"Suzanne works the robot in surgery at the UVA hospital," he said.

I nodded, happily uncomprehending.

"Do you live here in town?" Lacey asked. I explained that I lived in

Richmond (a 2.5-hour drive from Lynchburg), but that I visited Charlottesville (one hour away) every weekend to stay with a pregnant friend whose husband worked a lot. Because I was in Charlottesville on the weekend anyway, driving to Lynchburg wasn't a big deal. There was a layer of truth in that—my Charlottesville friend had generously allowed me to stay Saturday nights to get to Lynchburg early on Sunday, but didn't exactly require my company.

They looked at me as if I were turning into an immense, purple balloon. The more I talked, the stranger I sounded. I closed my mouth and did some vigorous nodding.

What I had interrupted, it turned out, was a PowerPoint presentation that Pastor Woody now resumed. On the hulking old monitor connected to a laptop were two titles: "What is this class about?" and "What are we asking of you?" Bullets under the first title told us the class would educate new members about the church and prepare us "to stand before Christ one day and not be ashamed." Under the second title, bullets instructed us to read through the Statement of Faith in our packet; to get involved at Thomas Road through time, talents, team, and treasure; and to participate in a something called a "membership interview."

At the bottom of the screen was a simple equation: Your (Time Talents Team Treasure) + Our (Vision Values Vehicles Views) = *A Great Church!*

All this alliteration struck me as infantilizing and as hard to warm up to as amateur polka music, but I would come to understand the rationale. Years later, on Washington's National Mall, a friend and I happened upon some kind of Christian rally. A hip-hop preacher at the microphone tried to rally the crowd to join in his chant: "Sin! Preach! Hear! Believe! Sin! Preach! Hear! Believe!" The preacher flogged it, but he couldn't get the crowd to catch on. We joked about how this sequence was weirdly hard to remember—*Spin! Peach! Jeer! Achieve!*—but I'd learned by then that the preacher should have embraced the power of unforgettable alliterative mantras.

Pastor Woody clicked to the next screen, which showed a brief history of the church. "You know, people all over the world listen to Pastor Jerry's radio broadcast every week and they call Thomas Road Baptist Church '*my* church.'" He discussed the church's size, explaining that churches tend to "peak out" when the parking lot gets full, as happened with Thomas Road several years ago. Having peaked out at 3,000 and desiring a larger congregation, Jerry Falwell began asking around about available alternatives. A supporter offered him a $59 million property in the Chicago area free of charge, but Pastor Jerry—as Pastor Woody called him—did not want to move his church from Lynchburg and so passed the offer on to an Illinois congregation.

A week later, Pastor Woody told us, God saw to it that the church was offered another property in Lynchburg—-the old Ericsson Telecommunications plant located on something Woody called Liberty Mountain. Lacey interrupted her husband to note that Pastor Jerry had *requested* this location, that it wasn't exactly heaven-sent. Ignoring her, Woody told us construction was now well under way on the new sanctuary, which was set to have a 6,500-seat capacity. Pastor Woody hoped this would allow the church to begin growing again. The move date was set as July 2, 2006, in the church's fiftieth year.

Large churches presented new challenges for the congregation and the ministry alike, Pastor Woody told us. He didn't use the word *megachurch*, although I knew Thomas Road technically qualified as such, and I wondered if he considered the term a pejorative. Pastor Woody said that to cope with size issues Thomas Road had adopted strategies from Rick Warren, author of the blockbuster *A Purpose-Driven Life* and pastor of San Diego's mega-mega Saddleback Church. According to Warren, breakout groups within large churches reinforce commitment on an individual level. This made a kind of intuitive sense—you feel more devoted to something if you're participating.

"We don't want our church to be the kind of place where no one notices you, no one knows you," Pastor Woody said. "We want it to feel like a small church." One of Thomas Road's strategies to that end was called bread patrol. The bread patrol visited each new member of the church to deliver a loaf of whole-grain bread.

Not living in Lynchburg, I would be missing such—Woody's words—*touches of love.* I was grateful that I would be able to compartmentalize my church experience, not have to worry about hiding the wine bottles in my fridge or my well-thumbed copies of *The God Delusion* and *Cults in Our Midst* on the bookshelves. I couldn't imagine living the way Evangelicals seemed to live—with church all the time, every day; with church people popping over with bread, with Jesus showing up in your dorm room when you're trying to get ready for a party. Maybe the church's omnipresence was benign and it was like a close-knit family, keeping in touch out of love and a desire to make sure everyone was all right. But I suspected something different. I suspected Foucault's panopticon—that the vigilance existed to scare members into policing themselves.

Woody then told us that he and Lacey had spent twelve years in Ireland working as missionaries. He remembered coming back to the United States on the plane, turning to his wife, and telling her, "There's nothing better a person can do in life than be a missionary." This was Thomas Road's position as well, that witnessing must be at the center of Christian life. Witnessing meant reaching out to unwed mothers, drug addicts, and alcoholics, Woody said, and saving them.

"Now, when we say *witnessing* to our members, some of them get scared, like we're going to bash people over the head with the Bible," Pastor Woody said. "But we've developed a new method of witnessing to people, and it's one of the most important things that we do—bringing people to Jesus."

Pastor Woody turned off the computer monitor and Lacey excused herself to go into a little washroom. Woody smiled at the empty seat she'd left behind. "My wife woke up this morning and said, 'Lately God has been talking to me and telling me I need to feed his sheep.' " Woody asked us to recall the story of Jesus confronting Peter after the resurrection, when Jesus asked if Peter loved him. Yes, Peter said, he did. " 'Then feed my lambs,' Jesus told him."

We've all been given a gift, Woody told us. In some cases, as in the case of Pastor Jerry, a person is blessed with many gifts. God wanted each of us to identify our gift and use it to feed the lambs.

Woody was sort of blowing my mind with his mixed metaphors: what *gifts*? And if we were Peter, who were the lambs?

Suddenly Woody said, "Let's pray." I bowed my head. Lacey was still in the washroom. Pastor Woody thanked God for bringing the church new members, and especially for something called the Living Christmas Tree, for which, he said, they used to charge $17 admission and now charged $5 so that more people could come and enjoy it. "In Jesus' name, amen," he said.

"Amen," the rest of us said.

As I filled out my information on the new member form—under the heading "Getting to know you!" and leaving the space for "Church History" blank—Pastor Navin hurried away, Reid blew out candles that had been burning on either side of the handout basket, and Lacey emerged from the washroom and engaged Rhoda in what looked like a private conversation.

When I was finished with the form, Pastor Woody took it and asked where I'd gone to college. Yale for undergraduate, UVA for graduate school in writing, I told him. He flinched happily, as if someone had pinched his rump. I had sort of expected this news would shock him—hyperactive education did not typically correlate with religious fervor.

Woody's son was a writer in Atlanta, he told me, working at a music magazine there.

"Neat," I said, not sure how to respond. Was this an effort to make me feel at home?

I pulled on my coat and Lacey clicked over in her ankle boots. "He's also an excellent guitar player," she said. Fresh pink lipstick rubber-banded her broad smile. "I was just talking to Rhoda about the singles ministry, EPIC, and I want to know if you're interested in joining, too."

"Oh," I said. "Heh. I don't know. I don't think so." I had a boyfriend, but I wasn't sure whether I should mention him.

Lacey's smile switched off. She picked up her purse. "I was going to have the girl call you if you were," she said, and she was gone.

Oops. EPIC had sounded like a fix-up thing, and I had meant something like, "No, I'm not interested in getting set up." But it seemed to have come across as "No, I'm not interested in dating." The last thing I needed was another red flag to add to my red flag gallery. I decided to revise my decision the following week.

Pastor Woody was working on Rhoda, who seemed to be looking at him with a kind of bored hatred, as if he was trying to guilt her into buying a magazine subscription. "Did you know," he was saying, "that fifty percent of Americans are single or single *again*?" Churches needed to create space for the unwed, he told her, and EPIC—short for Experiencing Personal Intimacy with Christ—was intended to do just that: meet the needs of people who don't have families.

"Uh-huh," Rhoda said.

Pastor Woody glanced at his watch; it was nearly eleven. I sensed he wanted to leave. So did I.

"See you next week," I said.

"I hope so," he said. "I hope we keep you."

* * *

THE CONNECTIONS CLASS HAD been far more intimate and intense than I was prepared for, and when it was over, as I burst out of the building and pushed past the churchgoers moving purposefully toward the main sanctuary, I felt as if I had just kicked free of grasping sea plants and was shooting back to the surface of the ocean. I locked myself in my car and gulped in the air. Then I started driving back to Charlottesville.

Though Rhoda and I hadn't really been asked anything about ourselves, and most of the stuff Pastor Woody had presented seemed like administrative church information, I was shocked to have been so *visible*—and then shocked to have been uncomfortable with a fact of existence I usually take for granted. I had revealed hardly anything, and already I felt watched.

Fifteen minutes outside of Lynchburg, I turned on the radio. Scanning through the channels, I counted six different stations broadcasting Christian sermons. I realized then that I had left church before church even started, and I wondered in a flutter of panic if Pastor Woody would judge me for not showing up to sermon.

It didn't take long to find Jerry Falwell on the dial: I recognized that well-oiled, baritone twang from his guest appearances on cable news channels. When I tuned in he was talking about the seven hundred lawyers he had on the "hunt nationwide for Grinches who try to steal Christmas." The battle to rescue Christmas from those who might insist on wishing "Season's greetings!" or "Happy Holidays!" was in full swing during the winter of 2005, prodded on aggressively by Fox News peddling newscaster John Gibson's book *The War on Christmas*. The heat on businesses to put the Christ back in Christmas was having some effect—Target had succumbed to pressure and promised to wish customers "Merry Christmas!" going forward.

On this particular morning, Pastor Jerry had taken up the mantle with vigor and told an applauding congregation that Christians were "winning for the first time"—funny, given President Bush's second-term situation—and he thanked God that "we do have the Left on the run." In the vein of Christmas, Pastor Jerry reminded congregants that commemorative Christmas ornaments were on sale for $10 in the lobby, where Living Christmas Tree CDs could be obtained for the same price.

He introduced a man he said seemed to have been around for all two thousand Christmases—Doug Oldham, a gospel singer. An ancient voice replied, "Sometimes it feels that way. But with any luck, this may be the last one down here." If those words had come from a younger Christian I might have assumed he was talking about the Rapture; from the feeble Oldham, it sounded as though he was all set to shed his mortal coil. He sang a song, his voice creaking like an old ship. Later I discovered that Mr. Oldham had at one point worked with Elvis Presley.

I was well into the woods and hills outside Lynchburg, but the Thomas Road signal was still strong. Doug Oldham ululated to a finish and Pastor Jerry returned to the airwaves. As it turned out, the war on Christmas was not the primary focus of his sermon. That Sunday morning he wanted to give the church a "biblical look into 2006."

"I want to suggest to you several things I believe will occur in the near future, many of them in 2006, having their origin or their continuation toward an ultimate end," he said, his tone light and colloquial. "Now, I can't read tea leaves and I don't know the future—only God does—but the Bible does give us certain indicators whereby we can know what God is up to." Pastor Jerry went on to discuss the way in which 2005 was blessed, citing the thousands of souls who had come to Christ, many through Scaremare and, again, the Living Christmas Tree. Pastor Jerry said he knew 2006 would also be a year of "great soul winning," particularly as a result of Thomas Road's move to the new facility.

He then unveiled his first prediction for 2006: Rapture. "No one knows the date or the hour," he said. "Date setting is forbidden. But there is no prophecy yet to be fulfilled. All the pieces are in place." Pastor Jerry said he wanted us to be ready for Jesus to return at any time, and he believed that 2006 could be the year we had been waiting for. He went on to talk about how Southern Baptists believe in the pre-millennial, pre-tribulational Rapture.

This is the eschatology most Evangelicals support, and it means that at some point living Christians will vanish from the planet, soaring up to heaven along with the resurrected souls of the Christian dead. Pre-tribulational means the Rapture is due to occur before the Great Tribulation, a global nightmare in which civilization will unravel into unprecedented chaos and violence. The Antichrist will consolidate absolute power, and God will turn the seas to blood, rattle the world with earthquakes, send the mountains crashing down, and unleash giant locusts with the teeth of lions and the tails of scorpions. Suffering across the planet will be so great that "men will seek death, but will not find it; they will long to die, but death will elude them" (Revelations 9:6).

During the Tribulation, nonbelievers will still theoretically have the opportunity to convert to Christianity, but they'll have to suffer incredible persecution at the hands of the Antichrist, as if enduring the Tribulation weren't bad enough. This period will culminate heinously at the Battle of Armageddon, where the Antichrist's 200 million–man army will confront a conglomerate of resistance forces. One third of mankind will be annihilated. Jesus will come back with his Christian flock to vanquish the surviving armies and win the devotion of the Jews who manage to live through it all. The Antichrist gets thrown in the Lake of Fire and Christ reigns on Earth for one thousand years, at the end of which all souls face final judgment. Then begins a new heaven, a new earth, and all of eternity.

So, as Falwell put it, this imminent, pre-tribulational Rapture creates in Evangelicals a "driving incentive to win souls, for this may be the last day to do it"—a cramming pressure many other denominations do not feel.

Prediction two: a record number of ethnic groups around the world will accept Christ. Falwell cited Matthew 24:14 as proof that the end of times would be preceded by the preaching of the Gospel to all the world. "China—with a population four times the United States—has six hundred million cell phones. Plus the computers and Internet and all the rest. We can get the Gospel out quickly because the world now has receivers to get it, and we have the message and technology to deliver it to them." According to Pastor Jerry, China already had a solid foundation of 100 million Christians (though the highest estimate my research turned up was 70 million), and with the technological capabilities available witnessing to the lost Chinese would finally be within the church's reach.

Islam's increasing strength would heighten conflict in the Middle East around the state of Israel. Opponents of Israel were inspired by the Antichrist, Pastor Jerry said, and their efforts to persecute the Jews would "culminate at the Battle of Armageddon, when Christ will lead his church and blood will flow in the streets up to the bridles of the horses for two hundred miles," he said with frothing relish.

Europe would become a resurrected Roman Empire. We would see increased anti-Semitism there as a result of the rise of radical Islam in Europe.

A global economy—manifested first by a cashless society—would come to be. When the Antichrist came, he would run a one-world government and a one-world economy, and he would exploit the infrastructure we were now building. Last year was apparently the first in this country when most transactions were completed electronically. One day, Pastor Jerry predicted, "you will walk up to the grocery checkout and you'll have no money. There'll be no currency. At that time, the mark of the beast will be necessary to buy and sell."

This prediction struck me as a pretty obvious trick of turning observation into prophecy. I mean, didn't we pretty much have a global economy and cashless society already? I was reminded of the time I visited a palm reader in high school. She contemplated my hand in silence and then told me I would end up in a career that would "make people happy." *Mystical!* Like you're a soothsayer for pointing out what everyone else can already see coming.

Wars would increase all over the world. While he was on the subject, he wanted to express his disgust with those protesting the war in Iraq. He accused them of forgetting the September eleventh attacks—which he called "nine-one-one." Two Sundays ago, Pastor Jerry told us, there was a man sitting in his front pew, listening to his sermon, and he couldn't tell if the man was a supporter. The man approached him after church. He said he had come to ask Pastor Jerry to bring the troops home from Iraq immediately. He stopped the man from saying more.

"I'm for getting the troops home when the job is finished," Pastor Jerry said. "When the last terrorist is either dead or converted."

"These are innocent people," the man said.

"Innocent people my foot," Pastor Jerry told him. "They blew up the World Trade Center and you're talking to the wrong preacher right now." At this, his congregation erupted in laughter and applause.

I suddenly felt very, very tired. The words *September eleventh* had long since become estranged from the actual factual events. It had become commonplace to hear someone wrenching people's pain and anger away from the attacks to use as a bludgeon against some unrelated target. Falwell was, of course, not the only puppet master doing this.

Hearing the enthusiasm of their applause, I wondered why the congregation still believed something that had been proved untrue. Didn't they read the newspaper? Was it so hard to admit being wrong? Or was it that war, any war, in the Middle East seemed to bring Evangelicals that much closer to Rapture and heaven?

It seemed Evangelicals could recognize a wrong (a global economy as harbinger of the Antichrist) and still consider it useful (all the better to convert the Chinese).

Whatever the reason, how was I to find a place among people indifferent to facts? How was I supposed to understand people who had developed antibodies against reality, who saw the world as they preferred to see it?

Pastor Jerry went on to say he founded Liberty to raise thousands of young people who would "charge hell with a bucket of water" and who wouldn't "turn left, socialist, or liberal."

"They call me the most dangerous man in America," he said. "And I want to stay that way."

The pastor ticked through the remainder of his predictions: the apostate church would grow stronger, wickedness would become more prevalent, the prophecy would become clearer and clearer to the church, and knowledge would increase at the expense of wisdom. He talked about lining America up for battle, and how he wanted his church to start campaigning for public schools to allow students to talk about Jesus, to let valedictorians preach on graduation day.

During the prayer, he reminded us that Christ died for us, and whosoever called upon him shall be saved. He urged anyone who hadn't given his or her heart and life to come forward. He had men to pray with the men and women to pray with the women, so that those who came forward would have company inviting Christ into their hearts. "Give your life to Christ," he said. "Come on down while we sing."

A man began to sing a bellowing hymn: *Have thine own way, Lord, have thine own way.* The multicolored voices in the congregation made the song a kind of hypnotizing rainbow swirl.

I switched off the radio and tried to imagine what it would feel like to come down that aisle through the disorienting billows of all that singing. I'd find Pastor Jerry pulpited at the end, and I'd approach him in a nimbus of light as a new believer, even as I held down the dark knowledge that I hadn't believed a word.

VEHICLES

———

DURING THE WEEK FOLLOWING MY FIRST SUNDAY AT THOMAS Road, I tried to better prepare for my second. I clicked around the Thomas Road website trying to figure out what was so special about the Living Christmas Tree. I had pictured a magnificent pine tree silvered with lights, but the ticketing page on the website showed only an indoor seating chart, no tree. Perhaps there was a hole in the floor for it? The next weekend would be my last chance to go. Most of the tickets for the Sunday afternoon performance were already sold out, but I found a single aisle seat available in the back, under the balcony, and I bought it.

I sat on my bed and reviewed the information packet from the Connections class. In it I found Thomas Road's nebulously articulated purpose to "bring glory to God by making a positive difference in the lives of people" and its mission statement to "*win* the lost, and *connect* them to the local church where they will *develop* into *servants* and *worshippers* of God."

A numbered list broke down the elements of the church's mission statement. One, win the lost to Christ and get them baptized (class 101). Two, connect them to a local church. Three, help every believer to develop (class 301). Four, encourage every member to serve in the church. Five, worship God with all our hearts.

The number assigned to Pastor Woody's Connections class was 201. Which meant I had skipped 101: getting won to Christ and baptized. Was there even a class for 101? I hadn't seen one on the website.

I flopped flat on the bed, amazed by my own cluelessness. I had enrolled in a class as if church was school. I had failed to understand the simple idea that I couldn't be connected to a church before I'd been turned on. Pastor Woody had assumed I was already a Christian; I had assumed he would know I wasn't.

At some point I was going to have to tell Woody I hadn't gotten around to giving my life to Christ—and, oh, while we're on the subject, I actually don't know what anyone means by that. Thinking about this exchange was giving me indigestion. It wouldn't have been strange if I had just told him at the start that I was "lost," but now, it would seem strange I hadn't said anything.

Well, I was going to have to give it a shot. My boyfriend had grown up a Southern Baptist, and he kindly signed on as my sartorial advisor. "No more mohair," he said. For my second church outing, he picked out a loose purple sweater, ordinary gray slacks, and ugly buckled job-interview loafers he called my Puritan shoes. My fingernails, which I was in the habit of painting glossy black, had gotten a gold coat for my first day at church. I didn't realize until I was digging my gold claws into my purse at Connections that this color was maybe even more transgressive than black, particularly when paired with my rainbow skirt.

The day before my second church outing I stripped the gold from my nails and redid them in good-girl pink. That should do it, I thought.

I OPENED THE DOOR to Connections looking ready for work at Banana Republic, and behind it Reid and the Buchanans sat smiling, looking at me as if I had entered on cue. No Rhoda. No Pastor Navin.

"I can't get over you went to Yale," Pastor Woody said, shaking his head with the metronomic rhythm of a cat's twitching tail. "I've been thinking about it all week."

What were those smiles all about? Were they going to kill me?

"What can I say?" I said.

"That's where our president went to school," Lacey said happily. Kill me not.

"And Bill Clinton," Woody added. Kill me.

"Bush's daughter was there when I was there," I said. I was still standing in the doorway.

"Which—? Oh," Lacey said. "The *other* one seems like a whole lot of trouble."

"I'll bet she's a handful," Woody said.

She and Woody gave each other a little high-five of a look.

I guess they weren't planning on killing me right away, because Woody invited me in. As I settled onto a folding chair Lacey asked me how I had chosen Yale. I told them I had been seventeen and sort of superficial and I had liked the look of the buildings. They asked me more about the academics, campus housing, my current job, my dating life, my writing. And I told my first three lies: I did not, as a matter of fact, love my job as a copy editor at Capital One bank; I omitted mention that my boyfriend was also my roommate; and I was *not* not writing anything at the moment. I was writing about them.

But I answered their other questions in detail, making eye contact as if they were computers assessing my ability to hold eye contact. I hoped that in dumping out all this personal information I would seem less mysterious to them, that Woody wouldn't be, *ugh*, thinking about me all week. On the other hand, there probably wasn't any way to get around being a jagged shape at Thomas Road; if my California license plates and Richmond address hadn't done it, my Ivy pedigree would.

As Lacey began to tell me again about their writer son in Atlanta, Woody pulled a folding chair out from behind the lectern and straddled it backwards. I asked where Rhoda was.

"Probably someone called her about EPIC," Lacey said. "She probably went there this week."

"Well, this class *is* all about making connections," Woody said.

Lacey said, "I guess she made a connection."

Woody laughed. "Ah. Let's pray."

I felt like a guest on a Japanese talk show. The rhythm of the exchange was jerky and unnatural to me, and I didn't know how to negotiate it. What were they laughing about? I looked at Reid in search of a sympathetic shrug, but his eyes were locked on Woody with a kind of velvety admiration.

The suddenness of group prayer struck me as a kind of narcolepsy: you're talking, you're talking, you're talking, then *poof*, you're praying. Not that it mattered, being a nonbeliever and all, but I didn't like the idea of group prayer. Woody delivering a message to God on my behalf seemed a little presumptuous.

Pastor Woody thanked the Lord for giving him so much and for bringing so many people to him. He thanked the Lord for the hundreds of spiritual decisions made at the Living Christmas Tree. He said he believed God had good things in store for the church, and he never ceased to be amazed at the gifts the Lord brought, whether they be "Yale grads or CIA operatives." Whatever *that* meant.

After we prayed Lacey asked me if I was going to go to the Living Christmas Tree. I told her I had bought my ticket online, but that I was going to have to go to Kinko's to get my confirmation receipt on email. Lacey said I should just use Woody's office to access email. They gave me directions for walking over there after Connections. I didn't even need to print out my confirmation—Woody would be working the door at the Living Christmas so all I needed was my seat number. It took me a few minutes to be sure that I'd understood correctly—they were suggesting I go alone to use Woody's computer. I was taken aback by this sudden gesture of acceptance.

We turned to today's class. Our kickoff point was "Connecting to Ministry/Serving." Pastor Woody explained that there were two types of ministries: pastor-centered and member-centered. Most ministries, he said, were pastor-centered: the pastor conducted the ministry, the members liked having their work done for them, and the growth of the church corresponded directly to the energy and gifts of the pastor.

"You know, hundreds of pastors leave the ministry each year because they get worn out," Lacey said.

They get worn out from the incredible pressure, Woody explained. In pastor-centered ministries, the members are all dependent on him, but the abilities of just one person are limited. For the pastor, Woody said, "it's a gilded cage." The members, bonded to God only by an overextended minister, begin to "slip-slide away from God, like that Paul Simon song."

I looked down at the sheet he'd given me. One bullet point under the pastor-centered ministry heading read, "Frustrated pastors and spiritually immature people generally do not have a dynamic impact on the world."

Dynamic impact? The corporate-speak here was just as bad as it was at Capital One. But there I had learned to ape the vernacular, estranged though I was from the words dribbling from my lips—*bringing things to the table* to *dialogue* with my *team* in order to secure an *integrated solution*—so I supposed in time I would pick it up here, too. Soon I'd be talking about dynamic impacts myself.

In member-centered ministries, Woody continued, the church mem-

bers were the ministers and the pastors were mere administrators. The
pastors still conducted ministry that required specialized training—
marrying couples, certain types of counseling—but ministry in the more
general sense of "meeting the needs of another" (which, I gathered, included recruitment) was relegated to church members. This disbursement
of duties increased commitment within the church.

Pastor Woody then laid out the "vehicles" of the church: the celebration service on Sunday mornings (did he mean the sermon?), Adult
Bible Communities (Sunday School?), cell groups (or was that Sunday
School?), classes through Equip U (more Sunday School?), and Sunday
evening services. Most people came forward for salvation and baptism
during the celebration service, Woody said. That I had not done so, not
come forward for salvation and baptism, not been to celebration service,
made me afraid to ask my dumb questions about the Vehicles.

"Sunday evening services are special because they emphasize the
family and preaching God's word," Woody said. He used to skip Sunday
evening services because he liked to watch football instead.

"And then you became a pastor and *had* to go," Lacey said.

"No, honey," Woody said evenly. He began attending *before* he became a pastor, as a matter of fact. But *after* he'd already passed a sheaf of
Sundays watching football. "And, you know," he said, "I didn't gain a
thing from that."

This concluded the Vehicles page of the packet and we were supposed to stop there until the next meeting.

Lacey was looking in a compact mirror, dabbing on lipstick. "Why
don't we just do Views today and the member interview next week, since
the Sunday after is Christmas?"

This would make Connections 201 three Sundays instead of four—
and push my member interview up one week sooner than I expected.
Pastor Woody thought this an inspired idea and we went straight into
the first portion of the Views section, which was titled, "The Bible Passages on Giving Living."

Satan, according to Pastor Woody, made a special effort to whisper
in your ear that you shouldn't tithe your money away to the church, because you might want it for something. Satan reminds you of all the wonderful luxuries you can buy with that 10 percent of your annual income.

"But God," Woody warned, "will find a way to sweep the slats out of
your false security." Reliance upon false security occurred at the expense

of reliance upon God, which meant that one was forsaking God for earthly delights. God would always find a way to punish such betrayals.

This was a rather sour idea: financial karma. Of course, God didn't need my money; Woody was talking about the church. The church needed my money, and to believe that not giving it up meant God was going to come after me—*sweeping out the slats!*—was to believe that the church was not only a place of worship, but an appendage of God.

As if in answer to my distaste, Pastor Woody pointed out that there was something in it for me: God rewards faithful givers. "One cannot outgive God," he said. Whatever sum you fork over, God will outdo it in recompense. "Some people," he said, "flip the percentage and live on ten percent of their income, tithing ninety."

I felt my eyes go round.

"We don't want you to *not* be able to pay your bills," he assured me. "We just want you to give generously, because it's God's money."

Lacey, sitting pertly on the edge of the couch, began to tell a story about one of their sons. One month, not long ago, their son missed a church payment—or as Lacey put it, he "robbed God of his tithe for a month." The next month, his car broke down and he took it in to the mechanic for repairs. The mechanic's bill was the exact same amount he robbed from God. Lacey smiled as she recalled her son saying it had been God "telling me I should have given Him that money."

Pastor Woody had another vehicle story to illustrate the point. Driving home from services one evening, his car began to buck and the engine warning light flashed on and off. He managed to coast to the service station. A trusted family mechanic reviewed the car and told Woody there was nothing he could do for it; it was finished. Woody surrendered to the decision—"It's God's car," he told himself—and sat in the waiting room while the mechanic cleaned up. But at some point, he looked into the garage and noticed his mechanic was under the hood, screwing in new bolts. Confused, Woody asked the mechanic why he was bothering with new bolts if the car was worthless. The mechanic happily informed him that the problem had only been bolts vibrating loose and all the car needed was some new ones. Elated and grateful, Pastor Woody paid only $129—which, he noted, included an oil change.

Woody delivered no capsule lesson with this anecdote, but I took the implication that being generous with God had its perks and rewards.

When Woody said his car was God's, I guess he was saying he accepted that whatever befell the car was God's design, and this freedom from false security in his car ownership led God to make his car problem easy to fix. Woody referenced the second Bible quote on my "Giving Living" page, Luke 6:38: "Give, and it will be given to you." Not that this should not be anyone's driving reason for giving, Woody wanted me to know, but it didn't hurt to remember it when giving felt like a drag.

Woody's father had grown up during the Depression, and throughout his youth his parents clung desperately to their money, so tightly that God turned it into dust in their fists. Pastor Woody smiled warmly at his wife. He said he was lucky to have met her, since she was the one who taught him to give it all away to God. Now he always gets it back.

Like some kind of card game strategy, I thought.

"That's right." Lacey swept her purse off the floor and rose. "Now you'll have to excuse me, I've got to go greet." Greeters, apparently, were member volunteers who stood at the entrances to the sanctuary, passing out church bulletins for the service.

"You *get* to greet," Woody corrected her.

"I *get* to greet," Lacey said, smiling a smile as flat as a refrigerator magnet and slipping out of the room.

Woody read 2 Corinthians 9:7 aloud: "Each man should give what he has decided in his heart to give, not reluctantly or under compulsion, for God loves a cheerful giver." My immediate sense of this quote was that the first two clauses dwarfed the third: give what you want to give, not what others want you to give.

But Pastor Woody began expounding on the third clause, and in particular, on the word *cheerful*. He said that the word *cheerful* was *hilarios* in Greek, a fact he liked a lot—the idea of giving hilariously.

"They always tell you to give until it hurts, but God wants you to give until it feels good," he said. To me, this sounded like the *opposite* of what the verse was saying. If it doesn't feel good right away, wouldn't you be giving reluctantly?

We moved on to Thomas Road's ordinances. Pastor Woody explained that although Thomas Road was not a sacramental church, they did have two ordinances. He didn't explain this terminology, and I didn't feel brave enough to ask. I knew Catholics had seven sacraments to abide by, so I figured that Woody was basically telling me Protestants weren't like

Catholics. Later I learned that sacraments are rituals where God is present, prerequisites for salvation, while the ordinances at Thomas Road are simply symbolic. You only have to do one thing to get saved.

The first ordinance was Christian baptism. This was not a cleansing baptism, so it wasn't baptism that saved you, although Thomas Road did practice baptism by immersion (meaning, I took it, the dunk as opposed to the sprinkle). Members of Thomas Road believe, according to Pastor Woody, that when you are baptized, your life until that point has ended and you die; you're buried under water, but as the baptizing pastor lifts you from the water he's lifting you from the grave, and you are born again.

At Thomas Road, you had to decide to come forward and choose Christ in order to be baptized. Pastor Woody likened this active choice to Lacey's choosing to marry him: the marriage worked because they *chose* to be together. Because you have to speak to choose, the church did not baptize infants, and children are only baptized once they are old enough to elect rebirth—although Woody didn't specify what he meant by "old enough."

The second ordinance was the Lord's Table, where you received the Eucharist while contemplating the details and meaning of the crucifixion. According to Thomas Road's interpretation of scripture related to communion, partaking in the body and blood of Christ was also the point at which a believer should appeal to God to reveal his "unforsaken sins" and confess to them, privately.

Pastor Woody lowered his packet and looked at me evenly. He told me that it was imperative to approach the Lord's Table with great reverence, since one was eating symbols of Christ's blood and body. "Taking the Lord's Supper in an unworthy manner and not believing in your heart while engaging in holy acts," he said, "makes you guilty of the body and blood of the Lord."

I nodded, feeling a little guilty already. Yes, I was planning to get saved unworthily. Yes, I was planning to take the Lord's Supper without believing in my heart. If I was going to understand Evangelicals, didn't I have to know what it felt like to do as they did? To try to see what they saw? The truth was, in spite of my spasms of guilt, in spite of trying to be open, I didn't take Evangelicals seriously enough to reckon with the gravity of what Woody said.

Woody checked his watch (it was about 10:45) and then briskly scanned the Thomas Road Statement of Faith, a two-page list explaining the basic beliefs of the church. These included the Triune God (the Father, the Son, and the Holy Spirit as one, which reminded me of nothing more than Dracula's ability to transmute into a bat or a mist), creation, inerrancy of scripture, sin (of which we are all guilty since our own conception), salvation through faith, and the imminent return of Christ.

"Christ is comin'," Woody said, slapping his packet shut. "Look busy."

Reid blew out the candles burning behind him and I pulled on my coat. We would tackle the Statement of Completion next week, Woody said, turning off a table lamp and knocking it over as he did so. He stood it back on its base. "Heal!" he shouted, his palm on its shade.

Out in the hall, Reid thanked Woody for his help.

"Help with what?" I asked.

Reid had recently had a problem: he had two credits to finish at Liberty before graduating but couldn't afford the tuition. Woody and Reid spent some time praying about the problem. Woody then emailed Pastor Jerry, who offered to pay for Reid's last two credits. I congratulated Reid on the money coming through, but I wondered why they had to pray if Woody knew he could just ask Falwell for the money. I had just read in a newspaper article about the $1 billion Liberty University fund-raising campaign Pastor Jerry had in the works to prevent ever having to turn a student away for an inability to pay.

Outside, Reid hurried off ahead. I asked Pastor Woody if he would mind walking me to the service since I was a little confused about where to go. It would be his pleasure, he said, and as we turned to descend the stairs, the church and parking lot spread out at our feet. People were moving in rivers into the round building to our left, a few groups chatting on the blacktop outside.

"What's going to happen to this property once the church moves to Liberty Mountain?" I asked Woody.

He told me it was up for sale for around $5 million. "I don't know if you can see across the street," he said, pointing across the parking lot, across Thomas Road and down a hill to some buildings barely visible through clusters of trees. "That's Lynchburg College. I think they're going to try to buy it because they're landlocked and they probably want to expand." I nodded. We walked down the stairs. "But it would be *really* funny if they bought it," he said quietly.

"Why is that?" I asked. He stopped, leaned in, and grinned, his eyes hard as a soldier's. "They're known as a *liberal* college."

Not having any anti-liberal arrows ready to sling, I simply volleyed back his smile. We entered a vestibule. There were a couple of little offices to our left, and to the right what looked like a waiting room, bisected by a long counter. I didn't know why we were stopping here—wasn't Woody walking me to church?

Woody led me behind the counter. The lights were off and blinds were drawn over the windows. I could hear the voices of people passing in the hall, muted as if they were talking through pillows. There were no personal effects—no postcards or Post-its, no tchotchkes or photos. Cardboard boxes were piled Jenga-style around the floor. Woody set to clearing papers off a laptop on a particleboard secretary set against one wall.

This was his office. We were here to get my seat number for the Living Christmas. I was so disoriented I had forgotten all about it.

I sat in Woody's desk chair drawing short breaths, looking into my lap as he leaned over me typing his login. Soon a logo illustration of a razor-beaked, fierce-eyed eagle appeared on the screen over the words *Liberty Flames*.

"Is that the Liberty mascot?" I asked.

Woody nodded. "A lot of people think it's too mean," he said.

I said, "I thought college mascots were supposed to be mean."

"Some people say, 'Well, we're a *Christian* college.' I tell them"— giving me a private, intense smile—"I *know* we are."

I navigated to email. I felt vulnerable with him standing there, worried that my inbox might contain a subject line something like "re: your big fat secret book." I quickly searched the pockets of my mind—what was the worst thing that could happen? With Woody, it didn't seem like I'd have far to fall. I mean, geez, he'd already paired me off with CIA operatives.

It occurred to me that after I'd taken a few more steps into Woody's world, once I learned to synchronize with the church rhythms and talk to Christians without fretting I sounded like the nonbeliever I was, once I'd gouged out a Christian narrative of my own, I would be connected to people who wholly bought my story. I might make friends in the church. And what then? What would happen when they learned who I really was? Would they be hurt and disappointed? Might they be angry, too?

I brushed away the troubling thought, found my confirmation email, scribbled my seat number on a scrap of paper from my purse and was ready to go.

On our way out, Woody stopped me in the doorway and looked me full in the face. He stared as if he were going to have to draw me from memory.

"I've really enjoyed getting to know you," he said.

Well. It was like a coconut had bonked me on the head. I looked at him. With his tender look, his white hair and his bulb-tip nose, he reminded me of Bill Clinton. "Me too," I said.

Did he mean it? I don't know. He hadn't gotten to know me, of course, and I was convinced that he didn't trust me. But it wasn't every day someone looked at you like that, as if they cared what happened to you. And even if Woody was being insincere, in that moment I felt *caught* by him, caught like I'd fallen out of a tree I hadn't known I was sitting in.

Back outside, passing kids pegging each other with icy Virginia snowballs, then to double doors that swung open at the sanctuary entrance, Woody recognized one of the ladies handing out programs and stopped to chat. I wandered off into a lobby area, drifting toward music as if toward a light. Pamphlets were piled on a mantel against one wall and flights of stairs curved up at both sides of the lobby. Ahead of me were more double doors, open, through which I could see dense rows of neatly dressed people on their feet, singing, "Rock of ages, Jesus is a rock!" The song I heard was Christian contemporary, I guess, played by a live band.

I began to advance through the doors, and suddenly Woody was behind me. "You can go ahead and sit wherever," he said. "You're by yourself, you can sit in the front row if you want."

I didn't know why, but suddenly I wanted to sit with Woody. I felt a little stung he hadn't asked me.

Two blocks of pews spread across the floor of the main sanctuary, bisected by a carpeted path across the church. The pews were nearly full and I didn't feel like parading in front of the entire church to the first row, so I took the path to find a seat in the rear block. The whole room was round, on a sweeping downward slope to the stage, like a clamshell. A large balcony extended above half of the main floor seating and curved to a taper along the side walls. There were several high windows on the walls opposite the balcony, and flat pieces of wood cut and painted to look like curtains hung over them, like window coverings in a dollhouse. Heightening this effect, cardboard set pieces painted to resemble stone towers and walls dripping with ivy were propped on either side of the stage. Hanging above the stage, two large blue projection screens displayed the lyrics to the songs. In the center of the stage was a preview of what was in store for the afternoon program: unmistakably the Living Christmas Tree.

The tree was a tall pyramid built from curved green layers. Each layer had white frosting gooped along the upper rim, more like a wedding cake than a Christmas tree. Every inch of the tree was festooned with fiber-optic lights and light-up gingerbread men, candy canes, and snowflakes. Along the frosted top of each tier were the heads and shoulders of actual people—I guess they were sitting behind the tree layers, although the short height of each layer made it seem impossible that they could fit their whole bodies back there. This created the odd visual effect of disembodied singing heads, though on this particular set piece they looked more like macabre Christmas ornaments. There were around ten such living ornaments on the bottom layer, decreasing in number to a single lady's head up at the very top just below a starburst. Most of the people were in middle or old age, with the ladies in silver sequin sweaters and the gents in suspenders and bow ties. As they sang, the fiber-optics on the tree did amazing tricks in time to the music. The lights swirled in a spiral up the tree like a soft-serve ice cream. They exploded from the tree's center point to its outer reaches, fading from red to orange, to yellow, to white. They shimmered subtly. They zigzagged, they made a flashing checkerboard, they rained, they bled. They brought on faint eye pain.

Downstage, seven or eight people were singing into microphones. There were musicians—violinists and horns and a college-aged boy with bangs hanging in his eyes playing guitar. A woman off to the side of the stage was performing the song in sign language. The choir director was a hugely obese man with rosy cheeks, who tugged and pushed the air with his hand as he sang. Stage right I thought I recognized Pastor Jerry, clutching his leather-bound Bible and singing into the air, jowls quivering like liquid. His suit was tailored snugly over his ship's hull belly, his white hair combed. A pair of frameless square glasses perched on his swollen nose.

But I wasn't at all certain it was Jerry Falwell. If you had put him in a lineup with six other men his age from the congregation I probably couldn't have picked him out. I hadn't yet left behind my prejudices. To me Jerry Falwell just looked like every other stuffy old white guy you could imagine being rude to his shoeshine boy.

I chose a pew near the rear and put my coat and purse on the floor. I stood with my hands behind my back and listened to the music, reading the words on the JumboTron but not singing along. I felt comfortable just reading: I am basically tone deaf. I thought I probably never would sing at church and I looked around to see if there was anyone else holding back. No one was. Everyone was singing with open-mouthed passion.

Two audiovisual technicians wearing complicated headgear managed several small television screens inside a box in the middle of the church. On the screens I could see video shot by cameramen roving around the church, the lyrics to the song being sung, and several different angles of the stage. The technicians were busy at work, cutting back and forth. I later learned that their edits were not only for the church JumboTrons but also for broadcast on television and the Internet—church TV.

The choir director asked us all to greet each other. I shook the hand of the man sitting next to me on the pew and was surprised when I became the target of outstretched hands from everyone in the pew in front of me, from two pews in front of me, hands reaching up from behind. Everyone who could reach wanted to greet. Woody had said this was how their church was—no one is overlooked—but I was still stunned to see everyone so eager to connect.

After a few more songs, Pastor Jerry took the pulpit and sent out the ushers to collect the tithes. Guests were supposed to fill out an attendance card in exchange for a free CD of Thomas Road music. Pastor Jerry described the CD as a bribe to fill out the card so Thomas Road could send out a letter and invite the guest back. In one of my books about Evangelicals I remembered reading, "Give Jerry Falwell your address and you'll never be lonely again."

He kicked off the sermon with updates on the battle to rescue Christmas. "It's the birthday of *Christ*," he said. "Why do we want to honor witches and Wiccans and everything? That's all right: Kwanzaa, menorahs—that's great! But don't leave out the nativity scene. This hostility against Christianity must stop."

According to Pastor Jerry, many companies (Wal-Mart, Target,

Sears) had agreed to acknowledge Christmas, but Costco was holding out. If they continued to hold out, he was going to organize the biggest boycott this country had ever seen. "C-O-S-T-C-O. Costco," he said. And when that boycott came down on them, he promised, "They'll get religion."

It had gotten so that everyone needed a lawyer, Pastor Jerry said, sighing. Not long ago a woman came to church for the first time and when she left after service she walked straight into a three-foot-wide column and broke her tooth. She sued Thomas Road for putting that column there. But over the course of her lawsuit, the Thomas Road lawyers discovered rogue columns had broken this woman's tooth at several other churches in Virginia.

"Thank God we all have a lawyer," Pastor Jerry said. "No charge and he's never lost a case. Whatever you plead of the Father, plead it through him." Ha! I thought. Jesus, Esquire.

Pastor Jerry talked about the Living Christmas Tree and the merchandise for sale in the lobby, and the move to Liberty Mountain, and how they were going to do the Lord's Supper right after the morning service on Christmas Day, and he generally droned on for some time with announcements he read from scraps of paper. When he was finished, we got a musical number (chorus: *He had the birthday—we got the gift!*) and then Pastor Jerry invited a state senator from Nebraska to lead the prayer. Adrian Smith had once been a student at Liberty University and now he was running for Congress back in Nebraska. Pastor Jerry said he knew there were people watching the sermon in that state.

"I can't *tell* you to vote for Adrian Smith"—religious leaders are legally barred from endorsing candidates from the pulpit—"but be dumb if you want to be and vote for somebody else."

Cheers and laughter geysered from the congregation. It struck me that part of what people responded to in Falwell was his prickliness—if you didn't agree with him, you were a fool and probably some other things, too, and he was going to tell you so. If you did, you could feel proud to be on the right team and safe from ridicule.

After Adrian Smith led the prayer, the choir director stirred up the band again and began to sing. When he had polished off a hymn, he talked about how amazing it was that God knew everything he was going to confront by taking the form of a man, but he went ahead and did it anyway. As he spoke, a man in a beige suit, his thinning hair gelled into doormat bristles, took center stage and lifted the microphone to his lips.

At this point I felt I knew what to expect from music at Thomas Road. Though most songs crescendoed dramatically at the three-quarters point, the intensity of the singing had not moved me. It seemed scripted and empty. Well, this man, whom I privately named the Weapon of Mass Salvation, had something mystical. I didn't know what he was doing or how he was doing it, but the rich sound that came out of him—I was hearing it with my whole body, as if it was a poltergeist possessing me.

And it was really a silly song, lyrically. In it angels watched Jesus put down his crown, take off his robe, and travel to Earth with arms outstretched. And why was he embarking on that great journey? Simply to "make your heart his home." Later, listening to the song on my computer to write down the lyrics, I thought, Give me a break! But in the moment, I was transported.

As the WMS sang, a light sheen of sweat broke on his forehead. "All of heaven watched as he released his crown, as he stripped away his kingly robe and began his journey down. To think that God would shrink himself into the Milky Way, reduce into the time of man to fit within our day." I didn't even consider what it meant for God to shrink himself into the Milky Way; I considered leaping over the pew in front of me. Singing about the marvel of Jesus' grace, the WMS went wild. His suit wrinkled as he thumped his chest and curled over, as if releasing this song was causing him abdominal pain. All across the rows of pews hands lifted in the air as if to better absorb the sound. An elderly man sitting in the middle block of pews rose up out of his seat and lifted both arms in the air, swaying gently side to side.

When the song was over and the church was erupting, I was sure people would be coming forward to get saved. Pastor Jerry and the Weapon were the perfect one-two punch: Falwell said you were a part of something true, everlasting, and endangered; the Weapon stirred your heart and made you feel it was so.

Pastor Jerry's message for the day was called "The Rest of the Story"—meaning what happened after Jesus was born. He asked us to turn to Hebrews 10 in our Bibles. As the only Bible I owned was the Oxford Annotated, which I would have had to bring to church in a shopping cart, I reached for the book stashed in the pew in front of me. I flipped it open and found that it was a hymnal. The man sitting to my right looked at me askance as I clumsily returned the book to its place. "Note to self," I thought, "get Bible."

Pastor Jerry worked through what he called "the incarnation verse," discussing God's transformation into man, into the body of Christ. When he was finished he asked everyone to please stay for the invitation, as it was the most important part of the service. He asked people new to the Lord to come forward, but he also extended his invitation to wayward Christians. "If you were thinking, 'I can't say for sure that I know that I know that I know that he lives in my heart'—for Christians who aren't very motivated—I want you to come back to Him today. We're moving into a new church on July second and we'd love to have you helping us."

He had men to pray with the men and women to pray with the women. The whole church sang as people came forward. Was the pew-leaping feeling I'd had during the Weapon's song real enough that I should go down? I hesitated. The feeling was vague, hard to describe, and didn't strike me as God-related. I wanted to try to integrate at Thomas Road without falsely claiming salvation, but I knew I was going to have to do it at some point. I was too afraid to do it just yet. It was all too new.

From my pew I had a difficult time seeing over everyone's heads, and I thought it might be rude to make a show of trying to get a good look, but I saw movement: several people coming down to the foot of the stage, where they joined other bodies, bodies ushering them off through a side door that I could hardly see.

WITH A COUPLE OF hours to kill between church and the Living Christmas, I went to get something to eat. The roads were clogged to a crawl and when I finally made it to a decent sandwich place in a strip mall, the line of churchgoers was so long I had to wait outside in the cold. I gave up after a few minutes and picked up a drive-thru chicken sandwich. I ate in my car in the parking lot, napkins papering my lap, coat on and everything. Doing this made me feel pretty depressed and alone. I found myself looking forward to settling into a pew beside some friendly people.

BACK AT THOMAS ROAD, families were showing ushers their tickets and then filing into the sanctuary. I didn't see Pastor Woody, who was supposed to wave me in without a printed ticket, so I walked around to the opposite entrance. No Pastor Woody there, either. I tried to tell myself it was ridiculous to let this hurt my feelings.

I folded into a little crowd and managed to snag a program and make it inside the chapel without a ticket.

The sanctuary blared with the noise of children's voices, and most of the pews were near full again. I found my aisle and row, at the end of which sat a man with a tan complexion, an all-black outfit, and a glossy black pompadour. The little brass numerical marker next to him on the pew was my number, but something was wrong—my seat was directly behind a column. On the Thomas Road website seats with obstructed views had been specifically eliminated from the matrix of available tickets. They had apparently overlooked the obstructive properties of this particular column.

When I sat down, I had to angle my knees into the aisle to fit. If I bent down to reach my purse, I would have knocked my face against the column. I had to lean out into the aisle to see the stage. I could make out the Living Christmas Tree, its lights glittering behind a thin maroon curtain. Downstage, a small white four-poster bed stood where the pulpit should have been.

I reviewed my program. On the front cover was a graphic of a few snowflakes, tilted as if they were gliding toward me. Inside I found a list of Christmas songs on one page and on the other an advertisement for Living Christmas DVDs, CDs, and tree ornaments along with invitations to upcoming events: the Easter SonRise service, the move to Liberty Mountain, the Celebrate America! festival. On the back of my program was a list of the hundreds of people who were participating in the Living Christmas Tree.

The lights dimmed. Under a spotlight shining down on the bed, a little girl in a white nightgown was tucked in, receiving a good-night kiss from her mother, dressed in a blue evening gown.

"Merry Christmas, Lindsay," the mother said before sweeping offstage. Is she going to a holiday party in that gown? I wondered.

Lindsay lay down to sleep and finally the maroon curtain behind her lifted to the tree. As the Living Christmas Tree began to work its eye-assaulting magic and the disembodied head–ornaments sang with glee, dancers came onstage and pranced around Lindsay's bed in a *Nutcracker*-inspired number. Little girls spun prop lollipops bigger than they were; Raggedy Ann and Andy flopped around with two big teddy bears; a jester twirled a curvy ballerina in a scandalously tight fuchsia leotard; and some intriguing international dolls danced with their partners.

After the doll dance, and after a line of soldier boys marched out pointing their rifles and singing, and the dolls lip-synched "Twelve Days of Christmas," the mother returned to Lindsay's bedside and delivered a slow song called "When Love Came Down" as violinists played at the foot of the stage. Love, I took it, is another name for Jesus. While she performed (and when she pinged the high notes I understood her diva gown) green laser lights crisscrossed the audience like a security system in a spy movie. The Christmas tree flashed and glittered. When the song was over the mother sat on the edge of Lindsay's bed.

"Wake up, Lindsay," she said. "It's Christmas."

Lindsay threw her arms around her mother's neck. "I love you, Mommy," she said, and they swept offstage together.

The living Christmas ornaments performed a few numbers, and then a few ladies dressed in black came out and sang "Pat-a-Pan" as little girls with ribbons on sticks wandered the stage doing, I guess, rhythmic walking. The choir director offered up an orgasmic performance of "Joy, Joy"; a woman with distractingly bouncy hair sang a honky-tonk number called "That Little Baby"; a Jesus look-alike in an all-white suit blinded us with his halogen smile as he grooved and twirled *American Idol*–style.

I was pretty bored. After listening to Woody and Lacey I'd expected a mind-blowingly powerful event, guaranteed to deliver souls right into God's cupped hands. Perhaps I was too old and jaded to catch the frequency, but so far for me the Living Christmas Tree had the depth and resonance of a cable-access talent show.

I wanted to feel as transported as I had by the Weapon's song that morning. It had been a good feeling. But the magic here felt rehearsed, canned, and slopped down on stage. Little Lindsay—now encumbered by a huge hair bow—minced back onstage to perform a creaky melody called "Happy Birthday, Jesus." She sang, "The shimmering lights, and the presents are nice, but the best gift is you."

Neatly dressed children appeared to accompany little Lindsay in repeating these verses over and over. And you know what? Watching them was like eating warm cupcakes. Children! Who could resist children singing? But then an elderly man lumbered onstage with his cane and loomed over Lindsay and her friends, apparently undetected. He interrupted their song, piano quietly playing under his voice. God loved them very much, he said, and that was why he gave his only son, who was the first person to get presents on Christmas. He quite suddenly broke into song, as if he had forgotten what he had come to say. My program told me this was Doug Oldham, whose name and craggy voice I recognized from the first sermon I'd heard—the man who hoped this would be his last Christmas. The children scattered to the edges of the stage while Mr. Oldham caned to its edge and delivered a feeble song called "God Sent His Son."

When he was finished, the head ornaments began to sing "Come All Ye Faithful," and the faithful—about ten people in vaguely biblical, drapey dress—came as bidden. A woman in a white robe and a Jesus look-alike huddled together, admiring the live infant the woman held, which kept kicking its leg out of its swaddling. Over the course of this song, the characters from previous songs streamed down the aisles and onto the stage, where they knelt at the feet of Mary, Joseph, and baby Jesus, and walked offstage again.

Mary retreated to a spotlighted corner downstage and knelt with her baby. Joseph strode off to the other side of the stage. The head ornaments began to sing a song, from which I only recall the morbid refrain, "Start at the manger—and end at the cross!" like a TV jingle for a children's board game.

As the lyrics told the story of Jesus' life, the actors actualized the words. A spotlight came up on Joseph teaching a young boy to sharpen the end of a little pole. After much miming and wood shaving, Jesus helped Joseph hammer the pole into a stool as the third leg. They set it triumphantly on the ground and little Jesus crashed into Joseph's embrace. The spotlight died on them and shone on Mary and baby Jesus again for the refrain. Then a spotlight came up on a boy of about ten or eleven pantomiming an argument with two old men. The old men kept brandishing scrolls at him, pointing at the pages and then pointing at the boy. The boy pushed their books aside and opened his arms—the *this much* gesture—seeming to indicate something greater than the scrolls.

The lights then come up on the whole stage as a grown-up, glossy-haired Jesus enters stage left, much to the delight of the small crowd congregated. He greets them with a warm smile. Two men come out carrying a stretcher on which another man lies, writhing in agony. The two men set the stretcher on the ground. Jesus bends over it, claps his hand on the patient's, and yanks him up to stand, teammate-style. The man, instantly restored to health, gazes down at his own body in amazement, as if he's just become visible to himself.

A man then presents a limp little girl to Jesus. Jesus takes the girl into his own arms and drops her without a thought. The girl stands on her own! As Jesus performs a similar miracle on a blind man onstage, in front of me a woman rests her head on her companion's shoulder. She is crying. And as her husband turns, holding her closer, I see he is crying, too. And looking around in the dimly lit audience, I see many others wiping tears from their eyes.

Now, I am no stranger to crying in an audience. I cry at the movies. I cry at weddings and graduations. I sometimes even cry during commercials for arthritis cream. But this? This seemed to me a corny pageant and I felt nothing. Why were people crying?

I couldn't see it then, but I was hung up on the low art of it, the disposability of the production. But the people in the audience apparently didn't need a sophisticated depiction of Jesus' life: any gesture would do. It stimulated the stimulus. And the stimulus was not something I grasped yet.

As Jesus stood among his followers, the Living Christmas Tree went dark and became a mountain at night. And then a huge red crucifix lit up on its dark face.

Time to end at the cross, I thought.

The music surged and out of the wings strolled the Weapon of Mass Salvation himself. Sliding forward in my seat, I felt my ear canals opening for the new pew-leaper he might have in store. As it turned out, it was the same one he'd sung only hours before, "He Came All This Way." I slid back into the pew. Maybe it was just the repetition, but this time I didn't even think it was very good.

When the Weapon had finished, Pastor Jerry took the stage. He stood in front of the big red cross and wished us a Merry Christmas. He asked us to please fill out the card in our programs, which the ushers were coming around to collect. The card asked for our names and addresses and how we had heard of the church, with a checklist in which we could identify the type of experience we had at the Living Christmas. My options were "I prayed to receive Jesus Christ as my personal savior," "I recommitted myself to Christ," or "I would like more information about the Thomas Road Baptist Church." I checked the third box.

Below the checklist was a space to write down whatever you wanted someone to pray for on your behalf. My pencil hovered over this empty space as I considered giving it a shot. But the usher came by with his wooden salad bowl and I placed my card in it with the others, leaving the prayer space empty. While Pastor Jerry pushed the Living Christmas merchandise, I whispered good-bye to the pompadoured man next to me and headed back to Richmond with the "Happy Birthday, Jesus" song stuck in my head.

SIN OF OMISSION

———

DETAILS I BEGAN TO NOTICE AT MY CAPITAL ONE JOB: ANGEL figurines praying on cubicle desks, jewel-studded crosses glinting in the Vs of collared shirts, postcards printed with psalms tacked to bulletin boards alongside phone extension rosters. Coworkers talking in the breakroom about church on weeknights, online Bible courses. One coworker—a devout Christian wife and mother with whom I found myself easing into a friendship—emailed me a picture of a boy praying at his bedside, his dog seeming to pray beside him, paws on the bedspread.

I was seeing better, noticing the synchronicity of church and corporate culture—the overlapping dialects, the solace in repetition, the remoteness of people in charge. One could ping-pong easily between the two. And it made sense to me that so many corporate workers would need to be elevated beyond the intersecting planes of gray-flecked plastic and the twitching racks of fluorescent lights, beyond the cabinets stocked full of generic powdered creamer to last through the end of days, that they would want to hear a hopeful answer to that small, high voice inside wondering, "Is this it?"

The expansive privileges of graduate school had receded into my past, and now I felt somewhat claustrophobic, bracketed on one side by the church and on the other by a corporation. Neither of these places were exactly my métier. But I was getting more comfortable by degrees. I started to use the word *workaround* with increasing regularity to refer to a temporary fix. A friend asked me how things were going with "the fundies" and was a little unnerved when I spoke protectively of Woody.

I started to consider crucifixes kind of delicate and pretty, and wondered if it would be weird if I wore cross studs in my ears. That picture of the boy praying with his dog? I thought it was sort of cute.

When I telephoned my mother in California to regale her with stories from church, she received them with a thoughtful silence, white noise glittering on the line, before saying, "Just don't convert."

IN THE CONNECTIONS ROOM on the second floor, Rhoda—seemingly a new Rhoda in a leopard-print skirt, brown sweater with diamond cutouts on the arms, and kohl-rimmed eyes—was cracking her gum and telling Woody about herself. She hadn't, as it turned out, made a connection. She had merely taken a week off and was back now, doing her membership interview. Woody and Reid were nodding as she spoke, as if in time to music.

In my lap was a checklist meant to determine in which ministries (*ministries?*) I would be interested in participating. Special events, women's ministry, drama, nursery school—in all, there were over fifty options on the page. I tried to read them while keeping an ear tuned to Rhoda, as if rehearsing my lines while listening for my cue.

She had divorced about three years earlier and had two daughters—one married and a teenager still living at home. "I don't really know what ministry I'm interested in," she said, a faint edge to her voice. She wanted to do outreach, be with people.

Pastor Woody brought up the singles ministry again—EPIC.

Rhoda said that when she thought of singles, she thought of people in their twenties, not middle-aged parents with children.

Actually, Pastor Woody pointed out, EPIC had a ministry specifically for people with children.

Rhoda felt they would be people with *young* children.

Pastor Woody smiled. "Rhoda, did you know *half* of Americans are single or single again? There's nothing worse than loneliness in a crowd."

"Yeah," Rhoda said, nodding slowly, working her chewing gum. "I remember you mentioning that."

Pastor Woody tried another approach, telling Rhoda about two women who had recently joined the church who took new members out to lunch—

"Yup, I remember you talking about that," Rhoda said.

If we didn't have lunch plans after church, Pastor Woody said, would we like to come to a great Japanese place called Sakura? "Every Sunday we just about fill that place up, and that's why they love *Thom-ah Loh!*"

Rhoda busted up in raucous laughter. I took a few seconds to upload a fake laugh.

Satisfied that he'd turned Rhoda around, Pastor Woody shifted his attention to me. "What about you, Gina? What's your church background?"

As vertigo tipped me forward, each word fell from my mouth like a boulder my tongue was too weak to hold back. "I have no church background to speak of." The sounds thudded onto the carpet, puffs of dust rising from their edges.

Pastor Woody choked on his coffee and began to cough.

"What do you mean?" Reid asked.

I felt slightly lighter, more balanced now that I'd released this rumbling avalanche of truth. "This is all pretty new to me. I've never actually . . . *been* to church," I said. "When I was looking at my Connections packet and saw the 101 class I realized maybe that's where I should have started."

Pastor Woody, recovering from his cough attack, said, "No, 201 is a great place to start. But how did you decide to come here? What is it you're seeking? What questions do you have?"

I lied and told him that though I believed there was some finite answer, some truth to explain everything, I didn't know enough to say what it was. I said that I was feeling lost and confused, and that the Baptists I knew—my boyfriend's family—all had a nice peace with things, with life and death and the general state of the universe. The idea that God takes care of everything. I liked the way they were in the world, and I wanted to maybe be that way myself.

Woody told me the key text for someone in my position was *Mere Christianity* by C. S. Lewis. This book addressed the questions many nonbelievers felt Christians never bothered to answer. It would be especially useful for someone like me, since Lewis had once been a nonbeliever himself.

Reid asked if I'd read the scripture. I said that I had read much of the Old Testament, and some of the New. Start with John, he said. "It's the most important scripture to read in terms of what we believe."

As I wrote this down, I thought of the nuts holding up John 3:16

signs at football games. I knew the verse: "For God so loved the world that He gave His only begotten son, that whosoever believes in Him should not perish, but have everlasting life."

"A lot of people who are thinking like you—that there has to be something else—end up Buddhists or Muslims," Reid said. "But the thing they don't realize is that Jesus said he is the way, the truth, and the life, and that there's no way to God but through him." As two-dimensional as his argument was ("He said it, so it's true!"), I was touched to see Reid take such an interest in my salvation. My ignorance inspired him.

"Are you very serious with your boyfriend?" Pastor Woody asked.

I told him I was.

"What are your plans?" he asked.

Plans . . . ? I frowned.

"Your *plans*," he said again.

"Oh!" I said. He must have wondered if I was trying to become marriage material for a Baptist. "We don't really have any plans . . . we're just, you know, boyfriend and girlfriend."

Pastor Woody's smile wilted at the edges. "Well, Reid has a really interesting testimony."

"I got caught up in drugs," Reid said. He hitched his slacks up by the knees as if getting ready to wade into water.

"It's so hard to believe." Pastor Woody shook his head and waited a second, but Reid didn't chime in. "Well, mine's not very interesting but I'll tell it anyway." Woody accepted the Lord when he was nine years old, but he only did it because he was afraid of going to hell. He said this mockingly, as if it was a cowardly reason, which I thought was a little odd considering the whole shake-'em-to-wake-'em conceit of Scaremare. When Woody was in college in Arizona, already having been saved in church as a child, some kids from Campus Crusade for Christ told him that there were three ways that people lived: they were either carnal, natural, or spiritual. If they were natural, they had no spirituality at all. They were deaf to the Holy Spirit. If they were spiritual, they were living righteously. If they were carnal, they paid lip service to God, but they were living in the flesh. This was Woody's testimony—the stunning realization that he had been living carnally. Enlightened, he accepted Jesus as his savior in earnest.

I have been told by friends that I do something facially when I don't understand, a kind of brow-furrowing, skeptical snarl. I guess I was doing it in that moment because Woody leaned forward and told me I couldn't expect God to give me more. "You have to give more to God first. If you don't give yourself to God," he said, "if you turn away from him, the more you turn away from him, the more you slip into darkness, the faster the slide, the darker it gets, the further from God, which—eventually—ends up in homosexuality."

Uh. Now the skeptical snarl was real. Pastor Woody said this was something they explored in detail at higher levels.

When he was in Ireland, ministering to Irish kids, they'd tell him, 'I don't want to give myself to God now, I like my life now. I'll do it when I'm older.' Pastor Woody would tell them, "You're holding on to this dime store pearl necklace, this piece of nothing in your life, when you could have a cultured pearl. Why *not* do it now? Why *not* have that pearl now?"

I nodded, processing. But this spiel didn't seem to apply to me. I hadn't told Woody that I believed in a Christian God but wanted to pack in a few more rock 'n roll years before doing as Jesus would do. Instead I told him I wasn't sure *what* I believed. Perhaps, just as I was certain you can't *choose* to believe anything, Woody was certain belief was a choice.

Woody referred to a passage in Matthew: "Come unto Me, all ye that labor and are heavy laden, and I will refresh you. Take my yoke upon you and learn of Me, for I am meek and lowly in heart, and ye shall find rest unto your souls. For my yoke is easy and My burden is light."

Reid's face brightened as if someone had turned up the lights in the room. "That's part of *my* testimony. That's the passage that brought me to the Lord."

Reid said he had been a cocaine addict since he was thirteen. When he turned eighteen, he was about to graduate from high school with no plan for his future. He had a terrible GPA because he never went to class. The only reason he had stayed in school was so he could play baseball. His girlfriend dumped him, which increased his anxiety, and he dropped twenty pounds.

Pastor Woody leaned over and said, "Now how'd you do that again?"

"You don't want the diet I was on," Reid said.

His cousin was always ministering to him, telling him about Jesus, but Reid wasn't hearing it. But he went to church one Sunday on a lark and the preacher read that passage about the yoke. That night, lying in bed, Reid felt his chest crushed under the weight of his sorrows and troubles and anxieties—there was too much caving in on him. I knew the feeling he was talking about, that leaden paralysis.

He couldn't bear it a moment longer. He spoke to God: "Lord, please take my burdens because I can't carry them anymore." And Reid said that God did. He lifted off the burdens. Reid felt it instantly.

I could tell his experience was real in a sense, that he really had felt revived, whether through some murky hormone secreted in his brain or because he believed that God had reached down and given him a new yoke for his burdens. Hearing about it I felt—I don't know. Empathy? Envy? Woody and Rhoda seemed to feel something, too, because we were all quiet for a little while.

Then Pastor Woody told us he always does a little exercise with students in an evangelism course he taught at Liberty. He asks them, Do you consider yourself a good person? *Yes*, they always say. He asks, Have you ever stolen anything?—the cost doesn't matter. Everyone nods. Have you ever told a lie? Yes again. "Then I'd ask, 'Have you ever wanted something someone else has?' For men I usually say a woman, and for women . . . something else," Woody said, seeming not to want to venture a guess as to what a woman might want. "Everyone says, yes, I've felt that way. Then I ask, 'Have you ever taken the Lord's name in vain?' And everyone says, 'Well, I'm not happy about it, but yes I have.' And I tell them, 'Well, you just told me that you're a thieving, lying, blasphemous adulterer. So what would you say if I told you someone wanted to take on all your punishment for you?' And everyone says, 'That sounds pretty good to me!' "

As Woody downshifted to a closing prayer, I thought about that bargain: accepting Jesus to duck out of the punishments due you. I guess I had started seeing it in a different way, that you were supposed to accept Jesus out of gratitude, not cowardice. That Jesus was supposed to have preempted your desire to have someone punished in your stead, so as to prevent you from even going there, from wishing for it, which would have been unconscionable. Woody's argument to his students seemed that way to me—immoral, chickenshit, an appeal to the lowest common denominator.

After the prayer Pastor Woody said I should find a mentor and that

Lacey would be good for me because she loves evangelizing and taking people on. He also suggested that both Rhoda and I could find a place in the older singles ministry.

Rhoda laughed and looked me up and down. "I think I'm a lot older than she is," she said.

I checked off some boxes on the ministries handout: for singles, for women, for special events. As I passed the sheet over to Reid his eyes locked on mine. "I think you're here because God's got ahold of you. I think God's got plans for you."

Pastor Woody agreed. "You drive so far, all the way from Richmond. It's the people who try the hardest for God that get the most rewards, and I think you're gonna find him. It's gonna change a lot of things for you."

I said I guessed change would be a good thing, which was bland enough. They said they'd pray for me.

SAKURA WAS ON A busy street, plunked castle-like in a huge, empty parking lot. At the host stand, there were little dishes of gummy bears and chalky mints, each with a tiny spoon dug in. We were the only table in the place.

The lunch menu was a sequence of permutations on the theme of surf and turf, each option available for five dollars. Hibachi shrimp and steak, hibachi shrimp and chicken, hibachi scallops and steak . . .

Rhoda was there, and Pastor Woody, and the two ladies he had mentioned were there with their husbands. I was seated between the husbands, both of whom looked to be circling in on seventy.

When I mentioned my difficulty finding an ATM on my way from church, Woody said, "I wouldn't have invited you to lunch if I wanted you to pay." Rhoda and I protested, but Woody said he wanted to do more for new members—he always felt he didn't do enough.

Lacey breezed in, neat and prim in a mint blue twin set. She kissed Woody and settled in her chair as he gestured at Rhoda and me: "Both of these women have just completed Connections 201." There was a polite sprinkling of applause. "Rhoda is a new member and Gina is here because she wants to learn more about Christianity. A friend of hers told her that Thomas Road would be a good place to start." He added that I'd gone to Yale, and that I was a copywriter in Richmond.

Everyone regarded me with alienating surprise, as if Woody had just told them I had recently been released from prison. I was a little surprised myself at the distinction Woody had made: Rhoda was a new member, I was not. I suddenly felt like I was outside a glass door, watching them settle down to lunch without me.

Lacey regarded me with a powerful grin, a grin that told me she could see more than I had revealed. "You know you're jumping into the deep end here—Jerry *Falwell's* church?"

Forcing myself to hold her gaze, I said, "I know that. But it feels right." Her smile seemed to harden and turn to wax.

I concentrated on my menu. Shrimp and chicken or shrimp and steak? None of the combinations sounded very appetizing to me at that moment. Couldn't I just get one thing?

Fielding questions from the older couples, Rhoda talked more about her family situation. She and her husband got divorced around the same time her eldest daughter moved away, which was very hard on Rhoda's youngest daughter, who was about fifteen at the time. Rhoda, obviously ill at ease opening up about her personal life, turned the family questions on Lacey and Woody.

They had five children, one of whom was adopted—the daughter of a Jamaican father and an African-American mother. They adopted the girl when she was nine. "We tell all Christians, 'If you have a family, adopt a child. Start a family and adopt one child," Lacey said. "If every Christian family adopted a child, things would be so much better." She urged us to think about how many children were in foster homes.

What was unspoken here was that this was buttressing for the argument against abortion—if pro-lifers were going to present adoption as a viable option, they had better be willing to open their homes. These were people trying very hard to live by their principles.

I stared as Lacey and the older man to my right sprinkled Sweet'N Low into their water glasses. We ordered our food. One of the ladies told Lacey, "You know, a lot of people just don't want to deal with the problems."

"Yup," Lacey said, "there are a lot of problems. Ours ran away nine times when she was a teenager."

"*Nine times?*" I said.

Nine times. She'd run to a friend's house or off with a boy. Each time they'd bring her back and tell her they loved her. I wondered if the girl had felt suffocated or steadied by their persistence.

Later, I found an article about the Buchanans and their adopted child on a website called "Passionate Hearts." They'd adopted the girl in 1994. She had lived in two foster homes until she was six, at which point she was adopted by an abusive woman. She went on to two different group homes before coming to the Buchanans. Lacey told the website, "We had prayed for a lot of things, including her temperament. And God answered all those prayers, including that she would come to know the Lord. She trusted Christ two weeks after she came to us. In fact, I didn't share the Gospel with her for two weeks, because I wanted her to feel settled and at home before I brought that up." Despite the happiness Woody and Lacey described the girl as having had in the Buchanan clan, she began to run away at age fourteen. Her ninth run came when she was eighteen years old. Each time she came back, the Buchanans would ask her why she ran. The girl never gave an answer.

I asked if they had ever met the girl's mother. They said the mother gave the child up when she was a year old, and the girl had never expressed a desire to meet either biological parent. Everyone nodded solemnly.

Lacey brought up another son who had an Internet company, kind of like an online Wal-Mart: you can buy anything on it except for perishable goods. The company produced some of their own products, like soap, but mainly they just sold goods from other companies. I couldn't quite see the point since there was already such a thing as Wal-Mart online, not to mention Target and Costco and Kmart online, to say nothing of eBay or Amazon. The kicker, apparently, was that at their son's company, the management and affiliates were all committed to Christ. In this way, their son was extending the concept of the megachurch, which would not only provide an alternative to secular community, but also to secular consumption. Whenever Woody and Lacey bought from retail stores, their son called their purchases "toxic goods."

During weekend conferences in Lynchburg, all the son's employees spent Saturday conducting company business and then Sunday was reserved for preaching. Nine times out of ten, Woody said, if the workers weren't Christians when they came to the conference, they were by Monday morning.

Our waiter, a young Chinese man named Ling, worked for their son. Ling had a Chinese girlfriend in Roanoke who Woody said was "basically an indentured servant" for a family there.

Ling served our orders. I was a little awed at the pink plastic plate before me: the shrimp and chicken came evenly coated in brown mucus, heaped next to what appeared to be a quadruple portion of Uncle Ben's. Next to my water glass Ling placed a bowl filled with pink mayonnaise.

I knew enough from movies and television not to dig in. We joined hands to say grace. I had not done this since childhood, under coercion at summer camp, and though I knew we were supposed to hold hands, I didn't know whether they were joined on the table or left hanging in the air. So I held one man's hand resting on the table, and the other in the air between our seats.

After the prayer, as we all flattened our napkins on our laps, Lacey told us that the bowls near our water glasses contained yum yum sauce, which got its name from the fact that it was "yum yummy." We nodded. "Ling," she called. "Ling, what's in the yum yum sauce?"

Ling stood at the edge of the table, looking down at Lacey's bowl. "Uh, mayonnaise . . ." he said, and paused to think. "That's all I really know."

Lacey told us to put it on everything.

As I drizzled it on my food, one of the women leaned over her husband to tell me about herself. She and her husband had recently moved to Lynchburg from the house they'd built across from their son's in Tennessee. She had loved her old house, where she could stand at her kitchen window and watch her grandchildren playing in the yard. But she couldn't ignore it: God was directing her to Lynchburg. Speaking to us now, she couched every decision in these terms: God directed me to build a house, God directed me to worship at Thomas Road.

"God gave me the grace to accept his will and move to Lynchburg," she said, smiling wistfully, "but God hasn't yet given my son the grace to accept it."

Rhoda swallowed her food and frowned. "Why did you *really* move here?"

I felt a little sparkling swirl of excitement. Rhoda did not mess around!

"Well"—the woman said, clutching back the words as if she didn't want to part with them—"I moved here to be near my daughter."

And God wasn't finished with her yet. Recently he had directed her to round up some friends from the development in which she and her husband now lived. Out of her seventeen lady neighbors, six came over for coffee. She evangelized at their social and was happy to report that one of them found the Lord right there on the sofa while another had pledged to begin her search. At our table, everyone congratulated her.

While the other lady began to talk about the saga of tiling her kitchen floor—the warping! the wobbling! the poor workmanship!—her husband leaned in close and asked me what I did for a living. I worked in knowledge systems at Capital One, I told him. He nodded, and apropos of work, I guess, told me that at one time he'd been a homebuilder, a realtor, *and* an insurer—"You get 'em all three ways." But one year God directed him to sell his business so that he could put himself through Bible college, and he hasn't regretted it for a single day. Now he ministers to lawyers and government officials. He used to be up in Arlington, but he moved to Lynchburg when he got tired of "the hustle and bustle."

"But I've still got a friend up there. What's his name," he said, as if I'd know—"the guy who lives on the border of Alexandria and Arlington?" He thought a moment more. "Oh," he said, "Jesse Helms."

These moments, "God directed me," "my friend Jesse Helms," made it difficult for me to focus on summoning my powers of empathy, to push past my alienation to see our bonds and commonalities. And worse, as lunch wore on I realized that introducing myself as an outsider, as a nonbeliever, might have been a royal, irreversible mistake. They were more obviously interested in Rhoda, impudent Rhoda who mocked their ideas and skipped their classes, because she was a Christian.

But what about Win the Lost? I wondered. Wasn't that the main name of the game? But I knew: I had revealed myself as being more interested in learning about Christianity than in being a Christian. I hadn't come across as lost so much as intentionally elsewhere. And that moment when I felt that Woody had caught me, when he said he'd enjoyed getting to know me—I wouldn't be getting that back.

After lunch, as everyone spooned gummies and mints into their hands, I said good-bye to Lacey and the two older couples. Lacey said she looked forward to seeing me after the new year, but her voice was sealed behind ice. Pastor Woody caught up with Rhoda, and didn't even try to say good-bye.

THE EAR OF THE HEART

———

AFTER CHRISTMAS IN CALIFORNIA, I DIDN'T REALLY WANT TO go back to Thomas Road. That last day had been mortifying, like one of those dreams where you have to take a test for a class you had completely forgotten you were enrolled in. I felt certain that Lacey and Woody had written me off as a gawker, and I worried about what the dead bud of our relationship might mean for my prospects of getting a handle on the evangelical enigma.

I read *Mere Christianity* while I was away. C. S. Lewis's argument seemed to be that our shared understanding of right and wrong, our collective conscience, was proof of God. Being a pretty dogmatic evolutionist, and seeing conscience as an advantageous trait that could have developed over time, I was not persuaded for an instant.

To my complete shock, just after the New Year Pastor Woody left me a phone message saying he'd been thinking of me and that he and Lacey had been praying for me. But when I went back to see him, he was cold. Though he crushed me into a side-hug and told me again he'd been praying for me, he barely looked me in the eye.

AND THUS I STARTED OVER. By reading my Bible and going to church off and on for about six months without talking to a soul I somehow found myself near the main sanctuary of Thomas Road Baptist Church one morning, in a gleaming white chapel airless with the scent of fresh paint, a Salvation Guide flushing Satan from my heart. The guide was sitting across from me in a pressed blue suit, her panty-hosed knees brushing mine, the two of us hunched in folding chairs under a stained-glass window, like study partners at the library. Her gray curls were arranged in the shape of an upended bird's nest and her full blue eyes seemed perpetually on the verge of tears.

A dry hand reached over to cover mine, which was curled awkwardly on the Bible the guide had provided as a flat surface for filling out my application card. Her glittering eyes closed and she began to talk to God.

"I pray that you will open Gina's heart," she said quietly, "and come into her life."

Around the chapel others who had come down the aisle with me after the Sunday sermon wept and blew their noses as they unburdened themselves. On my face a smile stretched and lifted and threatened to split my head in half.

It was July 2, 2006, Thomas Road's first day in the new facility. The church was set on high ground, called Candler's Mountain on my map but referred to as "Liberty Mountain" by Jerry Falwell. From the parking lot, a panorama of beautiful green hills rolled in the distance, like an inviting ocean. My white button-down was already drooping and sweat-creased by 10:30 a.m. when a shuttle bus deposited me at the church entrance a half-mile away from my parking spot.

The main building of the new church was a crucifix-less brick colossus with columns in the front like long white teeth. Passing between the columns and through the front doors, I had entered the vast lobby, packed solid as Macy's on Black Friday. The men wore suits and the ladies were shellacked and perfumed in their florals, holding large Bibles zipped into nylon carrying cases. The crowd was so dense it was kind of thermal, and it was impossible to judge with any accuracy where I was supposed to go.

The carpeted entryway of the sanctuary at the old church had reminded me of the lobby of a small movie theater. The new entrance hall, with its soaring ceilings and ornate details, called to mind the foyer of an opera house. Heels clicked on the marble floor, done in a handsome Prussian blue. The lobby, I would later learn, had been christened Main Street, as if presenting an alternative to Lynchburg's secular downtown. Kind light glowed from high overhead making everyone look camera-ready. At long tables groups distributed leaflets for their ministries, and farther down Main Street I could see a line snaking up to the register at the Lion and Lamb espresso café.

Against the walls small areas were designed to look like living rooms: each had an Oriental rug, plush club chairs, end tables, lamps, potted palms, and sideboards arrayed with books and bowls. These areas were being put to good use by Main Street congregants, who lounged in the chairs and reviewed their full-color church bulletins. Between the living-room arrangements flat-screen televisions were bolted to the wall, broadcasting church announcements and (I presumed) the service once it began.

Several sets of double doors leading to the sanctuary opened and closed periodically, offering glimpses of what I had guessed from the dense crowd around me: the sanctuary was at capacity. Overflow rooms were down the hall past an indoor playground featuring an enormous Noah's Ark structure and an even larger outdoor playground aswarm with children.

Armed with a map of the new facility and a program for the morning service, hopeful that because I was alone I would not be forced into overflow, I squeezed into the back of the sanctuary. From the last row to the retaining wall 15 feet behind it, there was scarcely room to stand. I picked my way along the crowd for a better vantage point. The sanctuary seats were cushy theater chairs, replacing the symbolically penitent wooden pews of the old Thomas Road. There were no hymnals shelved in the backs of these chairs because the song lyrics were broadcast on JumboTrons flanking the stage, allowing the congregation to keep their faces upturned and stay connected.

The rows were filled all the way to the front, and on the flanking staircases to the balcony people were standing pressed against the walls. The stage, which I squinted to see clearly, impressively spanned the width of the room and was presided over by towering rows of the new 300-person choir. Downstage was a wide white pulpit with an oak tree's air of age and permanence. Newness and anticipation shot in electric crackles over the chattering crowd. It was as if some important pronouncement was about to be made, and I was flush with the claustrophobic terror that anything was possible.

On video screens above the stage, a brief montage limned Thomas Road's fifty-year history—black-and-white photographs of the church's first sign and a boyish Falwell at the pulpit, an older Falwell admiring a baby, hugging an elderly African-American man, Falwell dunking a new Christian in the baptismal pool. The images were so fleeting as to almost have been subliminal, as in a promotional video for a summer camp. "Welcome home to Thomas Road Baptist Church," said an announcer. Then Falwell took the stage with his wife and a cloud of pastors as the church band burst into symphonious sound and the choir was ignited by three hundred voices ringing the same high note. The song was "Honored, Glorified, Exalted." The ominous enthusiasm of the singing pinned my ears. It was music I could imagine heralding the start of a great battle, music thrumming with bloodthirst. During the song, hands lifted all across the congregation. Nearby, a man swayed side to side with both arms aloft, as if he were planted underwater.

Falwell was standing stage left with a faraway smile, his hair white and neatly side-parted; his eyes contented slits behind his square, gold-framed glasses; his nose as swollen and shapeless as a fingerling potato. He wore a dark suit and red tie as he did every Sunday, which by contrast made his complexion even whiter, white as a powdered donut.

After several songs, he took to the pulpit and in his creamy baritone he introduced special guests: the state lieutenant governor, charter members of the church, a classmate of his from Baptist Bible College, a couple who had flown in for church that morning from Grand Rapids, Michigan, on their $40 million jet. After shilling for a coffee-table book and DVD commemorating the anniversary, Falwell introduced his own family: Macel, his wife and the church pianist until a few years back ("the gal I've been in love with fifty-four years"); his sons Jonathan and Jerry Jr.; his daughter Jeannie and her son Paul ("all the children, in-laws, outlaws, stand please"); and "one very private member of our family, totally unlike his twin brother, he doesn't like crowds, he doesn't like to be noticed, and if he'd known I was going to do this today he would have sat at the very back of the nosebleed section, my twin brother, Gene."

Intimacy sweetened the pride with which Falwell introduced his family, and it was clear this first day in the new church was an emotional one for him because of what it stood for—all around him was the future of the church, while his old body was the past.

According to Falwell, a photographer present was equipped with a special lens with which—standing on a perch above the choir—he could capture every face in the house.

Falwell invited the congregation to break out their checkbooks and asked his son, Pastor Jonathan, to give the prayer. Jonathan, he said, had taken over his office, and would also be taking over the 8:30 a.m. sermon, a move that was clearly preparation for Jonathan's eventual inheritance of pastoral duties.

Pastor Jonathan settled into place behind the pulpit. "I wanted the eleven o'clock service," he said, "but he only gave me the eight thirty, so I guess we'll figure that out." Jonathan had the patrician good looks of John Kennedy, red-haired and lean, his voice an urgent whisper—in short, totally unlike his father.

He began talking about building the church in which we were gathered, how it almost wasn't ready in time for service this morning, and how it wasn't built for the church members themselves, but to enable the church to go out and use God-given resources to reach the community with the Gospel of Jesus Christ.

"Every single one of us is tasked with this responsibility," Pastor Jonathan said. The church greeted this injunction with enthusiastic applause. "We've got the playland, we've got the lobby, we've got the sanctuary, we've got all the great educational space, but all of it is a waste of time, and all of it is a waste of money, if we don't go out and reach people with the Gospel."

Pastor Jonathan surprised me. I had never heard Jerry Falwell ask his congregation for non-monetary contributions. Instead he generally reported to the congregation everything he and other Christian leaders were doing to advance Christian causes and preached on the importance of tithing to keep funding the work. But here was Pastor Jonathan calling on Jerry's church to join in preaching the Gospel—and it seemed like a message the church was glad to hear.

Then he prayed, expressing humility in the face of God's blessings, and praying for the ability to reach thousands, even millions, in the name of Jesus.

Falwell released the ushers into the aisles to collect the tithes and offerings. Wooden bowls bobbed along the rows and we sang a little more. Jonathan Falwell did most of the honors that morning, reading a letter from President Bush, presenting his mother with a self-playing piano that would be displayed on Main Street in her honor, giving his father a signed copy of a book by Winston Churchill. Charter members of the church were honored and there were goals laid out for the future of the church.

At the end of the service, Pastor Jerry gave the invitation for people to come forward for salvation, membership, and baptism. "Have Thine Own Way," the invitation song that day, was a gentle, rocking lullaby I had heard before. But on that morning, I felt unexpectedly invaded by the song. In past services I had begun to soften to church music, as corny as it was. Belt anything out in a large group and you'll start to feel something stir inside, especially if you know the lyrics. And many of these songs were written to travel the spine, simulate or stimulate religious feeling. And so it was with "Have Thine Own Way," a hymn of surrender.

> Have Thine own way, Lord! Have Thine own way!
> Search me and try me, Master, today!
> Whiter than snow, Lord, wash me just now,
> As in Thy presence humbly I bow.

Singing the song at the very back of the packed sanctuary, in the wake of a service celebrating family, history, and hope, losing my orientation for a moment on the map of politics, emotion began to surge inside me. It was the first instance in which I was overcome by what I eventually came to think of as Feeling X.

I had never had Feeling X before. It wasn't happiness or sorrow, adrenaline or peace; it wasn't love or lust or misery or hate. It felt like the awakening of a new organ, an organ like the one described in a chapter on conversion by the thirteenth-century French mystic Bernard Clairvaux: "the ear of the heart." That was about right.

The closest thing to it I'd felt was vertigo, a sensation my grandfather once described to my mother as the urge to jump off a cliff. It was a kind of limitlessness, a sudden permeability, a sense of connectedness with all the living things around me, with all of time and space. It was a kind of instant corporeal understanding of infinity, and if a little unsettling, it still felt good.

So with a scary opening sensation in my chest and color bars scrolling across my field of vision I stepped out into the aisle, joining the converts and new members going down to the stage. I was shaking openly as I walked and was aware of the gazes of the congregation on my face as I passed. I felt bridelike. It was a long aisle, and I was slowed by the throngs of people coming forward. Watery song all around clogged my ears and I did a kind of mental pat down to check if I, uh, suddenly believed in God? Did I deserve to be cosmically punished for all the things I'd ever done wrong, for even just having the *potential* to do things wrong, and had the death of God's son relieved me of that punishment? Was I giving that knowledge a kind of 10-4, and accepting my passport to paradise?

No. Though I realized that Feeling X might have been the thing that seized people when they spoke in tongues or raised their hands in the air during church or decided to come forward to accept Jesus Christ as their Lord and Savior, for me there was no theology involved. I felt split open, but I couldn't make the connection to God or Jesus.

The pastor receiving people at the end of my aisle was, of all people, Pastor Woody. He put an arm around my shoulder and clasped my hands in one of his. "It's so good to see you!" he cried, and I could feel that he meant it harder than anything he'd said to me before. Then he asked if I had come for membership, a rather sterile question under the circumstances, as if I had arrived at the front desk in a health club. I said I had. He guided me on to be patted and smiled at by other pastors lining the stage. Jonathan Falwell clapped me lightly on the back.

As we all bottlenecked through one doorway and up a few stairs into a hall lined with soft purple carpeting, the singing congregation faded behind us. Along the purple-carpeted hall, men and women were leaning against the walls, Bibles and index cards in their hands, hopeful looks on their faces, as if they were working on commission. The way it went, I gathered, was that whichever one of these Bible-bearers you locked eyes with first became your Salvation Guide. Before I could even think to be strategic about it, I was walking down the hall alongside the woman with the little nest of gray curls, who had about her a librarian's fastidious tranquility.

We exchanged names and she led me gently by the elbow into Pate Chapel. The whiteness of the light, the bleaching effect of track lights overhead, reminded me of home, of California. The walls were crisp alabaster and the stained-glass windows brand-new, saturated with color. On either side of the room were columns of folding chairs, and each column was divided into groups of four chairs, two facing two. Dozens of new members sat with their personal guides in intimate caucus. My guide and I sat together under a stained-glass window, her back facing the wall.

"Why are you here?" she asked me.

This was a more searching question than the guide could have known. Even though I'd had Feeling X, even though I'd suddenly felt kind of punched in the back to come forward, I wasn't there because I'd had a revelation about God. And though I didn't yet have a deep understanding of how much it mattered to lie about this, about believing in God, I grasped the problem to the extent that I couldn't just say, "I'm a sinner, and I believe Jesus, the son of God, died for me." I couldn't say that.

Instead I explained that I had been coming to the church since the previous winter and I had been trying to fix things in my life that clearly needed to be fixed, and that I still felt a core emptiness. I told her that I had read *Mere Christianity* and I was ready to give my life. I left off the name of the recipient.

My salvation guide was confused. "So you're in the Singles Ministry?" she asked.

I wasn't in any ministry at all, I told her, but Singles had been my mentor's suggestion.

The guide gave me an application card and I filled out my name, my address, my phone number. My hand was trembling hard and my handwriting was freakishly jagged. There was a checklist on the bottom left, with the categories Membership, Salvation, Baptism, Statement of Faith, By Letter, By E-mail. I told the guide I didn't know what to check.

"Well, where are you going when you die?" she asked as simply as if asking whether I'd eaten breakfast.

"I don't know," I told her, "because I haven't been saved."

"You're coming to be saved?" she cried, zapped by joy. I told her yes. She shot out of her chair and threw her arms around my neck as if one of us had won the sweepstakes. She said, "Oh, God bless you! This is so wonderful, so exciting!" She settled back into her chair and looked deeply at me with her watery eyes. "Christ died for you on the cross. You know, we are all sinners. All it takes for you to be saved and go to heaven is to be able to admit that you're a sinner and to give your life to Christ. Because he died for your sins."

"Okay," I said.

She told me she was going to pray with me, and that this prayer would help open my heart to God, though she said it sounded to her like my heart was pretty open already. She put her hand over my hands, which were resting on my knee, and recited a soft, extemporaneous prayer, most of which was inaudible, under her breath. She prayed to God to open my heart and come into it, enter my life, help me take baby steps to live my life in Christ, and help me grow to be a young woman in Christ. She prayed to God to flush Satan out of my heart. She noted again that Christ had died for me.

"In Jesus' name, Amen," she said.

"Amen," I said.

The guide congratulated me and we hugged again. "Now," she said, "before you can become a member, you have to be baptized, and we baptize by immersion. Do you know what that means?" I said I did—dunking, not sprinkling. She told me to make an appointment for my baptism and then I could become a member. She told me to check off Membership, Salvation, and Baptism. And on a little line at the bottom of the card she wrote down the date that I was saved: July 2, 2006.

I should definitely do the Singles ministry, she told me.

The new members were being called back to the sanctuary, so the guide and I said unembellished good-byes and I joined the others in the purple-carpeted hallway, filing back the way we came. Conscious of being watched in the sanctuary, I walked gingerly toward the stage, as if my bones were suddenly built from the thinnest porcelain. The man in front of me stopped and we all turned to face the church. We were lined up along the foot of the huge platform, one hundred forty of us in all, stage lights burning us up to make filming possible. I couldn't see cameras, just a rising wave of congregation about to crash down on me. I stood just off the center point, near the pulpit, and looking back over my shoulder I saw I was so close to Jerry Falwell we could have reached out to hold hands.

Falwell was reading names from index cards. He had a whole stack in his thick fingers. These were the cards the salvation guides had delivered from the chapel. These were our names. I stared up at Falwell rather than look out at the church. Who was out there drinking in the sight of all us poor surrendered souls?

Pastor Jerry finally called my name, and I jumped as if he had struck a gong. "Gina Welch," he said, pausing to read the checked words on my card. "Here for salvation, baptism, and membership." The congregation clapped and cheered.

I know how this part should have felt. I was supposed to have a kind of flinty satisfaction and sense of homecoming, as if I could fall into the crowd and be received in a soothing embrace as instantly familiar as a relative's laugh. But I felt more like a knock-kneed fawn at a meeting of wolves, my wolf-hide disguise slipping out of place. Because even though I had just had my first hint of what Evangelicals feel that makes them so passionately devoted, and even though it would be some time before I found myself called upon to pray out loud, I was still not a Christian. And I had just set off on a long adventure pretending that I was.

IN THE LIKENESS

———

N O LETTER OR BROCHURE CAME IN THE MAIL, AND NO ONE called to welcome me to the flock. Where was my hand-delivered loaf of whole-grain bread? Wasn't I anyone's friend in Jesus? I was a little annoyed.

But mostly, being ignored was a relief. My approach to the altar had startled me, and I didn't really feel ready to act like a Christian. I had just quit working at Capitol One and moved back to Charlottesville in the wake of a difficult breakup with my boyfriend, with whom I'd been living for two years. Gas for the hourlong drive to Lynchburg was too expensive; I was flat broke, subsisting on my old hard-times staple of ramen-with-an-egg-stirred-in. I was depressed, distracted, and felt actually vulnerable when what I thought I needed was a simulacrum of vulnerability.

That summer I took work as an extra on a movie filming near Charlottesville called *Evan Almighty*, starring Steve Carell as a cynical congressman God calls upon to build an ark in his Virginia subdivision. For months I played an astonished neighbor, marveling at the size of the ark, gaping at the variety of the wildlife milling around, tear-assing up the ark ramp in rain pelting down from huge nozzles overhead. The director of the film was an evangelical Christian, a generous man who bought dozens of bikes for his crew when he heard a local bike shop was at risk of closing down, stocked an abundant buffet for the extras, and went on to open a homeless shelter in an old Charlottesville church. I thought perhaps working for a Christian I liked was a kind of preparation to pretend to be one myself.

But when the movie wrapped, I still didn't feel ready. Working as an extra hadn't exactly made me rich, and I thought maybe I should spend more time with my Bible before I tried to convince anyone I believed it was the word of God. In September I fell back into restaurant work, waiting tables full-time at an expensive French place in Charlottesville. My life was part Bible camp, part spring break. Mornings, I read from the camo-green King James version I bought secondhand at the Salvation Army, a Bible from which, when I'd slid it off the shelf, had slipped a school picture of a little boy with a black eye. Evenings, I put on a tight black dress to sell venison and quail. I mixed Old Raj martinis and poured out gallons of Chateâuneuf-du-Pape, and when the restaurant closed, my coworkers and I polished the silver while we polished off cases of beer. Waitressing satisfied several conditions: it paid well and it gave me the chance to be debauched before I went on Christian virtue lockdown.

But most important, waitressing gave me practice at being undercover. While my coworkers knew me as a writer, none knew what I was writing about or took my vocation any more seriously than if I'd told them I was a professional calligrapher. Being undercover, I discovered, meant learning to listen more often than I talked.

When winter came, I felt ready for church. I had some money, I knew my Bible well enough that I didn't have to hit the index to find Colossians, and I was ready to clean up my act. I started attending services again, and thereby remembered that I hadn't received any church mailings because salvation wasn't the only precondition of membership. Every new member had to get baptized. Including me.

THE DAY OF MY BAPTISM there was a terrible ice storm in Lynchburg, apt conditions for Dr. Falwell's sermon, "The Myth of Global Warming." The preacher, gazing out over a cold-whipped, half-full sanctuary, reported that some had told him there weren't going to be many churchgoers because of the weather; but look at us, faithfully braving the ice—he'd "never preached to sissies or softies."

I was looking forward to the novelty of baptism and I sang heartily in church, finding beauty for the first time in the airbrushed vocal stylings of Ray Masters, the evenly tanned music director with soap-opera good looks. I had heard him sing dozens and dozens of times, but that morning was the first that I detected the passion behind the Vegas sheen of his performance. He meant what he sang, just like the WMS.

In his sermon, Dr. Falwell acknowledged that the seasons were getting warmer—we can all feel that. But, he told the church, this was all part of the planet's cyclical change. He reminded us that thirty years ago we worried about global *cooling!* The people who were pushing global warming were doing so to distract Americans from more substantial issues, such as moral bankruptcy. Dr. Falwell condemned the eighty-six Christian leaders who had signed the Evangelical Climate Initiative for abandoning the Christian cause. He retitled Al Gore's movie *An Inconvenient Truth* as *"A Convenient Untruth"* and called it a scheme to get elected president.

After church, I spent the day in Lynchburg—shopping, eating lunch, driving around the beautiful but deserted downtown area and looking at the James River, which features a fountain that is just a stream of water spouting into the air. As with many small cities, Lynchburg's energy had moved elsewhere, and most of the shops lining Main Street were dark, For Sale signs in the bottom corners of their windows like misplaced postage stamps. Downtown's historic neoclassical buildings and cobblestone courtyards, and even the breathtaking Monument Terrace, with its granite and limestone stairs climbing up past war memorials and up a steep hill to the foot of the old City Court House—many Lynchburg residents had effectively cut the lights on all this. Town house developments, sprouting out of the ground like dandelions, were more convenient to the megaweb of superstores, shopping malls, and chain joints spanning out around Ward's Road, closer to LU and the new church.

AT FIVE, I CAME BACK to Thomas Road for my baptism and stopped at the information desk for instructions. A woman in a wheelchair told me I was too early, that I should come back at a quarter to six, fifteen minutes before the commencement of evening services. She slid a piece of paper across the desk, on which was printed a checklist of particulars I would need for my baptism:

- Towel
- Change of underclothes
- Hair dryer (optional)

I told her there was a towel in my car but that I hadn't brought any extra underclothes.

"Go on across the street to TJ Maxx," she said. "Get a pair for ninety-nine cents."

She then wheeled around the desk to show me the baptistry. She asked if my family would be there and I told her they would not. She seemed sad for me and didn't pry.

We entered the sanctuary, which was dim and quiet, as if it were the middle of the night. A cluster of men in suits sat in a row near the wall. She lifted her finger in their direction, and up above their heads, where there was a square hole cut into the wall.

"There's the baptistry," she said. The room beyond the hole was tinted dark blue.

One of the men shouted out, "Ain't no one up there yet! Come back at quarter to six!"

As we left the sanctuary, the woman took my hand in hers and told me, "I'm so glad you've been saved."

WHEN I CAME BACK to church, the sanctuary seats were filling up quickly, and through the square hole I saw that lights were on in the baptistry. Up some steps to the balcony and off the landing, opposite two men wearing exoskeletons of expensive camera equipment, I found the baptistry reception area: a small room featuring a sign-in podium and a long rack of deep–ocean blue robes. At one end of the rack were tiny child robes; at the other, robes as big as bedsheets. To my left were changing rooms for men and for women, to my right a prayer room, and straight ahead lay the doorway to the baptistry itself.

Two elderly ladies at the sign-in podium were assisting a teenage girl, Mimi, who had just come out of the changing room. She had lined her eyes in bright blue. The collar of her baptismal robe hung lower than that of the orange T-shirt she wore underneath. Hanging over her T-shirt collar was a silver pendant: a cross stacked on top of an ichythus. A boy about her age, stocky and bland as a potato in his baptismal robe, blinked at her through his glasses.

"Do I have to take my T-shirt off?" the girl asked nervously.

"Oh no," said one of the ladies. "Our fella is a whiz with Photoshop—he can make it look like the robe comes all the way up."

The elderly ladies—Lucille and Roann—greeted me and had me fill out an index card—all the basics, plus the dates of my birth and salvation. Roann's husband came in from the hall and struggled to refold Mimi's towel—a huge striped beach blanket. "You can tell I don't do the folding at home," he said.

Once I was all checked in, one of the ladies began flicking through the rack of robes, looking me up and down. "You're a tall one," she said. She pulled out a robe and held it against my back. "It ought to be long enough," she said, handing it to me.

Roann's husband showed me the baptismal pool. Through a doorway, short flights of stairs ran up to the right and to the left. We ascended the stairs, and at our feet was the pool: a powder blue tub sunk into the floor. Steps led down into the pool and back up on the other side. The tub was perfectly framed by the square hole, which afforded us a bird's-eye view of the entire sanctuary. Roann's husband told me someone would be waiting with my towel on the other side of the pool, and after taking it I would come back to the reception down the other set of stairs.

Lucille led me into a changing room, which had a long mirror with a counter below it and a row of locking stalls. She told me to get undressed and leave my personal items in the stall. I asked her what I should wear beneath my robe.

"You don't have to wear anything if you don't want to. Whatever you wear *is* going to get wet." Her breeziness made me feel as if I was suiting up for the log ride at an amusement park.

Locked in my stall, I put on my new underwear, preferring to keep my original pair dry. I examined my robe. The garment tag labeled the thing a Baptismal Culotte. It had a crotch. It wasn't a robe at all—it was a kind of billowy clown suit. The crotch, I presumed, would prevent the thing from floating up around my waist and revealing my 99¢ TJ Maxx panties. I stepped into it, and zipped it up to my neck. It was like a body bag with cutouts for my head, hands, and feet.

Back in the reception area, Lucille clipped my name tag to the top of my zipper. It was for the photograph, she said, and as a safeguard against the pastor forgetting my name once we were in the baptismal pool. Roann was saying she knew the Pennsylvania town Mimi and her boyfriend, Sam, were from—an Amish lady there had taught her how to de-ice a freezer using mayonnaise.

Mimi was a sophomore at Liberty, majoring in kinesiology. Sam was a car salesman for now, taking time off from school.

Downstairs in the sanctuary, Sunday evening service was getting under way. A choir of children was singing, their voices as bright and chaotic as confetti.

Enter our agent of baptism: Old Ray (*old*, Roann explained, to distinguish him from EPIC Singles Ministry Pastor Ray Fletcher and music director Ray Masters). Old Ray had side-parted hair, white and soft as down feathers; he wore gold squarish glasses and a handsome navy suit. His little brown eyes were watery, like oysters. He arrived with several men and introduced himself to us before Roann's husband whisked him into the prayer room to change.

While Old Ray changed, a man who had arrived with him spoke to us. Affixed to his lapel was a gold pin bearing the words *Jesus First*. He remarked on how fortunate we were to be baptized in such a blessed church with such a blessed history by a pastor who had been with the congregation for as long as Old Ray had. Old Ray, he told us, read the Bible cover to cover three times each year.

Jesus First decided (arbitrarily, it seemed to me) I was to go first, then Mimi, and Sam last. I was irritated by this order—I had never done this before!—when I realized that Mimi and Sam were first-timers, too, by definition.

Roann's husband suddenly emerged from the prayer room. "Old Ray wants to have a word with you three," he said.

The prayer room was Main Street in miniature—a bookshelf, a mahogany side table, a few lamps, a portrait of Jesus, and in the center of the floor an Oriental rug the size of a bath mat. Old Ray's dress shoes were lined up neatly next to the side table. Ray himself wore a solemn black judge's robe, his crisp shirt and tie visible at the neck. Neoprene booties poked out beneath the hem of the garment, and I thought I saw the pants of a wetsuit as well.

We stood in an intimate circle. Mimi, I noticed, was still wearing sweat socks. The sound of a lone child singing in the sanctuary thrummed the floor under my bare feet.

"You all understand what a baptism is?" asked Old Ray. His tone was subdued but warm with the joy of the occasion. We did. "You've all been saved?" We had. He asked us each individually and we assented again. I didn't snag when he asked me; my thought was, *I've been to that.*

"Good. Now, baptism is like a soldier getting his uniform. The uniform doesn't make him a soldier. It's what the man does that makes him a soldier. The uniform only marks him as a soldier. It's an identifier rather than something that gives the man actual qualities of being a soldier." Old Ray pointed to his slim wedding band. "It's like this ring. I've been married for sixty-two years. This wedding band doesn't make me a married man, but it marks me as one. I got saved at seventeen and married at twenty-one. I only needed one baptism and I only need one marriage."

Mimi nudged Sam. "Aw," she said. "That gives us hope."

"Well," Old Ray continued, as if he were a prerecorded hologram, "y'all are lucky today. When I was baptized at seventeen it was in the river during the wintertime. There were hunks of ice in the river. I still remember floating down that cold river." I imagined him there in the water, skin bluish, looking drowned. It seemed a more poetic approximation of death and rebirth, holier than getting dunked in a factory-issue plastic tub. "I didn't mind the cold," Old Ray said. "When I got out of the water, my mother was there and she gave me my daddy's overcoat, and then we walked home together."

Perhaps if the conditions had been different, if I'd gone down to some river's edge for a baptism rather than signing in on a clipboard as if I was there to get a fake tan, perhaps then I would have been awed by the seriousness of it. Perhaps not. In any case I didn't grapple in any kind of sustained way with whether getting a Christian baptism as an atheist was any worse than anything else I was doing. I labeled it a necessary step, part of my program to get closer to the heated core of evangelical life.

We prayed, and then Old Ray lined us up outside the entrance to the baptismal pool. The children were still singing, their voices high and happy. Two songs left, Roann told us. Today we would be doing baptisms before the offering, so after the songs, we were up.

Old Ray handed me a paper towel folded into a small rectangle, and instructed me to cross my forearms over my chest. I did so, holding the paper towel to my shoulder.

"Now," he said. "Have you ever seen a corpse hold anything?"

I thought of King Tut, clutching his crook and flail. He meant me—I was the corpse. "I guess not," I said.

"That's right," he said, taking my paper towel away again. "That's why *I* hold this."

Old Ray told me that when my time came, I would bend my knees a little and let him tip me back into the baptismal pool. He would hold the towel to my nose and mouth to prevent water from rushing in. He demonstrated this and I fell into his arm a little. The two photographers would take my picture. After I had been dunked, I would walk up the stairs leading out of the pool, where Lucille would be waiting with a towel. Soon I'd receive a photograph and a certificate in the mail.

Jesus First asked if I had ever seen a baptism. I said no—deciding not to mention the Catholic sprinklings I'd observed. He pulled a photograph from a stack on the reception podium to show me one. It was a picture of a pretty little girl—maybe ten years old—standing in the pool with an old man, looking up at him sweetly, arms in an X over her chest.

"This is going to be you," he said.

"That's going to be me," I said, "but older and bigger."

Old Ray told a story of the largest woman he'd ever seen baptized— he thought her to be around four hundred pounds. The pastor doing baptisms that day had a bad back. The woman came down into the pool, and the pastor held her in his arms, but when he tipped her back he couldn't get her up. He had to struggle, and as he heaved her out he shouted, " 'And RAAAAAISED up in the likeness of his resurrection . . .' The church all had a good laugh about that," he said.

One song left, Roann said. It was a lone little girl singing in a cracked tone.

Old Ray went up the stairs to the right. *Jesus First* suggested I wait at the entrance and go in when it was time. Air didn't circulate well in the baptistry, he said, and it was cooler down here.

I asked *Jesus First* when he was saved. He didn't know Jesus until his late twenties, he told me. But here at Thomas Road, he said, they baptize a lot of children who grow up in the church. When this happens, the child is often so small that he can't walk down into the pool—one pastor floats the child off into the arms of the baptizing pastor like a paper boat. When the child is immersed, sometimes he's so light that he has to be pushed under. And sometimes his legs fly up out of the water.

This seemed strange to me: Woody had told me they didn't baptize babies at the church because they believed a person had to *choose* to get saved, had to understand what it meant to be a sinner and to have Jesus sacrifice on your behalf. How could a little child apprehend these concepts?

Applause was clattering from the sanctuary, and Roann told me to go

on up the stairs. At the top, two men waited. Old Ray was already standing in the pool, wearing a wireless, flesh-colored microphone on his
head like Britney Spears. Under the water, his robe was a moving black
cloud. There was no stopping—one of the men took my hand and began
to guide me down into the pool. My sleeve caught on the handrail and
held me back, though the man kept drawing me down and Old Ray was
reaching out for me. "Wait!" I said, reaching back to unhook my sleeve,
nervously laughing off the snag.

In the water now, my robe was suddenly leaden, dragging on my
chest and back. Old Ray was standing at my side, speaking. He took my
paper towel. His voice was loud and his words seemed to float by in
compound shapes. I couldn't focus on what he was saying. I looked out
the square hole and saw a sanctuary of faces upturned at me, saw myself
pictured on the JumboTrons, saw Dr. Falwell sitting on the stage, slit
eyes turned up toward the baptistry. Flashbulbs glittered; the two photographers were already at work at the exit end of the pool. Not knowing where to look, I mimicked the little girl from the picture and gazed
up at Old Ray with a sweet smile that felt as leaden as my robe.

Old Ray was saying, "Today we have the baptisms of Mimi, Sam, and
Gina. You've been saved, haven't you, Gina?"

"That's right," I said.

He raised his right hand up in the air and held the paper towel before
me. "Gina, based upon your profession of faith in our Lord Jesus Christ,"
he said, "I baptize you in the name of the Father, the Son, and of the Holy
Ghost," and he brought the paper towel down over my face, swooping me
down under the water. Down there in the blurred blueness my eyes were
open. Old Ray was a shadow above me and water glugged into my mouth.
I heard Old Ray say, as if he were speaking into a pillow, ". . . buried in the
likeness of his death . . ." and then he launched me out of the water, and
bell-clear again, "raised in the likeness of his resurrection." The sanctuary
clapped and I waded over to the exit stairs, where cameras were snapping,
and took the towel Roann was holding out.

Shivering and laughing back in my changing stall, I peeled off my
baptismal culotte and wiped the mascara from my face. Mimi came in
laughing, too. "It is *so* cold!" she said. What was so funny? It seemed
possible it was just the childlike thrill of getting wet.

As we changed, we chatted a bit about how I came to the church.
When Mimi asked why I came all the way from Charlottesville, I told her

I found Dr. Falwell very entertaining. She said that if I thought Dr. Falwell was funny, I had to come Wednesdays to TRBC to hear Ergun Caner. "He's young and so exciting," she said. Dr. Caner, Mimi told me, was Turkish and a convert from Islam. "He preaches about things other people are scared to preach about," she said.

"Like what?" I asked her.

"Homosexuality, race . . . he says a lot of daring things. Like have you heard of the Blasphemy Challenge?" I hadn't. "It's this thing on YouTube where people videotape themselves denying the Holy Spirit, which is the worst thing you can do. Dr. Caner invited the creator of the Blasphemy Challenge to debate him, but the guy hasn't come down yet. They've only had email debates. But you *have* to come on Wednesday nights."

In drawers under the long counter I found an array of hair dryers and curling irons. Feeling relaxed now, I began to dry my hair as Mimi ran out to meet Sam and find her parents downstairs, born again not of the flesh, but of the spirit.

THE MICROWAVE EFFECT

THE PROPERTIES

———

T HE PRECISE LAWS OF THE RABBIT HOLE INTO WHICH I HAD
plunged were not clear to me for a long time. I thought I had to appear to know automatically how to behave, because if I were truly a believer God would make it self-evident to me. The Holy Spirit would
become a muscle in my tongue and Jesus would be living in my heart,
pushing levers. Asking questions seemed shameful, faithless. The reality,
of course, was that communities and cultural dictums shape native be-
havioral cues—the codes were in the water and I was a foreign body.

Eventually, I came to know the doctrine, and, struggling the whole
way, learned to mimic the native tongue.

To go to heaven, you had to believe that Jesus was the son of God,
sent to live and die atoning for our innate sinful nature, and that his resurrection served as proof of his sovereign divinity. Then you had to say
the sinner's prayer, admitting you were a sinner, and accepting with gratitude Jesus' sacrifice as a proxy for the punishment you deserve. That
was it. God liked church attendance and good Christian works—these
were expected of you and netted you karmic rewards on earth and in
heaven—but being a Christian slouch didn't put you in jeopardy of losing your pass to paradise.

Once you were bound by your contract with God, there was only one
way out: "And so I tell you, every sin and blasphemy will be forgiven men,
but the blasphemy against the Spirit will not be forgiven" (Matthew
12:31). Blasphemy against the Holy Spirit was typically interpreted as
witnessing God's miracles or knowing and understanding God's offer

yet denying their divine origin, thereby rejecting them. There was no for-giveness for apostasy.

Baptism was sacramental and symbolic of union with Christ. It was required for church membership, but not for salvation.

Jerry Falwell could be called Pastor Jerry or Doc, but most com-monly, Dr. Falwell.

Sunday morning services were held in the main sanctuary at 8:30 or 11:00. Featured in the services were announcements; songs to sing along with; songs to quietly admire; songs sung by the whole choir or by small groups or solo artists; a chance to shake the hands of the people sitting near you; the collection of tithes and offerings; prayer led by a guest or a church pastor; prayers for the sick and the dying, prayers for the families of the dead; the sermon (given by Jonathan Falwell at 8:30 and his father at 11:00); and finally an invitation of membership for non-member Chris-tians, salvation for the unsaved, and rededication to Christ for the slip-sliders. Sunday nights there were guest speakers and preachers, baptisms in the baptistry, and more singing and praying.

Sunday School was called Adult Bible Community at Thomas Road, and it was held at 9:15 every Sunday morning. The size of the church meant there were classes for every stripe and persuasion: for young cou-ples and for empty-nesters, for men only and for women only, for the military and for emergency responders, for college kids and for choir singers, for new members and those altogether new to Lynchburg, for motorcyclists and for Spanish speakers, for singles of all different ages. There were around sixty communities, all told.

Wednesday evenings dozens of Community Interest Groups met, like my 100% Effective Evangelism class, with member volunteers teaching classes on subjects as varied as debt reduction, Alzheimer's support, cross-stitching, and spring gobbler hunting. Dr. Falwell started the CIGs in 2006 in an effort to entice people who might not otherwise come to church. After CIGs, Campus Church featured a program in the main sanctuary for college kids—rock music and sermons from hip young pastors.

Throughout the week other groups met to plan events, fund-raisers, or just to get together and pray.

Bibles, I observed, were not carried to church in purses or bookbags, but in the hand.

Falwell had built an empire, a closed system. There was Liberty University, of course, which had over 10,000 students, but there was also the Distance Learning Program, or DLP, which boasted over 17,000 students enrolled online. There was the K–12 Lynchburg Christian Academy and Vacation Bible School for the summertime. *The Old Time Gospel Hour* broadcast Falwell's sermons on national television, radio, and the Internet. There was a team of lawyers called Liberty Counsel, who were employed to prosecute a Christian agenda. There were short-term and long-term missions, domestic and international. There was the Elim Home for alcoholics (men only). There was a program for homosexuals (men only until 2008). There was the Liberty Godparent Home, which housed single pregnant women and linked to Family Life Services, an infant adoption program.

Dr. Falwell often seemed more interested in politics than religion. Using the same rhetoric as Fox News and the Bush administration, he preached on current events during every sermon. He tunneled around the restrictions on political endorsements from the pulpit. In one sermon he specifically advised the congregation to ignore network news, the *New York Times*, and NPR, and to rely on the impartiality of Fox News and the Drudge Report (he mentioned no reliable newspaper). And Falwell went beyond merely recommending news sources, determining for his church which reports were false (a study on the failure of prayer to effect medical miracles) and which were true (an unsourced report on the link between oral sex and cancer).

Swearing was verboten. So were drinking, smoking, and premarital sex. Plunging necklines, spaghetti straps, facial piercings, and short skirts were frowned upon, and two-piece bathing suits at pool parties were considered scandalous and gossiped about long into the winter months. Out was any movie with a rating stronger than PG, along with dancing and pessimism.

New to my life was the intricate language, trance-like rhythm, and personal flourishes of group prayer, which often happened with little or no warning, and to which one had to instantly submit, head bowed and eyes closed. New was lifting my palms to the source of the music when I was particularly transported by a song. New was one-stop shopping at Wal-Mart (more commonly known as "Wally World"), sweet tea, and emails ending with Bible passages.

But once I got beyond the culture shock, there was an evangelical personality I came to know. More than anything the people I met at

Thomas Road tasked themselves with Jesus' Sermon on the Mount directive that they be the salt of the earth and the light of the world. As imitators of salt, they endeavored to be humble and preservers of purity. As sources of light, they believed that sharing their truth through evangelism was the most important thing they could do in this life.

These characteristics were derived from the Bible but had been so distilled over the descent of time that they seemed to have more to do with culture than scripture. A deep, abiding xenophobia, faith in feeling over logic, in prayer over Bible study—these were other patterns of thought and behavior that I noticed in nearly everyone at various moments. But these observations only became available to me once I stopped getting snagged on the rituals and allowed myself to be invaded by people's attitudes.

A preacher in my evangelism class said that the most effective way to make someone a believer was to evangelize like a microwave—heating the nonbeliever in his or her core, letting awareness cook from the inside out. In other words, the nonbeliever arrives at the knowledge rather than having it applied. With Christians, the microwave effect worked its powers on me, and in time, I was nuked into understanding.

GOD WHISPERERS

Y ou often hear Evangelicals use an inscrutable expression to describe their faith. They call it "a personal relationship with Jesus Christ." For a literal thinker like me, those words had a corporate-speak detachment from content. Why *personal*? Did it mean, as the Scaremare video seemed to imply, that Jesus himself was going to beam down and get all hands-on in the granular issues of your life, such as whether or not you go to a party instead of studying? And what was different about the Evangelicals' mode of belief that made them stipulate that believing in God was a *relationship*?

I found a clue on my first morning at the pre-sermon EPIC Singles Ministry which Woody had tried so hard to entice me into attending. At EPIC, a table piled with hundreds of name tags was manned by Laura, a plump, sparkle-eyed twenty-something with a shiny brown bob, dressed in a long skirt and sweater set. She was from Maryland and had gone to a small college in Pennsylvania. At the behest of another pastor, I had just spent several weeks attending the college student ministry—The Fellowship—and I felt relieved to meet someone who had not gone to Liberty.

Laura had me fill out a visitor's card. There was a box to check if you wanted someone to visit you at home. I told her I lived in Charlottesville and didn't want to make anyone drive that far. She told me to check Yes anyway, and if someone could make it, they would.

I really didn't want anyone coming to Charlottesville. I had a wholly separate existence there. The clothes I wore were hipper and tighter and cut lower, my hair was dirty and messy, just the way I liked it. At home I played my music loud and it was not Wal-Mart-friendly. I spent mornings writing in a room in my apartment which I'd set up as an office. Behind me were tall shelves of books about Evangelicals; scattered across my desk were dictaphone tapes of notes I recorded on my drives from church back to Charlottesville; and unmissably plastered to the wall, was a blown-up newspaper photograph from the 1970s of my father punching out a Klansman. Afternoons I'd hit the gym, and in the evening I'd have drinks with friends at a smoky bar, or I'd go on a date. With my evenings suddenly free, I was having a kind of dating renaissance, although I wasn't getting very close to anyone given that when my date would ask what I spent all my time writing about I'd tell him it wasn't any of his business. Few people in my life knew what I was up to: my closest friends and my immediate family. Friday nights I'd work at the restaurant. Saturday mornings I often had a hangover. My Charlottesville life wasn't very Christian.

Well, it wasn't like anyone would show up unannounced, right? I'd have time to—I don't know—stash my evangelical books under the bedcovers?

By the time I finished filling out the card for Laura someone was handing me a printed name tag strung on a shoelace—*Gina W.* I slung it around my neck and followed Laura down the wheelchair ramp into the EPIC meeting room, which still bore the Ericsson placard above the door: Communication Training Center.

There was a stage against the wall to our right, and some college kids were singing earnestly about Jesus, arms aloft under a projector screen displaying the song lyrics. The room was large, windowless, carpeted, furnished by a dozen round tables, trays of donuts, and a coffee urn set up on a long table in the back. There were about fifty people around the tables, all on their feet and singing. The age range was wide—from folks in their twenties to a few in their mid-fifties. Unease lay on the room like a fog bank. Necks craned to look for new members and people tugged at their shirt hems and tore their napkins to shreds.

I sat down at a table and was soon approached by a flannel-clad slab of a man with dime store brown glasses and on his forearm a tattoo of an arrow-pierced heart with the blurred name *Zelda* underneath. In a thick New York accent he introduced himself as Mitchell and handed me a black coffee mug. *EPIC Singles Ministry* was printed on the side.

After the singing, the group divided according to age. I went with the 25-to-34 group upstairs to a classroom. As we filed in, each person expressed dismay that the long conference tables had been pushed against the wall and the chairs were vaguely arranged in a circle. Several people said the same thing: "Now there's nothing to hide behind!" We pulled the chairs into rows.

The group's usual preacher—Donny—had just gotten married in Philadelphia and he and his new wife were away on their honeymoon. Our substitute preacher was Kip, a handsome man with the hoarse, strained voice of a sportscaster who was pacing the front of the room like a kenneled dog.

Laura wrote down our prayer requests and praises on the dry-erase board. One man wanted to offer up praise for having secured a new job at Liberty. A woman sitting in the corner wanted prayers for debt relief. Britney, a girl with a chocolate-brown pompadour and violet eyeliner, one of the college kids who had been singing downstairs, asked for prayers to help fund her upcoming mission trip to India. Alice, a woman about my age with shoulder-length hair the color of a new penny and a Bible bound in pink leather resting on her knees, asked for a prayer request for a woman she worked with at an orthopedic surgeon's office. The coworker's twenty-year-old son had been in a car accident and had just been taken off life support. Neither the coworker nor the son were Christian. Alice had accompanied the coworker to Richmond to visit her son in the hospital and was struggling to be a good witness to her friend without offending her. Listening to Alice's story, I found myself moved by her sensitivity.

We all bowed our heads as Laura sent up everyone's prayers and praises, and then Kip banged his palm on a podium and asked us what made the world go round.

A young man up front with neatly combed hair who looked like he could be president of a college conservative group quipped, "Inertia?"

Kip aped irritation. "No, *Wyatt*. Relationships. Ree-lay-tion-ships make *everything* possible. What is the Bible? The Bible is a *relationship* book, because the Bible enables you to have a *relationship* with God." Relationships were deepened in cycles, Kip explained. When first meeting people, you define your relationship with them. When you come to know and understand them, you may come to trust them and commit yourself to them. Once that happens, you redefine your relationship and the cycle begins again—define, know and understand, trust and commit.

The relationship cycle is the same between man and God, Kip told us. "When you're spiritually immature, when you're a new believer, you can't *instantly* have a deep relationship with God. It grows over time through the cycle."

The personal relationship with God, I took it, was somehow related to communication. But it wasn't until a couple of weeks later that I began to understand what that communication would entail. Fresh from his honeymoon, compact and lively as a hot coal, Donny Stillman was preaching to the EPIC 25–34s from Jonah. His new wife, Kelly, sat off to the side, nodding. During the main EPIC meeting earlier that day she and I had been seated at the same table and so were stuck with the sudden intimacy of exchanging a Stuart Smalley–like mantra. The lead pastor for EPIC Singles, Ray Fletcher, directed us to turn to the person sitting next to us and declare, "I love you in the Lord, and God has a plan for you and your life."

From the back of the room, someone called out, "Awkward!"

Now, upstairs, Donny's theme for the day was impatience. On the video screen, the words *I'm in a Hurry to Get Things Done* were superimposed over a picture of a dim blue sea.

Our age group was particularly prone to impatience and particularly oblivious to God's voice, Donny told us. We were oblivious to the fact that God speaks to us *personally*. Instead of listening, we restlessly plow ahead making decisions about our lives, afraid to wait around listening for a divine voice. "We analyze everything in our lives to death. We analyze our lives down to the skeleton, and then we analyze the skeleton to dust. But everything we need to answer all of our questions," Donny rasped, lifting his Bible into the air, "is right here. So often we get caught up in trying to think about what to do that we aren't listening to what God is telling us to do." Donny had neon blue eyes and the hoarse enthusiasm of a Little League coach. "Why would we be disobedient to God's will?"

I thought about this, ramming my head against the question. God's will: How are you supposed to know when it's God talking and when it's your brain?

A plump girl sitting next to me, corkscrew curls dripping into her eyes, said authoritatively, "We have a self-destructive nature. From the time we're children we want to do things that aren't good for us."

"Good," Donny said. "Our sinful nature."

From behind me: "We interpret God's will so it matches up with what we want for ourselves rather than actually listening to God."

"Good," Donny said. "We don't *listen!*"

Donny told us a personal story to illustrate this point, the focal point of his sermon. When he was younger, working toward a degree in business administration, he went with his church on a mission trip to Monterrey, Mexico. One day he found himself in a Pentecostal church. "It was one of those churches where people were falling out, and speaking in tongues, and laying on hands," he said. "*I* don't believe in that, but it's one of those little things: you say tomato and I say tom-*ah*-to."

In that Pentecostal church, Donny sat in the back, a vaguely amused observer. Believers were speaking in the Spirit, collapsing in the aisles, and then the preacher called everyone down to the altar for prayers and the laying on of hands. Obliging, Donny approached a woman who was lying on the floor near the altar. He put his hand on her and began to pray. Within an instant, the woman sat up and started yelling in Spanish. "If you looked up the dictionary definition of awkwardness," Donny told us, "it would be Donny, in Mexico, praying over this woman as she yelled. But I kept praying anyway."

Later Donny was told this woman had been deaf her whole life, and Donny's prayers had healed her. Interpreting the event as a clarion call from God, he swiftly abandoned business administration to go into ministry. Even in the midst of our cynicism, Donny suggested, God speaks.

"I believe that God speaks to each and every one of you," Donny said. "And it's hard to listen to him—but it's important."

Talking to God meant, of course, prayer: communicating with him, forging a distinction between your desires and his plans. Prayer is at the center of evangelical life, so regular and natural that it's almost a biological process. According to a survey conducted in 2007 by the Pew Forum on Religion and Public Life, 78 percent of Evangelicals pray daily (20 percent more than the national average), and 29 percent report having prayers answered on a weekly basis.

And prayer was everywhere at Thomas Road: opening and closing meetings and services, sprouting up in the middle of a song and at the start of a meal. At sermon, the pastors prayed from the pulpit on the church's behalf. In EPIC and at smaller gatherings, non-clergy volunteered to send up prayers for the group. Every Sunday EPIC broke into small groups for prayer, where each person submitted a prayer request, and one member of the group would spin all those requests together and send them up in a kind of prayer cloud. There was also a special EPIC delegation called the Prayer Ministry, which convened once a week to pray for items singles submitted via a *Prayer 911!* sign-up sheet.

Prayer seemed to be at the heart of the personal relationship with God—as in, *you* communicate with God instead of asking clergy to do it for you—and in keeping with the notion of a specific personal relationship, each person had his or her own style of prayer. But there were commonalities. To pray, you bowed your head and closed your eyes and called on God. Some folks got him on the line with a "Dear Heavenly Father," some "Lord Jesus"; some had a different opener altogether. Ray Fletcher always said, "Dear Lord, we do love you, thank you that you love us." You would find some things for which to be thankful and awed—the weather, the meal, the company of friends; and then you'd move on to ask for life guidance on matters large and small, for protection from harm, for help coping, and for things you'd like to have or have happen— provided, of course, that it was God's will. You'd close with a little more gratitude, and in His precious name, Amen.

The fact that most Thomas Roaders freestyled their prayer and embellished it with fluent personal touches made me absolutely *petrified* about having to pray in front of others. Sometimes I'd sit at my desk in my home office and practice, but I couldn't conceive of anything listening on the other end. I couldn't figure out how to arrange my face or where to turn my gaze behind my eyelids. I got bored and distracted and quickly ran out of things to say. The several times I was asked to do it at church my words were stubborn and unnatural, and I spoke as if I were choking on a long rope.

But the talking part I mostly understood: you just told God what you needed and what you were grateful for. The listening part was less immediately accessible: when Christians talked about hearing God speak, they didn't mean they heard words. They meant that God spoke to some supernatural organ inside them, the heart's ear. He created knowledge in that organ that felt distinctly God-originated. When they felt that knowledge they would say, "God put it on my heart" or "God was telling me."

I often thought about the Id and the Superego, the struggle between instinct and conscience. Maybe by "God talking" Donny meant what I thought of as conscience. The existence of conscience is at the center of C. S. Lewis's efforts to prove God exists in *Mere Christianity*. As in, our ability to distinguish right from wrong is God talking.

But God talking was more complicated than conscience, as I would come to see, because sometimes what God said wasn't a matter of right or wrong, but a matter of his preference. Donny told EPIC a story about his brother's wife, who was pregnant with a baby girl. The baby's arm was not forming properly. It wasn't growing past the elbow. And instead of praying for the arm to grow, Donny was praying that if it was God's *will*, the arm would grow. If not, Donny wanted God to grant them the ability to appreciate the baby as she was. I would never be able to understand that aspect of prayer—asking God to choose something rather than appealing for moral guidance. Why would you have to pray for God's will to be done? If it was God's will, wouldn't it just *happen*, since God was in charge? Was I overthinking this stuff?

On another occasion Donny gave a sermon on prayer that made me feel like less of an idiot because he acknowledged that praying wasn't easy. Christians often complained to him that God wasn't answering their prayers. It wasn't God's fault, Donny told us. It was ours: we were praying wrong. If we were having difficulty praying, Donny suggested we return to the original prayer, the Platonic ideal: the Lord's Prayer. "Our Father, who art in heaven, hallowed be thy name; thy kingdom come; thy will be done, on earth as it is in heaven. Give us this day our daily bread. And forgive us our trespasses, as we forgive those who trespass against us. And lead us not into temptation, but deliver us from evil. For thine is the kingdom, the power, and the glory, for ever and ever. Amen."

Address, awe, succor, protection, guidance, gratitude, Amen.

Practice that prayer, Donny told us, and you'll learn how to pray.

I mostly liked it when other people prayed. Their letters to God were rhythmic, humble rambles and often thumped me in the chest with their searing honesty. But one thing really bothered me about prayer at Thomas Road: the only prayers they sent up for non-Christians were for salvation. Alice's prayer for her bereaved coworker was the only one in which I saw a Thomas Roader express concern for a non-Christian that didn't pertain to conversion. I tried on a number of occasions to get them to pray for the troubles of my friends and family members. Once the chaplain of the Liberty football team offered to pray for someone in my family after I'd helped him edit part of his dissertation. I asked him to pray for my stepbrother, who was experiencing some personal difficulties.

"Now, Gina," the chaplain said, "what is your brother's religious status?"

I said he hadn't been saved.

In his work with the Liberty Flames, the chaplain told me, he was constantly in the position of reminding his guys that God puts them through hardship to create opportunity. He suggested that maybe my brother would find God through his own hardship, and that maybe God was using me as a vessel to expose my brother to the Gospel. He said he would pray for my stepbrother's salvation.

This was what always happened when someone asked if my loved one was saved and I said no: when my head was bowed and my eyes closed I'd hear my friend's name floating up in the general prayer cloud and then the hope expressed that he or she would "look to Gina as an example that will open their heart to You." To get God on your side, the message was, you've got to get on his first.

BROTHER'S KEEPERS

O NE NIGHT SOON AFTER I'D MOVED TO VIRGINIA, I WAS ZIP-
ping along Highway 64 between Charlottesville and Richmond at
80-something in a 65 zone when siren lights swirled in my rearview. The
highway trooper regarded my California license with suspicion and,
glancing his flashlight around the inside of my car, asked me if there was
alcohol in my soda can.

"I don't know what you're doing here," he said, ripping a ticket off
his pad, "but we don't drive like that in Virginia."

Years later I got pulled over running late for EPIC one Sunday
morning, going 80 coming into Lynchburg from Charlottesville. The
trooper again looked at my California license warily and then asked
why I was driving so fast. I told him, nerves buzzing, that I was late for
church.

"Don't be nervous," he said. "It's all right. Where do you go to
church?"

I mentioned Thomas Road, explained that I drove down on Sundays
and Wednesdays. Recognition smoothed his features like a cool cream.
"You come down every week . . ." he said, smiling and shaking his head
in wonder.

He asked me nicely to slow down, then let me go.

PERHAPS IT'S UNFAIR TO compare the two episodes: the first happened
at night, sixty miles away from the second, on an altogether different
road; the highway patrolmen might have had nothing in common beyond

their guns and badges. But I felt a certain secret handshake quality when I said I was late to church: I was signifying both that I was a good girl and I was part of a club—maybe he was, too?

This communal belonging was one of the agents that kept the weave tight at Thomas Road. Evangelicals believe they can implicitly trust and rely on other Evangelicals. Part of the general idea behind megachurches is that it's wise to transfer the better part of your life to church so that you're surrounded by other Christians on whom you can depend. The truth is, I was living on the fruits of this reliance: it was only by my profession of faith that I began to capture the trust of Thomas Roaders.

Of course, the desire to be near those like you and to trust them more than others is close to universal. But Evangelicals have particular reasons beyond the obvious to trust one another, and produce particular consequences as a result.

A CHINLESS, DWEEBY PREACHER named Jerry Prevo, who took over duties for Jerry Falwell one Sunday morning, illuminated this point in his sermon. Prevo was the preacher at Anchorage Baptist Temple but originally hailed from Tennessee. Syrup dribbled from his low voice as he warmed up the congregation: "Dr. Falwell, for the past thirty-plus years, has been an encouragement to me, and a real friend to me, and I just want to take this opportunity to thank you, Dr. Falwell. You have been a help to me and a blessing—but you have gotten me into a lot of trouble down through the years also. I remember he brought me down here to get me fired up for Moral Majority back in the late seventies and the eighties." He said this in a somewhat mocking tone. "I was young and didn't have any more sense than to go and do what he told me to do. And boy, it caused an uproar." One chuckle burped up from the congregation. Evangelicals, I was finding, were willing to laugh at a lot of things about themselves, but never their values. Prevo backpedaled. "But—it was a good uproar! Today, it's a great privilege for me to be here in your new auditorium."

After bombing with a lame comedy routine about how to recognize an Alaskan (the congregation, perhaps, withholding laughter to punish Prevo for his Moral Majority quip) the preacher delivered a sermon about being certain you were a Christian. "You cannot become a Christian by good works, Amen?" Amens murmured across the sanctuary. "We're not saved by works. We're not saved by a combination of faith *and* works. You become a Christian by faith *without* works . . . but you cannot be saved or become a Christian by a faith that produces no works." Prevo was no poet, but his message trickled through: being a good person couldn't make you a Christian, but being a Christian was guaranteed to make you into a good person.

Therefore, if a person claimed to have been saved, you could trust that God was triggering his impulses, determining what he did and didn't do. This method of generating good behavior, Evangelicals believed, was more reliable than a human's ability to produce works to please God. Born-again works, in a sense, are not human-originated at all: they come at the behest of God.

This God-originated goodness created an ecosystem of trust, interdependence, and freedom with favor-trading the likes of which I had never before experienced. Mostly, the climate in this ecosystem made living easier. If you needed a job, you'd naturally have help finding one. If you were moving, you would have to *turn away* volunteers. If you hit financial hardship, the pastor of your ministry might take up an anonymous collection for you. Particularly among the EPIC singles, the evangelical imperative to be brother's keepers meant having a safety net where otherwise there might have been open air.

But the ecosystem had the potential, I knew, to be cloying in its demands for service. I experienced the suffocating pressures to give and get early on, when I volunteered to help the Liberty football chaplain with his paper. I had first gotten involved with the chaplain when he offered to help me find a suitable ministry at Thomas Road. No sooner had he suggested a place for me than he asked for help on his paper. And no sooner had I agreed to help on his paper than he offered to pray for my brother. And five minutes after I hung up from that exhausting sequence of reciprocity, the chaplain's paper popped into my email inbox. And later that evening, I got another message from him. "I don't have the words to say how you helped me today," he wrote. He said he looked forward to serving me as pastor.

And the next day, he emailed to thank me again and to tell me he'd prayed for me. Below the email he included a reference to a Bible passage, Proverbs 3:5–6.

I went to my Bible to look it up. "Trust in the Lord with all your heart and lean not on your own understanding," it read. "In all your ways acknowledge him, and he will make your paths straight." *In all my ways!* Sheesh.

One morning at church the same chaplain told me he couldn't open a document I had sent, so I agreed to come over to his office after sermon to see what I could do. At the Football Operations Center, a single car was parked in the lot. The chaplain was standing alone at the top of the wide staircase leading up to the center, waving and smiling as if in the unpopulated universe of a dream. Inside, the air in the halls had the distinct tang of new plastic. As the chaplain led me to his office I felt increasingly laden with the weight of our new relationship.

I couldn't unlock the document. I had thought the chaplain would maybe just flutter his hand and tell me to forget it, but he was looking at me as if waiting for me to supply a solution. I told him I could drive home and correct the problem, send the thing again. He was very grateful and tried to get me to accept an apple and yogurt from a little refrigerator in the corner. I refused, afraid the gesture would somehow ricochet back in the form of a request.

The chaplain insisted on driving in front of me so he could lead me to the freeway. On our way out, he pulled over three times—once to tell me about a shortcut back to Charlottesville, again to direct me to a Christian music channel, a third time to tell me the channel might fade out somewhere along Route 29.

We drove side by side on the highway until my turnoff to Charlottesville, which I knew was coming because for a mile the chaplain had been driving with his arm out the window, pointing to the right. Then he waved and waved until he passed out of view.

I was eventually freed from the iron fist of kindness: the chaplain settled me into EPIC and then he was gone.

The ecosystem of trust and favors wasn't necessarily fertile territory for the best course of action: the safety net was sometimes more a wispy gesture more designed for show than a sturdy scaffold. Sometimes the ecosystem only tended to problems enough to make them compelling success stories to share with the ministry—the problems weren't really solved at all.

I began to recognize this on an evening when we had a guest preacher for the Wednesday relationships class I attended with other EPIC singles. He was pacing the room in long strides, delivering the final message in his series. I sat at a round table, watching Genevieve, a Liberty student, feed Rold Gold pretzel sticks to her new white bunny. She had the bunny in a red carrier with white polka dots and a dainty pink ribbon was tied around its neck.

"I can get you one if you want," she whispered to me. "They're free."

The speaker was crisscrossing the room, microphone in hand, his warm-up pants swishing as he walked. "The primary problem in every relationship is *you*!" he said. "The problem might be that you're speaking in error instead of truth. You might be saying, 'I'm having a bad day' versus, 'God created every day so every day is glorious.' If you're being negative, you aren't grateful and people don't want to spend any time with you! You've got to love yourself. Like David said, 'I am fearfully made!' "

Mitchell lifted a large, calloused hand into the air. He was wearing a September 11 memorial T-shirt tucked into his blue jeans. "How come in some towns you can get along with everybody and in other towns people ain't friendly at all?" he asked.

"Well, that has to do with geography," the preacher said.

Just then Ray Fletcher entered, coming down the wheelchair ramp with a middle-aged man in a tightly strapped-on helmet, who wheeled his neon green bicycle beside him. The man's facial features were set on a slant and he was clearly a little disabled.

"Hey, everybody? This is Frank." Frank's eyes darted here and there, pinging around the room of faces as Ray explained that a collection taken up the previous Wednesday had been for him. I had contributed— Ray told us that an EPIC member was having difficulty making ends meet and needed money right away and that another had a special need. Frank's bicycle was, apparently, the special need and physical proof that members were generous when it came to supporting their own.

Ray told us Frank lived across the street from church, which I had difficulty picturing since church was surrounded on three sides by vast parking lots and on the fourth by a shopping mall. "He's a single," Ray said, "but he works on Sunday mornings and can't come to sermon so that's why you don't see him."

Frank walked to work on busy roads and so Ray had taken up the collection to get him a bicycle, helmet, and lock. "Frank, buddy, there are people here who love you and want you to be here Wednesday nights."

The guest speaker swished over and said a prayer for Frank, laying a hand on his bicycle. "He was in danger of getting hit by a car before," the speaker said, head bowed, "but now he's going faster and is in more danger. Lord, please watch over him."

After the prayer, Frank said, "Ray, can I say something? I almost got hit by a car today on my bike."

Ray slapped him on the back. "All right, buddy," he said, "we're praying for you, man."

And with that, Frank's special need was considered addressed.

CONSIDERING THE EVANGELICALS' INCLINATION to trust and support their Christian brethren, it makes sense that there's a strong desire to work primarily with Christian businesses. To this end, there are dozens of Christian business directories online, where you can find companies and individuals advertising both their trade and their faith (similar searches for Jewish and Muslim directories turn up comparatively paltry results). In these listings you can find accountants and lawyers; grocers, locksmiths, and arbitrators; dog groomers, rug cleaners, private investigators, masseurs, maids—almost anything you need. You can open an account with a Christian credit union or order Christian checkbooks; you can hire a Christian clown for your birthday party or have a Christian give you a French pedicure.

One directory, Ohio's *Blue Pages*, polled its users and found that the top two reasons people used it were a "higher trust level" in Christian businesses and a desire to "be good stewards of their finances": payments to Christian businesses, the users assumed, circulated back to the church through tithes and offerings, keeping the money within the fold. Perhaps the best-known of these directories is *The Shepherd's Guide*, an annual print booklet with listings for 100 cities and a distribution of 3.5 million. The online *Shepherd's Guide* improves on the print model with event calendars and classified ads for each of the participating metro areas. If you want to limit your contact with non-Christians almost exclusively to evangelism outreach, you have the means.

Of course, when a person's faith is the quality that recommends him, disappointment often follows. The danger was that Christians were just like everyone else but cloaked in the golden robes of holiness.

A kid named Xander ran headlong into just such a limited Christian when he was trying to find a way to get himself out of debt. Xander wore gunmetal-framed glasses and encrusted the rims of his ears in hoops and spikes. He preferred a more rock 'n roll church north of Lynchburg to Thomas Road for Sunday sermons but often came to EPIC class and lunches.

After church one afternoon, at an Italian restaurant lit dimly by red lanterns, he unwittingly pitched what seemed like a pyramid scheme to me and Alice, the girl with the new-penny hair and the pink Bible. I was listening contentedly, in an excellent mood from the service. I had been zapped with Feeling X and reduced to tears during a song called "Something Special," and had found myself appreciating Dr. Falwell's message on perseverance during tribulations. More and more I was beginning to feel that church was kind of a wonderful idea—the accountability of weekly self-examination, the support of togetherness, the refreshing exhale of group song. I joked to my mother that I wanted to start the Secular Church for People Who Think Jesus Was a Good Dude.

Xander was applying himself to a large dish of lasagna. "Some members make $500,000 a year. It's appealing to me because I know I have to plan for my own retirement—Social Security barely gives you anything."

Alice hadn't touched her salad. "I know that," she said. "You do have to plan for your retirement. No one's going to support you. That's why I invest and save."

I asked Xander to explain the arrangement.

"It's a deal with stores at the mall. Whenever you make purchases you would normally make, you get bonuses, and all that adds up."

I didn't understand. Did you have to pay? Were bonuses actual money? Was he also working somewhere else?

Xander told us he worked as a stockboy at a chain store. He said with this business opportunity he wouldn't have to actually do anything. Even if he didn't hustle, he'd still be making money.

I asked again if he had to pay to participate. I suddenly realized my alacrity in interviewing him seemed like interest in getting involved in this scheme.

"Getting the information is free," he said happily, dabbing the corners of his mouth with a paper napkin. "After that it's two hundred dollars. And then I just have to get twelve people to sign on before I start earning."

Alice gave me a look of clear-eyed disbelief. Xander had been bamboozled, signed up for something he didn't understand. Alice pushed her plate away. "Who told you about this?" she asked. "Who got you involved in this?"

When Xander first moved to Lynchburg, he had worked at a cell phone store and a coworker there told him about it, showed him a check a company had cut him for $1,700, which was much more than Xander's monthly wages. "I was skeptical at first, too," Xander told us. But he started and discovered that one of the leaders of the scheme holds sessions where he brings his employees to Christ. "And once I found out the purpose was to lead people to Christ, I was sold."

Alice pulled her plate toward her and ate her salad with her head down, saying not one word more.

Xander leaned back from the table, tipping his chair and rocking. He was just a kid: twenty-two, with a crisp, fresh energy and movie-star good looks; flawless olive skin, long-lashed yellow-hazel eyes, a fine, symmetrical nose with flared nostrils. He blinked at me and smiled, his teeth gorgeously white. I felt sorry for Xander, who seemed to have been inveigled into this scheme by someone capitalizing on his belief that one Christian can always trust another.

He told me that the next time we saw each other he'd have brochures to give me, that I should sign up with him because if he brings enough people on board he gets to go on a retreat.

"I think I'll be able to retire off this by the time I'm twenty-seven," he said, pausing to probe his teeth with his tongue. "And I don't know about you, but I don't want to be seventy or eighty years old and working at Wal-Mart."

BIBLE BELIEVERS

———

Upstairs in Donny's class one morning, the projection
screen was uncharacteristically blank. Donny stood behind his
lectern, jaw set, his electric blue eyes searching our faces as if he didn't
recognize us. He and Kelly, his wife, had just returned from a conference
in northern Virginia for pastors who cater to young Christians. A seminar on evangelism was the most popular session at the conference, he
told us, drawing around one fifth of the 750 conference attendees. It was
led by a pastor from California (Donny rolled his eyes when he named my
home state and I slunk down in my chair), who introduced himself as an
adherent of the emerging church, a diverse, postmodern movement of
evangelical Christians. Right then, Donny knew there would be trouble.

The emerging church had taken a very different approach to attract-
ing new members than had Jerry Falwell, who, as everyone knew, had
accelerated his spread of the gospel using the catalysts of negativity and
unyielding exclusionism. When NPR's Neil Conan asked him in a 2006
interview how his church had grown, Falwell replied, "A pastor needs to
be media savvy if he's going to reach everybody. I don't mean to be ugly
and harsh, but to be forthright and candid. And the result is that people
who don't like you start listening."

The emerging church, recognizing the natural ceiling on a stubbornly
reactionary model in an inexorably liberalizing world, took the opposite
approach. Not a unified denomination at all, the emerging church is actually a broad category of formulas designed for inclusiveness. It builds
on the principle that in order to keep the evangelical movement growing,

certain ideological sticks have to be retired and some carrots introduced. Emerging churches are more politically progressive, less restrictive on lifestyle, and typically encourage their worshippers to refocus on the issues Jesus promoted in the Sermon on the Mount—hunger, poverty, disease.

Donny told us about the things the emerging church pastor he met abided in his congregation: women deacons, social drinking, all manner of dress—things to which Donny applied the same expression he used for Pentecostals: "You say tomato, I say tomahto."

But Kelly was pursing her lips and shaking her head, and swiveled in her chair to appeal to the class. "Can you imagine Dr. Towns"— cofounder of Liberty University—"sitting down with a Corona and talking about the Bible?" Heads shook in response. "No, because it's wrong."

Donny agreed, but didn't see this point as one that would irreparably split the evangelical church. But then the pastor had said something that Donny thought would do just that: *The Bible is inspired, but not inerrant.* At this, our EPIC class oohed as if Donny were telling about the lead-up to a bar brawl.

In the moment, Donny hadn't wanted to make a big scene in front of his wife, so he'd simply raised his hand and began directing the pastor to scriptural passages that indicated the Bible's inerrancy. "I was so angry because this guy was insulting *my* Bible, the word of *my* God," Donny said, eyes rounding. "Every word in the Bible is *literally* true, it *literally* happened. My Bible contains no errors. I would die for my Bible."

Now Donny wanted help from us gathering information on the emerging church. Rick Warren, of the famous Saddleback Church, was becoming so powerful "that his people are going to figure into our lives somehow, make no mistake about it." At Liberty, there would be incoming freshmen reared in emerging churches; in our jobs we would find them stirring their coffee in the next cubicle; at home they'd be waving to us as they watered their lawns. All around us, people would be invading our world with corrupt theology, and we needed to prepare ourselves to parry their arguments.

Although many Evangelicals wouldn't include Rick Warren among the ranks of emerging church acolytes (because, for example, he did believe in biblical inerrancy) he was unequivocally an ally: he had written a foreword for Santa Cruz, California, pastor Dan Kimball's movement-defining book, *The Emerging Church*, and by championing issues like global warming and stopping the genocide in Darfur he had become a natural envoy to the left. *A Purpose-Driven Life* had sold 25 million copies and his approachable image, with his goatee and Hawaiian shirts, was becoming as familiar as that of Bill Gates. His "five giants"—the five gravest problems facing the world: spiritual darkness, poverty, disease, ignorance, and lack of leadership—made him seem like some kind of human Venn diagram of Jerry Falwell and Barack Obama. Whither Rick Warren went, it seemed, so went the future of evangelical Christianity.

It excited me that Donny was so worried about the potential of the emerging church, because the institution was open to transformation in a way that Jerry Falwell was not, in a way that made me think the tethers attaching Evangelicals to the sinking barge of right-wing politics could be untied. And so I was probably one of the few Americans adamantly in favor of gay marriage who cheered upon hearing that Barack Obama had asked Rick Warren to give the invocation at his 2009 inauguration. Obama drew heat for picking Warren, who had compared gay relationships to incest and whose Saddleback Church had a statement on its website effectively discouraging gay people from even thinking about membership. By choosing an anti-gay activist, Obama, the critics said, was turning his back on a community that had supported him. But by including Warren with such a grand gesture, Obama, I thought, was indicating respect for Evangelicals, when Evangelicals only expected to receive ridicule.

This was the beginning, I thought, of an effort to plant a stent in the obstructed ventricle between the left and the traditionally insular evangelical base. The only hope for Evangelicals to ever reconfigure their hard-line views on any issue was precisely this way: through exposure to the moderating influence of the left.

I saw Obama's invitation to Rick Warren as a long-term investment in changing evangelical attitudes—exactly what Donny was afraid of. Sure enough, days after Rick Warren agreed to step onto Obama's stage, the anti-gay language disappeared from his church's website.

JOEY'S LITTLE BROTHER PERFORMED a card trick for the whole EPIC group one Sunday morning. As he triumphantly held up Donny's card, the King of Clubs, Ray cracked from the back of the room, "He's a witch! Hang him for sorcery!"

Upstairs later that morning Donny preached the emerging church sermon he'd been working on since the conference in northern Virginia. He called it, "Why I Believe the Bible." The emerging church pastor had told his seminar that he wanted to teach them to be fundamentalists with a lowercase *f*, as in, Christians dedicated to the fundamentals of the Bible, who also eschewed the inflexibility of the capital-letter designation. "There's a contradiction there," Donny shouted, "and I am not afraid of being marginalized."

But perhaps Donny was missing the pastor's point. It seemed to me that the pastor was referring to a "Fundamentalist" as a divisive cultural archetype not necessarily rooted in the fundamentals of Christianity. It seemed to me that the pastor was calling on Christians to get back to the Bible.

Now we all knew there were things on which Christians would never agree, Donny allowed: music and movies, women's place in the church, alcohol, six-day creation, clothing, worship, and preaching styles. All of that, to Donny, was a gray area about which it was okay to disagree. Looking at the lonely hearts club around me, I wondered if marginalization could be added to Donny's list, if these people were willing to be exiled to the fringes of culture as willingly as Donny was ready to cast them.

But the issue that was not a matter of perspective, the issue that divided Christians from non-Christians, was biblical inerrancy. "God is perfect," Donny said, pounding his fist on the air in front of him as if to dent it into a shape, "so his word is perfect."

Donny laid out the evidence he had collected to prove the Bible was inerrant.

Inspiration: The Bible, Donny told us, is God-inspired, God-breathed. And since it is the breath of God, it is perfect and true.

Preservation: Donny used the Internet to trace the origins of the Bible. It had survived so much, he told us, it had basically been fact-checked over hundreds of years.

Revelation: Here Donny pointed us to a passage in Hebrews about God revealing himself through his word.

All in all, Donny's case felt a little underresearched, a little anemic, as if it were an oral report for a class he knew he was going to ace. But the problem wasn't his apathy, it was that the means had been patched together to justify the ends. The Bible *had* to be all true because if it wasn't, it was mortal and meaningless. And, seriously? A document's preservation was proof of its truthfulness? This reminded me of another thing I'd read in Clairvaux—that curiosity is vanity. Who are we to question what centuries of Christians have believed to be true?

Hearing Donny's rebuttal to the emerging church pastor helped me understand why many Evangelicals felt they had to be Fundamentalists to be Christian. If they allowed some parts of the Bible to fade from certainty it cast the entire book into question—even God's promise of paradise.

CLOSETED AND FEARFUL

———

E VANGELICALS HAVE WORKED HARD TO EARN THEIR REPUTA-
tion as core constituents of our country's homophobic base: preachers
rail about one man–one woman marriage from the pulpit and liken homosexuality to incest; many churches refuse membership to gays and lesbians;
some host reeducation programs to preach the gay out of you. And though
Mormons get all the shame-on-you credit for funding the ads for proposi-
tion 8, California's 2008 ban on gay marriage, they couldn't have pulled it
off without Evangelicals: 85 percent of California's two million Evangelicals supported it, compared to 42 percent of the state average.

Thomas Road did not disappoint when it came to displays of homophobia. Gay jokes got tossed around as blithely as commentary on the
weather, same-sex marriage was a dangerous threat to the very institution,
and church membership was not available to the openly gay—though
church attendance was encouraged. "We have many gays and lesbians
who attend our church," Dr. Falwell told CNN in 2002, "all seeking help
and spiritual deliverance from their abnormal lifestyle." Such deliverance
was formally offered through the Freedom Ministry, which was the umbrella title for Thomas Road's different support groups for the depressed,
the divorced, the chemically dependent, and the unsung "victims" of
abortion—women who have had them. During my tenure at Thomas
Road, deliverance was available to gay men only, through a group called
"Freedom's Quest." I nurtured a suspicion that Thomas Roaders simply
did not believe in lesbians—their thinking seemed to be homosexuality is
lust, lust is male, homosexuals are men, Q.E.D. But sometime in 2008 a

group for women "struggling" with same-sex attraction popped up on the Freedom Ministry website: True Identity.

The arrival of True Identity didn't totally prove my theory wrong; the titles for the two support groups suggested that same-sex attraction for men and for women was still classified as two different abnormalities. Freedom's Quest implied men were prisoners of their sexuality (an analysis supported by the title of the men-only pornography addiction support group, Every Man's Battle). True Identity seemed to suggest lesbians were merely confused. In either case, homosexuality was treated as a perversion or a delusion, not understood as an orientation.

Nevertheless, there was something about the texture of attitudes of many individual born-agains that made me think their homophobia was a delusion, something they could unlearn. If it wasn't an orientation, why then it was curable. But I knew re-education camps wouldn't set them straight. They would have to get used to gay people the same way an atheist like me had been able to get used to believers: through prolonged exposure.

I wasn't alone in my thinking: Reverend Mel White—openly gay and openly evangelical—had made it his mission to find the cure, citing Mahatma Gandhi and Martin Luther King Jr. as the inspiration for his activism. White—formerly the ghostwriter and friend of such prominent Evangelicals as Pat Robertson, Jim Bakker, and Dr. Falwell himself—moved with his partner into a house across the street from the original Thomas Road Baptist Church in 2002 to persuade Falwell and his congregation to become more tolerant of gays. In 2006, White founded a gay rights organization in Lynchburg called Soulforce, intended to confront "religious and political oppression" against the LGBT community through the use of "relentless nonviolent resistance." Though in an interview with CNN's Kris Osborn he called Lynchburg "closeted and fearful," White seemed certain that just by living by example, by showing straight Evangelicals that "our lifestyle is just like [their] lifestyle," he and his community could convert the unbelievers.

ONE NIGHT AFTER ATTENDING Campus Church, a Wednesday night service for Liberty students, I lingered in a shiny linoleumed hallway near the EPIC room with Genevieve, Alice, and Britney, who were giving the parking lots a little time to clear out. The Liberty Praise Team had played a straight-up rock concert that night, recorded for a CD and

DVD they'd eventually sell. All the seats had been filled and the roads would be congested for a while.

Genevieve unzipped the hatch on her pet bunny's carrier and reached in to massage its ears—the concert had been quite loud. "Hey, did that new Chipotle open in Charlottesville yet?" she asked me. I told her it had. "Cool," she said. "I want to come up there and eat sometime."

I said, "You should all come see me whenever you want." The invitation traveled the conveyor belt of my tongue before I could inspect its implications. I was just feeling friendly; I'd bonded with these girls. I hung out with them before and after sermon and EPIC, sat with them at lunch, talked to them just as I'd talk to my other friends, about family, work, love. I had recently cleared the language barrier, finally unpacking idioms that had signified nothing to me when I first started at Thomas Road. Now I knew what it meant to speak in the flesh or the Spirit, I knew what it meant for the Lord to put something on somebody's heart. I knew what Clementine meant when she told me she could "just see how much Britney loved the Lord"—I even felt I could see it, too, in the brightness of her lifted face when she sang on her praise team. Knowing the language—even though I never employed it myself—made me less sensitive to our differences. It was like Kip had said in his sermon about the relationship cycle: define, know and understand, trust and commit. I was learning that I didn't have to pretend to be somebody I wasn't to get along with Evangelicals. And I liked being around them: they were happy, and their happiness made me want to be happy.

My Charlottesville life was also beginning to change in such a way that I was no longer afraid of having Christian visitors. I was in the early morning writing habit now, so I was almost never out drinking. This development coincided with the fact that I couldn't tell anyone in Charlottesville what I spent my time doing or why I was out of town two days a week, and the result was that I'd essentially stopped dating. Intrigued by my secrecy at the start, men eventually felt rebuffed by it.

Maybe this wasn't the only issue. My bland church style had bled into my Charlottesville life by necessity: not only had I stopped zipping around the restaurant full-time, but EPIC fellowship had increased my donut hole consumption tenfold, and with the increase in hours I spent slouched in front of my laptop I'd ballooned several sizes. I stocked up on muumuu-style shirts at Old Navy, not wanting to spend much money on what I thought of as a temporary wardrobe for my temporary church body.

My Charlottesville friends had dwindled to a couple of girls I was close to, girls I wasn't afraid to have the Lynchburg girls meet. Besides, the Thomas Road girls knew I had non-Christian friends. People at church thought of me as an oddity in my secular family and my liberal hometown, even though there were moments when they'd ridicule my background. One Wednesday night, over dinner, Vaughn learned I was from California. He said, "The land of fruits and nuts."

"Heh," I replied.

"And grapes," he added.

"Yes!" I said stupidly. "We grow grapes!"

"Sour grapes," Vaughn said.

My home state and even Charlottesville were the subject of loathing, sure, but Evangelicals believed apples had the power to fling themselves far from the tree.

"I've never been to Charlottesville," Britney said, adjusting the bobby pins securing her pompadour. Alice made a sour face.

"Alice apparently doesn't want to come to Charlottesville," I said.

"No," she said, "I like C-ville, but I'm a Tech girl."

"Well, I *live* in Charlottesville and have no real UVA allegiances," I said. "I didn't even know what the mascot was at UVA until I was half done with grad school."

"What's the Tech mascot? A Hokie?" Britney asked. "What's a Hokie?"

"It's a bird," said Alice.

"What's a Liberty Flame?" Genevieve asked.

"An eagle," Alice said.

"So we're the Liberty Flames, but our mascot's an eagle?" she said, narrowing her eyes. "What's up with that?"

"Maybe it's an eagle on fire," I said. "A flaming eagle." As soon as I said it, I knew where we'd wind up, and I regretted teeing the ball.

"Maybe it's a gay eagle, a flamer," Alice said.

Britney suddenly leaned in, making our group a huddle, the flush of humor draining from her face. "You know, there are some gay people at Liberty."

Alice regarded her with a wisp of a sly smile. "Yeah, I know," she said.

There was a quality in Alice's smile and a restraint in her answer that made me think she understood gayness better than the other girls.

I asked if they were out.

"A few of them are, but most of them aren't," Britney said. "They all live in a house together. They even have girlfriends." Genevieve nodded, grimacing.

I asked how anyone knew they were gay.

Britney sighed at my naïveté. "Secrets come out, people learn about someone's history. You know, it all gets spread around."

Alice said she had known gay people when she was a student at Liberty, and the matter-of-fact way she said it made me think she hadn't judged them. Part of me wanted to find another time to talk to her more about it, to test my suspicion that she was more tolerant than the other girls, but I knew doing that would be risky. There was also a scandal while Alice was at Liberty. A staffer at the college had come out of the closet and then immediately left town. The suspicion was that someone was on the verge of outing him.

"Where is he now?" Britney asked.

"I think he moved to California, and I don't know what happened to him after that," Alice said.

"If that was me I'd move to California, too," Britney said.

I took in the other girls' faces, their complexions sallowed by the fluorescent lights pulsing overhead, the little etches on their lips visible. I was getting that million-miles-from-home sensation. I had learned to lift so many subjects and rotate them so that they caught the light differently. This meant appreciating Christian priorities like positivity and community. It meant understanding the evangelical desire for prayer in schools and even their objection to abortion, although I would never agree.

But homophobia was one feature of the evangelical mind I was unable to tolerate. It was sanctioned hate, the thick-skinned blister bubbling up from ignorance and prudishness, a failure to comprehend human sexuality, all slathered with a transparent biblical gloss. Ridicule and animosity were weapons I almost never saw Christians wield. But with homosexuals, it was different. "Love the sinner, hate the sin" only went an inch deep if the sinner was gay.

Non-Christians I knew seemed to think it was a staple of the faith, but I felt that if evangelical hatred was mostly a product of insularity and naïveté, well—*show* them. If somehow Evangelicals were forced to co-exist with gay people—if everyone who came out didn't have to immediately flee to a less closeted place—Evangelicals would eventually learn that their ideas about gayness were wrong. Their opposition to homosexuality would go the way of their opposition to suffrage and school integration.

In the hallway, the girls were very quiet and I wondered if they could tell how upset I was by the tenor of the conversation. But when Genevieve zipped the hatch on her bunny carrier, flopped out her tongue and said, "Yecch, sick," I knew my own revulsion had gone unnoticed.

AT CELEBRATE AMERICA! there were fair booths, food booths, and a moonbounce outside the football stadium, and inside a stage was positioned center field for the night's entertainment. After sunset, there would be a fireworks show over on Liberty Mountain. EPIC was running a concession hut, and I stood ready at my assigned register, prices memorized.

Before the acts came on, a deejay played country and adult contemporary over giant speakers. In the concession hut, Cintra was doing a grapevine step to "I Hope You Dance." Wyatt made fun of her, telling her Baptists don't dance.

"Well, I was born Baptist," she said, "and I love to dance."

Business picked up almost immediately. Wyatt was the runner for my register, grabbing hot dogs and Pepsis as I rang them up, telling me all about his world travels and military service between transactions.

Frank, the man for whom EPIC had raised a collection to buy a bicycle, came to my window and ordered a hamburger and a soda. From his post by the grills, Ray saw him and came over to make sure I didn't charge him for anything. I did as I was told, although as I watched Frank strolling off with his free burger and Mountain Dew, I felt surprised: Ray had once told me he considered Frank one of several guys who only came to EPIC to "eat, lust, and leave." And now Wyatt leaned in close, wanting to tell me another secret about Frank. Wyatt's nose was beaded with sweat and reflections of my face appeared in each polarized lens of his wraparound sunglasses. I looked uneasy.

"Frank is the only person I know who has ever been fired from

Liberty," he muttered through a private smile. He said that Frank had been a janitor, until one Friendly Friday—the day Liberty opens its campus to visitors—when Frank followed behind a tour group and finally said to one of the visitors, "You look like a queer to me." The tour guide reported the incident and Frank got fired.

I sneered, of course—because of the image of Frank lunging at a person that way, because of such searing homophobia. Frank was mentally disabled and couldn't exactly be held accountable for his behavior. But I was upset because this place—maybe it was how he was raised, maybe it was this church, probably both—sowed in him the poison seed of hatred.

But it was something else, I was surprised to find, that bothered Wyatt. "One of the only things I don't like about Liberty is that they promote snitches," he told me, hands on hips, now gazing off at the jiggling moonbounce. "If you *don't* report somebody for something you know they did wrong, you're guilty of it, too."

"Well," I said, for a moment not caring how I came across, "it *is* aiding and abetting not to report somebody."

Wyatt chuckled, shook his head, and stalked off to the grills.

Maybe I had contracted too much of the evangelical optimism virus, but I couldn't help believing that in the end people like Frank would be left behind with their anger. The emerging church was the future for born-agains, as it acknowledged that Christians needed to mold to the shape of the world—not the other way around. Signs of hope were everywhere. In December 2008 Richard Cizik, the chief lobbyist for the National Association of Evangelicals, a man who had added his signature to a full-page ad accusing the LGBT community of "anti-religious zealotry"—went on *Fresh Air* and told host Terry Gross that his position on gay marriage was "shifting." Cizik wasn't in lock-step with the Thomas Roaders; he was one of those controversial Evangelicals who acknowledged the urgency of global warming, in spite of the implications for creation theory. But he was also a self-described pro-Bush conservative, and for him to concede any ground at all on gay marriage was a jolt. "I'm always looking for ways to reframe issues," he said on *Fresh Air*, "give the biblical point of view a different slant, if you will, and lookit, we have to. The whole world, literally, the planet is changing around us, and if you don't change the way you think and adapt, you may ultimately be a loser."

Cizik paid for shifting position, turning in his resignation to the NAE a week after the interview aired. But he and Mel White were first wavers on the front lines of progress, felled by a doomed resistance. Even if other aspects of the emerging church were blockaded at Thomas Road, gay rights were inexorably civil rights: to stand against them was to stand against the natural passage of time.

EMOTIONAL THINKERS

—

D ONNY STOOD BEFORE A PROJECTION SCREEN AGLOW WITH A photograph of three wooden crosses, the crosses themselves back-lit by a fiery sunset. Laid over this image were the words *The Cross Paid It All*.

"It's an exciting day," Donny said. "We have a movie." He noticed a little girl sitting quietly with a book of word searches, a *My Little Pony* tote bag with looped rainbow handles at her feet. She was the daughter of Vaughn, a red-complected man at the high end of our 25–34 age group. The girl was eight or nine years old, visiting from her mother's house in Chattanooga. "Perfect for you!" Donny said to the little girl.

From her seat against the wall, Kelly was frowning at her husband. "It might be kind of graphic, Donny." She leaned into Vaughn's ear and told him what Donny would be showing. Vaughn nodded gravely. I guessed, with Good Friday coming up, the movie might have something to do with the crucifixion.

Evangelicals are a little obsessed with the crucifixion. This you probably surmised if you paid any attention to the throngs flocking to Mel Gibson's *The Passion of the Christ* in 2004. I remember feeling shocked at the enormous success of the film, at the footage of moviegoers surging out of theaters in tears. I hadn't guessed that anyone would be so eager to see Jesus abused. And despite the fact the movie had been made by a Roman Catholic, Evangelicals wholly embraced it: congregations bought out whole showings and set up screenings at church once the movie came out on DVD. Morris H. Chapman, a leader in the Southern Baptist

Convention, told the *New York Times*, "I don't know of anything since the Billy Graham crusades that has had the potential of touching so many lives. It's like the Lord somehow laid in our lap something that could be a great catalyst for spiritual awakening in this nation." *The Passion*—criticized by many for its anti-Semitic overtones and enthusiastic grisly torture scenes—struck many Evangelicals as a pitch-perfect depiction of one of the main elements that keeps them in the faith: the magnitude of Jesus' suffering.

It's always seemed to me that religious people seek some way to express unworthiness, some official means of feeling shameful and thereby beholden to God, who graciously accepts them in spite of their failings. For Catholics, unworthiness is expressed as guilt. But Evangelicals don't believe in guilt. Not only do they feel that negativity is an offense to God's gifts, they believe that if you're feeling guilty, it's a sign you're not perfectly immersed in your faith, that you don't possess the smooth, flawless orb of belief that Jesus' death counts as atonement for every last Christian sin.

So, guiltless, they express unworthiness by immersing themselves in the details of Jesus' sinless sacrifice. Constantly refreshing their exposure to Jesus' suffering binds them closer to God and to the church, because it reminds them of the price of their pass to heaven. And so they talk about the crucifixion, they sing about it; they love *The Passion* because they want the crucifixion expressed so vividly that they can nearly feel the nails piercing their own raised palms.

Now, before the image of three crosses—two for thieves, one for the son of God—Donny began the day's lesson with the Latin, Greek, and Aramaic origins of the place-name Calvary. In each language, he told us, the name translates to "place of the skull."

"Has anyone been to Israel?" Donny asked. Several people lifted their hands, including a woman with short, hairsprayed curls and a leopard-print scarf knotted around her neck. "What does Calvary look like?" Donny asked.

"A skull," the woman said.

Hands on hips, Donny nodded, his lips tight. A skull.

Later, I looked at pictures of Calvary online, trying to discern the skull on the chunk of sloped white rock, which was sprouting black bushes and pitted with holes. It was possible to perceive two hollow eye sockets, perhaps below the angle of a forehead. But it was a little like trying to see a sailboat in one of those Magic Eye posters.

Calvary, Donny told us, was a place of destination, a place of execution, and a place of salvation.

Donny had done a research paper on crucifixion, he told us, and he found it was a common means of execution until around AD 313. With great intensity, he began to describe the act of crucifixion. "The person was beaten and scourged," he shouted, "stripped naked!" After carrying their own cross to the place of crucifixion, the person would have their hands and feet nailed to the planks, either lying on the cross before it was erected or else ascending a ladder to be nailed standing.

Arms outstretched, Donny said, "When you're up there, in order to breathe, since your body is slumped, you have to push up on the ledge with your feet." Donny drew in a hideous wheezy gasp, straightening as he did, an expression of anguish crossing his face. I looked at Vaughn's daughter, who was concentrating on her word search. "If you don't die of asphyxiation, you die of blood loss, which can take days." He let his arms fall. "It's hard for us to imagine how great Jesus' suffering was. You need to remind yourself that all that suffering was for us."

At this point, Kelly nodded to Vaughn, who packed up his daughter's tote bag and escorted her from the room. Donny cued up the movie. "When I saw this movie—even though *The Passion of the Christ* is probably as close as we can get to understanding the extent of Christ's suffering—when I saw this movie I felt it explained what Christ did for us." Kelly shut off the lights.

The clip was from a movie about American prisoners of war in Japan during World War II. An American soldier is weeping on his knees in the dirt, hands bound behind him, about to be beheaded by a Japanese soldier. A bare-chested American man halts the execution and volunteers to stand in for the soldier. A Japanese commander considers his offer and then shouts his agreement. The executioner slices through the ropes binding the pardoned prisoner and tells him, "You are free." Then, in a gruesome display, Japanese soldiers nail the volunteer to a cross and raise him up. A single tear slides down the Japanese commander's cheek.

When the clip was over, several EPIC singles were crying, too.

AT SERMON IN THE SANCTUARY, Dr. Falwell announced that he was going to share with us the three reasons why "secularists" hate the cross. Dr. Falwell often preached sermons like these, such as in his "War

Against Christmas" series, inventing a cabal of secularists where there was none, providing his congregation with something to define itself and unite against. Dreaming up a monolithic opposition for Evangelicals also did the work of making the Christian cause seem insurrectionary, which inspired more intense, defensive devotion.

"The cross," Dr. Falwell boomed from the pulpit, "is an aesthetic offense." The cross is grotesque, an emblem of suffering. Cicero called it "the most disgusting pencil" and called for the very word "crucifixion" to be "far removed not only from the person of a Roman citizen, but his thoughts, his eyes and his ears."

Dr. Falwell claimed that someone told a friend of his that he didn't like talking about the crucifixion or the cross because it was so ugly. Falwell's friend replied, "I agree with you. It is ugly. It's ugly because it stands for *your* sins."

"The cross," Falwell continued, "is an intellectual offense," meaning that a Christian must approach the cross as a child, without trying to understand it. Dr. Falwell described the scene at Calvary, where Jesus' cross was planted atop the skull-shaped rock, which he interpreted to mean that man can't comprehend with intellect the sacrifice Jesus made. "In this case," Falwell said, "a PhD can be more of a hindrance than a help."

This was a common theme at Thomas Road—the subordination of the mind to the heart. Brains could rationalize sin; hearts would hold us accountable. And so Evangelicals acted according to what God told their spiritual organ, following whatever feelings were glowing inside them. Pastor Woody, recognizing me as more of a thinker than a feeler, had sent me to the book that was supposed to prove the evangelical version of God using logic and reason. But at the center of *Mere Christianity* was the argument that God is conscience—that *feeling* the difference between right and wrong is God; and so that, too, is a book for the heart.

Taking direction from visceral feeling spills over from the private realm into the public. Evangelical positions on political issues are also largely determined by a visceral response: sonogram pictures of fingers on a fetus's hand stir outrage over abortion; the physics of gay sex prompt knee-jerk discomfort with homosexuality; semi-articulate politicians who seem familiar, who strum the charm strings, gain evangelical support despite having no clear plan to implement their agenda.

In the sanctuary that morning Falwell finally concluded that secularists hate the cross because it is "a spiritual offense." The idea that God accepts man on the basis of his son's sacrifice and not by virtue of any good thing man can do is, according to Dr. Falwell, spiritually abhorrent. There is simply nothing man could ever offer to match Jesus' sacrifice.

As Dr. Falwell gave the invitation and many came down the aisles to accept the offenses of the cross, I thought about the portrait of Christians Falwell had drawn in the negative space of his sermon: by embracing the inscrutable cross, Christians were comfortable not fully comprehending the concepts around which they built their lives.

AFTER RAY'S CLASS ONE NIGHT, Alice and I, growing ever closer as friends, decided to go over to Campus Church. My friendship with Alice had taken me by surprise; I never expected to automatically identify with someone whose belief system was so different from mine. Wouldn't we always be arguing about abortion?

But the daily texture of our friendship was just the same as the texture of all my close friendships: we processed the ongoing dramas of our lives, shared the minutiae of our days, laughed and wondered at the spectacles we observed together. And even though our beliefs were fundamentally at odds, I didn't think that meant our principles were; and anyway I felt a kinship with her that seemed to transcend all that, a common orientation toward being in the world.

Campus Church was usually held in the Thomas Road sanctuary, but tonight it was on the Liberty campus, at the Vines Center sports arena. Red crosses were painted on the sidewalk leading up to the Vines Center, which was a textured white dome, like Epcot Center. Inside, the arena was huge and dim and filled almost entirely with college kids. It was disorienting to be with so many people in the near darkness and I thought I might trip on the stairs as we descended a few rows to find seats.

Below us, a blue mat covered the floor of the arena and a couple dozen students were down there kneeling or standing, holding their hands up in witness as a rock band played onstage. A banquet table in the shape of a cross was set and positioned in the center of the floor. It seemed to have silvery circles all over it, but from up in the stands I couldn't see what they were.

After a few songs, the band left the stage. The four JumboTrons hanging in the air went black and then displayed the words *Woe Is Me. Examine Yourself.* Everyone began to pray, including Alice. I bowed my head, but I wasn't sure what I was supposed to be examining.

A preacher named Wayne Parsons was leading Campus Church that night, and he walked the mat, delivering a sermon about Barrabas, the prisoner Pontius Pilate pardoned on the day of Christ's crucifixion. "If Barrabas were alive today, he would have to say that Jesus died for him, and not only that, but that he suffered for him." The same was true for us, Parsons said. "All the punishment due to you, everything you deserve for your sins you don't have to bear because Jesus bore it for you."

The JumboTrons lit up with the words *For You.* Ushers had given us each a paper flyer as we came in; printed on the front was a dark gray cross. Parsons instructed us to write our own names on the cross as well as the word *sinner.* "This may be the first time you've really confronted the fact that this is what you deserve for your sins—death, suffering, and crucifixion. But you don't have to endure those things because Jesus endured them for you." After Parsons's sermon, ushers began to move through the arena, releasing rows to come down to the floor in turn to exchange their flyers for the Lord's supper.

I wrote my name on the cross and then sat quietly, watching rows of young people stand and stream down to the floor, crowding the banquet table. In the row in front of me, a girl used a Sharpie to write *Michelle* and *sinner* and then she drew a frowning stick figure, strapped to the cross at the wrists.

It got darker and blue lights came on. Over the stereo system an aura of ambient sound started to waft. The arena was beginning to feel like an enormous cocktail lounge.

Eventually, an usher tapped our aisle and Alice and I descended to the arena floor. Down there, expressionless kids were coming and going in slow, silent chaos. The light coated everything in blue and with the swishing of bodies all around and the rising seats above me, I felt as small as if I were on the ocean floor. Reaching the edge of the table, I saw that the silver circles were platters, some holding little plastic thimbles of grape juice, some with crumbles of matzo crackers. I was hungry. Is it wrong to think of this as a refreshment? I wondered. I collected my Lord's supper and picked my way to the stairs through groups of kids who were spontaneously gathering in prayer circles on the floor.

Back in my seat, I meditated on Isaiah 53, which was now beaming brightly from the JumboTrons. *But he was wounded for our transgressions, he was bruised for our iniquities; the chastisement of our peace was upon him; and by his stripes we are healed.* I liked the sound of that—*by his stripes.* I dissolved the matzo on my tongue and concentrated on picturing Christ's agony on the cross.

During the long series of rock songs that followed, Liberty kids rose from their seats and held their arms straight up in the air as if to rocket into space. Some came back down to the mat on the arena floor to kneel. Some of them threw themselves flat on their stomachs.

Outside, Alice and I walked to our cars in the numbing stillness after the loud jolt of Campus Church. Alice had graduated from Liberty six or seven years earlier but had been returning to Campus Church lately. The pastor who typically led it, Ergun Caner, the formerly Muslim preacher Mimi had told me about in the baptistry, had been giving a good sermon series on being unhappy. Alice disliked her job and felt ready for a change, but she said she felt like Caner was talking right to her when he preached on being patient until "God touches you at a particular time for a particular task." He warned against fighting God's plan for your life, against missing the blessings of the status quo.

Caner reminded Alice that God would tell her when he was ready for her to move on, and that he probably wouldn't do that until she was able to find happiness right where she was.

GOD'S COMMISSIONERS

———

WHEN I WROTE A LETTER TO MY FATHER YEARS AGO TO COM-
plain about religious overtones at my summer camp, his reply assured me that I'd been spared a worse scenario: at my sister's camp, two
counselors had told some of the girls they were going to burn in hell unless they accepted Jesus. The girls were terrified. They complained to the
camp director, and the counselors were fired.

If someone had asked me to isolate the purest essence of what unnerved me about Evangelicals before I began at Thomas Road, I would
have distilled it to the force behind what those counselors had done: the
drive to evangelize, irrespective of context and propriety. Because even
though I strenuously disagreed with the Evangelicals' every political
view and gagged at every cultural expression, none of that would have
deeply bothered me if megachurches were fortresses, built to block out
the world. But the churches were boot camps: Christians laws were
meant for all of us.

This was arrogant, I thought. Besides being dull, it was anti-democratic
to want everyone to be just like you.

I realized early on that the reaction of people like me probably only
fortified the desire to evangelize: the more Evangelicals felt ridiculed and
cast out of mainstream culture, the more they wanted to convert it (consider the mania around the war on Christmas). But this was no chicken-
and-egg issue: it was clear that they were cultural castaways *because* of
their desire to hammer the Bible into the lives of the rest of us. My

sneering attitude didn't create their evangelistic determination, it certainly intensified it.

So what were the origins of evangelistic zeal? Why did the faithful require everyone to share their specific narrative of the universe? I had assumed that evangelism was arrogance alone, an insistence on uniformity, a childish refusal to coexist with people who could not believe, say, that God made a virgin pregnant. But my assumptions weren't born out in my actual interactions with Evangelicals. There was, I would find, a gentler purpose behind the gale-force wind of their proselytizing.

EVANGELICALS EMPLOY SEVERAL DIFFERENT tactics to spread the word: living by example, witnessing, and mission trips. The targets for evangelism are quite simply every person who has not said the sinner's prayer in earnest, including Jews and atheists—although I noticed most church people were disinclined to go toe-to-toe with others who followed a firm interpretation of the Bible, like Catholics. Almost every Evangelical will say they live by example, following their understanding of the Bible's life instructions, hoping that unsaved neighbors will notice their happiness, remember their faith, infer causation, and come down to the altar. I met several people who had become Christians by observing the tranquility of someone else's life and wanting that feeling for themselves.

Witnessing, or faith sharing, was a soft sell that most Evangelicals I knew dabbled in but wished they had the courage to do more often. It meant bringing up church, faith, and Jesus as a tangent in casual conversation (and most felt this was important, but very awkward), or suggesting someone turn to Jesus when going through a personal hardship (also important, but worse than awkward).

Mission trips were the pinnacle service achievement for born-agains, as they represent a focused effort to rescue people from hell. The missions page on the TRBC website states "every believer" should feel tasked to do missions, citing the Bible's "Great Commission" to bring the world to the Lord: "Go therefore and make disciples of all the nations, baptizing them in the name of the Father and of the Son and of the Holy Spirit, teaching them to observe all things that I have commanded you; and lo, I am with you always, even to the end of the age" (Matthew 28:19–20).

Heeding the call to round up all the nations, the Southern Baptist Convention has both International and Domestic Mission Boards that help organize and support thousands of missionaries each year. Domestically, the SBC chooses "Strategic Focus Cities" each year in order to match evangelistic and church planting efforts to reach exponential population growth in metropolitan areas.

Mission trips are not always solely evangelistic efforts but are always concerned with evangelism to some extent. Most trips use the expressed purpose of providing some other community service—homebuilding, child care, disaster relief—and append evangelism as a kind of silent rider. The SBC reports, for example, that in 2007 "missionaries and volunteers shared the gospel with more than 580,000 people because of the opportunities provided through hunger ministries."

Christianity Today reports that between 1 and 4 million American Christians go on short-term mission trips each year, and true to that bulging number, almost everyone I met at Thomas Road had been on at least one. Mission opportunities for students and singles came up most frequently; it was easier for the young and the unattached to find time to get away. If you were raised in the church, you usually began mission work as a high school student. You didn't have to be rich to do it, either: other Christians were usually happy to support missionaries, combining credit with God and tax deductions in one gesture.

Britney, the pompadoured Liberty student who sang on the EPIC praise team, had no difficulty finding people to support her mission trip to India: Donny made a plea for EPIC to underwrite all $1,400, and as a collection bowl bobbed around the EPIC room one morning, everyone seemed eager to ante up, adding bills of different denominations. Britney was standing onstage, looking grateful and a little embarrassed.

Britney planned to travel to India's northeast corner, near China. She'd prayed a lot, and felt that was where God wanted her to go. She was excited because so many of the world's "lost people groups" could be found there.

I walked up to Donny's class with Candice, the curly-haired girl who wore a leopard-print scarf knotted around her neck. Candice had given up her job as an elementary school music teacher to become a professional missionary and now spent much of her time traveling to small churches to minister to children. She was at a different congregation every week, and so almost never came to sermon at Thomas Road anymore. She had been greeted with a hero's welcome by many at EPIC that morning, who admired her commitment to God's heartbeat.

Candice worked with what she called "native missionaries"—foreign Christians recruited, trained, and funded to minister to their country-men. Her efforts, she told me, were primarily centered on the "10/40 Window"—a region stretching from West Africa to East Asia, between 10 degrees and 40 degrees north of the equator—also called the Resistance Belt. The countries in the 10/40 Window had the greatest concentration of "lost people groups" anywhere in the world, Candice told me sadly. It was a lost region.

"When I go to India," she said, "with my blond hair, blue eyes, and white skin, people see me as money walking. It makes it hard for me to go in and do missionary work when I stand out in that way." So instead of interacting directly with lost people groups, Candice operates via Iranians in Iran, Indians in India, and Ugandans in Uganda so that cultural and language barriers don't obstruct the spread of the good news.

ON THE FIRST NIGHT OF 100% Effective Evangelism—the Wednesday night Community Interest Group I thought might put me in the engine room of the church—I followed Ray Fletcher with the two men I'd waited with in the wrong place. Ray navigated yellow-lit halls, telling us how special this course was to him. We might be surprised to know that it was rare that church people volunteered to evangelize, he told us. "Most Christians don't *want* to be leaders."

We ended up in Jerry Falwell's conference room. A glossy mahogany table spanned the length of the room, rimmed by buttery leather chairs. A soft-focus portrait of Falwell hung near the door, centered so that the preacher appeared to be sitting at the head of the table, and a nameplate nailed to the bottom of the frame read *Dr. Jerry Falwell, Founder and Chancellor*. Opposite the portrait, at the other end of the conference table, a projection screen was pulled down. To the right of the screen was a door, which led, I later learned, to Falwell's office.

The conference table was almost full with people waiting for class to begin. Some of my church friends were already settled in their seats—Connie and Joey, Ingrid, Bethany, and Alice, who waved at me cheerfully. Xander, hair spiked like a burr, had his feet on the table.

"Now, Xander," Ray said, "would you want Dr. Falwell to come in here and see you with your feet up on his table?" Xander slid his feet down without a word.

A guest speaker would be teaching our first class, as Ray had to attend a meeting with Dr. Falwell himself. But before he left, Ray wanted to tell us that even though he had led 6,200 young men and women to the Lord in his post as a chaplain in the U.S. Air Force, he couldn't personally save a cockroach. "All you have to do is expose people to the word," he told us, "and the Holy Spirit will do the rest. People don't save people. *God* saves people."

The guest speaker, Floyd Greene, queued a video and dimmed the lights as Ray excused himself. "When this class is over," he said, "I want you all to be agents for Christ."

Onscreen, an African-American football player in greasepaint and a blue jersey was seated in front of a fluorescent cross. "Why did I want to be the evangelism linebacker?" His voice had the electric punch of a preacher's. The tape cut quickly to the linebacker sacking an unsuspecting college kid. Back to interview: "Let me put it this way. As a fish was created to swim in water, as a bird was created to fly, I was created to knock people out who don't evangelize."

Two teenagers, a boy and a girl, approached a suburban home.

"All right," said the boy, "it's all you. This house has your name on it."

"I'm not ready yet," the girl whined.

"What makes you think *I'm* ready?" said the boy.

The linebacker flattened them on the lawn. "God loves ya," he growled, crouching over them. "Now get off the flo' and go do the door!"

Another boy was at home on the phone, declining a friend's invitation to come out and evangelize, when he was clotheslined by the linebacker.

"The world needs a message!" the linebacker shouted, pointing his taped fingers down at the boy. "For God so loved the world he wants to communicate his message through *you*! If you procrastinate you will open up the gate to a *beatdown*!"

"I think it's fitting," the linebacker told the camera, seated in front of his glowing cross again, "when people are too prideful to share their faith, what I do is I"—punching his palm—"knocks the pride out of 'em."

It seemed pointless to show this video given that we all had elected to pass Wednesday night in an evangelism class, but when the video was over Floyd revealed some surprising statistics. Ninety-three percent of Christians have never saved anyone, he told us, and 55 percent of pastors have not shared their faith in the past six months. But anyone can evangelize, Floyd revealed. It doesn't take any special talents, and you don't have to be trained as a pastor. The first person he ever saved was his wife. They were teenagers on a date, and he asked her if she knew Jesus. She didn't, so he stumbled through the good news and saved her.

"It doesn't matter what your gifts are," Floyd said. "All you have to do is be willing to expose people to the word." In other words, no sales pitch is necessary when one is simply passing along the truth.

Standing in line with his daughter for cake batter milkshakes at the Cold Stone Creamery the other day, Floyd noticed two teenagers behind him who looked "straight out of the Goth handbook." If ever there were people who had the wrong idea of what Christians were all about, these were two. When Floyd approached the counter, he told the clerk he'd like to buy the order for the kids behind him in line. Later, as he was pressing the lids onto his cups, the Goth kids approached him, clutching milkshakes, eyes wide pools. There was some mistake, they said. He assured them there wasn't. The kids were so grateful they willingly opened up to Floyd about spirituality. "It was probably the deepest conversation these kids had ever had," he said, "and all it cost me was six bucks."

Churches are not houses of God; they are where the houses of God gather to worship. God lives in us. "And when you go to Alaska," Floyd said, "you have to remember you're not away from church; you are church."

When you go to Alaska.

I looked around at the others, everyone jotting notes. One recent Sunday morning I had followed Laura and Alice to the EPIC room so that they could unplug the coffee urn and cover the donuts before sermon. Waiting for them, I noticed a stack of letters printed on Thomas Road Baptist Church stationery. The form letter, signed by Ray Fletcher, was a financial sponsorship request for an upcoming mission trip to Alaska, the theme of which was "Salt and Light." Fletcher had written the letter on behalf of the fifteen EPIC members who were preparing to go on the trip to Anchorage and Fairbanks. "We want to serve our fellow man/children to hear the good news of God's love," the letter said. The missionaries would be working with Anchorage Baptist Tabernacle and Pastor Jerry Prevo in the inner-city ministry, "sharing the gospel with the homeless," and with the Children's Bus Ministry, "sharing the gospel with children."

Each missionary needed $1,000 to go on the trip. This would cover room, board, and travel. The letter asked for prayers and tax-deductible financial support, payable directly to the missionary. "Our goal," the letter said in bold print, "is to lead 100 men, women and children to Christ." I imagined bodies, one hundred of them—why that perfect round number?—traveling upward in a beam of golden light. A coiled fuse burned in me: I wanted to be on this trip.

In the hall on our way to sermon, Alice had asked if I had ever been on a mission trip. Between them, Laura and Alice had been missionaries in Russia, Ukraine, Vermont, Massachusetts, Florida, and the Bahamas. I asked Alice if it was too late to sign up for Alaska. She didn't think it was, although if I was planning to have the whole thing covered I'd better get started. *Covered by whom?* I made a mental note to look into it.

But I hadn't realized that night's class was the first meeting for the trip. I was always enchanted by coincidence, and this one brought jets of anticipation to life in my chest.

Now Floyd asked us, how does one go from starting the spirituality conversation to winning the soul?

Evasion won't do it, Floyd told us. Judging and avoiding people wasn't going to get an evangelizer anywhere. Christ didn't pick certain folks as his chosen ones—he loves everybody. "When you guys go to Alaska," he said, "people are going to look really different from you and people are going to smell really different from you. You can't run away from them." A preacher friend of Floyd's once gave an invitation at the end of his sermon, and a homeless man came loping down the aisle. The preacher thought, "Oh no, he's coming to ask for money." The homeless man, hair wild and spiked, stank from yards away—of booze, of barf, of urine. The preacher asked him what he wanted and the man said, "I need Jesus." Chastised by God for judging this man and not discerning his spiritual hunger, the preacher began to pray over him. As he prayed, the aroma began to change in the preacher's nose: he could smell the sweetness of Christ in the man.

Pervasion doesn't win souls, either, Floyd told us. Christian rhetoric can be a bludgeon to the nonbeliever. People don't like to be lectured, people don't like to hear that Christ died for them. Effective evangelism requires personalization and listening.

Invasion is the only effective method of evangelization, Floyd revealed. To win souls, you have to "get inside of people to produce an awareness of God's love in them." And in this moment he introduced the Microwave Effect, the method I was co-opting to turn myself tolerant: souls are cooked from the inside out.

Be simple and fun, he told us. Be real and authentic. "All your efforts can be undone by plastic Christianity."

Ray Fletcher, whom Floyd named as one of the greatest examples of authenticity, was back from his meeting, passing around a sheet of paper that we were to fold up into a pamphlet. Salvation can be done over the telephone, Ray told us, and you can do it using this trifold transcript.

"When you get on the phone with somebody, you just say, 'Can I talk to you about this? Will you just relax while I talk to you about this? And when I'm finished you can ask me as many questions as you want.' Ninety-nine out of a hundred people will listen to you. And ninety-five out of the ninety-nine will allow you to pray for them at the end."

The transcript did the work for us, making the argument for salvation, pulling those specific verses from the Bible that, Ray said, "hit people with a whump." He wanted us to read the transcript out loud three times per day. We needed to become so well versed in it that we could evangelize to people as ourselves, without them feeling like what we're saying is learned. "They need to feel like it's coming from within *you*," Ray said.

To demonstrate, Ray started reading through a part of the transcript that quoted Galatians 5:19. "Now the flesh is susceptible to all these sins: 'Adultery, fornication, uncleanness, lasciviousness, idolatry, witchcraft, hatred, variance, emulations, wrath, strife, seditions, heresies, envyings, murders, drunkenness, revellings and suchlike.'

"Wyatt," he said, aiming a finger across the conference table, "have you committed any of these sins?"

Wyatt shifted in his chair and chuckled as he looked at the rest of us, as if we might vouch he hadn't.

"It's okay, Wyatt," Ray said.

Wyatt chomped his gum a few times and then said, "Yessir."

"Well, I'll tell you what," Ray said and patted his own chest. "I have committed every one of these sins but two: I've never adultered, and I've never murdered anybody. But I've committed every other one of these sins, and I'm a sinner."

Despite the platitudinous ring of that declaration, and the fact that

Ray was merely performing a demo, he appeared to deeply mean what he was saying. He believed himself a sinner.

He read us some of the positive attributes the Holy Spirit offers us: love, joy, peace, gentleness, goodness, faith, meekness, temperance. "So if you have to choose between grace on the one hand and all these sins on the other, what are you going to choose?"

The class nodded and wrote more notes.

Ray approached a woman wearing tarantula legs of mascara and closed his hand over her shoulder. His intimate pose with this woman, the way she smiled up at him, her pretty lips glazed in magenta, told me this was his wife. "The idea is to get y'all to a place where if there are lost people in your family, you can just call them up and read off the script," Ray said. "They won't even know you're doing it. You *can* save those lost people in your family."

As we stowed our notebooks and pushed back from Falwell's conference table, Floyd told us why saving people feels so good: you are personally making sure they get to go to paradise. It was like being in the birthing room at the hospital. "It's the same thing when you're saving people," Floyd told us. "You get to be a part of the birthing room, the excitement that is new life."

IN APPOMATTOX, about a dozen EPIC singles gathered in the home of one of the members for turkey sandwiches and soda. The house was on an empty lot, fragile and cheaply constructed, like one of those structures you see on a wide-load trailer swaying down the freeway. Seams snaked across the center of the ceilings as if the house could be folded up and stowed away. As children of some of the single parents in the group ran around playing, the floor shook under our feet.

I was drinking orange soda and talking to Connie and Joey, a young couple from my 100% Effective Evangelism class. They'd met in EPIC and had recently gotten engaged. Connie was my age, a teller in a bank, but Joey was still in college and only twenty. She was quiet, voluptuous, with a cute, rabbity smile and a cameo necklace picturing a woman at prayer. He was a computer geek with a scraggly goatee, majorly into the Harry Potter books and fond of message T-shirts I never understood (on this day he wore one that read, "Your wheel is spinning but your hamster ain't moving"). When they flirted I was reminded of their probable virginity. They dropped ice down each other's shirts and squirted each other in the face with whipped cream; they embraced awkwardly, as if in a high wind.

They were definitely going to Alaska, and I told them I had submitted my deposit that morning. Connie said she hadn't been sure she'd go, but had been able to come up with the money and get time off from the bank, and she took those occurrences as signs that she should. "The thing that interested me about this trip is that it's an evangelism trip. Every trip I've done before has been a service trip. Like last year I went down to New Orleans. It's out of my comfort zone, but that's why I want to do it." Connie said she hoped that Ray's course would give her practice so she could get more comfortable doing it.

We were two weeks into the evangelism class, but I had been out of town for the second meeting. I asked Connie what I missed. She told me that each person in the class had to explain a Bible passage from the tri-fold transcript. Connie's passage was "Let the flesh be in the flesh and the spirit be in the spirit." I told her I didn't know if I would be able to do that one.

"Oh," Connie said, "if I can do it you can, too!" She'd started by saying if you're living in the flesh you're living carnally. Ray had told her that was too complex, that she needed to make it really basic. So instead she said, "When you're born, you're born in the flesh. But when you get saved, you're elevated to a higher level and you're in the spirit." Joey looked at her proudly.

A lanky woman in a turquoise sweatsuit had been listening. "You know, I was thinking about going to Alaska," she said as she munched on a cookie, "but I ain't into evangelism." The woman had gone on the New Orleans mission the year before and had been disappointed that only the men were allowed to work on gutting houses. The women were relegated to Vacation Bible School. She hated it. "I want to see people won to Christ, but I don't want to be the one to do it," she said.

"I just want to get one," Connie said, squinting. "I just want one real convert."

IN RAY'S WEDNESDAY CLASS, Amy and I were sharing anxieties about Alaska, sitting knee-to-knee in a couple of wingback chairs against the wall of Dr. Falwell's conference room. We were supposed to be practicing our witnessing script.

"I haven't always lived a Christian life," Amy confided. She was maybe the most beautiful woman in EPIC, around forty, with a halogen smile and a soft cloud of blond hair, but the gritty quality of her voice supported her confession: she sounded as if she'd seen things.

I wasn't an angel, either, I told her, but I didn't think we were alone in feeling unprepared to evangelize.

"I'm not a preacher," she said, her blue eyes blinking earnestly behind her frameless glasses. "What if somebody asks me questions I can't answer? I mean, I know the basics, but . . ."

Ray, aviator sunglasses pinched in his hand, walked past and gave us a look of mild reproof for chatting. I asked Amy if she wanted to go first. She had been busy at work and hadn't practiced the transcript as much as Ray asked, but she would give it a shot.

As she struggled through the transcript, skimming a passage with her eyes and then trying to find her own words, I found myself instinctively playing the easy convert, wanting her to succeed in this endeavor she felt was so important.

When she was finished, and I confirmed that if I dropped dead right then I'd be going to heaven, she shrank in her chair. "I did a terrible job," she said. I told her I thought she had done a fine job, and anyway it seemed like the important thing was learning the turns and folds of the argument.

When it was my go, I softened the transcript with charm, making it up as I went along, reading the lines when my own words failed me. *Can I sell a product I believe to be defective?* I wondered.

I told Amy I was worried about memorizing the Bible verses. This was true, but extending this information felt like letting her in on a risky secret. Mercifully, she understood. We began to brainstorm ways to etch the argument into our minds. I suggested writing it out on another sheet of paper in our own words.

"Ten minutes," Ray came over to tell us, putting his hand on my bare neck, squeezing. "No chitchatting, ladies," he said. "You're not at the mall."

"We're just trying to figure out how to do this so it's not so stiff," I told him.

Ad-libbing was fine, he said. "If there are things that a woman would say to another woman, you're going to know about that more than I am. Or if you have personal testimony that you feel would be helpful to other people, you should go ahead and plug that in." And a tip: "Always ask somebody if you can pray for them first. You say, *Now I just want you to sit back and relax. When I'm finished you can ask me as many questions as you want to ask me.*"

Leaning in, Amy whispered, "But I'm worried I don't have the *answers.*"

Ray flipped his hands open, as if releasing a bird. "None of us have all the answers. If we did, our God would be about this big," he said, holding his index and middle fingers centimeters apart. "If someone asks you a question and you don't know the answer, you say, 'That's a good question, and I don't know the answer. Can I get back to you on that?' And you write it down."

Sometimes, Ray told us, people will ask us things they shouldn't. When he was a chaplain in the air force, he had a kid ribbing him, saying, "Chaplain, chaplain, chaplain, is it possible that God can make a rock so big he can't move it?"

Ray answered him with a line from Proverbs: *Do not answer a fool according to his folly, or you will be like him yourself.*

When Ray was gone again, Amy told me she was new to Thomas Road. She had been attending a small church in the area, but she and her husband had recently divorced and the small church had been theirs together. Not only did she not want the constant reminder of her old life, the church was mostly elderly people and married couples. "I felt lonesome there," she said. But there was always something to do at Thomas Road, always someone new to meet.

Ray shouted from across the conference room, "Jesus is coming in two and a half minutes, so you'd better save whoever you're talking to!" Ray wore polo shirts and a heavy-looking gold watch, a gold class ring on his hand like an extra knuckle. His head was always shaved and shined and his white goatee was trimmed close. His wife, Clementine, matched him well with her tanned skin and her orange-blond hair teased and sprayed, gold tennis bracelets glinting from her wrist. It was clear she was a pretty woman, but it was hard to tell exactly what she would look like without the layers of rouge, mascara, and lipstick.

As we all settled back down at the conference table, Ray told us he had been going around and listening to people. Some of us sounded natural, he told us. "And some of you sounded like you were reading *See Spot Run*," he said. Amy smiled shyly at me from across the table. We hadn't been doing our homework, and Ray knew it. "Once it's memorized, you can make it your own. It works. If you find something that's as effective as this, then you should use it. But until you do, you should use this."

Sometimes you won't have the time to go through the whole trifold with somebody, he said. "You should have something ready for whatever amount of time someone has to give you. When I said Jesus is coming in two and a half minutes, that means you're not going to have time to go through this whole thing. So what are you going to pull out and use?"

We all examined our trifolds. Alice suggested Ephesians 2:8: "For by grace you have been saved through faith, and that not of yourselves; it is the gift of God, not of works, lest any man should boast."

Ray thought this was an excellent suggestion for a "drive-through" passage, since it highlighted that there was only one way to get saved. "And don't forget you should always ask to pray with the person first. Opening with a prayer opens their heart and gets the Holy Spirit knocking, okay? And if they say no, you say, 'Well, God loves you and I hope someday He'll open your heart to His word. Have a nice day.' Because you know, if they won't let you pray a prayer they're not open."

Walking to our cars that night, Alice told me that she and Clementine had been practicing in Dr. Falwell's office. Ray kept coming around the corner and busting them chitchatting. He told them they shouldn't be talking back and forth. The person getting saved is just supposed to sit there and listen. Alice asked him why.

"If you're asking too many questions," Ray told her, "you're not getting the message."

AT OUR ALASKA CAR WASH FUND-RAISER, the women were not expected to do any actual car washing, so we took turns holding a hand-drawn sign at the roadside and eating snacks in the shade by the church entrance while the men worked on the cars. Ingrid and I stood out by the road for a while talking about missionary work.

She told me she dreamed of going on a mission to someplace really poor because she thought it would be life-changing and eye-opening. She and her husband, Ethan, had vacationed in Jamaica, where she saw incredible poverty: people living in tin shacks with pillowcases for windows. "But I guess everyone there lives that way, so they don't even know what good living standards are."

I didn't point out the obvious—that affluent tourists probably provided poor Jamaicans with a sufficient comparison point. Instead I told her about the shantytowns in South Africa, how people I met there were frustrated, did feel disenfranchised, could identify themselves as have-nots.

Ingrid turned a vacant gaze on the passing cars. Somehow what I'd said was off-topic. I had been thinking a lot about why getting people saved was so important to Evangelicals, why so many of the people with *Jesus First* pins on their lapels put much of his platform second. What about poverty? What about discrimination? What about human rights abuses? Where was the Christian outrage at so much heinousness in the world? Why was the rhythm of God's heartbeat Preach the Gospel and not Help the Needy? Why not Practice Christian Charity and Let People Believe What They Will? Why the need to capture souls? Was it for personal enrichment? For power?

Waiting in the cataract of Ingrid's silence, I felt I was beginning to understand. There wasn't much point in helping the needy if they were just going to end up in hell anyway. Focusing on corporeal problems made as much sense to Christians as offering people pool floaties in the middle of the ocean; getting them saved would allow them to live underwater.

When I thought about it, I wasn't sure I would act any differently if I believed what they did, that non-Christians are going to suffer eternally in hell. I imagined sitting next to a stranger on an airplane, watching him sip a diet soda from a plastic cup, and somehow knowing absolutely he was going to die a terrible death, a death I could prevent. Wouldn't I try to tell him? After all, that's the central conceit of so many movies and shows about psychics and time travelers—If you could prevent accidental death, wouldn't you try?

Amy came out to relieve us, her ivory smile gleaming. "Now y'all step back and let me reel in the old men."

Ingrid and I joined Alice on a bench stacked with pizza boxes and began to speculate about opportunities for exercise in Alaska. Ray, who had been surveying a team of men as they hosed down a white Nissan, came over to chat with us. In casual clothes, Ray looked like a football coach—his baseball cap low over his eyes, his polo shirt pressed and tucked into khaki shorts, his tan calves thick as hitching posts. He told us he might be able to take us to a gym at Eielson Air Force Base in Fairbanks, and he was hoping to get some of us to come salmon fishing with him. I told him I wanted to go, but that I'd only caught sunfish out of the Twin Lakes in Wisconsin, which I'd always thrown back.

He didn't expect that I would be able to pull in a salmon by myself—he'd have to help me. "When you reel in a big fifty-pound salmon," he said, "it can be like holding a rope tied to a Suburban." Ray had caught salmon aplenty, and sometimes vacuum-packed them to ship back home. He'd also hunted deer, caribou, moose, bears.

A man waiting for his car said he'd shot deer before but could never imagine shooting a bear. "They make a sound when they die."

Ray nodded contemplatively. "You know, a woman once asked me how I could shoot a bear," he said. "I said, 'Well, ma'am, you just aim the X at their shoulder and pull firmly on the trigger.'"

But for all his swagger, Ray didn't hunt bears anymore because bear hunting was for sport. Now he only killed animals whose meat he could use.

GREAT CASCADES OF fresh spring rain were spilling down on the night of the last 100% Effective Evangelism class. I arrived in Dr. Falwell's conference room drenched, mopping my hair with paper towels. Everyone who had signed up for the Alaska trip took seats around the conference table, Dr. Falwell squinting down at us from his portrait.

Ray wanted to kick things off right away. Dividing the transcript into six parts, he assigned each person a number corresponding to a part. We were each to perform our assigned section, and in the end we'd have a vote to see who was the best evangelist. Ray promised a very good prize for the winner. "I promise it's something you'll want," he said.

At the front of Dr. Falwell's conference room Ray placed two chairs facing each other. We would each sit in one of the chairs and perform our assigned segment, with someone else in the opposite chair acting as a lost person. Ray asked everybody to remember what it was like when they got saved. "You just saved that person and they might be feeling a little weird," he said. "It won't necessarily be a bad feeling, but be sensitive."

Ethan went first, handing Connie the Bible and having her read from John 3 rather than reading for her. Ray told him he should read the Bible passages aloud, since he "might embarrass somebody if you don't get a reader."

When Amy performed her section from Galatians, listing the sins to which the flesh is susceptible, she had difficulty with many of the words. Afterward, sounding a little defeated, she said, "I don't even know what some of these things mean."

"You need to know what *all* these things mean," Ray said. "If somebody asks you, you can't be stumbling through as if it's the first time you've read these things."

Amy frowned down at her trifold. "What does *revelings* mean?" she asked.

Ray thought a moment, squeezing the back of Clementine's chair. "It's like, 'Hey man, they're having a reveling down the street.' "

Ethan cut in, a superior smile drifting across his lips. He was an ex-Navy boy and the only married man in EPIC. He and Ingrid said they felt they'd been called to help the Singles, and so Ethan often slipped into an authoritative role. "No, no, no," he said. He turned to Amy. "Reveling is basically abusiveness. It's like if a mother is being overly strict with their child and it verges on abusiveness."

Alice looked up from her Bible. "Mine says revelings means orgies."

"Well, Alice," Ray said, "I guess you've got the *Playboy* edition."

Clementine peered up at her husband. "Mine says orgies, too."

Ethan tried to wave off a mist of tittering. "It's definitely abusiveness," he said.

Performing his section next, Mitchell, the six-foot-six New Yorker with the *Zelda* tattoo on his forearm, struggled to fit in culturally at church. Others rolled their eyes when he announced he had to "go to da jahn" or cackled with his mouth open, fillings glinting in his molars.

"Who knows what Mitchell's problem was?" Ray asked after Mitchell had finished, smacking his lips together.

"Chewing gum," everyone replied.

"Some people hate gum chewers. Dr. Falwell is somebody who hates gum chewers. If you chew gum in front of him, he'll just put out his hand and say, 'Can I have that?' " Ray said. "The Devil is as real as God and he's going to be looking for ways to foil what you're trying to do. So don't let it be over something stupid like chewing gum or moving a mint around in your mouth."

During Joey's turn he accidentally transposed the words leading up to the prayer, saying, "While your head is closed and your eyes are bowed." Everyone laughed.

Connie then took the part of evangelist, starting the transcript over from the beginning. She asked Amy where she was going when she dies.

Amy scoffed. "Well, what do you mean?"

"Um"—Connie looked nervously at Ray—"well, when your body dies, do you know if you're going to heaven or hell?"

Amy shrugged. "I don't know."

"Do you believe in God and the Bible?" Connie asked.

"I'm not really sure," Amy said.

"Time out!" Ray shouted. "Now don't be mean, Amy, or we're going to have to save somebody else tonight."

Xander rushed through his section as if he were reading the fine print on a warranty.

Bethany, in patterned nurse scrubs, long curtains of blond hair swaying around her face, read through her section and into a prayer without changing tone at all.

Ursula rushed, too; she was pathologically quiet and seemed uncomfortable in front of the class. Often when Clementine or Alice would try to get Ursula to open up—asking her what she looked for in a man or what she had enjoyed best about an event—she would shrug and say, "Nice guys, I guess," or "It was all pretty good."

No one could understand poor Lyle, who seemed a little slow, blinking through his Coke-bottle glasses and fingering his bushy mustache as Ray gave his critique.

Wyatt left out a passage of scripture. He was an ex-Navy boy, too, but less assured than Ethan. And when replying to Ray he always affected a low voice and addressed him as Colonel. He often prefaced his opinions by saying, "I've been all over the world . . ."

Carter was nervous and didn't seem to like being watched. When he finished, Clementine said, "I'm just glad you came tonight, Carter." Carter was EPIC's treasurer and right-hand man of the Falwell family. He was in his thirties, very short and perfectly round. He seemed shy, smiling with only one side of his mouth as if he were afraid a whole smile might attract too much scrutiny. But I heard stories about his love of entertaining. Once, for Dr. Falwell's birthday, Carter did a Barry Manilow impersonation that reduced everyone to hysterics.

Someone thought Pamela was chewing gum, but she said no, it was pure nerves. Pamela once told me she'd quit her job as an elementary school teacher because the endless demands of course preparation and the children's short attention spans had given her panic attacks. She suffered from chronic anxiety. She was now an academic advisor at Liberty, in charge of making sure students completed coursework toward their majors.

In spite of her lacquered look, Clementine was natural and soft, maternal as she performed the trifold transcript. Alice and Ingrid both had an easy command of the material, and an enthusiasm that was pleasant to watch.

"You've got to watch out," Ray told Alice as she sat down at the conference table. After she had listed sins, Alice had told her partner, "You're guilty of some of these and so am I."

"They're going to feel convicted enough," Ray said. "When they start identifying as a sinner, they're going to feel the Holy Spirit working in them. They might even need something to lean on."

When it was my turn, Clementine sat across from me, playing my nonbeliever with a friendly smile. My section traced the genesis of our sinful disposition, discussing Adam's punishment for original sin—death—and the sin nature transmitted through subsequent generations to us, so that we're natural-born sinners. I knew this little circuit of the argument pretty well and thought it was a neat folk story, so I held Clementine's eye contact with relative ease.

When I sat back down at the table, Ray asked the group, "How did our newest member of EPIC do?" Several people hooted and said I'd done great, and Alice and Carter chanted my name.

When everyone finished, we voted (leaving Clementine out of the running), and I beat Ingrid as best evangelizer by a hair. As I laughed through my desire to dive under the table, Ray pulled my prize out of a paper bag. It was a black umbrella, emblazoned with the yellow U.S. Army logo.

"It's good it's going to you and not Ingrid," Ray said. "Ethan was in the Navy, and you know those Navy guys." He began to open the umbrella, but everyone cried out that it was bad luck.

As we packed up to leave, Ray reminded us that this was our last evangelism class. Next week we would be joining the ongoing EPIC Wednesday night meetings on successful relationships. "Don't come up here and wonder if we've all been raptured out of here," Ray said. "Maybe we will be, but if not, we'll be downstairs."

* * *

AFTER DONNY'S CLASS ONE DAY, I caught up with Britney following her return from India. She told me about all the people she'd met there who were already religious but didn't have a sense of peace from their beliefs. This was her most persuasive point when doing street evangelism, she told me—sharing the secret to her peace. Once she led her first person to the Lord she just wanted to lead more and more, and she felt confident that her passion for evangelism—what she called being "on fire for Christ"—would continue here in Lynchburg.

But she was not exactly on fire tonight, a little frustrated, she told me, because her makeup bag had been stolen from her housing complex. "The thing is, everyone's black in my neighborhood so no one can use my makeup anyway," she said, pouting. "They're from Africa on one side of me and Ghettosville on the other."

In spite of her recent trip, Britney remained young and sheltered, her mind a tight bud. I wasn't sure how to respond to her blithe racial insensitivity. But whenever I saw her after that day I wished I could find something to say that would help her shed the simple-minded attitude that the only redemptive quality in others was their ability to become more like her.

CHEERFUL GIVERS

———

BACK ON THE FIRST NIGHT OF RAY FLETCHER'S 100% EFFEC-
tive Evangelism class, guest pastor Floyd had asked whether anyone had ever worked in a restaurant. Several of us raised our hands. "So
you know firsthand how hard it is for restaurants to staff Sundays,"
Floyd said. We nodded. "Why is that?"

No one answered. In my experience, you couldn't make any money
on Sundays: not many people went out to eat and those who turned up
didn't drink much, which kept check and tip totals low. But I had the
feeling that wasn't exactly what Floyd was driving at, so I kept quiet.

"It's because waiters know church people don't tip," he said. "Waiters think church people are meaner, more high-maintenance, and worse
tippers than the drunk at happy hour on a Friday night."

I muzzled a nod. Not because I had had any memorable run-ins with
Evangelicals from my waitressing days (although a Christian diner once
left a friend of mine religious tracts in lieu of cash), but because what
Floyd had said aligned with my experiences eating out with Thomas
Roaders. At every meal I'd had with them the orders were persnickety
and the group tip always rang up well short of 15 percent. Several times
I stayed behind to throw a few extra bucks on the table.

But I couldn't think of Evangelicals as simply stingy. Whenever the
collection bowl made the rounds at EPIC to support a mission trip or a
fellow member in need, it was a salad of green bills by the time it came to
rest in front of me. And at sermon when the ushers sent the bowls up and
down the aisles to collect the tithes and offerings, I rarely saw anyone pass

it on without slipping in an envelope. In fact, I too had to start dumping cash in the collection bowls, only to keep from seeming peculiar.

There is, of course, a glaring distinction between these modes of giving—in restaurants, we give to a stranger; in church, we give to God's house. It seems obvious that Evangelicals' purse strings would be looser in church. But in time, I learned there was another motive behind the cheerful generosity in church, a motive that implied the tithe was less a gift than an exchange.

One morning, Alice, Laura, and I were sitting close to the front of the sanctuary, and Dr. Falwell was preaching about making a miracle church—his rather unsubtle way of impressing upon us the importance of tithes and offerings. He told a long joke about the penalties awaiting "tippers and tightwads" in heaven—they would be chained to ugly folks on Hallelujah Boulevard, with ugliness in direct proportion to the soul's stinginess. I had never thought of heaven this way—better for some than for others. I thought maybe Falwell was fudging theology to get laughs from the congregation. But later in his sermon, he confirmed the sincerity of the foundation for his joke: "We will have different levels of rewards in heaven, depending on our actions and choices on Earth." Just as there are circles of hell, it seemed, there are circles of heaven.

Dr. Falwell limned the details of the exchange—financial support of the church becomes credit for heavenly rewards. Money given to the church is automatically touched by immortality—it becomes currency repaid exponentially in heaven. Implying a kind of capitalist nature to Christianity, Falwell told us that desiring rewards was a valid motivation for serving Christ. But still, I thought to myself, the church is not God. I felt like I was watching a 3D movie without the glasses—I understood what was supposed to appear so vividly before me, but all I saw was how the illusion was created. And as if to quell my doubt, Falwell pointed out, "You put money in the offering plate a moment ago. The moment you gave it to the Lord, you didn't put it in the plate for man—you gave it straight to Jesus."

After church, I said good-bye to Alice and Laura, and on my way out to the parking lot, in a side hall off Main Street, I passed framed displays of mementos from each decade of Thomas Road's history. As I scanned the newspaper headlines and yellowed church bulletins, the Falwell family photographs and ticket stubs, I decided I would definitely go to Alaska, and I would definitely pay for it on my own.

At the end of the most recent decade's display was a blown-up fish-eye picture taken in the sanctuary on July 2, 2006, Thomas Road's first day in the new church. And in the photograph, inches away from Dr. Falwell's face, I saw my own—dark, tipped down.

THOMAS ROAD OFFERED a free dinner on the night of Easter Sunday, which Dr. Falwell began advertising several weeks before as "The Feeding of the 5,000." EPIC had been cancelled that morning so the singles could go to the early service, and I had attended the later service alone. Dr. Falwell's sermon was a clear reaction to the recent media frenzy over a television program called *The Lost Tomb of Jesus*, which claimed to have discovered the location of Christ's remains. Dr. Falwell angrily flogged the notion that if "Jesus is not bodily risen then your faith is in vain and you are yet in your sins," as if by pointing out how disastrous such a discovery would be made the discovery impossible.

After church I tried to go shopping to pass the time before the Feeding, but all the little antiques places along the river were closed, and the Wards Road superstores were closed, too. The only store I could find that hadn't closed for Easter was Barnes & Noble.

Easter dinner was held on an indoor running track deep in the network of church buildings, and twelve long tables were set up for food service. There were platters of chicken fingers and roast beef, waterlogged green beans and corn niblets. To drink, there were huge jugs of sweet tea and punch.

I didn't know where the EPIC folks were sitting and the room was unmanageably vast, so I decided to find a seat alone at one of the hundreds of tables. Walking with my plate of food, I ran into the Liberty Flames football chaplain, the one I had helped with his dissertation. He pulled me over to meet his wife. "This is the girl who helped with my paper!" he told her. She smiled coldly. He squeezed my shoulder. "Don't think I forgot about you," he said.

I chose an empty seat near the front of the room and the stage, at a long table where a couple of people were already eating. One table away, in a Rockwellian tableau, Jonathan Falwell was sitting with his wife and children, everyone's rosy cheeks lifted by smiles. The table beyond that hosted Dr. Falwell and his wife, who received many well-wishers.

It turned out that I had taken someone's seat, and I had to move a few seats down. The man whose chair I had been sitting in was Old Ray, the man who baptized me. I introduced myself, but Old Ray showed no spark of recognition.

Ergun Caner gave the speech during dinner, provocatively titled "Tithing Is for Wimps." I had expected a speech about doing more, evangelizing, volunteering at homeless shelters, something in the spirit of what Jonathan Falwell had said the day I joined the church. "Tithing," Caner said, "is nothing to be proud of. It's what's expected of you. It's the obligation, the bare minimum." *Tithing* was only referred to in the Bible 18 times, Caner told us, while *offerings* got 500 mentions. *Tithing* was obligational, *offering* devotional. There was no obligation, manipulation, or stipulation in *offering*. Caner likened *offerings* to giving to his sons and wife, telling a humorous story about something his wife wanted from "Bed, Bath, and Beyond My Budget." When Caner gives to his family, he doesn't think of cost or limits; he thinks of giving something commensurate to what he feels inside.

I let my meal go cold in front of me. This dinner was a sleight of hand, a fund-raiser disguised as an amazing act of the church's generosity.

"If we wanted to manipulate you," Caner said, pacing energetically, "we would say we need to raise $5 million tonight and we'll give you *this*"—he gestured grandly at nothing—"in return." But the church wasn't being manipulative, Caner told us. "You should give with free will and an open heart."

Caner acknowledged that there might be some skeptics among us. "*God wants me to give to him*," he imagined the skeptics saying, "*but what happens when I give to the church? What's Jerry Falwell doing with my money?* Now I love Jerry, but people wonder. Well, you don't need to worry about that. If people are being sneaky with your money, God will take care of that problem for you. It will be between the sneak and God." Caner got a standing ovation on this point.

I had always wondered how Evangelicals regarded the gap between church and God. The answer, apparently, was that they didn't worry about it. When they gave, it wasn't that they implicitly trusted the church. They trusted God, who would see their offering and furnish their reward in heaven.

Dr. Falwell took to the microphone. "Please don't leave," he said. "I want to share with you six parts of my vision for the next five years. You've had your free dinner, now do me the favor of listening to this vision." Falwell talked about building and expanding, deals and budgets, asked not only for offerings tonight but also for written commitment to increase tithes over the next five years. Checkbooks fluttered all across the track.

Before he let us go, Falwell wanted us to know that the beautiful potted lilies decorating our tables could be purchased for five dollars apiece.

I poked at my heap of cold corn niblets. More like the Fleecing of the 5,000.

SEEKERS OF A SILVER LINING

———

NEAR THE BEGINNING OF DAVID LYNCH'S *MULHOLLAND DRIVE*, Naomi Watts's ingenue arrives at LAX chaperoned by a gentle-seeming elderly couple, who wish her luck becoming an actress. As the elderly couple rides away from the airport, their smiles stretch and stretch and endure so long they seem to dry out and turn sinister, and there's the faint suggestion that they've done something to Watts's character. When we see this couple again, they appear in miniature, scrambling under the ingenue's door, laughing fiendishly, happily terrorizing the fallen actress just as she seems on the brink of suicide.

When I saw the movie, the elderly couple somehow aligned with my notion of evangelical Christians. I thought of them as monstrously cheerful, certifiably happy, in a cirrostratus cloud state that had no filamentary attachment to the difficult terrain of reality I knew: occasional sadness, anxiety, and existential woe. Their denial of turbulence and darkness only served to make me more acutely aware of it. Their happiness gave me the willies; I didn't think it was real. It was surely a proselytizing tool, either a way of advertising openness to conversation (about Jesus) or inviting inquiries as to the source of their satisfaction (Jesus again).

But the smiles of Thomas Roaders never turned hard or flat, even when there was no one around to convert. They were just *happy*. In fact, along with Orthodox Jews, Evangelicals have the highest reported rates of happiness in the country. Some social psychologists believe this happiness results from strict moral order, the neatly trimmed hedges they maintain around their lives. Dr. Jonathan Haidt, author of *The Happiness*

Hypothesis, has found that "when people believe that anything is permitted, it's a recipe for existential emptiness, for anomie." We fare better, Dr. Haidt suggests, when we have a rigid sense of right and wrong.

But in addition to the relief Evangelicals find from structure, they seem to have, as I came to appreciate, a kind of bottomless spring that keeps their happiness lush. I started to believe it was perfectly authentic, and I wanted some for myself.

ONE WEDNESDAY EVENING, Donny asked us to divide into groups to generate ideas about why we complain. At my table, Cintra folded her arms across her chest. "I complain to stop from hurting somebody."

Everyone at the table tightened their lips in gentle disapproval.

"I complain when I want someone to feel bad for me," Connie said.

I thought about it. Lately I had been cultivating a personal philosophy that was probably influenced by the cheery Christians all around me—the same Christians I used to consider plastic in their cheeriness. Whereas I once thought clever negativity and cynicism were part of my charm, I was beginning to believe that even if they won me a laugh now and then, they actually made me sort of unpleasant and miserable. I called my new philosophy "Positive Out, Positive In," and it was simply about acceptance and adaptability: the more easygoing I became, the easier things were. It really worked.

Part of this new philosophy was that I had vowed to stop complaining. Not only because it was intolerable to others, but also because of the reason I shared with my group that night: "I complain when I don't want to actually do the work of solving the problem."

I repeated this notion after Donny asked our groups to share ideas with the entire EPIC class.

"Er—huh," Donny said, searching for a grip on the idea, "so the problem is . . ."

"You complain when solving the problem is too daunting," I said.

Gasps and oohs fluttered all across the room, as if the word I'd used had been a sudden swirl of cold air. *Daunting! Big word!*

Several people settled intent, inscrutable expressions on me.

I sank down in my chair. I was so careful: no cussing, controlled cultural references, muzzled political opinions—and somehow with this innocuous twitch of a word, I had drawn the searchlights on myself. I suddenly felt very nervous about having to be *on* all the time in Alaska: there would be no Charlottesville to which to retreat.

I hadn't been listening for awhile—suddenly breathless from anxieties, as if anxieties were thousands of bats blasting from the mouth of a cave, suddenly realizing the extent to which I would be cut off in Alaska— and when I finally regained my focus, Donny was saying, "When you complain, you're not understanding that God has a vision for you, and you're not thanking God for your health and your blessing. When you feel like complaining, you ought to just praise God. Because God destroys complainers. Complaining gives place to the Devil."

After Donny's sermon, the Alaska group met to discuss final preparations for the trip. Ray had an itinerary for us: we would begin in Anchorage, doing bus ministry and work at a homeless shelter, and Anchorage Baptist Temple had asked the women to prepare a lesson for Children's Church. After working in Anchorage, we would have a couple of days for sightseeing in North Pole and Valdez. Ray wanted to make one thing very clear: in Alaska we would not be allowed to go anywhere alone, ever.

We would begin meeting Monday nights at Ray and Clementine's house. Our "Salt and Light" T-shirts had been made. An Anchorage rental service would be offering us two vans for free.

"God has really lined things up for us," Ray said.

BUT HOW DID EVANGELICALS maintain the bright and even tone of their happiness even in the face of incomparably heartless cruelty? Or in the face of an implosive tragedy that suggests godlessness? What did they think that Monday morning in April, when a student gunned down thirty-two people at Virginia Tech, an hour and a half southwest of Lynchburg? By Wednesday, with the killer dead and his name released, it was becoming clear that no one was alive to be truly angry with. Not the campus police, not the Virginia Tech president, not Seung-Hui Cho's teachers or classmates, not his parents. Everyone appeared to have tried their hardest to intercede. So what about God? Could we be angry at Him?

Pawing through the wreckage for lumber to feed the 24-hour news chipper, the media found workable material in gun control and mental illness, and they talked and talked. But in Virginia, a black tide of grief swelled. Everyone wore memorial ribbons and Tech paraphernalia. On

Ward's Road in Lynchburg a billboard the color of dried blood read, *There Is a Hokie Heaven.* In Charlottesville, one wall of a stone bridge on which UVA students paint messages, a bridge that almost never bears the same messages two days running, was painted with the rival-uniting slogan "Hoos For Hokies," and set a record by remaining untouched for fifty days.

That Wednesday whoever wasn't dressed in Hokie red at the EPIC relationships course was in head-to-toe black, including Ray Fletcher, who managed to still look tan and dapper in spite of his sober expression. Many in EPIC had Virginia Tech associations and a few were even connected in some way to victims of the shootings.

A guest speaker gave a lecture on the importance of communication in relationships. Nobody seemed to be listening.

Donny read us Psalm 46: "God is our refuge and strength, an ever-present help in trouble. Therefore we will not fear, though the earth give way and the mountains fall into the heart of the sea, though its waters roar and foam and the mountains quake with their surging."

We would engage in a few moments of small-group prayer, Donny said, "to pray for the families of the victims, for the witnesses, for the professors and the students, for the secretaries and the janitors, for the Blacksburg community—everyone you can think of—that God uses this time to appear to them. That he uses MSNBC, Fox News, and CNN to reveal his Word to them and to make himself known."

My prayer partner was an obese man with a voice like a foghorn. He kindly offered to pray first. Panic batted its wings inside my head, making it difficult to plan a prayer. This would be my first time praying aloud. I had tried on several occasions to practice at home, but I always felt irritated at how phony I sounded.

"God," the large man called out, "we can't know why this occurred. Only you know . . ." The deep, vibrating plush of his voice was striated with held-back tears. All around me I heard the language of horror rippling, one voice rising above another and then dipping below a third in a terrible chorus. *The screaming, deaths, that killer, bloodshed, bullets, massacre . . .* My ear couldn't follow any of these voices past a word or two, and I suddenly felt short of breath and claustrophobic. I imagined the voices as battering rams at my ears, weapons of brain invaders. Blurred spots of red and yellow light stained my eyelids and I tightened my fists. I was going to faint.

The large man was weeping now, and he cried out, "Bring revival to Blacksburg, revival to Virginia, revival all across this great nation!"

My dizziness abated some, diluted by my shock at the opportunism of his suggestion. Was this really an appropriate moment for evangelism?

"In your name I pray," the man said.

My turn. I heard Alice praying softly nearby, her southern rhythm natural and understated, a comforting island in the ocean of voices.

"Dear God," I said, pausing, hoping to suddenly be borne up on the crest of the Holy Spirit, for a Christian tongue to pick up naturally where my own tongue left off. It didn't. My mind was as dry and blank as a swept stage. *This man is listening*, I reminded myself. *He is paying attention!* I turned out the words effortfully, as if trying to press handfuls of dirt into bricks. My eyelids fluttered and my voice was froggy and deep. "I just want to pray for all the families of the victims, and all the students, and the whole community of Blacksburg," I said. *Nothing wrong with unoriginality in this instance.* "I just want to pray that you ease their pain and carry them through these trials, and that you would enter their hearts to bring them peace." *Too short! Go on!* "I also just want to pray that the lost find you in their time of need." That was the tonic, I thought, but it was black and sour in my mouth.

Then Ray said, "God has called me and Donny to this singles ministry, and we're not just here to help you find a mate, okay? We're here to glorify God and find ways to serve him and bring people to Christ." I understood this to be Ray's way of drawing a larger point from this moment—that even though we each had needs, it was important to remember that we hadn't been put on earth to minister only to ourselves.

After class, I asked Alice if she was going to Campus Church. She wasn't sure, she said, melancholy and distracted.

Campus Church was packed, and I heartily joined in the singing. I was beginning to find that no music drove me to sing quite as passionately as Christian rock, a genre I still recognized as vacant of artistic merit.

After one song, the pianist asked his bandmates to silence their instruments. Removing his hands from the keys and turning to the audience he said, "I feel like this week has been really *awkward*, and that all the services have been really *awkward*. And it's like we don't know if it's appropriate to sing all this happy, exalting music . . . But He wants to tell us, God wants to tell us that what He's doing in these moments is

He's jarring us out of our complacency, our satisfaction with our lives, our rhythm, making something *awkward* happen to show us what really counts, which is this"—and he lifted his Bible from where it lay on top of a speaker—"this is what we need to be focused on. This is what's important."

THE FOLLOWING SUNDAY, EPIC was full. Ray showed slides announcing several EPIC activities for the week, and then clicked to a slide in which two shot glasses, empty but for lime wedges, rested on a bartop. A blurred businessman slumped in the background. Alcohol was not permitted, Ray reminded us, at any of the EPIC functions.

Age groups would not be meeting separately today, Ray said. We would all remain in the EPIC room for a special guest speaker, Misty Bernall, the mother of a girl killed at Columbine High School, the girl who allegedly said yes when one of the Columbine assailants asked if she believed in God, the girl who was allegedly shot point-blank for her faith.

Misty began crying as soon as the microphone was in her hand. She was small, a wispy-haired blonde with a chapped complexion and a swollen ski-jump nose. "The last week has been hard for me—hard for everyone," she said, and then steeled herself. "But we need to know that there's this window after a tragedy like this, a window when people are open. There's an opportunity to win people to Christ, but it's a short window and it *will* close." She gripped the microphone and her voice quavered with intensity: "*Use the window.*"

She told us her daughter's story. A preternaturally engaging narrator, Misty's free hand fluttered expressively, her chin dimpling at the more painful memories. The raw metal ore of Cassie's life became a shape in Misty's intricate retelling, a shape we all knew would taper to a knifepoint. The singles ministry was silent with dread.

Misty had been a Christian since childhood, and her husband came to Christ in the military. They had two children together and believed they were raising their kids according to God's wishes. In spite of their efforts, Cassie fell in with a bad crowd. Misty and her husband unhappily rode the turbulent waves of Cassie's disobedience, until one afternoon Misty found a three-inch high stack of letters in a drawer under Cassie's Teen Bible. Misty began to cry again, the shock seemingly fresh. The letters contained references to suicide, drug and alcohol use, cutting school, Satan worship, and more. Most chilling were graphic drawings depicting how Cassie and her friends could kill Misty and her husband.

Misty brought the letters to the sheriff and pulled Cassie out of public school, enrolling her in a private Christian school. Cassie was miserable in Christian school, and Misty prayed constantly for her to meet a friend: "someone who understood her but was on fire for Christ."

Such a friend did appear in Cassie's life, a girl who shared the language of counterculture but spoke it within the confines of Christianity. Cassie's intense relationship with the girl—which, as Misty described it, seemed laced with the infatuation common in many inseparable teenage friendships—brought her to a mountaintop on a retreat, where Cassie's friend and two boys prayed over her, and Cassie felt her burdens lift away.

Now a passionate Christian, on fire for Christ herself, Cassie begged her mother to put her back in public school, where she thought she would be more useful as a witness. Cassie started at Columbine in the fall of 1998.

From their fence, Misty and her husband looked down at Columbine High School on Tuesday, April 20, the following year and watched thickets of police surround the school. By now the whole world knew of the shootings at the school, but the details were vague. They assumed everyone was okay simply because of the huge numbers of police present.

But after two days, they had only heard from their son, who was safe. Shuffling from waiting location to waiting location with the other parents, they heard nothing of Cassie.

Finally the coroner called Misty at two in the morning on Thursday and said Cassie had been among the dead in the library, and that's where her body still was. Misty said she went crazy—she just wanted to collect her daughter's body, take care of it, unable to bear the thought of her child all alone, dead in the school library.

One morning, as Misty was blow-drying her hair, she felt what she described as a strong presence. She turned off her hair dryer and sat on the bathroom floor. She heard God speaking to her. He said, "I'm taking care of Cassie now. And I'm going to take care of you." Her husband experienced something similar as he walked out to feed the rabbits and wound up on his knees in the dirt.

Using her faith to trim the wilds of grief, Misty began to work on the idea that Cassie was not lost, not gone, but with Christ. She was still connected to her family, still in existence. Misty remembered a time after Cassie's salvation when her children were sitting at the kitchen table, talking about how awesome heaven was going to be. Cassie said she couldn't wait to get there. Misty said she sat next to her daughter and asked what she would do without her.

You'd be happy for me, Mom, Cassie said, *because I'd be in a better place.*

"And I *am* happy for her," Misty told us, adding that Cassie had dreamed of being an incredible witness for Christ, and in death that is what she had become.

Misty had written a little book about Cassie, detailing her trials and salvation, her new life as a Christian, her death as a martyr. She expected the book, *She Said Yes*, to sell around 10,000 copies. It sold two million.

"There is a veil of grief," Misty said. "But Jesus has the power to turn ashes into crowns, to make tragedy triumph."

After a hearty standing ovation, Misty fielded some questions. Donny asked her what we could say to people who ask why God could let something like the Virginia Tech tragedy happen.

"My faith has been tested and is stronger and more real now than it ever was before," Misty said. There was a time, she confessed, when she had been asking questions about God, when her faith had wavered thinly over the abyss of her grief. But then she and her husband visited Breckenridge, a resort town in Colorado and one of Cassie's favorite places. Surveying the majesty of nature, Misty felt her faith become more powerful. "There is a God. But we have free will." On this subject Misty hesitated and made a few false starts, as if she were prying open a locked box. "He knows everything that is going to happen, but he has to allow us to make choices." As Misty struggled to explain her answer, I thought of a friend in Charlottesville who stopped believing in God at a young age because she identified a Christian paradox: if God knew everything already, free will was an illusion.

Misty recounted that through their classroom windows students allegedly saw Columbine killers Eric Harris and Dylan Klebold walking the halls after the shootings, guns down. They had plenty of ammunition left when they killed themselves. Misty believed God had put his hand down and said, "*Enough*—you have free will, but this is *enough*," and stopped them from taking any more lives.

When asked how we could protect our kids, Misty emphatically urged parents to keep kids off the Internet, calling it an unfiltered source of evil. "Information is just *dumped* on kids." Also, Misty said she wouldn't let kids go to public school if options were available. She home-schooled her son for his remaining high school years after Columbine. "It's not so much a safety issue as a matter of heart," she said. "There's some heart missing there."

Surprisingly, Dr. Falwell didn't give the sermon that morning. Instead a stooped older man named Ed Hindson preached on tragedy, his thin hair dyed the brown-black of charred wood, his unusually large, flat hands moving like fans.

DAPPLED BY LIGHT from the disco ball rotating overhead, the EPIC ladies gathered in the middle of the roller rink on a Saturday afternoon, divvying up chores. The rink was owned by Master's Inn, a Christian summer camp in a little town south of Lynchburg called Altavista. On a water tower planted by the side of the road Altavista's motto was printed in large, black letters: *A place to live, a way to live.*

The previous Wednesday Ray had urged us to help clean up Master's Inn: "Even though you won't be working there in the summer, you can still participate in a great platform for bringing children to Christ."

Certain areas of Master's Inn were rented out and used over the course of the year, but the roller rink remained dark. It hadn't been touched since the end of the previous summer. So while the EPIC men joined a group of Liberty kids to paint, shovel mulch, and blow leaves at the main grounds in preparation for the arrival of that year's campers, the EPIC women tackled the rink. We were giddy and felt glad to be distracted from the pall of the Virginia Tech shootings; we all wanted to skate. I felt wacky and hyper, laughing at anything. I wanted to race the others to the skate shelves and then zoom around, giggling.

But there was too much work to do, so we bent our energy toward labor. Kelly put on a danceable Toby Mac CD in the rink stereo system. Alice said she'd been a janitor one summer at Liberty, so she volunteered for the bathrooms. A Liberty senior named Genevieve strapped on roller skates to sweep the rink. Britney steered a Zamboni-size vacuum cleaner to do the carpets. Ingrid took to the purple and turquoise kitchen. Laura and Kelly organized the skate and hockey rooms. I was on trash.

My duty was more involved than I expected. No one had emptied the cans at the end of the summer, and there were rainbow scraps of childhood detritus everywhere: Starburst wrappers and pieces of candy wadded into the carpet; stickers curling from the walls, adhesive gray with lint; pen caps and barrettes discarded like cigarette butts; rubbery neon toy fish with dead lights in their bellies, strewn across countertops as if spilled from a net; and dozens upon dozens of lone colored socks. Mired in a tar pit of chocolate syrup at the bottom of a waste bin, I found a ripped-up love note written in colored pencil. As I indiscriminately filled garbage bags with these items, I felt as though I was cleaning up some old rotten corner of my own memory—as if this was my abandoned playground, this was my forgotten trash. All the while, Genevieve skated big loops on the rink, sweeping with a long broom.

And for what spectacle were we setting the stage? Interspersed with familiar scenes of summer youth—girls pushing bunk beds together so they could whisper after lights out, counselors idly teaching how to make French braids and play cards during free time, first kisses minted in the streaky light of empty cabins, nurses treating knee scrapes in the infirmary, small hands folding the American flag into a triangle at dusk— there would be the Christian fare. Children picturing Christ's agony on the cross, nurturing an abiding dread of hell, trying to parse and digest the sophisticated notions of sin and salvation, of being entered by the Holy Spirit. This would be no military outfit, as portrayed in the drumbeat documentary *Jesus Camp*, with wailing and speaking in tongues and talk of armies for holy war. But children would be expected to develop a personal understanding of Christ, and such a relationship could not be wrung from dry catechism.

As I collected Alice's trash in the girls' room, she told me that the toilets hadn't even been flushed before the place had been locked down for the off-season. I told her tales of moldering socks.

She sighed. "Oh well, when I'm picking up something and it's grossing me out, I just have to remind myself I'm doing it so when the kids come here they can focus on what's important."

Later I was at the kitchen sink, washing my hands and arms: Kelly, Laura, and I had been absently gathering up heaps of fiberglass in the hockey room, and we had all broken out in stinging rashes. Ingrid was mopping and had the purple and turquoise kitchen looking as good as one could hope for.

She was slim and athletic in her red workout pants, her eyebrows so perfect and dark they might have been swept on by a calligrapher's brush. She told me she had grown up in Florida and West Virginia but had been living in Lynchburg the last ten years since matriculating at Liberty in 1996, where she met Ethan. For seven years Ethan served as an officer in the Navy, before "God had put it on his heart" to become a minister. He then enrolled in Liberty Baptist Theological Seminary and became Liberty's Dean of Men in 2003. Ingrid was working part-time at a gym as well as mentoring Liberty girls seeking romantic wisdom. Ethan really wanted to be a youth pastor and he was looking around for openings wherever they turned up.

"Have you paid for any of the Alaska trip?" Ingrid asked. I dumped dirty mopheads and an avalanche of soda bottles into my trash bag. I said I'd taken care of my deposit and was saving for the next installment. Had she?

"Ethan and I are . . . struggling to put the money together," she said.

When Kelly's Toby Mac CD ran out, I volunteered to find something else in the deejay booth. Pawing through the binders of CDs in the booth, I became a little frantic—I didn't recognize any of the artists. They were all Christian. It seemed critical to choose wisely. I selected a compilation of Christian rock, figuring it would bear some resemblance to the U2-style arena rock everyone loved so much at Campus Church. It was blistering heavy metal. Through the booth window I saw Genevieve and Kelly exchange bemused looks by the snack bar and I quickly swapped out the CD. I had a CD labeled *R + B Mix* on backup.

As I hauled bags to the front doors, we made it through a couple of songs with semi-oblique sexual references—Ginuwine singing, "*Is there room in them jeans for me?*"—before slamming headlong into "Stroke It": "*Stroke it to the east, stroke it the west . . .*" I had unleashed '70s disco-innuendo fever on the EPIC group. Blushing purple, I began to drag my trash bags outside. When I came back in, Genevieve was repeating a line from the song to Alice: "Baby, have you ever made love before ten in the morning?"

Lucky me. This was the silly icebreaker we all needed. All the girls began dancing at the edge of the rink. Our work was almost finished. Al Green's "Let's Stay Together" came on. Kelly got on the microphone in the deejay booth and said, "This couples' skate has been specially requested by Laura. Laura, this one goes out to you."

We were all goofing again, in the mood for girl talk. Laura started telling us about a guy she'd gone on a date with to see *Pan's Labyrinth*.

"It was *really* weird," she said. He hadn't called her after—it had been ten days.

"Men." She sighed.

Britney told Laura she would burn her a CD of a sermon a young pastor named Johnnie Moore had recently given on relationships, called "The Organ." Everyone began gushing over how cute Johnnie was. Genevieve said he was choosing to be single. "He has options," she said. "He definitely has options." Britney said he was the leader of her mission trip to India. She twitched her eyebrows, Groucho Marx–style.

"You know, his voice is more normal in person," Genevieve said.

"Yeah," said Britney, "it just gets really high when he's in front of a crowd."

"He's such a spaz," Laura said, "but I love that about him."

Britney gave us all a naughty look, as if she was thinking something she didn't dare say. "I have a theory about men," she said. We all perked up. "Okay. My theory is that when men get past a certain age and they don't get married, they get *frustrated*." She paused, wrestling with a little smile. "*Sexually* frustrated. And then they become spazzy."

"I think I know a lot of sexually frustrated men," Alice said dryly.

"With men, if they don't get that release it gets all backed up and bottled up in there," Britney said, making a strangling gesture with her hands.

"With women," Alice said, "it doesn't affect us as much. We can last a lot longer before becoming frustrated. And we never become *as* frustrated."

A little tide of silence lapped around us. Laura was gazing out at the glossy rink. "I don't know." She sighed again.

Back at the main camp, we prayed over peanut butter and jelly sandwiches and Doritos. Alice had invoked the prayer but didn't eat—she wanted to save her Weight Watchers points for something good.

Kelly was talking about how so many people had been at EPIC the previous Sunday, trying to entice the participation of a cute Liberty boy who had stopped by our table to say hello. "We had, I don't know, a couple hundred," she said, scrunching her lips.

"Okay, Jerry Falwell," Alice sniffed, "multiplying everything by ten."

WE WERE DOING PRAYER requests in Donny's class. Donny wrote the prayers on the board, and Bethany copied them into her journal; she would get the prayer team to pray on the requests again later. One woman's brother had just gotten saved in Boston, and she wanted prayers for discipleship for him.

"I don't want to say Boston is a *lost* city," she said, "but let's just say my brother definitely needs a Philip"—the determined evangelizer in Acts.

A woman with drippy curls had a mother in liver failure. Donny wrote on the board, "liver failure stubborn." He turned to the class, snapping the cap onto his pen. "Doctors take you to a point, and then there's God."

Donny's message that morning was about surviving storms. The video screen behind him displayed the message's title, "Peace in the Middle of It All," over a gray sky and sea. So often, Donny told us, we're in the midst of a storm, struggling to get out of it so that we can embark on God's will, not realizing that God's will resides inside the storm. A couple was coming to see Donny for premarital counseling. Only the woman had been saved. "They had so many storms, so many struggles, and I just wanted to get up on the desk and shout, 'How else can I make this clear to you?'"

The lesson in Jonah, Donny told us, was that "the reason we cannot find the cure is we have not discovered the cause." It was for Jonah that God created the terrible storm his ship encountered on the way to Tarshish, and it was only Jonah's submission to the storm that would quell it. "Storms are inevitable," Donny said. "They are for our testing, and for our discipline."

By allowing himself to be swallowed by a whale, by releasing his life to God, Jonah was saved. "And just so you know," Donny said, tapping the air with his finger, "this *literally* happened." On the Internet Donny had found research that proved it scientifically possible to survive in the stomach of a whale for three days and three nights. "God made some people who claim this is mythology, but scientists have proved that the gases inside a fish make it possible that this *literally* occurred."

The singles scribbled notes, nodding. A new guy with a crewcut and a green rayon shirt raised his hand. "Couldn't the Jonah story be about Jonah using his testimony to convert sailors?" he asked.

Donny bugged his eyes and looked around, indicating that someone else should answer.

"Well," Alice said, "he didn't have a testimony yet."

"He needed his 'come to Jesus' moment," Connie added.

The new guy nodded his head slowly. "Well . . . then how does being proactive jibe with letting God do his will?"

"If you're a controlling person, you have to listen for God telling you to pull back," Donny said tentatively. "And he'll tell you via other people."

SITTING NEXT TO ALICE and her mother in the sanctuary, I was surprised to hear that Dr. Falwell, too, had planned a sermon about storms. He preached from Acts, telling the story of Euroclydon, the great wind that wrecked the Apostle Paul's ship. Storms come, Dr. Falwell told us, when we least expect them. "Here the south winds are blowing softly," he said, "when everything is under control, everything is going well. And in an instant almost—Euroclydon."

We must expect and endure these sudden storms, Dr. Falwell told us. "If you've never been to a place in your life when all human hope was taken away, the scripture says, brace yourself. You're likely to go there someday."

But so long as we were Christians, we needn't be afraid. A newspaper had recently asked Dr. Falwell if his pulpit was bulletproof. "No," he replied, "but I am. And so is every believer until he has finished the work God has called him to do." Because God made the storms, he also controlled the extent of their damage. "No waters can swallow the ship where lies the master of ocean and earth and skies," Dr. Falwell said, quoting a gospel song. "Just because things don't make sense to you and me doesn't mean they don't make sense to God. Even when we cannot trace his hand, we can always trust his heart."

Surrounded on all sides there in the congregation, I remembered something from Dr. Falwell's official website—"Trials and calamities are God's tools to perfect our life and character."

Even tragedy is an act of love. Ergo, there is always a happy ending.

MANAGERS OF GRIEF

———

As part of my Positive Out–Positive In philosophy I'd begun making a point of trying to redress wrongs and let go of old grudges. It was not lost on me that this was the sort of thing recovering drug addicts did.

So in May, I made a coffee date in downtown Charlottesville with a professor from graduate school. I'd once felt a tremendous amount of bitterness toward this woman for being very hard on my short stories. She was hard on everyone, but sometimes I felt as if she was mocking the very notion that I considered myself a writer.

Once, after a particularly brutal workshop in which she suggested that an atmospheric detail in a story I'd written should have been its main subject, she said, "Will you call me in a year and tell me I'm right?"

Though I didn't say it, I placed my pen on my desk and thought, *I'll call you in a year to tell you to go fuck yourself.*

The sentiment seemed to have traveled through my silence, because in class the following week she asked, in an artificially gentle voice, "Gina, are you still talking to me?"

I looked at her dead-on. "Aren't I talking to you right now?"

Whoa. I cringed to think of that time, the anger I carried around. Where had it gone? I never felt it anymore. I saw that the tension between us had been my problem as much as hers. Probably more so.

Now, sitting outside a coffee shop on the pedestrian mall, I could feel her taking in how I'd changed—my long blond hair, how heavy I was.

In school I'd been rangy, a smoker with short messy hair cut by my boyfriend.

I told her there were morsels of advice she'd given in workshop that I initially rejected because I didn't understand them, but that they'd become fundamental pieces of my writing process.

"I'm sorry I was so difficult for you," I told her.

She smiled charitably and shook her head. "Oh, I don't remember it that way," she said, and complimented my shoes.

When we said good-bye, I felt lighter.

The Christians I knew were masters of letting go. And it didn't take them years to do it. Their minds seemed uncluttered by remorse or bitterness, unhaunted by the idea of what could have been. It wasn't only because they accepted hardship as a character-building process given by God, it was that they believed they'd already been forgiven for what they'd done by the only one who mattered. And besides: why should they stay mired in the sorrows of this life with the bounty of delights awaiting them in the next?

THE HARDEST TEST of this faith came to Thomas Road unexpectedly. Around noon the day after I met with my professor, I popped on my computer while waiting for someone to come service my oven. And at the top of the list of headlines on my home page was an AP bulletin reporting that Jerry Falwell had been discovered unconscious in his office and was in "gravely serious" condition at the hospital.

I felt scalped by surprise. He had preached on Sunday, same as ever! He had cracked jokes while he dedicated babies, helping parents acknowledge God's sovereignty over the child until it was old enough to choose Jesus. And his last sermon, the Mother's Day sermon, had been so banal, about becoming a highly honored mother.

And just the day before, Dr. Falwell had driven his SUV up on Candler's Mountain to see the LU monogram, which was emblazoned in the grass as if with a giant branding iron. He had lingered at the monogram, snapping photographs and chatting with the Liberty students hanging around the new white gazebo. Jerry Jr. was with him, and Dr. Falwell told his son that he was feeling better than he had in some time.

The worshippers heard the announcement at the Thomas Road main sanctuary during a 2 p.m. emergency meeting and it quickly began traveling the wires: Dr. Falwell was dead. He had taken a working breakfast with a colleague at a Bob Evans on Ward's Road, returned to his office at Liberty for work, and in an instant almost—Euroclydon—he had been called home for good.

DISTURBED BY MY OWN SADNESS, unable to explain the odd couple of my affection for Jerry Falwell and my loathing of his ideals, I drove down to Thomas Road that evening to mourn his death, even though I'd long since missed the gathering of worshippers. News vans bristling with satellite dishes jammed the parking lot, and reporters and cameramen shuffled here and there loaded with equipment like astronauts uncertain of their coordinates.

Main Street was ghostly, only six or seven people around the living-room areas, reading their Bibles or checking the news on their laptops.

Entering the sanctuary, I smelled chemical ash. Everything was dead-television gray—great lakes of empty theater chairs, carpeted aisles running down to the stage, JumboTron screens blank charcoal. It felt like a burned building. An elderly couple and a group of teenagers were praying, and a man was playing an organ that had been pulled to the foot of the stage, where the pulpit should have been. Sitting with my forehead pressed against the chair in front of me, I conjured up Dr. Falwell's powdered donut face and his trampoline voice.

Beneath my sludgy, unwanted sadness over Dr. Falwell's death there was an active spring of curiosity about how his passing would affect his church, his university, his vision. *He* was the gravitational pull at Thomas Road. How would they let him go? Would the church fragment and scatter?

THE FOLLOWING MORNING, the TRBC website featured a picture of a red rose with a gold *Jesus First* pin resting in its petals. In ancient-looking script the message below the rose read, "This faithful servant of God will be most remembered as a beloved husband, father, grandfather, pastor, and educator. Dr. Jerry Falwell. August 11, 1933–May 15, 2007."

Beyond this page was information about the viewings and memorial services, as well as the coming weekend's Liberty graduation events. "Dr. Falwell would want Liberty University's Baccalaureate and Commencement programs to be held as scheduled," the website read. Newt Gingrich would still be the commencement speaker at Saturday morning's graduation. Dr. Falwell would lie in repose for four days at the Liberty University DeMoss Center and then in the TRBC sanctuary, and he would be buried Tuesday, a week after his death. "In lieu of flowers," the website read, "and to further Dr. Falwell's vision of spreading the gospel around the world, the family requests that memorials be made to the Founder's Scholarship Fund at Liberty University."

COMMUNITY INTEREST GROUPS WERE canceled Wednesday evening, and the church gathered in the sanctuary for a prayer service. Ushers handed out prayer sheets at the door—long lists of names of ministries, servicemen, missionaries, the sick, and the bereaved, and at the very top of the list, the names of the surviving members of the Falwell clan.

A pastor who looked like Elmer Fudd vivified and aged forty years brought the church to order, releasing the ushers to take a collection. He said that if they didn't take a collection tonight, Dr. Falwell would send thunder and rain from heaven. It was already raining, and anemic laughter wafted up from the congregation like a thin trail of smoke.

The corpulent choir director sang "I Am Not Ashamed," and then pastors took turns leading the congregation in prayer for each of Dr. Falwell's surviving next of kin. The Elmer Fudd pastor led the prayers, talking about the first time he saw Macel in church. He remembered what she wore: a black velveteen dress with white lace trim. He took notice of her, he said with a smile. But Macel married Jerry and this pastor met his own wife. He now prayed to God that Macel would be lifted up to Him. A picture of Dr. Falwell and his widow glowed on the big screens.

Another pastor led a prayer for Jerry Jr. and his children, and referred to "JJ," the new Liberty University chancellor. We prayed with a different leader for Dr. Falwell's daughter, Jeanne, a doctor in Richmond whom Falwell always referred to as his "only perfect child."

Ray Fletcher took the pulpit to pray for his best friend, Jonathan Falwell, who was expected to be named the new senior pastor at Thomas Road. Ray remembered when he started working security for Dr. Falwell many years before and he first met Jonathan, who was thirteen at the time. Ray traveled with Dr. Falwell and also worked at the Falwell residence. He remembered Dr. Falwell pointing to his redheaded teenage boy and saying, "That one's your responsibility—watch over him." Ray said he could now tell the story about bear hunting with Jonathan in Alaska, or flipping a golf cart at Ivy Hills, or choose one of any number of embarrassing chestnuts, but Jonathan was going to be senior pastor now, and Ray didn't care to lose his job.

Two more pastors prayed, one for Liberty University and one for the church. Finally, the man who baptized me, Old Ray, closed us in prayer. He and his wife had been with the church for twenty-eight years, he said, and he came to the church because of Dr. Falwell's heartbeat—getting people saved. That is still our work, he told us, and we must continue on.

I pondered Old Ray's claim to know Dr. Falwell's heartbeat. News commentators were already speculating on the sincerity of Falwell's Christianity, the possibility that he was just a huge hypocrite, a con man. A friend of mine said she was surprised he wasn't found dead on top of some hooker.

I wasn't. Falwell never seemed hollow. Though there's no way one can determine the depth and purity of another's belief, one look at Jerry Falwell's life showed that he was no hypocrite: he lived precisely according to the message he preached, bilious as it often was. And though I didn't agree—there were *plenty* of examples of people who were both incredibly magnetic and incredibly corrupt—Evangelicals believed that Falwell's magnetism was proof of religion—it was the Jesus in him. Ray once told EPIC that Falwell had been driving down the street and waved at the driver of an 18-wheeler Budweiser rig. Just that wave, just the sight of Dr. Falwell acknowledging him, sent the driver to Jesus. "Now that's power," Ray had said. "And it's not the power of Dr. Falwell. It's the power of God."

The power of God. Yes, the details of Falwell's biography—the political maneuvering; the shady takeover of Jim and Tammy Faye Bakker's Praise the Lord network; the frequent commentator appearances on news programs (rumor was that he was always in TV makeup to be ready for the air at a moment's notice); the ballooning of the church and the university; the perpetual appeal for more money, more, more—all suggested that Dr. Falwell's heart beat not for people, as Old Ray believed, but for that power.

What was less clear was what Falwell hoped the power would confer. Ray Fletcher always said Dr. Falwell never went on television without incorporating the Gospel message in his appearance, and he seemed persuaded that Falwell was only interested in power because it forced open channels through which the unsaved could be led to the

Lord. But I wasn't so sure about this. Falwell was a divider, not a uniter, and openly aspired to be the most hated man in America. To me, this meant he wasn't interested in building the flock, but in cementing its—and his—dominance.

Elmer Fudd returned to give the invitation. He said one night they'd neglected to do it and someone called the following day saying they had wanted to get saved and hadn't been given the opportunity. Dr. Falwell had telephoned all the pastors and chastised them.

That night there would be no Campus Church, and in the morning, Dr. Falwell would be lying in repose at the DeMoss Center.

When the service was over, I was struck by the sensation that I'd just been to a concert where the headliner had failed to appear. No one who had taken the pulpit had a smidgen of Falwell's magnetism or humor. What would happen at this church now that Falwell was gone?

On my way out of the sanctuary, I saw Ingrid and Ethan standing with Bethany, the nurse from my evangelism class. They all greeted me warmly. Bethany had that troubled expression, her lips screwed to a dot. Ingrid's eyes were puffed to slits and pink from crying. She and her husband had heard about Falwell's collapse together, while Ingrid was visiting Ethan in his office. They had come down to the sanctuary at once.

Bethany had been working at the hospital where Dr. Falwell ultimately died and was shocked when another nurse told her what had happened. Bethany said her hospital was one of the top 100 in the country for heart medicine, and Falwell's doctor was the absolute best. It was hard for many of the hospital workers to do their jobs when Dr. Falwell was brought in because so many of them were members of his church. Even Falwell's doctor told Bethany he was more than a patient. Now Bethany's face crumpled and she began to cry.

Alice and Laura came up the aisle with Kelly, Donny, and Kelly's twelve-year-old son. We all embraced. Everyone had been crying, and each of them said they'd come to church at some point the day before just to pray. I noticed that everyone was wearing the little gold *Jesus First* pins on their collars.

Donny was carrying a plastic bag containing several copies of the day's *Lynchburg News and Advance*. Tears gleamed in his eyes. "What happened to Hezekiah's prayer?" he whispered. Several weeks before his death Falwell had told reporter Christiane Amanpour that he was going to be praying Hezekiah's prayer for another fifteen years, "with an option to renew." He told her, "I need about twenty more years to accomplish everything."

Crowds flowed past, up the aisles and through the double doors onto Main Street, and we watched them pass in silence for a while. Finally, Alice said she hadn't been able to get anything done at work. Kelly said Donny had been unable to so much as write one email. "But we have to keep going," Kelly said, shaking her head. "He wouldn't want any of this. He'd tell us to knock it off." Everyone nodded, seemingly chastened by Kelly's words.

Donny said some sick people had been flooding the Liberty staff with emails about how they were glad Falwell was dead and that he had probably been sent "down below." He clamped his lips tight before adding, "And did you see that atheist last night on CNN? The guy who wrote that book?" He was referring to Christopher Hitchens. "He was being interviewed across the street from church, outside the Sleep Inn. I just wanted to go down there and . . ."—he tightened a fist around the handles of his plastic bag.

Everyone nodded again. There was a lot of grave-dancing out there.

Alice was looking off in the middle distance, hugging her arms around herself. "My thing is, even if you didn't like him and didn't agree with his politics, for now you have to respect that he was somebody's husband, and somebody's father, and somebody's grandfather."

I found myself nodding like a horse pulling at its bridle—this was how I felt. For now, snagged on Falwell's humanity, I was temporarily blindered from the content of his preaching.

Donny said we would go on, we would keep working. That the church was prepared for this. That we hadn't expected it to happen so soon, but we had expected it. "And anyway this isn't Falwell's church—it's God's church, and we can't question whether or not we will pull through. It's in God's hands," he said.

Kelly's son had asked her whether Dr. Falwell was talking to Moses and the Disciples. Kelly told him he was. "That's cool!" her son had said. And when Kelly's son had seen Donny crying in the sanctuary, he had told his stepfather not to cry: Dr. Falwell was with God now.

"I do take comfort in that," Donny told us. Earlier in the day, Mitchell had dropped by Donny's office with a theory. What if Dr. Falwell had eaten breakfast, come to work, and entered his office to find

Jesus swiveling in his desk chair? And what if Jesus had looked at Dr. Falwell with a smile and said, "Why don't we call it an early day?"

A dear friend of mine who was suffering through the loss of a close family member once told me, "Death is messy." This seemed to me the truest thing one could say on the subject: the regrettable things we said and didn't say, the mysteries and secrets forever buried, the million filaments of pain and longing, the flotsam and jetsam of belongings and affairs: it's a jagged, unremitting mess. But for Christians, death is different. For Christians, in a way, death is tidy: it fulfills a promise. And ultimately, the dead are better off.

I STAYED AT Lynchburg's Kirkley Hotel that night. I ate jelly beans for dinner, drank a tall boy of Budweiser I'd purchased at a nearby gas station, and watched news clips on my laptop. Every commentator had what seemed to be a prefabricated opinion—a necessity of the instant news cycle, I guess. No one seemed to need a few days to sculpt their analysis. I disagreed with Christopher Hitchens on many topics, and I knew he was a polemicist with a book to promote, but nonetheless I admired his light-speed intellect. When I heard him sneer to Sean Hannity that "if you gave Falwell an enema he could be buried in a matchbox," I suspected that many people from my cultural homeland shared his point of view. Suddenly I feared that my homeland was no longer my home.

Curled in a strange bed, I telephoned my mother. "How are you feeling?" she wanted to know. Pretty confused, in fact. I missed Falwell acutely, even as I knew it was probably good he was gone. Days after Falwell's death, my own personal king of comedy Bill Maher showed a photo of Pastor Jerry and said, "New rule: death—isn't always sad." He had done much harm to the country, to polarize and isolate and plant fear and suspicion where there was the opportunity for understanding. He had, as Maher said, "figured out that you could launder your hate through the cover of God's will." He had institutionalized homophobia and painted issues of great complexity in stark black and white. If you didn't agree, you weren't a Christian and your opinion wasn't worth a lick anyway.

And yet . . . against logic, as a liberal secular Jew, born to a Communist father, raised in Berkeley, educated in the Ivy League—I had been charmed by Jerry Falwell. He was an entertainer. I could have listened to him read an engineering textbook. That was one of the main reasons he had such a large following, I think—he had tremendous charisma, and you had to reason your way out of liking him.

THE NEXT MORNING, I went to the first viewing at the DeMoss Center, which also housed the small Falwell Museum. Liberty students had erected tables at the foot of the center steps for people to sign guest books and purchase the Falwell memorial pin: a black loop of ribbon wearing a little red paper necktie. Falwell almost always wore a red tie.

I stood in line on the wide stone steps leading up to the columned DeMoss entrance. A kid standing next to me was chatting on his cell phone. "I'm about to go see this dude's body," he said.

The procession from the building's exit was by turns somber and indifferent. People came out pressing tissues to the corners of their eyes, pinching the bridges of their noses. And then a Liberty boy galloped down the stairs, stopping to greet a girl standing in front of me.

"What did he look like?" the girl asked.

"Like he's about to sit up and start talking," the boy said.

Inside, the casket was propped open in the center of the high-ceilinged entrance hall, a sunny blue room with white trim that would have looked appropriate in a wing at Monticello. A red carpet marked the path from entrance to casket to exit and people moved along it efficiently, gazing with brief respect at Dr. Falwell as if he were the Magna Carta. Police officers stood guard here and there, watching from the corners of their eyes.

For a moment, I stood over the casket alone. Jerry Falwell's was the first dead body I had ever seen. He looked compact lying there in his casket—huggable. His hair was combed neatly and his face slathered with orange pancake makeup, which gave his skin a waxen quality. His lips were pushed into a tiny, faraway smile, as if he'd just thought of a rainbow. His hands had orange makeup on them, too, and they were crossed over his chest, a Bible held in one hand, his founder's ring on the other. I shuddered as I thought of Old Ray and my baptism—*Have you ever seen a corpse hold anything?*

I lingered for a minute, trying to let the viewing accomplish its mission: make the dead seem dead. But Falwell didn't appear dead, exactly. He looked like a terra-cotta statue. He looked as if he'd never been alive in the first place.

* * *

THAT NIGHT, I DREAMT that Macel and I were in the blue entrance at DeMoss, visiting Dr. Falwell's body. She was sobbing. Dr. Falwell was not holding up well. His body lay crooked in the coffin, as if he had been dropped from above. His white hair was wild like Neptune's, his mouth was agape and his eyes wide, irises whitish blue. His chest bulged with gases as if he had some great breath to exhale. Four days of viewings, it seemed, were too many. Suddenly, the body began to jerk around like a hooked fish, though the face was static. *Not dead*, I thought, backing away from Macel, who only cried harder. Just as suddenly, the body fell still.

"Unless you are Dr. Falwell," a police officer shouted, "you are not to move the body!"

IT WAS THE FIRST Sunday without Jerry Falwell and out on Ward's Road every store and fast-food joint with a signboard had tributes to him spelled out in tall black letters. Newt Gingrich had been in town the day before as the commencement speaker for Liberty's graduation at the football stadium. Addressing a huge graduating class, including the school's first law school graduates, Gingrich gave the "salt and light" advice, paraphrasing Matthew 5:15. "Light moral lamps," he said, "and put them out for all to see." The graduation had an unfinished, diluted quality without Falwell there to run it.

Now Thomas Road was filled to capacity. Ushers were doing actual ushering, finding seats here and there for people to wedge in. There was a special church program, one heavy stock page with no announcements or bulletins, no birthdays or upcoming events. On one side, the picture of a plush rose with the *Jesus First* pin resting in its petals, and on the reverse the list of songs and speakers for the day. I was alone, as almost everyone in EPIC had decided to attend the early service hoping it would be less crowded.

The sanctuary was much dimmer than usual, and though it was full, the chatter was quiet, at a low boil. I was sitting next to a four-year-old Latino boy, the apparently adopted child of fair-skinned, blond-haired parents. This was not an uncommon family makeup at Thomas Road: an entire Anglo group with one child of color. Pastor Woody's wife Lacey once explained it to me this way: "If you're going to be against abortion, you've got to be willing to adopt."

The little boy, legs tucked up under him, drew a stick figure in a dress on the back side of a collections envelope. When he was finished, he held it up and told me it was a picture of me. I thanked him.

"I like you," he said.

"I guess I like you, too!" I said.

He dipped his chin and looked up at me through his soft eyelashes. "Jesus first," he said, as if repeating a phrase he'd just learned in a foreign language. I grimaced. I was uncomfortable with religiosity in children, the lurid gestures they mimic but surely can't understand.

Onstage, the curtains drew back noisily as if they were hung on rusty rings, and the 300-person choir was revealed. All the singers were seated, memorial ribbons pinned to their purple robes. They stood up together, the shuffling of their shoes audible on the floor. Piano keys rumbled and they began to sing one of my favorite songs, "Days of Elijah." Except they slowed it down, crying out each word at the tops of their lungs, each of the three hundred voices distinctly heard, just a hair off-key. Jesus would appear in the heavens, they sang, "shining like the sun at the trumpet's call." We would lift our voices and salvation would come to us.

It was the sound of grief, all those voices singing together, yet split apart by the axe of sorrow. Ray Masters wandered downstage, as tan and gelled as ever, but somehow a facsimile of himself. "Well, let's stand to our feet and welcome the presence of the Lord here today," he suggested. "I know some of you just don't feel like singing, but folks, we're here to worship the Lord even in the midst of our sorrow. Joy comes in the morning."

"Days of Elijah" is a heart-lifting song, and the church began to rise into the pleasure of the music, singing it exuberantly. It felt like tossing off a heavy hood, and I suddenly wished I had gone to the early service so that I could have enjoyed the moment with Alice and Laura, Donny and Kelly.

When Jonathan Falwell finally took to the pulpit after an unusually long musical program, you could feel the church lean forward. He wore a light blue tie and his strawberry blond hair was trimmed neatly. In an energetic whisper he told us that the class that had graduated the day before had been Liberty's largest graduating class yet. He said a few kind words about his brother, Jerry Jr., and assured us that there was "no one more prepared to lead Liberty University than the man I call brother."

The two men embraced amid a clattering of applause, and tears stung my eyes. "And I would like to note," Jonathan continued as Jerry Jr. took his seat, "that today is the first day in ten years my brother has worn a pair of shoes not called a Croc."

Jonathan preached from Joshua. "After the death of Moses the servant of the Lord," he read from his Bible, "the Lord said to Joshua son of Nun, Moses' aide: 'Moses my servant is dead. Now then, you and all these people, get ready to cross the Jordan River into the land I am about to give to them—to the Israelites. I will give you every place where you set your foot, as I promised Moses.'" God's promises did not expire with the death of our leader; they would be fulfilled.

"This message was a message of hope, a message of peace, a message of joy at a time when the people of Israel were so distraught. A message that would bring them through the dark days," Jonathan said. "Today, we are all Joshua. This message is aimed at every one of us. We are all called by God to cross this Jordan."

I was instantly struck by the perfect fit of Jonathan's characterization, and I thought it was an appeal not only to Thomas Road but to all Evangelicals to find a new way forward. Indeed, a little over a year later, Barack Obama's campaign would steer into an eerily similar channel with the Joshua Generation Project—his appeal to young Christians to vote on a broader set of Christian values to move America beyond static partisan lines.

The promised land the Thomas Road ministry had been laboring toward for fifty-one years was a world reached with the Gospel of Jesus Christ. And even though our leader had perished, our calling would continue; we would pick up the mantle just as Joshua had done after Moses. "God promises us that he will give us victory," Jonathan said. But victory was going to require our commitment, he said, as well as "personal holiness."

Jonathan told us that when they were making plans for the new church, Dr. Falwell had specific notions for what he wanted in the main sanctuary. He wanted the stairs to descend directly from the balcony to the altar without going outside so that when people came to get saved they didn't have to exit the sanctuary. And he wanted a long stage, an altar that stretched the length of the room so that there would be space for people to kneel in prayer. Dr. Falwell said, "There are times when the altar needs to be full of God's people calling out for God's direction."

And now, Jonathan said, we were going to put that altar to good use asking God for direction in crossing this Jordan. "There's never been a better time for God's people to call out for God's direction. There are people across this city, across this land, who need to hear about Christ. We must give them Christ. God loves people. He loves all people. He doesn't care if we're rich or poor, he doesn't care if we're good or bad. He doesn't care if we have a shameful past. He doesn't care what bad things we've done. We are all precious to him. White or black, short or tall, fat or skinny." Dr. Falwell would tell us to rise up and cross this Jordan, Jonathan said. "Because you have a BHAG to reach." BHAG was Falwell's often-used acronym for Big Hairy Audacious Goal. "You have a world to reach. Preach the Gospel. Love the people. And don't quit. Don't ever, ever, ever quit."

Jonathan asked the congregation to come down and fill up the altar, and he didn't have to ask twice. People came rumbling down from all parts of the church and knelt on the steps to the stage, and when the steps were filled, they knelt in the aisles, and when the aisles were filled, they turned around in their chairs, knelt on the floor, and rested their elbows on their seats. On the screens, a blurred image of tree leaves shone behind a favorite saying of Jerry Falwell: "Nothing of eternal importance is ever accomplished apart from prayer." During the prayer, I felt petals of affection moving inside me; I felt the good intentions all around.

After the prayer, Ray Masters asked everyone to hold hands. He sang the Lord's Prayer and the congregation shuddered with tears. When it was all finished, I joined the crowd heading outside, stopping at a little table on my way down Main Street to purchase a *Jesus First* pin for a dollar.

THE CONGREGATION WAS ASKED to line the streets all the way to the DeMoss Center, where a horse-drawn carriage would be loaded with Dr. Falwell's casket and proceed to the church. He would lie in repose in the sanctuary for his second and final viewing before burial. I selfishly wanted to be at the entrance, wanted to see the processional into the church itself. I still couldn't believe he was dead—gone.

The crowd around Thomas Road's entrance was packed to discomfort, heavy perfumes converting to fog in the Virginia heat. Jammed in next to me, a group of women in gem-colored rayon suits discussed that morning's service. They had all been surprised by Jonathan's marvelous sermon, inspired by the story of Joshua, optimistic for the church's possibilities.

One of the women, whose bright red hair was dove gray at the roots, told her friends she had heard that Dr. Falwell had told Jerry Jr. "he was plannin' on stepping down after graduation anyhow." Her friends clucked approvingly, eager to put a positive gloss on things.

A photographer squatted down across the way from us, snapping photographs of me and the ladies. His huge camera obscured his face and press cards dangled between his knees. I looked down at my high heels. I had become uneasy about starting to feel like a legitimate member of the church and the implications of that for my real identity. By photographing me posing as a church lady, it was as if this man was actually turning me into one.

I felt a cold ping against my chest. I looked down and realized it was my *Jesus First* pin.

Shushing passed through the crowd and police officers pushed everyone back. A police car rolled through followed by the horse-drawn carriage—burnt-brown horses with black bridles and reins. The carriage was black, too, and fringed butterscotch curtains hung in the windows. People began to applaud, but the horsemen, in top hats and coattails, gestured for silence.

The surviving Falwells arrived and eight police officers marched to the back doors of the carriage, unlatched them, and extracted the long, black casket. They carried it to a wooden gurney placed just in front of the entrance, lowered it, and began to wheel it inside. The Falwells followed the casket, all of them stonefaced except for Macel, who was crumpled into her son Jonathan's chest. The crowd was silent, watching, until a woman shouted, "God bless y'all!"

Once the Falwells had been given time to enter the sanctuary, the entrance to Main Street was flung open. Hordes jammed through, waiting for the viewing to begin. The Falwells were inside with the body, saying their good-byes, although the funeral wasn't until Tuesday.

The crowd was so dense that there was no space for even a cocked elbow or a stretch. Down near my right hand, a little girl managed to fish out the craft project she'd made in Sunday School—a popsicle stick with a frowny face glued on one side and a poem glued on the other: "*A grumbler, a grumbler, Satan wants me for a grumbler.*"

Time dragged, no announcements were made, and we all grew hungry and uncomfortable, the lights overhead roasting us. Church programs people had saved for posterity became fans. People took off their shoes to cool their feet on Main Street's marble floors. Several older ladies gave up, irritably pushing through to go for lunch. But most who had been waiting seemed determined not to have wasted the time already spent.

A tiny Ecuadorian man proudly showed me a picture he'd had taken with Dr. Falwell last August. Another man, his chest piled with camera equipment, explained why he had driven up from Charlotte, North Carolina: "People have been saying these demonic things about Falwell, worse than what they said about the Virginia Tech killer. But I didn't believe all those bad things. He was a man of God, and has done so much to give conservatives a voice in this country and to get Christians to vote. I wish people would listen to people like Falwell rather than letting the liberal media make decisions for them."

Finally, after an hour and a half, I squeezed through the single door to the sanctuary, a droplet from the steaming reservoir on Main Street. A guard told me to take all the time I needed, and I was soothed by his words.

The sanctuary was pleasantly cool and dim and red velvet ropes lined the aisle on either side down to the stage. Couples and families walked the aisle together, accepting tissues from the handsome Liberty men stationed every fifteen yards or so with Kleenex boxes.

Expensive-looking floral arrangements crowded the stage in neon sprays, fireworks frozen in time. The casket was propped open before them. After a couple spent a moment praying over Falwell's body, I approached the casket alone. All the guards seemed instantly far off, and I had the impression of privacy, of space and time. The black casket was accented with bronze and lined with white satin. And nestled within like an expensive pen was Falwell again—this time looking disarmingly like himself. The makeup used on him now was different than at DeMoss, whiter and less waxen, more faithful to the powdery stuff he wore on television. There was also a compression about him—something waterless, dried up. The hands over the Bible looked hard and flat, as if the flesh had turned to carbon. He looked both like himself and also like a corpse.

Accepting a few tissues from a Liberty hunk and exiting the sanctuary into the warm spring afternoon, I felt that the viewing had achieved its purpose: Falwell seemed as dead as he was.

* * *

FALWELL HAD BEEN GONE a week and buried a day when EPIC finally reunited on Wednesday evening. Somewhere in the church, deacons were meeting to decide if Jonathan Falwell would be their new candidate for TRBC senior pastor. In the EPIC room, Ray was distracted, wandering around with a microphone as if looking for somewhere to put it, no message prepared.

The funeral had been the day before at church, a monumental affair attended by Rick Warren and Tim LaHaye, Pat Robertson, Ralph Reed, and George Allen, who had recently lost his Senate seat to Democrat Jim Webb after using a racial epithet against one of Webb's staffers. Even though the line had formed at one o'clock the night before for an 11 a.m. church opening, I had been fortunate to snag a seat in the main sanctuary. Great numbers had been bumped to the football stadium to watch the funeral on JumboTrons. The Westboro Baptist Church had traveled from Topeka to protest across the street from Thomas Road with "Falwell in Hell" and "God Hates Fags" signs, because they resented what they called Falwell's "God loves everyone" message.

"This has been the most emotional week of my whole life," Ray told us now. "It would have been different if Dr. Falwell had been in the hospital, like he was in 2005. I could have prepared myself. Like this, though, it was like he died in a car wreck."

On the morning Dr. Falwell collapsed, Ray told us he had slipped into the hospital to see him, had seen Dr. Falwell prone on the gurney. He had taken Jonathan's hand and told him he'd be there for him. When Falwell was declared dead, Ray returned home. His adult children arrived; he thought they wanted to comfort him, but he needed to be alone. He packed up his gear and headed out to Smith Mountain Lake to fish. "I didn't have fun fishing," he said, "but I needed the time to think." And in that time, he realized that his children may have come over because they needed him. In a way, he thought he had been selfish.

And sure enough, his children had taken it hard. He brought his son to see Falwell's body before they closed the casket, but the son refused to look. He wanted to remember Dr. Falwell the way he had been.

Ray hadn't been keen on Falwell at first. "I'd only heard, 'Send me five dollars and you'll get this, ten dollars and you'll get that.'" But when Ray came to know Falwell, he saw what a great man he was. "Whatever you thought of his politics, he preached the birth, death, and resurrection of Christ, and that's why I loved him." Every time he went on television, Ray told us, Falwell always got around to the Gospel. He always used his public platform to preach the Word. "If that man had been alive when the Bible was being written, he would have been written about in Hebrews. If he had been around hundreds of years ago, he would have been a founder. He could have been president if he had wanted to. Can you imagine the look on Jesus' face when he got to meet one of his most faithful servants ever?"

Rich, poor, it didn't matter to Dr. Falwell. He treated everyone the same. And Ray had seen him do things for people behind closed doors and never talk about it. "He was just being a good Christian. And if Dr. Falwell was about one thing, it was second chances. I saw him done wrong so many times, and I knew he must have felt it somewhere inside, but he would always just put his arm around that person and give them another chance."

Ray walked over to the wheelchair ramp and leaned on the railing. "Y'all see that video they showed at the funeral?" he asked. During the funeral, a montage of photographs and videos of Falwell had played on a loop. Family pictures, pictures with Republican presidents and talk show hosts. Falwell wearing patchwork overalls and climbing up to the ledge of a dunk tank; Falwell sprawled in a hammock with someone in a giant frog costume leaning over him; Falwell in a skin-tight Sunkist T-shirt, swinging a strike on a baseball field; Falwell napping with a Tinky Winky doll, the purple Teletubby he called a role model for the "gay lifestyle," based on his triangle-shaped antenna and his habit of carrying a red handbag.

I'd recognized a video clip from the documentary *The Eyes of Tammy Faye*: it took place at Heritage USA, Jim and Tammy Faye Bakker's Christian-themed amusement park and resort, during a 1987 fund drive in which Falwell raised $20 million to keep the park solvent. Shortly after the fund drive, just before news of Jim Bakker's sex scandal hit, Falwell took over Heritage USA and the Bakkers' Praise the Lord network. He called the Bakkers "the greatest scab and cancer on the face of Christianity in 2,000 years of church history." For their part, the Bakkers contended that Falwell had pledged to partner with and help them and wound up stealing all they had and slandering them to boot.

In the clip, Falwell plummets straight down a waterslide in a business suit: eyes closed, ankles crossed, arms folded across his chest. At the funeral, this clip elicited cheers and applause. "That video they showed, that was him. Knocking people on the head, joking around."

That was indeed the message of the video, I thought—that all the scandal, all the drama, all the dangerous screeds and hate speech—all of it had just been in good fun.

"He had God's wisdom and God's hand upon him," Ray said. "And he was more of a father than *my* father. He was my rock. Not *the* rock, but *my* rock. I would have given my life so that he could live."

Dr. Falwell was also a stickler for good grammar, Ray told us, correcting the speech of those who worked for him. Ray once saw Dr. Falwell editing a legal document "as long as a Bible" all the while standing up and having a conversation.

Ray began telling us about a survival school he'd been to where he developed claustrophobia, but he lost track in the middle of the story. "Now why was I talking about that?" he said, squinting down at his feet.

Clementine twisted in her chair to look at us all, sweetly apologetic. "We've both been doing that a lot this week."

Seeming to surrender to the melting circuitry in his mind, Ray shrugged the spotlight off himself onto us, asking us to share our memories of Dr. Falwell.

Alice told us that when her grandfather died twelve years earlier, Dr. Falwell took time out from his busy schedule to perform the funeral in Canada.

Cintra told us her little girl hadn't been feeling comfortable as a new student at Liberty Christian Academy until one day Dr. Falwell came for a visit and pointed a finger at her. "I baptized you," he told the girl. From that day forward, the girl felt she belonged.

Xander met Dr. Falwell only once: "I shook his hand and he pulled back my fingers."

"I was so messed up in high school," Ingrid said. "I'm thankful he started Liberty because going to school there taught me to start each day with the Word, and to know Him."

Growing up in Indiana, Bethany used to watch Falwell on *The Old Time Gospel Hour*. "I remember hearing Doug Oldham sing about unborn children and thinking I wanted to be a nurse," she said.

Donny said Dr. Falwell had been a guest at his wedding and had to step out twice during the ceremony. Later Falwell apologized to Donny—he had to field two calls from the White House.

A portly man I didn't recognize told us he was a Lynchburg native, and that the town had always divided neatly into two groups: those who were for Jerry Falwell and those who thought he was a crook and a phony. This man had once been in the latter group. But as he got older and as he experienced marriage and divorce and wound up alone, he came to realize he had never found a place to belong, didn't have anyone to look after him. One day he finally came to church out of curiosity and listened to Dr. Falwell. "I realized things people had been saying about him weren't true," he told us, "and I finally found a place to belong."

Ray took the microphone again, seeming to remember what it was good for. "You may have seen me with Dr. Falwell and Jonathan and you may have thought either I'm a brownnoser or I really love those people. Well I'm no brownnoser. I'm a nobody. I'm nothing. I just love that family—like I love you. I know if I don't love you and you and you," he pointed at Connie and Lyle and me, "God's not going to give me anyone else to love."

But the church wasn't going to suffer long from the death of Dr. Falwell, beloved as he was. "Thomas Road is going to be even better and the next fifty years are going to be more amazing. Now if we could take a stethoscope and put it to God's heartbeat, what do y'all think we would hear?" Ray lifted an invisible stethoscope to the chest of a very tall person, and listened. "*Preach the Gospel, preach the Gospel, preach the Gospel,*" he whispered to the rhythm of a heartbeat. "We've reached some of Lynchburg, we've reached some of Virginia, some of the country, some of the world, but there are still so many people who need to hear about the Gospel." There were even those in our midst, Ray reminded us, members of EPIC who came Sundays and Wednesdays, who were not believers. "We have to try to reach out to those people, too."

We had all heard Jonathan's vision for the church—a vision of expansion and missionary work, a congregation that would test the limits of the sanctuary's capacity. For EPIC, Ray told us, "there's no reason with 22,000 members that the Singles ministry can't have 250 people. Once we get those numbers, I want a Singles complex with keycard access, movies with decent language, popcorn machines, Ping-Pong tables. It doesn't have to be a place to meet the opposite sex—just for fellowship." Eventually, with an incentive like that—especially in ho-hum Lynchburg—we could be looking at 500 to 1,000 singles.

After class, as Alice and I rubber-banded bags of Chex Mix and capped the sweet tea, Ray came over and dropped a solid arm over my shoulders. "We need to get you a man," he said.

Over on the wheelchair ramp, Lyle was nervously fingering one end of his mustache as Donny leaned over him, hoarsely shouting, "Show me the money! Show me the money! Alaska's coming up, Lyle!" Lyle stammered an excuse, saying he was still pulling it together, his eyes lowered behind his Coke-bottle glasses.

Clementine came over and pulled Ray off me like a winter coat. "Gina's *fine*," she said.

ON FATHER'S DAY, Mitchell stopped to say hello as I sold tables for EPIC's upcoming flea market on Main Street. He was clean-shaven, in slacks and a blue blazer. It was a shocking departure from his usual anti-uniform: stubble, an old T-shirt, and blue jeans. EPIC was in session, and I asked him why he wasn't there, and why he was wearing a suit.

He was in the choir today, an all-male choir for Father's Day. "They got me in this monkey suit," he said, yanking at the collar.

He shuffled his huge, sneakered feet and regarded me through his brown plastic glasses. "Lemme ask you something," he said finally. "I see you in EPIC, but you don't say hi to nobody. You just go and talk to your friends." He fluttered his hand, as if comparing me to an irritating little bird. "Maybe you don't like men."

I told him I did like men, that I sometimes felt shy.

"Gotcha," Mitchell said.

What I didn't tell Mitchell was that at church I chose to talk only to men I knew were not going to ask me on a date. I didn't talk to the men who flirted with me or whom I caught staring full bore. I didn't want to have to turn anyone down or have them develop romantic feelings toward me.

"You get your Alaska money yet?" Mitchell asked.

I said I was almost paid up.

Mitchell told me his money was all set; now it was just a matter of getting his Virginia State ID in time. He didn't have a valid picture identification. "But I got all my money from asking the people who have a lot—Falwell, Rusty Smallwood, Ray Masters. You just show them that letter Ray wrote and they write a check because they gotta write it off anyway. I know a guy who said he'll sponsor the whole missions trip next year. He's worth billions." He raised his eyebrows as if to allow me a moment to express amazement. "He won't carry any bill smaller than a fifty, and he won't take change back."

I said that seemed wasteful.

"Yeah, well I work at Tuesday Morning," a closeout retailer nearby. "Our customers are all upper-middle-class snob types, so I'm used to it. I know how easy it is to get them to spend."

I told Mitchell I was glad he was able to get all his money together for the trip, and I hoped his ID would come through. He asked where I was going to sit in church and said he'd look for me from the choir.

Two special videos had been prepared for the Father's Day service. In one, children of Thomas Roaders were interviewed about their fathers, and clips of their answers played over the backdrop of whimsical piano music.

What do you do for fun with your dad? the children were asked.

"I jump on him and he tickles me," a little girl giggled.

What does your dad look like?

"He has blond hair," said a boy. "That's all I can think of."

"He goes to church with spiky hair."

"Uh . . . I don't know. I don't remember," said another.

Does your dad cook?

"Sometimes he cooks popcorn when we're watching a movie."

"He can cook really good grilled cheeses and that's about it."

What is your dad's favorite food?

"He likes to eat mashed motatoes," a towheaded boy said after some consideration. "He likes to eat carrots and all that."

"He likes to eat meat."

"Steak."

"Steak."

"Steak."

"He likes shrimp and steak. And pies."

How is your dad special?

Onscreen Jonathan Falwell's little daughter, whose strawberry blond hair was bobbed around a face undeniably like her grandfather's, dipped a worried gaze at her feet. When she looked up again, her brow was furrowed. "How he loves the Lord so much," she said, jutting out her jaw and raking her teeth across her lip.

In the second video, fathers discussed fatherhood. "They're great kids," said one father. "They all love the Lord, all serving the Lord, all share their faith readily. I'm also thankful for God's grace because he turned them out like that even with us as their parents."

Passion gurgled up in Jonathan's voice as he asked his congregation to make a fresh commitment to Christ. "Follow me as I follow Christ," he implored. "Follow me as we claim together it is not us—it is always Christ. *Not I, but Christ.* My friends, I believe the victory God has in store for us is nothing short of revival.

"I believe God has given us a new vision and a new passion, a renewed passion for souls. That's what it is all about. To reach out to those who need to hear that message. My friends, that is where revival comes from. I believe firmly today that revival is just around the corner."

The *Jesus First* pin would be offered for free on the website because Jonathan wanted to see it twinkling on lapels all across the country. "Revival's not something you buy. Revival's not something you sell. Revival is something that begins in the heart."

My jaw went slack: Apparently Jonathan had not inherited his father's habit of chumming for checks.

Dozens of people came forward at Jonathan's invitation, more than I'd seen since the day I came forward almost a year earlier, the congregation's first day at the new Thomas Road. The new members lined the stage, facing the congregation like actors taking a bow.

"This is what revival looks like," Jonathan said proudly.

RITES AND PREPARATIONS

———

A S WE SAT ON MY FRONT PORCH IN THE PURPLE SHADE OF MY yard's crepe myrtles, my mother—who was visiting from California— wanted to discuss religion. I sometimes got the impression she was disturbed by my growing affection for Evangelicals. I understood them well enough to fit in now, to consider it reasonable to go to Alaska with them, and in some ways I guess I was beginning to act like them, too. I was sunnier, gentler, friendlier to strangers. I didn't have that infinite pasture of happiness like Evangelicals, but I had a kind of miniature golf course approximation. A yoga teacher once told me it takes the same effort to sit up straight with your legs extended in front of you as it does to be a nice person. This was how I was living—making constant microadjustments. I listened better, swore and gossiped less, and had gained fifteen pounds. My mother was unnerved.

Often after I'd tell her a story from church she'd let a little poison cloud of silence float past before saying, "I'm going to send someone out there to deprogram you."

On this afternoon we were preparing for a visit to Thomas Road. She said she'd recently heard Philip Roth tell an interviewer on NPR that he didn't envy the religious because he wouldn't wish to be delusional. She didn't have to explain that she felt the same way.

I told her that what I envied most about Christians was not the God thing—it was having a community gathering each week, a touchstone for people who share values, a safe place to be frank about your life struggles, a place to be reminded of your moral compass. Having a place to guard against loneliness, to feel there are others like you. For some of the people I knew at Thomas Road, it seemed that without church they would have no community at all. And without community, I told my mother, a person might risk losing a grip on the humanity of others, might look into the eyes of humans as if humans were wild animals.

I was beginning to understand the need for certainty, the desire to tighten the straps on the universe by claiming to have a handbook written by the guy who made it. Sometimes I too wanted something to make the wilderness seem hospitable—or at least manageable.

But more specifically, I found parts of the Bible helpful even for me, and I thought it was too bad Jesus had been hijacked by religion and politics since the Sermon on the Mount seemed like a pretty good moral code. Jesus had laid out a beautiful plan for responsible personhood, I told my mother, and the Sermon was essentially the skeleton of liberal thought. I thought all these things, and yet she still needn't worry, because thinking them didn't make me a Christian.

We went to Thomas Road on a Wednesday evening. I was so buzzed with nerves driving down that I could barely focus to speak. My mother had recently expressed irritation at being wished a "blessed day" by a checkout clerk at PetSmart, and I was petrified about how she would react to the worship at EPIC. I was afraid, specifically, of how her revulsion would reflect upon me.

"If you're so nervous, why are you bringing me?" she asked.

It was true that I was bringing her to church in part to further reveal myself to the EPIC singles—chiefly to a very noisy doctor who had taken to asking heaps of aggressive questions in what I hoped was only romantic pursuit. But there was a more important reason on my mind. I knew how uneasy my mother was that I was going to Alaska with this group, and I wanted to prove to her that they were good people. And besides, she had asked to come.

As we drove into the Thomas Road parking lot, my mother surveyed the custard-colored complex. "Where are the crosses?" she asked. "It looks like an office building."

Clicking down Main Street together, I watched her expression, nervous she'd give us away, knowing she was secretly distressed by the vision of me walking into a church with a Bible in my hand. But she wore a friendly smile. "It's like a shopping mall in here," she said through her teeth. (Later she revealed that my stepfather had advised her not to come, afraid she'd be rolling her eyes the whole time.)

We came down the wheelchair ramp of the EPIC room during fellowship time. I was disappointed to see that Ray and Clementine weren't there that evening and that my mother wouldn't get the chance to meet them. I introduced my mother to several acquaintances, who were pleasant but a little tentative, as if unsure of my mother's grasp on English. Those who knew me well weren't tentative in the least. Alice and Kelly both rushed over and wanted to know how my mother liked my apartment, what she thought of Virginia. Donny—who would be preaching that evening—eyed my mother nervously, and she did the same to him, aware of his scrutiny. Later she claimed she overheard him telling someone he'd had "a Jew lunch"—a ham sandwich, oddly.

The doctor approached, as I knew he would. Just the sight of him unnerved me. He kept his Bible on a Palm Pilot, which he tapped at with a stylus, and he always wanted to show me camera phone pictures of his large new house, his shiny kitchen. He seemed more technologically savvy than the others in EPIC, and I was pretty sure that if he hadn't Googled me yet, it wouldn't be long until he did. He was the self-appointed photographer at every EPIC gathering, and he was too eager to take my picture. The photos always appeared on his website mere hours after the event. Once he asked me, "When did you get saved anyway?" I told him it had been about a year earlier. "Aw," he cooed, "you're just a baby Christian."

That night his hair was violently side-parted and he stood too close, tilting his chin as he lobbed questions. *What's the name of the restaurant where you wait tables? Can I get a discount? Aren't there any churches in Charlottesville?* My mother watched with meticulous neutrality as I bobbed and weaved, hitting all of the doctor's questions as they sailed at me. It seemed possible he had done reconnaissance on me and was trying to unravel my story.

Finally, Donny released us to pray in groups, asking that we include several special cases in our prayers. Someone's three-year-old niece was having surgery; another woman's mother had just had a heart attack; and Donny himself "coveted prayers for the sperm donor situation." The sperm donor was Kelly's ex-husband, the father of her eleven-year-old son. Donny had been trying to adopt Kelly's son, but the boy's father was being non-responsive. Donny vented about this man for a few minutes, muttering insults and tightening his fist for comic effect.

We gathered at the round tables to pray. My mother and I joined a group that included Alice and the doctor. The doctor asked us to pray for his new job. I submitted a request for a friend who was scheduled to have a benign tumor removed.

"That doesn't make any sense," the doctor said. "Why does he have to remove the tumor if it's benign?"

I said I really didn't know. I said maybe I'd give him the doctor's phone number. The doctor was silent as a chess player.

The man on the other side of my mother seemed to know implicitly to skip her in prayer requests, and he asked that we pray for his ex-wife's health. Alice submitted prayers after him, and then the doctor cut in: "Don't *you* want to pray for something?" he asked my mother as if she were a forgetful little girl.

I felt a terrible spike of rage at him, even though he was probably just trying to be polite.

My mother, amazingly, was unruffled. "I'll pray for my husband's youngest sister, who's struggling with alcohol addiction," she said earnestly. That she submitted something so personal, something she was so genuinely concerned about, moved me. I knew she had done it because she didn't want to make something up—my mother never lied about anything—but I wondered if there wasn't just the shortest blip of a moment where she thought, *Might as well, couldn't hurt.*

Donny's message that evening was about out-of-control tongues. "How many of you gossip?" Some hands raised, then more, then—with Donny's cajoling—hands lifted all across the room. "If you don't have anything *positive* to say, don't say anything at all," he said.

After the sermon, I saw the doctor prepare to lean over to say something to me, but I collected my mother and headed for the ramp. On our way out, we stopped to say good-bye to Donny.

"Good sermon," my mother said.

"Thank you," he said, regarding her with wary surprise, as if he suspected there was some second meaning in her compliment.

"And good luck with the adoption," she added.

"Well," he said, "it's whatever the Lord wants."

Over Carolina-style barbecue and hush puppies at The Silver Pig, I explained to my mother what Donny had done in that moment, refuting luck as the granter of wishes.

She told me she didn't like Donny. She couldn't believe how oblivious he was to his own hypocrisy: warning against gossip moments after he had sliced and diced Kelly's ex-husband like a TV chef. I was beginning to agree with her. Donny had not thought his positions through carefully enough to preach them. I felt incredibly disappointed that my mother hadn't had the chance to meet Ray, a man for whom I was developing a great reservoir of respect.

Overall, my mother was surprised at how nice and normal almost everyone seemed, how easily she related to them. I was glad to hear it: this discovery might put her mind at ease while I disappeared with them in Alaska.

She had noticed there were a few social misfits and she included the doctor in their ranks. He was a creep, we agreed, but she didn't think he was suspicious of me, just clumsily flirtatious.

"You should still stay away from him," my mother said.

RAY AND CLEMENTINE INVITED the Alaska group for dinner at their home. They lived in a bucolic suburb west of Lynchburg, their two-story brick house settled on a spacious square of land. Comforting homemaker touches were all around—scented candles and folk art tchotchkes crowded side tables; wallpapered walls bore wildlife photographs and hangings with embroidered phrases like *Peace Be Upon This Home*; a smiling rag doll perched on the tank of the commode.

Clementine had prepared lasagna and salad with a strawberry cake for dessert. We took our paper plates out on the deck overlooking the backyard. Below us, a small swimming pool twinkled at the edge of a sweeping grassy backyard fenced by tall, tall trees. It was a luscious summer evening, daylight loosening its screws, the dewy air cooling.

Ethan squinted at two tall trees on the far edge of the yard, separated by about twenty feet. "It's the little boy in me," he said, "but I see the perfect trees for a giant slingshot."

Wyatt leaned back in his lawn chair. "I was just thinking if there weren't neighbors here how this would be a great shooting gallery."

I shook my head and Ingrid leaned in conspiratorially. "Boys are always wanting to throw and shoot things," she said.

Sitting next to me, Ray entertained us with bear-hunting stories while we ate. One summer, sleeping in a tent in the Alaska wilderness on a hunting trip with his brother, Ray told us, "God woke me up in the middle of the night." He awoke in darkness, quiet but for his brother's ragged snores. Suddenly he heard galloping—the distinct sound of paws on dirt. He unzipped the tent flap and started hollering and just like that—the galloping stopped. Ray's brother woke up and he started hollering, too. They shined flashlights, shot Ray's .44 six times into the black. In the morning, though he found no evidence of the bear, Ray remained convinced that the bear existed and that God had granted Ray the chance to survive.

Tonight we would select roommates, Ray told us, and before those words calcified into a concept in my mind Alice was looking at me delightedly: she was planning to be mine. I had been hoping she would want someone else, a more Christian Christian, considering that our roommates were also going to be our soul-winning partners. But she wasn't thinking about soul winning, I knew; she was thinking of the person she wanted to spend time with.

I felt queasy: we were *defining, knowing, committing,* and *redefining* our way into a deepening friendship. We were going to be close, and my deception was going to hurt her maybe more than I had ever hurt anyone. I could never have imagined I would be in this position. When this started, I thought I would seem so peculiar that no one would really want to be my friend. The only thing I needed to do to spare feelings, I'd assumed, was not date.

Our group had seven women, and Ray said three of us would have to share a double room. "You can sleep one on top of the covers, one under 'em," he said.

"We're girls so it doesn't matter," Alice said.

" 'Cause I know for the guys, if it's one thing we don't do, it's touch legs," Ray said.

In addition to Alice and me, Pamela and Ursula would room together; Xander and Joey; Lyle and Mitchell; Carter and Wyatt; and Connie, Amy, and Bethany would squeeze into a double room. Ethan and Ingrid would share a room, naturally, and Clementine and Ray.

To prepare for soul winning, Ray wanted us to start fasting one day each week. "That's just to remind yourself who y'all are doing it for— that you're doing it for God. Fasting is time to pray. You can learn a lot through prayer. Like, it's okay to ask the Lord for a number, for how many people you're going to lead to Christ."

Ray told us about the time he asked God for a number. He had been at the lowest point in his life, training to be a chaplain, living on a military base in Myrtle Beach. He only realized it in hindsight, but the lowness—"it was the enemy." The Devil was in his life.

He prayed for help leading people to the Lord, he prayed for a number. God answered, telling him he would lead fifty people. And for a while, the souls rolled in according to God's promise. When he had forty-nine souls, he went to see a guy he knew who was laid up in a hospital bed. He knew the guy was unsaved, he knew where to find him, fish in a barrel. But when Ray arrived, the guy was irritable and told him he wasn't in the mood. Ray said okay, "because if someone's not in the mood, they're not in the mood." On his way out of the hospital, through a door opened just a crack, Ray saw a woman in her hospital bed watching *The Price Is Right*. He poked his head in.

"Hey, ma'am, how you doing today?" he had asked her.

"Well . . . okay," the woman said.

"Can I talk to you for a minute?" Ray asked. The woman turned down the volume on her television. "Ma'am, I'm a chaplain-in-training," Ray told her. "If you died today, do you know where you'd go?"

And in that clumsy, blunt instant, the woman began to cry. Ray saw that the Lord had already been working on her heart. He told her about the Gospel and led her to the Lord right then, with Bob Barker giving away brand-new cars on the television above.

Ray had to leave to catch a plane and he told her, "Ma'am, I know you're not going to believe this but I asked the Lord for fifty people. You're number fifty and now I've got to go." He patted her on the shoulder and left for his flight.

Now, on Ray's back deck, the darkness of evening was settling easy and silent as silt in a jar of lake water. Ray said, "Even if your faith isn't very big—and at that time my faith wasn't even as big as a mustard seed— but if you have just a little bit of faith you can plant it and grow from there, and God will sprout things from it. And once you win souls, you'll just want to win more."

We should bring cameras to photograph the people we save so that when the whole Salt and Light group goes before the Thomas Road congregation after the mission ends, we can do a slide show on the JumboTrons. "Part of it is I want to brag on you, and part of it is I want to brag about what God's done. Because it's okay to do that: it's okay to brag on God."

Street ministry might be a little treacherous, Ray warned. There were a lot of drunks around the area where we'd be staying. There was a big alcohol problem among the homeless Athabaskan Indians. "The Indians there look just like . . . who are the guys near China with the beards and the . . ." Ray pantomimed a spear.

"Mongolians?" Ethan suggested.

"Yeah, they look just like the Mongolians," Ray said. "Anyway, if they're drunk you'll be able to smell it. Don't bother talking to them. Don't go around the corner with them."

As for our flight, Ray reminded us not to bring any weapons, "especially with what's going on in London."

"What's going on in London?" Xander asked.

A few days earlier, British police had discovered and dismantled two car bombs. Everyone looked at him in disbelief; anyone who paid a smidgen of attention to the news would have known about it. His voice low and pebbled with impatience, Ray said, "You go turn on the Fox Channel and you'll find out all about it, okay?"

We had finished our dinner and cake and now people were shifting in the chairs, ready to leave. Ray seemed a little far off, the wrinkle folds around his blue eyes rendering them barely visible. Finally, he spoke: "There's one place I'll always want to go back to, and that's Alaska."

Clementine was leaning on the door frame with her arms folded. Her magenta lipstick had worn off with dinner and I could see the character of her face better, the easy charm of her smile. "You can move there with your next wife," she said.

"Maybe I will," Ray muttered as everyone laughed. "Alice, how 'bout it?"

Clementine sprang upright, eyes popping. "What did he say? What did he say, Gina? What did he say?"

"I don't know," I told her. "I can't hear out of that ear."

Before we scattered, Ray offered a final slip of advice. "Now, the Devil knows we're going to Alaska to try to win one hundred people." He was serious, and looked each of us full in the face. "The Devil doesn't mind us talking about Jesus, but he knows that once we get somebody to pray that sinner's prayer—they're gone. So the Devil will do anything he can do. Be on the lookout. Don't fear him. You don't fear the Devil. The Devil just gets your body. Fear God. Because God's the one who has a say about your soul."

* * *

IT WAS THE SECOND Sunday of the fifty-first year at Thomas Road. I was selling tables for the flea market on Main Street again during Sunday School, next to a room reserved for prayers for revival. The prayer room was full.

I felt a sweet breeze of relief that I was skipping EPIC. I was beginning to feel as if the moments I had alone were sips of fresh oxygen, my last before diving under with the Alaska group.

After I sold a table to a man who wanted to get rid of his deceased wife's earrings and baby yarn, an elderly woman in a rayon skirt suit approached to rest nearby, dabbing her upper lip with a handkerchief.

"It's eighty out there already," she told me.

"How hot's it going to get?" I asked.

"Ninety-seven."

"What's a person supposed to do when it gets that hot?"

"Don't get old like me," she said.

"Aw," I said.

Her hound dog eyes went blank and glazed with tears. She said, "Jerry and I was the same age."

At Main Street's entrance, a woman was slowly pushing the wheelchair of Doug Oldham—the man Bethany had heard singing about unborn babies when she was a girl. I had seen Oldham perform at Living Christmas, and he had been crumbling then, his voice brittle, his high forehead as scarred and ancient as igneous rock. Now he seemed scarcely to know where he was, staring in my general direction, his legs kicking and twitching involuntarily, his mouth an open black hole.

At 11 a.m. Jonathan preached his sermon on building the church, *Not I, But Christ* spelled out in lights on the wall behind him. There was a heap of dirt onstage that he said represented where we were as a church: we had the soil in which to plant our future. Planting was evangelizing, because if we stopped evangelizing we would cease to be an evangelical church, and worst of all—we would be allowing people to go to hell.

AT OUR NEXT MONDAY night dinner at Ray's, the men hung around the pool while the women met under the awning of a large shed in the yard, planning for Anchorage Baptist Temple Children's Church. Pamela had the most experience as a teacher, so she would take the lead, working with Clementine to develop a lesson to pair with a craft and the Gospel message.

There was general openness as to which Bible story we would teach. "You can basically take any story from the Bible and use it to teach the Gospel," Connie said.

Bethany suggested we use Esther or Zacchaeus. On a mission trip to the Bahamas, she had paired a lesson from Esther with a craft in which the children made bracelets with colored beads representing the Gospel message. Black for sin, red for Christ's blood, white for salvation, green for growth as a Christian, and yellow for heaven's rewards—streets of gold.

After our meeting, the whole group reassembled under the shade of the awning. Ray asked me when I was moving down to Lynchburg. I told him I had no immediate plans to do so but, suddenly tossed up on a little gust of fantasy, I pictured myself making church my real life. I was loved here, and I might eventually feel at home. "I would consider it," I found myself saying.

"We gotta find you work down here," he said. "Do you have a degree?"

I told him I had a BA in history and an MFA in creative writing.

"If you have a master's then we can probably get you an adjunct professor position at Liberty," he said. "Where they really have gaps is in the humanities. But I hope you're not too educated because we can't get you *that* good a job."

He told me to submit an application the next day and then give him a call. I froze. There was no way I was going to apply to teach at Liberty—*right?*—but it suddenly seemed that I wouldn't have a choice: how was I going to explain turning it down?

Ingrid told us she was looking to get her PhD, having already obtained a master's degree from Liberty. Many in the Alaska group held a master's from Liberty: Alice, Pamela, Ingrid, Ethan. They all emphasized how easy the master's program was—"easier than my undergrad," Ingrid said. Ethan said Ingrid might not even have to take the GRE, that he might be able to get her into the program without it. "It's like the military," he said. "If one officer asks another officer for a favor, you get it done."

It was time to go, but I wanted to use the bathroom before getting back on the road to Charlottesville, so as everyone loaded into their cars and drove away Ray directed me through the garage and into his basement. Turning into a hallway where I was almost stabbed in the eye by the bill of a huge wall-mounted marlin, I noticed a dim room to my left. I stood in the doorway and peered in. Here were Ray's hunting spoils: an elk, the large head of a deer, a grizzly bear reared up in the corner. I stared at these animals for a little while, thinking about the strange distance between their lives in the wilderness and now in Lynchburg.

I pictured Ray stalking that bear and putting a bullet in its shoulder, his heart knocking like a fist as he knelt over its body and pulled out its innards, tall, silent pines at his back. Now here the bear stood in the shadows of Ray's basement, positioned to look alive but unmistakably empty and dead, seemingly forgotten, snarling forever as Ray and Clementine prayed over steak dinners upstairs. It seemed to me at that moment that the desire to hunt was a desire to possess the mystery of something wild, to seize its powers and maybe understand it a little better. But once you held it, the mystery vanished: the bear was no longer a bear.

Out by my car, Ray was talking to Alice about the way men and women behave in relationships. "Women are dealing with their emotions from an early age, so they can cope with them. When men have emotions, they have no idea what's happening to them." Ray said that often when he did couple counseling the woman would have a whole list of complaints about the man while the man would not have been aware of them at all. "By the time a woman has decided she wants a divorce, there's no turning it around."

I told him how right I thought he was, and Alice shrugged. "I've lost forty-six pounds and I'm ready for a man," she said.

"It doesn't matter what your body looks like as long as you've got a pretty face," Ray said.

"I'm pretty on the inside," Alice said.

"Y'all are both pretty," Ray said. "I can't believe you're still single."

I told Ray I'd seen his man room in the basement, with all his animals.

"Most of my stuff's in the shed, unmounted," he said. "I've got a moose and I've got nowhere to put it."

I suggested he position them all around the swimming pool as if they're there for a drink. He laughed and we all said good night. In a little under two weeks, we would be traveling back to the homeland of all Ray's creatures.

* * *

THAT WEDNESDAY, after Ethan gave a message from Philemon about being productive even when you're in prison, after Donny gave me my size Large "Salt and Light" shirt, which fit like a pup tent, Alice told me something that froze the motherboard in my brain: Ray had talked to Liberty higher-ups about an adjunct position for me and they were waiting for my résumé.

Lucky for me, I was about to go to Alaska.

SALT AND LIGHT

WHAT'S IN ALASKA?

———

THE ALASKA MISSIONARIES PARKED IN A ROW IN THOMAS ROAD'S lower lot. Over the next week other cars would come and go while ours remained, as if we'd all gone missing.

A large bus destined for the Roanoke airport idled in the upper lot, and several men were busy chucking suitcases into the baggage compartment. Everyone was there but Bethany, who was flying to Alaska separately, and we were all somewhat lost and distracted with excitement. Jonathan Falwell was there, too, making the rounds, squeezing shoulders and getting grinned at, and Donny was there, looking, I thought, chagrined at being left behind. Ingrid handed me the Children's Church materials and I flipped through them a little blindly, as if they were operating instructions for a machine I'd never heard of.

Mitchell, in a Wrestlemania cap, was swaggering around happily: he'd gotten his Virginia ID card at eight that very morning. He hadn't thought it would come through. A few days before, Ray had fooled a nerve-racked Mitchell into believing he knew people at the airport who could arrange things so that Mitchell could be sneaked into the bag screening hangar and then stowed away in the cargo hold.

"But Mitchell—it's gonna be cold in there," Ray warned him.

"I'll wear my TRBC fleece!" Mitchell said.

He was reliably clueless. When Jonathan had invited the Alaska group to the front of the church to be blessed on Sunday, Mitchell went all the way up to the pulpit.

Once we were all loaded onto the bus, Jonathan boarded and told us how proud he was of our group: we were the first 17 of the 500 missionaries he envisioned setting forth from Thomas Road over the next five years. We were the first wave of Thomas Road's journey across Jordan.

After leading a prayer for safe travel and God's hand upon us and also for hearts to begin opening in Anchorage in anticipation of our arrival, Jonathan asked us to look after Ray. "He'll be fifty on Monday," Jonathan said, "and he may need your help crossing streets and reading restaurant menus." The two men shared a warm, tight hug.

As we rode, I looked over the Children's Church materials. Ingrid had given me the Zacchaeus story we would be performing at Anchorage Baptist Temple Children's Church, and Pamela handed me a Xerox of the posters we would be using as illustrations to accompany the play.

In Roanoke, we filed into the departure terminal and formed a neat line in front of the self-check-in stations. From midway back in the line I saw that up front, Ray and Clementine were waiting patiently for a check-in clerk to appear. Everyone was waiting. These were people who didn't get out of Lynchburg very often.

Eventually—with a little prodding from me—Ray and Clementine figured out the protocol and our group began to move through. As those who had checked in went to wait for the rest of the group in a seating area, Ingrid and I noticed Clementine sitting in a cluster of chairs with a frail woman clad in a heavy floral frock. Sympathy knitted Clementine's brow as she listened to the woman talk. Later, before we boarded our flight, Ingrid and I confided to each other that we both thought the race for 100 souls had begun, that Clementine had been witnessing.

"I thought, 'Go, Clementine!'" Ingrid said.

But the woman wasn't lost, as it turned out: she was Lyle's mother, there to see him off and to thank Ray and Clementine for taking him along to Alaska.

When we were all checked in, Ray called the group together to remind the men not to make any jokes about anything as we went through security. "They will take it seriously, and they will pull you out, okay?"

At the X-ray machines, people dumped all manner of things out of their bags: wallets, loose cash and change, keys, cell phones. Joey—who unloaded a great array of electronics into a gray bin—took pictures as Ethan posed with blue paper booties on his feet. As I walked through the metal detector, I saw Mitchell alone in the pat-down area, shoeless, lacing his belt through the loops.

"Did they take something from you?" I asked him.

"Besides my dignity?"

Air travel—so banal to me—was part of this group's exotic adventure into a land potentially hostile to its principles, and suddenly the differences I had learned to elide at church were shifting into focus so sharp I was sure I wouldn't be the only one to notice them.

At the gate, as Alice walked laps around the terminal with a heavyset man she was trying to witness to, I called my sister, who was visiting my mother in Berkeley, where an earthquake had struck the night before. I couldn't really talk plainly. Even our good-bye felt scrambled in a code, stripped of its direct meaning. When I hung up, I was unsettled by the notion that it might be my last conversation with my family until I returned because my phone might not work in Alaska.

Wyatt was my seatmate for the Chicago leg. As we took off, he announced, "That's the nose coming up now. That's the landing gear," as if I were a first-time flier. He kept trying to get me to accept his neck pillow, but I didn't want it.

Across the aisle from us, Mitchell was fidgeting, his large hands wrapped around the armrests. With the jet's every shudder of turbulence, he would blurt something and adjust his ball cap. "Hey now!" "Oh, brother!" I could tell he wanted to cuss.

Wyatt leaned over and blinked his flat penny eyes at me. "Just watch," he said. "If this trip is anything like New Orleans Mitchell will blab to everyone, everywhere we go." He shook his head, chuckling. Wyatt seemed to want me to dislike Mitchell. I preferred not to cooperate. I picked up *SkyMall*, reading about a nose-hair trimmer built to endure several lifetimes of use.

As the plane shifted in the air, Wyatt talked loudly about more terrifying flights he'd been on—long ones, bumpy ones, stormy ones through the night. At one point, as the plane banked left and Mitchell cried out, Wyatt barked, "Do you know how many planes are in the air that we're trying to avoid right now?"

Eventually I dozed off in spite of having no neck pillow, and when I awoke again we were circling over the gleaming geometry of downtown Chicago, little gasps of clouds evenly spaced around us, as if plotted on a grid.

As Wyatt detailed the miserable time he once spent in Chicago for basic training, Mitchell made little sounds to match each dip and bump in the descent.

"All planes land," Wyatt announced. "It's just a matter of how."

Walking to our connecting flight in Chicago, I confessed to Ingrid that I, too, was afraid of midair turbulence even though I knew most plane crashes occurred during takeoffs and landings.

Ingrid told me she and Ethan were once on an overnight trip coming back from Hawaii, flying in the dark through a terrible storm. Lightning was visible through the cabin windows and they could hear the roar of thunder from inside the plane. But even though Ingrid was convinced the plane would crash into the sea, she found serenity by saying to God, "Okay, Lord, if this is what you want—I'm ready."

ON OUR FLIGHT TO Anchorage, as Amy and Lyle quietly read self-help books in the seats next to me, I took a Unisom and conked out during a Sandra Bullock thriller called *Premonition*. When I woke again, it was because I heard window shades zipping open all around. I opened mine and what I saw set off depth charges of fear in my stomach. The landscape below was an alien planet: all white, the cleanest white, not a speck or streak of color visible, flat and smooth but for white mountain ridges and peaks cresting up, like a roiling white sea. It looked as though the very mountains were buried in thousands of feet of snow, only their highest peaks visible, and even those were bathed in white. Reality was thudding down on me: Alaska.

Looking at the white sea scrolling out below, I suddenly felt very small and unprepared, as if I were a zoo creature about to be released alone into the wild.

A CAMERA CREW WAS waiting at our gate next to a huge grizzly, snarling from the confines of a Plexiglas case. I joined several members of the EPIC group trying to figure out which famous person had been on our flight.

"It's Justin Timberlake," Xander said excitedly. "The flight attendant said."

Soon a handful of girls in Ugg boots came giggling off the jetway and the camera crew swarmed around them. They were filming a reality show about women so desperate to find a husband that they pack off to the Last Frontier—where there are a disproportionate number of single men—to land one.

ANCHORAGE IS THE KIND of place that makes you wish civilization could have left well enough alone. Car dealerships and big box stores sprawl pointlessly along the banks of four-lane roads. You might be anywhere if not for the cold black mountains rising in the distance.

It was nighttime but solidly light out and we were tearing down a main drag in two taxi vans. In my van, the driver—a native Alaskan—had his window down, and was shouting above the sound of the wind roaring in, telling us that many people he drives think of natives as foreigners. "Sometimes people compliment me on my English!" he shouted, disgusted.

The Econo Inn matched the grimness of the surrounding streets. Its office was enclosed in glass, its small lobby dominated by a battered leather couch and the somber head of a white ram. In the corner, a cloudy aquarium featured three koi bumping their noses against the glass and rolling over each other like nervous hands.

Alice and I were assigned a small, dank room with a thin slice of window overlooking a parking lot. We set our bags down and ventured out with the group to get snacks and drinks at a nearby gas station, congregating before bedtime in Ray and Clementine's suite. Bethany had arrived, having flown in separately. She told us that on the plane to Anchorage she had sat next to a businessman who threw back nine drinks. Stunned by his shameless debauchery, Bethany tried to witness to him.

"Are you a Christian?" she asked.

"I'm a devout Methodist!" he told her.

"But have you ever asked Jesus into your heart?" she asked.

He scoffed, "I do that all the time."

The EPIC group erupted in a great bubbly foam of laughter.

We prayed together and made arrangements for the morning. We were due early at Anchorage Baptist Temple to organize for the bus ministry. Alice and I returned to our room. As I was finding pajamas in my suitcase, Ray rang and asked if I could come back to fix his television.

Walking down the dim hall to Ray's room, my neck bristled with nerves. *Why me?* I thought maybe he knew something was up and wanted to get me alone, get my story straight. But when Ray opened the door to his suite, barefoot and in shorts, he merely passed me the remote and said, "I can't get it to work right."

I toyed with the controls and got the cable on, but the staticky picture indicated a loose connection somewhere. Clementine went behind the television and jiggled the wires. The picture cleared up.

"Now you stay back there until I'm ready for bed, honey," Ray said.

Back in my own room I washed my face and came out of the bathroom as Alice was coming in the front door, cartoonishly embarrassed. She had knocked on the wall our room shared with Pamela and Ursula's suite to say good night, and when they didn't respond, she knocked harder. Finally, thinking the walls were thicker than they seemed, she went over and knocked on their door. Pamela opened up and told Alice they had been praying. When she told me this story, Alice and I exchanged identical winces, and went to bed without prayer.

THE LAST FRONTIER

IN ALASKA, THE SUN WAS SEEMINGLY INDIFFERENT TO ITS OWN laws—dipping and floating deliriously, leaning down to the western horizon around midnight and twinkling eerily on the opposite side of the sky a few hours later.

At bedtime, it was hard to shut down my body because the sun was still up. My rest at night felt like an imitation of sleep, as if it were some sleep-flavored powder astronauts ate to replace the real thing. I tried literally counting sheep, but got caught up wondering if I was supposed to be picturing cartoon sheep or actual sheep.

In the morning, I woke easily at six, as if I had only been on pause, anxious to write notes without anyone looking over my shoulder. For the duration of our trip, I would get up before the others, zip a sweatshirt over my pajamas, and sneak off to a common area with my notebook. At the Econo Inn, I wrote in a strange room set in the center of the motel, several stories of balconies ringing the open air above me, no ceiling above but the motel roof. This room had a few scratchy couches that looked as if they had been salvaged from a frat house porch and a buffet table on which the motel staff laid out the Continental breakfast: jumbo muffins, two gurgling coolers filled with pink and yellow juice, and coffee, brown-water style. I christened this room the Grand Ballroom, and while we were in Anchorage, it was my office.

When I couldn't get to the Grand Ballroom, I took notes in the van, in bathroom stalls, during every idle moment, intentionally screwing up my handwriting so that it would be legible only to me. I split events across pages so that everything was out of sequence. My journal had a lock, and I used it.

My morning writing time was one of my two moments alone during the day. The other was in the shower, where I would sometimes swear, filling my mouth with water and saying *fuck, shit, goddamnit* as the water gurgled back out.

My phone received service only intermittently, in one corner of our room at the Econo Inn and once in a parking lot outside a hospital. I couldn't say much anyway, as I was never alone. I had no email access.

After a few days in Alaska, I realized I'd feared the wrong thing looking out that airplane window. I wasn't like a freed zoo creature at all. I was a free creature, trapped.

TWO NOTES WIGGLED UNDER the door as Alice and I were dressing Saturday morning. They were from Pamela, one for each of us. Mine was written on stationery picturing two cartoon polar bear cubs trying to climb onto a floating hunk of ice, which to me seemed pretty macabre, given the actual polar bears actually drowning in some cold sea not very far away.

In curlicue cursive, the note urged me to *"not be afraid of the people I send you to." I am with you and I will save you, announces the Lord.* She said she was praying that I would enjoy God's creation and be aware that he was with us.

The gesture was thoughtful, but as I folded the note and slid it into my Bible I had the acrid aftertaste of condescension on my tongue.

Sometime early that morning, Anchorage Baptist Temple deposited two vans in the Econo Inn parking lot for our group to use while we were in the city. One of them needed a jump, so Wyatt made a big show of attaching cables. The rest of us greeted each other and stretched our legs in the parking lot. Ray was wearing a striped button-down tucked into stonewashed jeans, and for the first time I noticed that his big-buckled brown leather belt was embossed with the words *Deer Hunter* and his last name. He was tuned in to a different signal, shuffling off by himself, checking out a group of three native Alaskans sitting on a curb at the edge of the parking lot. There were two men and a woman, all three with long, black hair.

The engine growled to life and we began to pile into the two vans. Alice, Pamela, Ursula, Carter, Bethany and I got into the van with Clementine in the front seat, and the rest of the group loaded into Wyatt's van. But Ray was lingering in the parking lot, watching the three natives. Finally he swung open the driver's side door of our van, grabbed his thick, leatherbound Bible from the center console, and walked straight over to the Alaskans sitting on the curb, squatting down in front of them. Our van fell silent. Clementine opened her door and stood, watching her husband through the window. Ray had his back to us, but we could see that he was talking, and we could see from the calm faces of the Alaskans that they were listening.

Clementine drew her camera from her purse and began to take pictures through the window. After a few minutes, she whispered, "They're holding hands."

And they were. Or rather, they had all stretched their hands into the middle of the huddle, Ray too, as if they were a football team about to return to the field. Their heads were bowed and their eyes closed. Soon, the prayer had ended and Ray came back to the van as the three Alaskans stood and walked off together. Ray climbed into his seat and slammed his door shut. "Ninety-seven to go," he said.

Cheers and applause burst from us like candy from a piñata. "What did they say?" Alice yelled.

"They said they believed in God and the Bible," Ray said, starting the van and steering it onto the road. "It's amazing how many people believe that much but still don't know Jesus," he said. Only the woman had offered any resistance to Ray's witnessing, wanting to know what denomination Ray was, where he was from. He respected her caution. After they'd all prayed the sinner's prayer, Ray told them he'd buy them breakfast at the Country Inn buffet down 5th Avenue. They were walking over there to meet us now.

"There they are," he said, pointing to the three Alaskans as they crossed another parking lot at a diagonal, heads down. I could see that they were conferring soberly, and I wished I could know what they were saying. Had Ray snared them? Or had they snared Ray?

We pulled up in front of the Country Inn and Ray put the van in Park. "Anybody got that hand sanitizer?" he asked. Bethany passed some forward and Ray squirted a dollop into his palms. As he rubbed it in, he dipped his head to look into the restaurant windows. "I bet these folks are going to love me bringing these stinky people in here with me." Clementine gave him a look like a mother who was trying not to yell at a father in front of the children. "And I mean that respectfully," he added with a smile.

The Alaskans arrived and Ray stepped out to escort them. Watching him walk into the Country Inn, Clementine shook her head and muttered, "Thirty-one years and I can't do nothing with him."

On our way now to Anchorage Baptist Temple to organize for the bus ministry, passing espresso huts and strip malls, brown mountains cresting in the distance like silt-filled ocean waves after a storm, Ray was telling us that the poor were the easiest to save, " 'cause they ain't got nothing." He looked into his rearview mirror to address us in the back. "The Bible says it's easier for a rich man to pass through the eye of a nee— Wait. What is it?" We all laughed and fed him the correct line, nearly in unison. "Yeah. A rich man says, 'I got all this . . . ' " Ray trailed off. Our van was idling at a red light, and his attention snagged on a homeless man in a trenchcoat walking down the sidewalk, shoulders hunched against the day.

I worked to finish Ray's thought: I guess he was twisting the line to suggest that the rich have it hard getting into heaven not because they're bad, but because they're so materially satisfied that they can't detect their own spiritual deficit.

Ray's eyes were locked on the homeless man. "Now look at that fella," he said. "That's who Jesus would have hung out with."

THE ANCHORAGE BAPTIST TEMPLE was made up of a series of tall, Saltine box-style buildings attached with walls of windows, silvered and opaque like solar panels. A high white spire spiked up into the sky and a giant signboard planted by the road announced the next morning's service would feature a sermon by Franklin Graham, son of Billy.

We had breakfast in a basement cafeteria called The Heavenly Cafe, whose logo reminded me of the Starbucks logo, but instead of the double-tailed mermaid there were twin angels. I was exhausted and disoriented, forking eggs into my mouth without really closing it to chew. When I finished eating, I felt like putting my head down on the table.

But after breakfast, it was time to organize for the bus ministry. There were about fifteen volunteers from the church, including a young couple tending to their several small children. A red-faced man with muttonchops explained how the bus ministry would work. We would divide into teams, going door-to-door to pass out information about the church, offer Sunday morning bus rides for children whose parents didn't or couldn't go to church, and, if the opportunity presented itself, witness. The man with muttonchops indicated the piles of paper on the long table behind him, stacks of materials we'd be taking with us: maps, sample ABT programs, Vacation Bible School pamphlets for the children, sign-up sheets for the buses.

Everyone in the EPIC group wore a look of bleary consternation, clutching styrofoam coffee cups and staring a little gape-mouthed. Maybe we were all too exhausted to understand what we'd be doing, but from the sound of it, bus ministry wasn't going to get us any closer to our soul-winning goal.

A man with a white crewcut in a Hawaiian shirt raised his hand and stood up without being called on. He had a tip for the Lynchburg group: "When you're speaking with children, just get the first names and phone numbers, because some kids aren't sure of their last names, but they all know their phone numbers."

Ray stood, and excusing himself for butting in, said, "Where we're from, we don't talk to kids without the parents around."

Backpedaling furiously, the man in the Hawaiian shirt claimed that wasn't what he meant—of course we wouldn't speak to children without their parents there. "What I *meant* was that in the neighborhoods we're going to, children in a single family can sometimes have different daddies, and so different last names."

Ray politely conceded that this was a possibility, and so we shouldn't worry about pressing the children for their last names.

We collated our handouts. The director of Children's Church offered to take the ladies down to see the room we'd be using in the morning. The room was large, high-ceilinged, windowless, with a rug the color of a basketball and a tall stage along one wall. The air was hot and perfectly still, and the stench of old sneakers was so potent it was as if thousands of them had been buried under the floor. The director told us that the next morning the children would sign in with church staff in the hall, and then they would be left with us for an hour. We had been under the impression we'd only have them for half that time, supplementing the existing Children's Church curriculum. All of us were a little confused, but Pamela looked particularly unsettled, shaking her head and pinching her lips tight.

Ray and Clementine drove Alice, Pamela, Ursula, and me to a subdivision near the church. The homes were large and paneled with cheap-looking wood, as if they had been built for a movie set. We had followed the Children's Church director from ABT, and now he was leaning into Ray's driver-side window and delivering a very repetitive speech on the best practices for going door-to-door. His eyes were empty and he wore a soporific smile, and Ray broke in now and again to poke fun at the things he said. The director seemed not to notice. He gave us a sample opening line: "Hi, I'm with Anchorage Baptist Temple, and we're just going door-to-door to invite people out to church. Do you have a church you attend in the area?"

"We'll see if we can remember that one," Ray said.

Alice, Pamela, Ursula, and I unloaded from the van with our literature, and Clementine and Ray drove away to tackle another loop of houses.

The four of us stood on the sidewalk. It was a recklessly gorgeous day: sky so sharply blue you felt you might hear its metallic ring, sun a soft incubation lamp. I tipped my head back and stretched my arms, refreshed not to be on an airplane or in a car, not in a moldy motel room, not in the bacon-grease-smelly basement of a church in Alaska.

But I was alone in my reverie. Alice looked up and down the subdivision streets warily, Ursula remained in her frozen pond of silence, and Pamela was rubbing her elbows, eyes averted, eyebrows elevated to Code Orange. I asked if she was okay. She was a planner, she said, and she wasn't good at coping with the unexpected. She suffered from anxiety.

"How is this different from what you had expected?" I asked.

She had expected to go door-to-door with people from ABT, she said, not to be dumped out on the streets of Anchorage alone, and she didn't feel comfortable representing someone else's church.

"Do you feel like a Jehovah's Witness?" Alice asked.

Pamela nodded, miserably amused.

"We'll make it work," I said.

"Can we pray?" Pamela asked, as antsy as if she were asking for a cigarette.

We drew in close and bowed our heads together, the sun warm on our scalps, and Alice prayed for us. She thanked God for the beautiful day and said that even though our job wasn't what we had expected it to be, we knew He would guide us and prepare the hearts of people we were going to meet.

Off we went, holding our Bibles like boxes of Girl Scout cookies. Our first street was a cul-de-sac, so Pamela and Ursula took one side and Alice and I took the other, and we would work toward meeting in the middle.

Alice and I came up the stairs of our first house and saw that the front door was open, revealing two sets of stairs off the entranceway: one leading down, and one leading up. Talk radio blared from somewhere inside the house. We hesitated, checked each other's expression. I was blinded by nerves. What was I supposed to say? We were meant to be looking for people to lead to the Lord, but I didn't know the language well enough for it to flow, and how were we supposed to find a window anyway with these armloads of ABT materials? Just as Alice was leaning forward to knock on the open door, a petite Southeast Asian woman came into view at the foot of the stairs leading down, white lapdog in tow. She saw us and nearly screamed from surprise, and her dog burst into a machine-gun spray of high-pitched yapping that drowned out our attempts to apologize for scaring her.

When she had settled the dog and finally came to the door, she smiled kindly at us, though she kept touching her face with shaking hands and pushing her hair around as if we had come with video cameras like the Publisher's Clearinghouse people. We introduced ourselves by name and told her we were visitors from Virginia, here on a mission trip. We had to speak loudly, as the radio was still blaring from somewhere inside the house. The woman introduced herself as Nhu. Alice asked her if she went to church anywhere. Nhu shook her head, but told us she had been wanting to go back. Her mother had been ill and it had been a hard year. Nhu's eyes filled easily with tears, as if she had been crying before we arrived. She didn't seem in any hurry for us to leave.

Alice asked her if there was anything we could pray for for her.

"Yes, please," Nhu said. "My mother."

Alice prayed. "Dear Lord Jesus, thank you for this beautiful day . . ." She prayed for Nhu's struggles, prayed that God would watch over her and take care of her mother, ease her pain. I was waiting for Alice to push the prayer in the direction of salvation, but she closed instead: "In your precious name, Amen."

We gave Nhu some literature on ABT and asked her to come see Franklin Graham at church the following morning. Nhu said she would make an effort to attend.

Something was missing. Something was unsaid. I felt a powerful urge to hug this woman, invite her on a walk. And I could tell that Alice had a similarly strong urge to ask her if she knew Jesus. Instead, we had a good-bye as floppy and disappointing as a deflated balloon.

As we walked down her driveway, Alice and I agreed that Nhu had seemed open.

"Her heart was ready," Alice said. Ray would have known what to do, she said. Ray would have steered that woman right into the arms of God.

At the next house, no one answered the door. From our vantage point on the porch, I could see a woman in the backyard sleeping in a lawn chair, legs outstretched, a cigarette burning in her hand. Alice and I watched her for a moment in silence.

"Should we go back?" Alice asked. She seemed anxious, as though if ruining her opportunity with Nhu meant that God wouldn't give her one with anyone else.

"We planted the seed," I said.

The rest of the cul-de-sac turned up only Catholics and Mormons. We met Pamela and Ursula in the middle and walked back to the mouth of the street. All of us were a little mortified, even after the promising encounter with Nhu.

Sitting on her stoop opposite the mouth of the cul-de-sac, a little African-American girl waved at us and said hello.

We went up her front path. The four of us stood there—four sweaty white ladies holding Bibles—as the little girl, hair half-done in braids, told us she was getting ready for her brother's second birthday party. He was peering at us through the screen door, palms against the screen. We were nodding, standing at a distance. The children's mother came to the screen door and swept her son into her arms. "Can I help you?" she asked.

Alice stepped forward. "We're just going door-to-door for Anchorage Baptist Temple, inviting people out to church," she said. "Do you have a church you attend in the area?"

The woman visibly relaxed. "We go to Counterpoint," she said, opening the door. "I thought y'all were Jehovah's Witnesses."

We talked church a little bit, talked about her son's birthday party. I felt weirdly threatening—the four of us standing shoulder to shoulder in this woman's front yard. But the woman said, "I'm glad you guys are doing this. I'd do it, but I'm too busy."

Alice and Ursula were encouraged by the mother's relief that we were Baptists, as if her reaction were a good weather forecast for the afternoon, but Pamela's face was still a chopped salad of anxiety. "I would just feel better about this in Lynchburg," she said. "Like if they said they went to another church in the area, I would know the church they were talking about."

We split into pairs to hit the rest of the neighborhood, and Alice and I found that at most homes people were friendly and took literature. The neighborhood seemed so open that some people came to the door in towels or allowed their children to answer the knock. One teenage boy seemed to flirt with Alice, telling us he was too busy working to ever come to church as he bored his eyes into her. But in none of these open houses could we locate the secret passageway to talking about spirituality.

Once I realized we probably weren't going to be leading anybody to the Lord while their children watched Saturday morning cartoons in the other room, I stepped up and did some of the talking. At one house, a Subaru was parked in the driveway, festooned with liberal bumper stickers. The man who answered the door was about my age, handsome, outdoorsy, with a beard growing in. In an instant, I felt he could plausibly be a friend of a friend. I wanted to seize him by the wrists. Feeling the dotted line connecting us, I cheerfully began to deliver my explanation about why we were going door-to-door. He held his body angled away from Alice and me, and before I could finish my spiel he said, "Not interested," and closed the door. I knew him, but he didn't know me. And standing on his front steps with that door closed and, *click*, locked, standing there with Alice—who was smirking at the man's unbelievably bad manners—was like looking up a periscope at my old life, not knowing if my submarine would ever return to the surface.

After rounding back up at the Econo Inn, we all headed to the Anchorage Gospel Rescue Mission. It was a two-story brick building with dirt-filled planter boxes in the front windows and dry vines snaking up the facade. Inside, there was a Plexiglas-fronted office to the right, a chapel straight ahead, and down a hall a small cafeteria.

Our group settled into pews in the low-ceilinged chapel to wait for instructions. At the front of the chapel a simple plywood cross hung above the piano and pulpit, and along one wall, a couple of benches were arranged under a sign that indicated they were reserved for ladies only. While we waited, a toothless man with one leg swallowed up in bandages shambled in on crutches, and, saying a few words to himself, collapsed onto one of the red-padded pews.

Finally, Freddy, an ambassador from the Mission, stalked in to speak to our group, wiping his hands on his apron. Freddy was tall and lean with the dry, tight lips of a surfer and a complexion that colored easily with emotion. He called himself a "programmer" at the Mission, which I assumed meant he scheduled speakers and activities. But then I saw it: the overeagerness, the performative jokes, the constant clapping for emphasis, the rocking back and forth, the tense shoulders, the rapid-fire tongue flickering behind his yellow teeth, the live-wire eyes and loud laugh. And sure enough, Freddy told us, "When I came here, my problem was cocaine." A number of the staffers were recovering addicts, committing to the New Life program for two years in which they lived and worked at the Mission while receiving treatment for their addiction.

The Mission also served the homeless, providing clothing and food, chapel services, and separate dorms for men and women. We were at the Mission to help serve dinner, and then Ray would deliver the chapel sermon for the evening. Women and the disabled came to eat at four, men at five, and then Ray would preach at seven.

Freddy took us back to the kitchen and cafeteria. There were already women at the tables, hunched quietly over their dinner trays, so we went back to the kitchen to team off. There was a dishwashing area, a cooking area, a serving line with a window onto the cafeteria, and a well-stocked pantry with everything from cumin to cream of salmon soup. There was a back door to a yard where donations were sorted and processed. Food came in from all over—weddings, grocery stores, restaurants—but the Mission couldn't use anything that had been opened.

Some of our group was relegated to the dishwashing sinks, some to sort incoming food, some to serve, and others to roam the cafeteria, wiping down surfaces with a bleach rag. Clementine, Amy, and I got cafeteria duty. Because the cafeteria was small and wiped clean in a jiffy, we expanded our duties to become soup kitchen waitresses: refilling plastic cups with milk and iced tea, asking if anyone needed condiments, supplying piles of napkins where the need arose. One woman set down her fork and leaned over her tray to ask the woman across from her, "What's going on here today?"

Certainly it would have seemed odd—the last suddenly the first and the first the last, a white-smiled blonde like Amy wiping up a gelatinous smear on the dessert buffet and bringing salt packets to an old homeless lady. But this was Ray's way, the method we'd learned in our first evangelism class. *Buy their ice cream. Add coins to their washers. Give them your umbrella. Drown them in the milk of human kindness.*

Ray called my name from his post, leaning against the wall near the cafeteria entrance, strong arms folded across his chest. He smiled at me appreciatively. "If I were twenty-seven and single . . ." he said. He said he would want to set me up with his son, if only his son didn't already have a girlfriend. He couldn't believe I was still single. "We gotta find you a man," he said, yet again.

There was a commotion across the cafeteria. A woman in a denim vest and enormous eyeglasses was standing up from her meal, shaking a finger at Bethany. "You can't just come in here and take pictures," the woman yelled. "Some people don't want their pictures taken. Some people have warrants out!" Bethany began to apologize a little helplessly, dangling her camera at her side, as if she had been chastised in a language she didn't understand, but Ray came over to broker a peace, apologizing to the woman and announcing to all our group that we weren't to take pictures of anybody before asking first.

Later, as the men began to come for dinner, as I was sweeping pie crumbs into a rag, Ray asked me to go around and witness. I realized that his earlier come-on was just a way to soften me up for this moment. Clementine, I saw, was sitting in conference with a woman with long gray hair spilling down her back, and Ingrid was settled in with a regally beautiful young woman with a large tattoo on one of the lean, brown arms folded on the table in front of her. They both had the same large-eyed, slender beauty, and for a moment they looked like sisters separated at birth.

I squatted down beside a group of ladies as they picked over shiny clumps of spaghetti. What could I do to help these women? I supposed merely showing them some respect and engaging them in conversation would be revolution enough. I sure wasn't going to carpet-bomb the calm of their dinner with an unsteady lecture on the new birth. I asked where they were from—Alaskans, all—and we had a conversation about Anchorage, about fishing. I told them I'd seen some people fishing down at the river's edge the night before, and they recommended several good places to find salmon. I started to lose myself in the tide of the conversation, in their knowledge of the place, when I heard raised voices at the end of my table. Down at the end, Bethany—apparently recovered from the camera incident—was sitting with a man and a woman, her face in a rictus of confusion. The man had shouted something final, words I hadn't made out, but his tone was a sort of warning shot, a tail rattle.

"But have you ever asked Jesus to live in your heart?" Bethany asked the man. "Did you know he died for us, and his blood washes away our sins?" I was surprised to feel more embarrassed by Bethany than for her. We were appendages of the same body. I sat in a chair next to the women I'd been talking with, turning my back to Bethany, and asked if any of the women had recommendations for our trip to North Pole.

Later, without a word to anyone, I reassigned myself to the pantry to organize the spice and sauce shelves, relieved to be interacting with jars and bottles, little canisters indifferent to my ability to broadcast spirituality. I was irritable from the day's constant interaction, from the pressure to demonstrate religion, which was so much easier when the demonstration wasn't supposed to result in someone becoming a Christian. Was it okay to be irritable? I'd never seen any of my fellow missionaries get irritable. Would irritability reveal that I wasn't really a Christian? I began to feel flattened under the enormous boulder of the week ahead, which now seemed so large and dark and close I couldn't make out its shape or qualities. I carefully wiped down shakers of celery salt and concentrated on generating energy and kindness from reservoirs that felt distinctly shallow, distinctly unenriched.

Carter came into the pantry and smiled his lopsided grin, eyed me with his tired yellow eyes. "Can I tell you something?" he asked.

"Sure," I said.

"You are a beautiful woman." It was an unthreatening compliment, offered as guilelessly as a simple carnation, and it was enough to turn me around. I felt personally redeemed by Carter's gentleness. He asked if I had thought any more about moving to Lynchburg and I told him I was thinking it over.

Ray called me out to the cafeteria. He had his black sneaker up on a chair and was holding court over several homeless men who were leaning back from their dirty trays, heaving breath as if dinner had been the last straightaway of a long-distance run. Ray slung his heavy arm over my shoulders and cinched me to his side. I knew what was coming. I was the silvery bait he was going to dangle before these weary old fish. "This is Gina. She's going to be at church, and she's going to sing!" He raised his eyebrows.

"I'm tone deaf," I warned the men. They looked at me blankly.

"And she's single!" Ray shouted.

One man with a leprechaun's ruddy complexion and chin-strap beard told Ray he would love to come to chapel tonight, but he had somewhere to be, and he had to go to court the next day about some Failure to Appear charges. He would come to chapel following night instead.

"No more FTAs," Ray said. "We'll see you in chapel tomorrow."

We shut the cafeteria down, carrying pans and platters to the dishwasher and stacking chairs. Freddy had made some smoked fish and reindeer meat especially for us and some of us washed our hands and ate. I noticed that several people seemed not to want to eat from the same kitchen as the homeless, and when Freddy then offered to make us a full dinner, Ray politely explained that we had other plans.

As we cleaned up, Wyatt kept trying to micromanage me, offering me fresh gloves with a twinkle in his penny eyes, trying to pull dirty tubs out of my hands to carry them for me. I gave up thrashing against his iron-fist chivalry and just let him take over all the carrying. I joined Ingrid in wiping down the cafeteria tables. She told me that the woman she had spoken with claimed she didn't really need to come to the Rescue Mission but does it to stay humble and experience everything in life. She said to Ingrid that she had gone out to a $100 dinner just the night before.

When the woman learned that our group was from Virginia, she claimed not to like our state. "Everyone there is so narrow-minded," she said. "They think there's only one way, one God, one spirituality." Ingrid told me this with an amused smile: the woman couldn't see her own narrow-mindedness for not considering the truth in that angle.

Seats in the Mission's chapel were beginning to fill up with some of the characters we had just served. I picked up a newspaper from the front office and took a pew. Deep inside the paper I found an article about the Bay Area earthquake my sister had reported when we were in the Roanoke airport. It had registered a 4.2 on the Richter scale, and in one photograph a shopkeeper was bent over, collecting bottles that had toppled from the shelves. The earthquake was nothing, a land shiver, but reading about it in that Anchorage chapel felt like hearing news of the unimaginable life events of a friend with whom I'd long lost touch.

When the pews were almost fully stocked, Freddy sat at the piano. Ray took his position at the pulpit. "Well, I promised you the ladies would sing, so ladies, would you please come up here?"

A little reluctantly, we all filed to the front, and Ray coaxed several homeless women into leaving their benches to join us. We sang "Jesus Saves," a rollicking classic that made our embarrassed giggles balloon into robust belting, and primed my heart for the next song we sang: "Love Lifted Me." I felt transported by this song, moved to Feeling X by the earnestness with which some of the homeless congregation sang it back to us without referencing the hymnal. One man in a grease-stained denim shirt, the lenses of his spectacles yellowed with age, black hair drooping to his jawline, gripped the pew in front of him and sang straight out, as if calling to a lost dog.

> *I was sinking deep in sin, far from the peaceful shore,*
> *Very deeply stained within, sinking to rise no more,*
> *But the Master of the sea heard my despairing cry,*
> *From the waters lifted me, now safe am I.*

When the song ended we settled back in our pews, the music still rippling out in concentric circles in my ear, and Ray began to preach. "Isn't it great? God loves you if you're black, white, red, or yellow. Amen?"

"Amen!" shouted the congregation.

"There's a thing they do in black churches," Ray said. "God is good?"

"All the time!" everyone shouted.

"All the time?"

"God is good!"

Ray said he was going to tell us what the saddest verse in the Bible was. Were there any guesses?

"Jesus wept," someone said.

"It is finished," said another.

"Why have you forsaken me?" offered a third.

Ray nodded as the suggestions rolled in. "Those are all very sad," he said. "But I'm going to show you what the *saddest* is."

He called for two volunteers to come to the front of the chapel. An elderly African-American man and a Native American woman with a clear, broad face stood at the head of the aisle, below the pulpit. Ray asked us to pretend that it was God's altar and that he was God and that this man and woman were souls wanting to enter the kingdom of heaven.

"Now," he said to the two street people standing below him. "Why should I let you in?"

They blinked at him placidly.

Ray descended from the pulpit and stood beside the man and woman, facing the altar. "Would you say"—and now he threw his arms aloft—" 'Lord, Lord! I've done all these good things in my life. I've gone to church! I worked at the Mission! I read my Bible every day!' "

Then he walked back to the pulpit. "You know what God would say?" He turned to face the man and woman, his face loveless and strange, as if he suddenly suspected all these people might turn on him. He raised his strong arm and pointed a finger at them. "*I. Never. Knew. You.*"

The words settled over the chapel like a fine layer of stardust. Ray nodded, as if momentarily struck dumb by the power of his own speech.

Finally, he shook his head, shaking the dust away. "Life isn't fair, is it?"

Murmurs of agreement from the crowd. Ray seemed to know intuitively how to manage this group. It required a different rhythm, more audience participation, literally three dimensions—a Gallagher sermon. He had to go among them to make them feel something. He had to act it out.

"But God is always fair. God always fulfills his promises." He took his Bible and came down to stand in front of Clementine, who sat pertly in the first pew, one khakied leg folded over another. "Now my birthday is on Monday," Ray said. "Let's say this Bible"—and he held up his thick old copy—"is the present Clementine bought for me." He had Clementine hold the Bible and offer it to him. "I can point to it and say, 'That's for me.' But it isn't mine until I take it, is it?" He lifted the Bible out of Clementine's hands: *take it.*

The little chapel churned like an old machine, heads pumping like pistons, processing this analogy. "Put it this way," Ray said. "Does the Devil believe in God?"

"Yes!" came the confident shout from the chapel.

"Does the Devil believe in Jesus?"

"Yes, he does!"

"Then why"—Ray leaned forward to whisper, as if what he were about to say would lead us to information worth thousands of dollars—"why isn't he in heaven?" He somehow held the gaze of all of us at once. "Because—he rejects them!"

You didn't have to go so far as to scorn God and Jesus to reject them, Ray told us. You could know about the gift, believe in the gift, but never accept it. And if you didn't accept it, you didn't get to have it.

"Now I can't open up my heart and say, 'There's Jesus!'" Ray said, goofily pantomiming a cuckoo clock in his chest. "But I promise you: it *will* change you when you let him into your life." I remembered a story Donny had told us about Dr. Falwell. A pastor had asked Falwell how he could help a fellow pastor who was troubled, unhappy, confused. "Well," Dr. Falwell said, "is he saved?" He was. "Does he believe in the Bible?" He did. "Then what's the problem?"

Ray wasn't promising riches or a life without trials. "I'm not saying you'll get everything you want," he said. "I haven't, although I've gotten a lot. But once God gives you the gift? God is no Indian giver. And I say that respectfully." A twitch in Ray's face showed us that he knew he had misspoken. "He gives it forever."

During his first year in the seminary at Liberty, Ray recounted, he had lived in a government HUD apartment. He had no furniture. His mattress was flat on the floor and he had a black-and-white TV plugged into the wall. He had a briefcase his aunt had bought him and just three suits from a local department store. And yet he was as happy as he's ever been because he was living by faith.

After we did Ray's affirmation—"I love you in the Lord and God has a plan for you and your life"—he invited those who hadn't yet received Jesus as their personal savior to repeat the sinner's prayer in their minds as Ray said it. "Heavenly father, we love you. Thank you for loving us . . ." One woman said the prayer aloud. Later, Ray told us that when he asked those who had prayed the prayer to lift their hands he had counted twenty-three.

* * *

DINNER WAS LATE, at nine or ten, but the sun was still out, shedding its heatless light. We ate at Outback Steakhouse, Ray's favorite restaurant. Everyone was a little field-trip slaphappy and loud, livened by the sensation that a restaurant was more than a restaurant because it was in Alaska. For a reason I couldn't quite grasp, everyone was in hysterics because Lyle wanted to save the pineapple that came with his dinner to add to his dessert. Several people videotaped him talking about it. I sat near the end of the table, virtually catatonic with exhaustion.

Xander was impatient to order a soda, and kept standing up from his chair to crane his neck. "Where's that waiter?" he whined.

"Chill out," I said under my breath.

Mitchell was chattering good-naturedly about his day, telling me about how he came close to saving a girl at a music store in the mall. The girl was a heavy-metal fan and Mitchell told her that he used to be into all that stuff, too—Megadeth and Slayer—and then he came close to saying he had dropped all that when he got saved. But he couldn't bring himself to do it.

When the check came, we had issues with people not leaving enough for the tip. Not for the first or last time.

After dinner, some of us wanted to go straight back to the Econo Inn, and others wanted to cap the day with a trip to Wally World. I hitched a ride in the Econo Inn Express and went to the room with Alice, complaining about Wyatt to her, who had kept calling for the waiter to refill my water glass. I lifted the lid on my boiling irritability and let billows of it blow off. Alice agreed he was too controlling. She described herself as an "independent woman" who didn't need to be helped out of the van like an old lady. She and I, I felt, were more alike than different.

A little later, Carter and the women met in the Grand Ballroom and had a Children's Church meeting, divvying up the narration we would be presenting the next morning. Pamela was positively wigged out and convinced no one was taking it seriously enough. Several people were working hard not to fall asleep. Clementine wasn't. She curled up and closed her eyes. Carter went to try on his Zacchaeus costume, a floor-length burlap robe the color of dried seaweed and a rope slung around the hips. He tied some kind of Bedouin scarf around his head.

"That's slimming on you, Carter," I told him.

We packed the half-size sandwich bags with the elements for the bracelets, including a strip of leather and five beads. Black for sin, red for blood, white for salvation, yellow for rewards, green for growth. The beads were the size of molars.

After the meeting, Carter came over to our room for pillow talk and confessed that Wyatt was driving him crazy, too.

EVEN ZACCHAEUS

———

AFTER SEVERAL WATERY CUPS OF COFFEE AND A SESSION OF hand-cramping, heart-racing early-morning note-taking in the Grand Ballroom, I joined Ingrid and Ethan to drive five sketchy city blocks to get coffee at what Mitchell called "Fourbucks." Ethan looked wan and serious; his black leather belt was cinched around his shrinking waist. He had been fasting since we left Virginia. I asked Ingrid how long he planned to keep it up.

"He doesn't want to talk about it," she said.

Ethan asked the barista for a pack of matches and on our way back to the van, he told me he needed them for the sermon he had planned for the junior high school kids at ABT. Ethan had worked out a trick that would contrast the reliability of wealth and marriage, and thereby the fleeting and the eternal, and thereby the flesh and the Spirit. He would wrap his wedding ring in a dollar bill and light the dollar bill on fire. The dollar would burn, duh, but the ring would remain intact.

Ethan's metaphor flambé reminded me of a trick a friend of mine, a physics teacher, had done for her high school students. She threaded a wick through a stick of string cheese and lit the wick on fire so that the cheese appeared to be a candle. She then took a bite out of it. She did this to demonstrate that the assumptions you make based on observation are not always reliable—that things are not always what they seem. Ethan and Ingrid really liked this story.

Later that morning, as we pulled into the ABT parking lot, Clementine squinted up at the signboard and said, "I wonder if Franklin Graham is staying at the Econo Inn."

"I saw him in the Grand Ballroom this morning," I said, "eating one of those big muffins."

AT CHURCH, ETHAN WENT to teach junior high, Ray to teach high school, and all the other men were supposed to help out with the preschoolers. As the women walked to Children's Church, we passed through a darkened basketball court and found Xander there. He was alone, his back to us, shooting hoops. Everyone fell silent in unanimous disapproval. They didn't like mavericks.

"I think they're looking for you up there, Xander," Alice said firmly.

He dropped the ball and let it bounce away without a word. A couple of the women clucked their tongues as if he were an unpleasant nephew.

In Children's Church, Carter stood at a table near the stage in full Bedouin regalia, his belted robe trailing to the floor, his freckled face dwarfed by a kind of maroon do-rag Alice had swaddled around his head. He was playing Zacchaeus, managing piles of coins we had donated from our purses. Rows and rows of folding chairs were filled with around a hundred children, the youngest sitting in front.

I stood in the back of the room with the other EPIC women, waiting for our cue, and realized that—having never gone before a group of children in adulthood—my only point of reference for a performance like this was from my own childhood. Watching Carter drip coins from one hand to the other, I remembered a theater troupe that had visited my school when I was about eleven, acting out skits about insecurity and performing a musical number that went, "Normal! Am I normal? What is normal?" I remember thinking it was stupid they were even bothering to ask, the performers seemed so normal and so nameless as to be almost interchangeable, like flash cards of twenty-somethings, and I wasn't sure what any of it had to do with me anyway, since I didn't particularly care about being normal.

"Clink, clink, clink," Pamela said into a microphone, reading from her script. "The coins dropped, one by one, onto two piles on the table. One pile he set aside. 'I'll send this tax money off to Rome tomorrow,' he noted. Then his eyes fell, gleaming, on the second pile—just a little larger than the first. A smile curved his lips as he ran his fingers through the coins. 'This money—this is mine! Payment for a job well done,' he congratulated himself." Carter gestured accordingly, fingering the coins.

"This Jewish man was a publican," Pamela continued as I strained not to roll my eyes, "a tax collector who lived in the city of Jericho."

Carter cinched up his coin purse and passed down the aisle to the back of the room to join the rest of us. All the round-cheeked children turned to watch their Jewish villain pass, and I felt seasick. This might have been the first time many of them had heard about Jews, and here we were, clumsily handing down that unkillable gray-skinned zombie of anti-Semitism, the myth of the greedy Jew. I never encountered direct anti-Semitism at church, but I certainly caught a few glimpses of its antecedents: ignorance and ridicule. Once Ray made fun of Carter for chuckling too wildly: "You're like one of them Jews at the Wailin' Wall."

Pamela read on, evoking the beautiful city of Jericho, "its tall palms and lovely balsam-wood trees, its gardens of sweet-smelling roses making the air like perfume. One day great crowds were gathering in Jericho in anticipation, and Zacchaeus tagged along to see what the fuss was about, though he couldn't see over the heads of those gathering. 'He's coming! He's coming!' the shout rose from somewhere. The people pressed forward, crowding into the street. He felt the excitement building all around him."

The EPIC women shuffled down the center aisle with a couple of older children we'd tapped for volunteers. We whispered dramatically to the children and each other—*Where is he? Have you seen him?*—as Carter grunted and jumped behind us, unable to see over our heads. There was nothing to see anyway, which I thought must have been confusing for the children in the audience. The stage was empty. Alice was going to read Jesus' lines from the back of the room. I felt certain the whole exercise was going to fall apart, like an old car bumping down a rocky path with none of its parts screwed tight. I only hoped it fell apart before it was my turn to speak.

"Why did this tax collector want to see Jesus?" Pamela asked. Perhaps, she suggested, he felt guilty about stealing from his fellow Jews, who in turn considered him a sinner because he worked for the Romans. She showed the children a couple of giant, laminated flash cards. The first read, "GOD LOVES YOU And Has A Wonderful Plan For Your Life BUT All People Do Not Have This LIFE. WHY? BECAUSE OF . . . SIN." In the bottom corner of the flash card was a red cartoon apple with a bite taken out (in this context probably more evocative of Snow White than the Garden of Eden). Pamela's next flash card read, "Some Things That Are SIN: Disobeying Parents, Being Unkind, Telling A Lie, Stealing Something, Cursing, Doing Wrong Against God."

Connie was the next narrator and took the microphone as we kept up our whispering and neck craning in the aisle. Holding up another card, she explained that Zacchaeus was not the only sinner. "Who has sinned?" her card read. "The Bible says . . . all have sinned. Does all include you?" It struck me that these cards looked a lot like the large-print end-of-days posters that street-corner apocalypse prophets thrust at passersby.

"You and I are sinners, too," Connie said in a soft voice, as if trying to break the news gently. "We are born that way. Sin is wanting your own way instead of God's way. Any time you talk behind someone's back, steal money from your mother's purse or go along with friends to do something wrong, like painting graffiti on walls, you show that you don't measure up to God's perfect standard of right. You sin because you are born with a *want* to do wrong. Your sin separates you from God."

Connie lifted up another card: a picture of a drawbridge opening for a plump tugboat. Planted on one side of the drawbridge was a yellow sign bearing the silhouette of a robed man with arms lifted in invitation (Jesus); on the other side, a sign bearing three non-robed silhouettes (the rest of us scoundrels). On the broadside of the little tugboat, SIN was printed in large letters. Toxic-looking ripples formed in the water around the boat. The split-screen story of Zacchaeus, the tugboat, and the apples had to be confusing. I looked at the children, who were paying attention, but didn't seem exactly transported to a higher dimension.

Amy's narration sent Zacchaeus up a sycamore tree for a better look at Jesus and his disciples, who were entering Jericho. Carter scrambled up on the stage and shaded his eyes from the jaundiced fluorescent light, looking out over our heads and the heads of all the children to the back wall, where Alice stood next to a guy working the AV cart. Jesus, Amy told us, went straight to Zacchaeus' sycamore.

"Zacchaeus!" Alice boomed from the back of the room in her best James Earl Jones. "Hurry and come down, for today I must stay at your house." Carter gave a look of cartoonish disbelief. Who was this man who not only knew his name, but also wanted to stay at his home? Amy told us who: "The son of God, who knows everything and loves unconditionally, who reaches out even to those rejected by others."

When it was time to deliver my part, I stood before the children and gripped my script as if it were the last floating scrap of a shipwreck. "Regardless of what Zacchaeus had done or what people thought," I croaked, "Jesus, God's son, reached out in love to Him." I made a mental push to think of something non-scripted to say, but beyond the written words was breathlessness and vertigo and inarticulate sounds.

"Jesus reaches out to you, too," I read. Here I was, preparing hearts. Planting seeds. Little eyes watched me with a spookily uniform neutrality. "He came to earth to help sinful men, women, boys and girls to find the way to God. Soon after this time, Jesus, who lived a perfect, sinless life, willingly gave up His life to save you and me from our sins. He died on the cross, giving His blood to take the punishment that we deserved."

I held up my first card, which was a giant picture of a wooden cross with clouds drifting in the background. On the vertical beam of the cross was "SINS"; on the horizontal, "IT IS FINISHED." Idiotically, I read these words, as well as the abstract caption printed next to the cross: "Jesus the savior took our sins to the cross." I didn't offer a further explanation. Back to my script: "The Bible says, 'and without the shedding of blood is no remission.'" I was doing my best to drizzle syrup over my speech, but I still tasted the bitterness of the language. I didn't like making children picture bloodshed. How could this crap not fuel nightmares?

"Jesus' blood, given on the cross, is the only way to have our sins forgiven," I warbled on. "Three days after he died, Jesus rose again. He is alive in Heaven today. Jesus made the way for you to know and love God. He reaches out in love to save you no matter what you have done wrong or what others think of you." Insisting on the love part of the bargain felt like a blow-softener, a way of declawing the monstrous notion of someone tortured and murdered for our benefit.

In the front row, a little boy with fine platinum hair clamped his hand on his crotch. He was as cute and clueless as a baby monkey, and I felt relieved that this concept probably wasn't even penetrating. I could barely sustain an understanding of the Gospel, and at that point I had spent a lot of time trying very, very hard. There was no way these children had any idea what we were actually prattling on about. I probably sounded to them like, "Blood, blood, blood; love, love, love."

When I finished my segment I virtually ran to the side of the room.

Bethany described the changes in Zacchaeus that Jesus' love produced: the end of greed, a willingness to atone for his past crimes. Bethany said that if you have been saved people should see a change in you, a difference in your life. And a saved person gets to ask God for guidance when facing temptations.

Ursula held up another card—the drawbridge again, but now the bridge was lowered, and the SIN tugboat was capsizing. The bridge now connected the scoundrels to Jesus, with a helpful sign that now read JESUS. The top of the card read, JESUS SAID "I AM THE WAY." Jesus was the way to Jesus.

Ingrid improvised the final piece. Her script was supposed to be about how if the children want to see changes in themselves as they saw in Zacchaeus, they had to let God in, whatever that meant. And though her script made no mention of afterlife, she described heaven and hell anyway. Heaven, she told the children, was a wonderful place where we got to be with God forever. Hell was a place where our bodies suffered forever and we would always be separated from God.

"Jesus' sacrifice on the cross was a gift to us," Ingrid said. When she said "Jesus" it sounded like "Gee Sauce." "Gee Sauce gives us this gift," she said. "And once it is given, it can never be taken away."

Ingrid asked us to raise our hands if we had sinned. All the other EPIC women raised their hands so I did, too, and little hands lifted in the air all across the room. "Who wants to go to heaven?" The hands stayed in the air. "If you don't accept the gift," Ingrid said sweetly, "then you have to go to hell."

She gave the invitation, asking the children to repeat the sinner's prayer in their heads if they were ready to accept Jesus into their hearts. After the prayer, she asked them to keep their eyes closed but raise their hands if they had prayed with her. I counted eighteen hands, but noted that Ingrid hadn't specified that the children should only raise their hands if it was their first time saying the prayer.

Pamela then asked all the children who hadn't raised their hands to proceed directly to craft. She told them about the bracelets we would be making, and asked them to remember the order of the beads: black for our sin, red for the blood Jesus shed on the cross, white for the blood washing our sins "white as snow," yellow for the streets of gold in heaven, and green for growth in God. It struck me as counterintuitive that heavenly rewards should come before growth, but I knew this was because no one wanted to give the impression that rewards stemmed from growth. Good deeds, which were what Thomas Roaders meant by growth, were filigree touches around the crown jewel of salvation. Rewards were for accepting Jesus, and for that alone.

I passed out the baggies of beads and leather strips to the children and helped them remember the color order.

"This is yellow, not gold," one boy pointed out.

"Well, use your imagination," I said, like zillions of adults before me.

They held out their little wrists for me to knot their bracelets. They were sweet and orderly, and quite matter-of-fact about doing craft. One knot, slip the beads on in sequence, another knot to keep the beads from sliding, and then a final knot to tie it on their wrists. The bracelet's symbolism didn't appear to overpower the simple pleasures of assembling and wearing it. I didn't see anyone staring intently at their wrist.

I was called over to another table to help the children who had prayed the sinner's prayer fill out their cards. Ingrid was talking to a little girl who said she knew she was a sinner because sometimes when her little sister came into her room she yelled at her to go away. The crotch clamper was telling Clementine, "I've said the prayer lots of times but I keep forgetting it."

I helped a girl named Kim, who said she had prayed the sinner's prayer before, but she hadn't yet filled out a card. She was seven, a large-eyed foal clumsy with the pen. She wrote down her name and address, her phone number, the name of her school. She didn't know her parents' first names. I felt a sudden maternal flush for Kim.

Down the table from me, I saw that Pamela was counseling a Native American boy who had his eyes screwed shut in concentration. Pamela had her face down close to his, talking into it with the intensity you normally only see when children are getting a scolding. Her hand was gripping his wrist like an eagle on a perch. I heard her say, "Jesus loves you very, very much, and he shed his blood to wash away all your sins."

Ah. So that's what we were supposed to be doing. I looked down at Kim, whose snow jacket was sliding off her shoulder. The message—it's okay that you do bad things, because everyone does bad things, and everyone can be forgiven, but you should try to be as good as you can be anyway—was a nice one. But the phrasing of it—Jesus loves you in spite of the fact that you're a dirty rotten sinner—how could that provide children with solace? I spared her. We hugged, and off she went.

After the children were gone, we circled for a prayer. Pamela was crying, gutted by the effort. All the other women looked at her with pity and appreciation. Ingrid said she had been trying very hard to make sure her little girl understood what she was agreeing to, and the little girl kept insisting she did.

"Are you sure?" Ingrid had asked. *Do you know that you know that you know*, I remembered Falwell saying during the weekly invitation. The little girl swore she understood. "And maybe I make it too complicated," Ingrid said, shrugging. "Maybe I should learn from childlike faith."

We had lunch at the air force base BX, which was a huge department store with a food court. CNN was playing on a television hung from the ceiling of the food court and I saw that Tammy Faye Bakker had died. I dropped my hoagie. Tammy Faye! I loved Tammy Faye! I had seen *The Eyes of Tammy Faye* early on in my church adventure, which depicted her as someone who had been dragged down by a corrupt husband and then trampled by an imperial televangelist, Jerry Falwell. In the documentary, Tammy Faye copped to having been naive and greedy, to having made mistakes and struggled with addiction. But she seemed redeemed and remorseful in her old age. She became an activist for gay rights and AIDS research. And she had a sense of humor about herself and her mascara as well as rich reserves of forgiveness. After Falwell's death, Tammy Faye told Larry King that she had wanted to make amends with Falwell. "I wanted to give him a hug and say it's all right," she said tearfully. "We're all human and we all make mistakes. Let's start all over again. Yesterday is yesterday, and today is today." She told King that she was praying for Falwell's family and that maybe one day she and Jerry would see each other in heaven.

At the BX, I informed the group that Tammy Faye had died. A few twisted to see the television, but returned to their lunches without comment. At first I felt astonished that no one had anything at all to say about her, good or bad. But as conversation trundled on—Ingrid and Ursula talking about what souvenirs they wanted to shop for at the BX, Clementine instructing us to pass her our purchases to get the military discount, Mitchell filling us in on Franklin Graham's sermon, Lyle telling about giving a $10 love offering to rebuild churches in the Sudan—I began to understand why. It was sad when people didn't know or accept the truth, but when someone had it and chose to give it up, or maybe had just *pretended* to have it in the first place, it wasn't sad— apostates were simply out of the family.

I RAN DOWN ANCHORAGE'S 5th Avenue, flying past laundromats and diners, pawn shops and furriers, gold nugget jewelers and souvenir boutiques. I felt calmer. But not free. My iPod and headphones were crunched in my sweaty fist because Ingrid was running with me. I had decided after the BX that I needed to break out for a little while, needed to sweat and feel some Jay-Z thumping in my chest, but Alice had insisted I couldn't run alone. I was planning to go out no matter what anyone said about it. What were they going to do—lock me in the van? I needed a second to breathe, and my mornings in the Grand Ballroom weren't cutting it.

So Ingrid came along, even though she wasn't really in the mood to run. She looked incredibly fit and strong, but she was a little slow and we kept having to stop so she could catch her breath. She had been curbing the cardio lately because she and Ethan were trying for a baby. We talked fitness for a while, and Ingrid told me about her gym job in Lynchburg. "It's a great witnessing opportunity," she said. She was "working on" a woman—a Unitarian. The woman wasn't convinced there was one way to heaven, but she always asked Ingrid to pray for things on her behalf. So if she believed in prayer, Ingrid reasoned, the woman was open to believing in more. At the gym, people were already there to work on self-improvement and felt inclined to share things about themselves in a way they wouldn't anywhere else.

This struck me as so true—at a gym, perfect strangers who might normally try to conceal their bodies could be found rolling around on the floor with their legs in the air, clinging to machines with sweat stains in their pits and crevices, hunching naked in the locker room as they stepped into their underthings. Their vulnerability and desire for embetterment could be exploited, sure. In fact, I once saw that happen. After a morning spinning class at my gym in Charlottesville, everyone was lying on the floor with the lights out, stretching and cooling down as Rob, the spinning instructor, walked among us, stepping over our ankles and wrists. "I pray a lot," he said. "And this morning I was doing my devotionals and thinking about what I could share with you all in class. And I read one of my favorite verses, John 3:16. It goes, 'For God so loved the world that He gave His one and only son, that whoever believes in Him shall not perish but have eternal life.' So I just wanted to share that with you all—God loves you." There was a moment of silence like a ball tossed into the air, and then a woman cried, "We love *you*, Rob!"

Ingrid and I ran along a green belt that spilled down to a neighborhood of large, handsome homes around the Westchester Lagoon. The lagoon was glassy green and gentle-looking. On the far horizon, snow-streaked mountains stood mute and huge like distant cousins of the mansions behind us. We found a little running trail along the edge of the lagoon and took it. Through puffs for air, Ingrid asked me about my friends in Charlottesville—were any of them Christian? No, I told her. And my family? Not them either. She asked if I witnessed to any of them. I told her I didn't, and she asked me why.

I told her about the chrysalis of silence that grew around my family and friends whenever I talked about Christianity. I told her that most non-Christians I knew (and I was privately including my old self here) saw being Christian as a cultural identity and a political identity more than a religious identity. That in order to be a believer, you had to already subscribe to a certain lifestyle. That therefore the conversation was over before it began. This was a risky thing to say, I knew. It implied not only that my friends and family were culturally and politically different from Thomas Roaders, but that I might be, too, and didn't see it as a barrier to belief. Ingrid entered her own chrysalis of silence, our padding feet continuing their conversation below us.

"Well," I said, hoping to change the frequency a little, "I guess I also feel a little weird witnessing because I haven't been a Christian very long."

Now we were at the crest of a hill, inside a little ring of trees overlooking the lagoon. Ingrid was ready to turn around. We stopped to catch our breath and stood facing each other, hands on hips, panting. Ingrid told me I was in a great position to witness because I could easily recall what it felt like to be lost. I had a recent reference point and so could potentially relate to the lost better than anyone else.

"Look at Paul," she said. "He became a believer long after any of the other disciples, but God used him more than anyone else." When she spoke, she jutted her face out a little and opened her eyes wide. Her face was dewy and flushed and she smiled with her mouth open.

"Maybe," I said.

As we ran back along the edge of the lagoon, I told Ingrid I thought a person needed to be at a dead end and ready for change to convert, and until a person arrived at that moment in his or her life, there wasn't really any point in lecturing. She shocked me by agreeing, though she pointed out that sometimes lecturing planted seeds.

I asked Ingrid how she became a Christian. Her mother had been Catholic and her father Protestant, and they both came forward to get saved during a church play her older brother performed in as a child.

How strange, I said, to have a religious awakening at a children's play.

Ingrid agreed it was very strange and sudden, and said that her mother's Catholic family had a difficult time adjusting to it. The strife forced her parents out of Florida, to West Virginia.

Growing up, Ingrid said her parents were very "legalistic" about Christianity, focused on laws and rules and certain ways of behaving and dressing. So the God Ingrid came to know as a child bore similarities to her father: doctrinal, aloof, authoritative. What Ingrid mainly learned about God growing up was what God sanctioned and forbade.

Of course, she did all the forbidden stuff in high school. She got in with a bad crowd, and got sucked up in a cyclone of drugs, drinking, and—she confided in a low tone—sex.

"I was very troubled," she said.

Aware of her misbehavior, Ingrid's parents told her that if she agreed to spend her freshman year at Liberty University she could then pick any college she wanted and they would pay for it. She agreed, not realizing then what a generous offer that was.

Her first semester at Liberty, she met girls on her hall who were good Christians, who loved the Lord, who were spiritually strong.

"How could you tell?" I asked her.

"They were always happy," Ingrid said, "and they cared about my life." They would check in with her often, and they set a good example— they showed Ingrid that having a relationship with God wasn't all about rules and restrictions.

Ingrid said she had a bad-news boyfriend who she thought cheated on her. "I was just—broken," Ingrid said, emotion blooming in her voice like ink in water. During Spiritual Emphasis Week at Liberty, she came forward to get saved for real.

Ingrid's new relationship with God was now causing a lot of friction in her family. "My dad's more works-oriented," she said, "and I see my relationship with God as personal. I used to think God was mean and stern, somebody who told you what you could do and what you couldn't do." Now her relationship with God is love-based.

I still had a hard time holding on to an understanding of these words— a *personal* relationship with God. As in you and God stay up late talking? As in you and God are secret sharers? I mean, I knew the rhetoric—an intimate relationship with God and a willingness to put Jesus first was the outward manifestation of real Christianity. It was somewhere beyond *What Would Jesus Do?* and using the Bible as an instruction manual for life. It had to do with perpetual prayer for guidance, with a life in which every single action was a micro-tribute to God. But there was more: as Ingrid said, Christianity wasn't works-oriented. Evangelical language was a language of its own, where the rhetoric often didn't mean what the words seemed to signify in English. Words were encoded symbols used to describe feelings Evangelicals understood. Sometimes I was able to understand these feelings and crack the code on a turn of phrase. But not so with the *personal relationship with God*. With this I scraped and scraped for a more direct meaning, but each layer I revealed was just another picture of a picture.

THAT EVENING WE RETURNED to Anchorage Baptist Temple wearing our "Salt and Light" Singles Ministry shirts. Holding the door open for our group was a man who bore such a striking resemblance to our recently departed preacher that we all paused to stare.

"That man looks just like Dr. Falwell," Clementine said.

The ABT sanctuary was smaller than Thomas Road's, less modern. Fake plants crowded the edges of the small stage and the choir was dressed in street clothes. The choir director was loud and kind of atonal. When we sang at TRBC, the overall sound blended and was then laminated with the best of our voices, so that the songs sounded just right. At ABT, the songs sounded like expressions of agony, ragged and human.

Jerry Prevo, the pastor of ABT, welcomed our group, and EPIC stood to receive the church's applause. Prevo introduced Ray as the guest preacher for the night and said a few warm things about Jerry Falwell.

Wyatt was supposed to run a slideshow biography of Ray, showing photographs of his Air Force service, but he ran into technical difficulties and the slideshow froze, so he had to pull the plug on it.

Ray took to the pulpit and paved over the moment with ease, saying something to the effect of "When it rains, it pours." Similar problems had plagued Franklin Graham's sermon that morning.

He thanked Prevo for his kind words about Dr. Falwell. "I still cry about once a week," Ray said, telling the church how Dr. Falwell's parking space was right under Ray's office window, and how he used to hear him pull up every day in his SUV, blowing his car horn built to sound like a train's. Prevo reminded Ray of Dr. Falwell in that he was a controversial figure, too. If you went to his church you always had to be ready to "pucker up or duck"—people either loved you or hated you, with nothing in between.

Tonight Ray was preaching to those people who were 99 percent sure they were saved and going to heaven but still had a "gnawing on their heart."

"I was that way growing up," Ray said. "Even though I got baptized twice, I still wasn't sure." This uncertainty was part of what made Ray's religion tangible and attractive to me. His faith wasn't a lawn ornament. The history of his belief was marked by doubts, erosions, uncertainty, the desire for truth. This process of self-examination worked on Ray's faith as if it were raw marble, shaping it into something lasting, something with unusual resilience and profundity.

When Ray was a junior in seminary, after he had already led a number of people to the Lord, after many years of the gnawing and many years of hiding the holes in his faith while he preached, he came to a seminary professor and confessed his uncertainty. He hadn't told *anyone* the truth, that he didn't know that he knew that he knew. The professor simply told him about the Gospel. He told Ray as if Ray had never heard the Gospel before. Ray knelt there in his professor's office and said the sinner's prayer. He begged God. "Please save me," he said.

And he didn't feel anything. He said good-bye to his professor and left the office, still not feeling anything. But once he got outside, heading to his car, Ray said he suddenly felt something radically different: a peace in his heart. This peace, he told us, was the Grail Cup. The perfect assurance.

He came straight home and told Clementine he'd gotten saved. He'd already been a Christian many years, had led people to the Lord, but he hadn't been saved until that day. Needless to say, Clementine was a little surprised.

Sitting in my pew at ABT, I was a little surprised myself. Just the other day at the Rescue Mission, Ray had said that in his first year at seminary he was the happiest he'd ever been because he was living by faith. Now it wasn't like Ray was preaching under oath, but it unnerved me that his personal history was subject to edits and revisions for the sake of persuading the audience. And I wondered if all the trouble I'd gone through to get the truth undercover was for nothing, if I was even being manipulated inside the fold.

"You may be six or sixty-six," Ray said. "If you aren't a hundred percent sure, you need to come forward tonight. Don't be ashamed."

People poured from the pews to pray at the altar as we sang. I wondered if this was an unusual occurrence for their church, but it seemed rude to ask. Afterward, Jerry Prevo came over to greet our little group. He told us that he had once flown around Mount McKinley with Jerry Falwell.

Ray wanted us to meet the ABT singles group, so we went upstairs to their lounge. I heard Ray behind me on the stairs, counseling a young member of the ABT group. "You surely don't think you're the only one who has ever felt this way," he told him.

The singles had a musty rec room with pool and Ping-Pong tables, couches and TVs. They were playing pool when we walked in and though they greeted us warmly, our group stayed near the door, as if we'd mistakenly walked into a roadhouse. After cracking some jokes about how we should all date each other, Ray invited the local singles to join us for dinner at a restaurant called Sea Galley.

"Who's paying?" one of them murmured.

I was in Wyatt's van for the drive to the restaurant, and he was making me nervous. He was talking to himself almost inaudibly, in a kind of tight spin of rage after having messed up the slideshow. A few of us said encouraging things, pointed out that there had been problems at Franklin Graham's sermon, too, but Wyatt didn't reply. At a stoplight, he made his right hand into the shape of a gun and pointed it at a squirrel skittering across the street. "Pow!" he said. "Street rats."

Sea Galley was all sticky polished wood, brass fixtures, and dim light from stained-glass chandeliers. Moldy-looking fishermen's nets were cast over everything with starfish and sand dollars glued to them. A roaring stuffed bear was sealed up in a Plexiglas box next to a refrigerator case of heavy-looking cakes. The sunlight filtered in bleakly through the tinted windows. *Sea Dungeon*, I thought privately.

Over my little heap of iceberg lettuce, I told Ray I had enjoyed his sermon. He didn't seem to hear me. He was worried, I could see. We weren't on track to make our soul quota.

And so dinner was sort of a bummer. Wyatt was pissed, Ethan was fasting, Joey felt sick, and Carter made a joke too blue even for our increasingly raunchy group, telling Alice his "banana can't wait forever."

When we were outside, about to load into the vans, Mitchell made a belch that vibrated in my ears.

"Thunder from the mountain tops," I said.

"Better than the thunder from down under," said Alice.

SPIRITUAL GIFTS

AFTER ANOTHER SURREPTITIOUS WRITING SESSION IN THE Grand Ballroom and a run to Fourbucks, we did more ABT bus ministry, this time in groups of three. Carter accompanied Alice and me, and Wyatt went along with Ursula and Pamela, and the six of us were back in the neighborhood my group had visited on Saturday. Wyatt made a big deal of how picturesque our neighborhood was, how he and Carter had braved a trailer park and harassment and streams of expletives.

The day was another blue sparkler, with warm sun and abundant light. It was Monday morning and, naturally, we had no success. Alice spoke at virtually every door, and I got the sense that Carter was even more apprehensive about approaching strangers than I was, usually standing behind us on the steps as if he were our bodyguard.

Eventually, we called Ray to come get us early because we all had to pee.

We regrouped and prepped for street evangelism at the Econo Inn. I sat on my bed reviewing my salvation cheat sheet in case I was forced to do some saving. If I had to explain it to a friend, I could, no problem. Original sin, passed to us as sin nature, someone's got to pay for our crimes, Jesus did it, say thanks and go to heaven. But when I thought of having to convince someone of it, really convince them it was true, my brain gummed up and the thread of the argument sank into the murk. I hoped I could just hang back.

We set out for street evangelism in bands of four, two men and two women. We had two hours to canvass and Ray urged us again to avoid drunks. "You'll know if somebody's been drinking," he said. "You'll smell it on their breath."

If we found it difficult to approach people, Ray reminded us that a good icebreaker was touching someone's shoulder and saying, "Hey, can I pray with you?" Although this seemed like the most natural thing for Ray to do, for the rest of us it was pretty awkward.

The men were supposed to provide protection should we find ourselves in danger. And we were courting it. The neighborhood we were pollinating was on the grizzled fringes of the struggling downtown commercial district. Garbage clotted the gutters and the few pedestrians we did encounter walked hard and fast, hands fisted.

Alice, Carter, Wyatt, and I scanned doorways and side streets in silence, eyes peeled for bodies. My tongue was a dry snake in my mouth, nosing around for something to say.

We had made it a few blocks down 5th Street when a man in brown rags, on crutches no less, cutting the very figure of a soul in need, hobbled across the road in our direction. A little zing of energy traveled through our group and we quietly agreed to approach him. But just before we reached him, Clementine and Ray came around the corner of a building and cut us off. While Clementine introduced herself to the man, Ray leaned over his own shoulder and murmured at us as we passed, "Get yer own."

On we walked. I peered into the doorway of a bar but the others didn't slow. I felt like a predator, scanning for the herd's vulnerable. And then, as we crossed a broad street, we noticed three homeless people sharing a bench on the other side. They sat at the foot of the featureless slate expanse of an office building. We steered in their direction.

One of the homeless, a Native American man with a long black mustache and a deflated baseball cap on his head, was hand-rolling a cigarette in his lap. A Native American woman, her hair shining with oil and dirt packed into the creases of her face, watched his hands work. Sitting next to them on the bench was a tall, lanky white man in a battered sports coat and yellowed glasses.

We walked toward them and slowed gradually as if approaching animals in the wild. I expected wariness, reservation, a wall we would have to scramble up, but kind greetings floated in our direction. Suddenly Alice began to walk faster down the block.

"Keep walking," she said. "They're doing pot."

Before I could think to censor myself, I caught up and told her, "It's just tobacco."

The moment's pressures seemed to occlude anything I might have revealed about myself. We circled back. Wyatt zeroed in on the man in the sports coat, who stood to speak to him. Carter stood back at the curb, clasping his hands in front of his windbreaker.

Trying not to look like a thug for God, I removed my sunglasses and smiled. I felt sweat-slicked and creepy. Alice looked clean and sweet in her polo shirt and khakis. Kindness seemed to glow on her cheeks.

"How are y'all doing today?" Alice asked the couple, standing several yards away at a diagonal.

The woman nodded and smiled as if we were passing on a hiking trail. Her partner leaned back on the bench and dragged on his cigarette, looking at the sky.

"Enjoying the beautiful weather?" Alice asked.

"Yes," the woman said. "It is very warm today."

"Good," Alice said. We all nodded. Good. Good. Opening hearts. Planting seeds.

Was I expected to jump in? I nuzzled into the down feathers of Carter's silence.

Off to my right, Wyatt was getting a lecture. I stole a glance. The man in the sports coat was saying something about the war, drawing his face close to Wyatt's. Wearing his aerodynamic sunglasses, Wyatt had a curling smile on his face, his hands on his hips. He looked maniacally at ease.

"Well . . ." Alice said to the couple, "we're here with our church on a missions trip, visiting all the way from Virginia, and we're just going around and talking to people today."

"Oh," the woman said, smiling without comprehension, as if Alice had just told her we wanted to order three double cheeseburgers. Maybe her English wasn't good, maybe she was dumbstruck, maybe softspoken, maybe higher than the highest snowcapped mountain peaks. Her partner nodded serenely, listening.

"Okay," Alice said, "let me ask you a question. If you died today, where do you think you would go?"

The strings of the woman's smile were instantly cut. "I don't know," she said, shaking her head.

"You don't know?" Alice said, sounding truly sympathetic. I sensed a process occurring in her brain, some lever lowering behind her eyes, some stone rolling out of place. She stepped forward and pressed her fingertips to her chest. "I believe when I die, I'm going to heaven." Alice explained why she believed this, how God had provided a route for her. "Do you believe in the Bible?" she asked.

"Yes," the woman said, her eyes suddenly scanning the air in front of her face as if a teleprompter had appeared before her. Her partner fished a small white pamphlet out of his pocket and began to page through it.

"What is that?" Alice asked.

The man explained that they often went to a chapel nearby and someone working there had given them this little pamphlet. Alice and I looked at it. It contained a few Bible passages, some instructions on prayer, exhortations to attend chapel regularly. No information about getting saved.

She asked if they had ever prayed the sinner's prayer. The couple looked at each other and shook their heads. It seemed too easy.

Alice explained that all we have to do to go to heaven was say a prayer acknowledging that we're sinners and that Jesus died on the cross to atone for our sins. "Would you like to pray that prayer right now?" Alice asked.

The woman sat forward on the bench and the man stubbed out his cigarette. "Yes," the woman said earnestly.

"You would?" Alice asked, surprise brightening her voice. She asked for their names: Anna and Wagner. She asked them to bow their heads and close their eyes and repeat the prayer silently in their minds. I saw Alice open her Bible to the salvation trifold she'd slid into the pages and find her place. Then I bowed my head and closed my eyes, too. I couldn't believe what was happening, how ready to surrender they were.

"Dear Lord Jesus," Alice said, flipping her Bible open and reading from Ray's transcript. "Please dear Lord, be merciful to me a sinner. Because I believe Jesus died for my sins on the cross and rose again the third day. I repent of my sins. By faith I receive the Lord Jesus as my savior. You promised to save me, and I believe you, because you are God and cannot lie. I believe right now the Lord Jesus is my personal savior, and all my sins are washed away through His precious blood. I thank you so much for saving me. In Jesus' name, Amen."

When the prayer was over, I looked up from my sneakers. The sunlight was twinkling down on this crummy little Anchorage side street in pretty beams, as if we were in an aquarium by a window. Anna tipped her head back and tears spilled down her cheeks. Stunningly, there really was something renewed about her, a sudden epiphany visible as light on her face.

She sucked in a deep breath and pressed the heels of her hands to her eyes. "Wow," she said, her voice low in her throat like fog on a lake. "Oh, wow." She pressed her hands to her chest and looked into my eyes. "I feel like a weight's been lifted off me." I looked at Alice and a bolt of recognition shot between us. Wagner rolled another cigarette and smoked it, concealing whatever he felt behind the gesture.

Giddy tears were filling my eyes. "Congratulations," I said. I could have swooped down to kiss them. I was wired with delight, and I wasn't even a believer. But one didn't have to believe to see that this was indeed the birthing room, and if it wasn't the birthing room of God in that moment, it seemed to be the birthing room of fresh possibility.

Alice told them what ought to come next: Bible study and regular worship at chapel. Whatever questions arose, Alice assured them, someone at the chapel would be able to help guide them.

We weren't sure how to tie off the encounter, so we shook hands with Anna and Wagner—long, hard handshakes—handshakes signifying a future together. Anna thanked us profusely, and Wagner said a few words of gratitude himself before leaning back with his cigarette.

We turned away from Anna and Wagner to find Wyatt hawkishly smacking his gum in the face of the man in the sports coat, who was talking about American wrongheadedness. Not only were we fighting the wrong people in the wrong places, he told Wyatt, "we're praying about the wrong things." Wyatt's jaw muscles worked the gum. I didn't know it at the time, but Wyatt had a handgun tucked into the waist of his jeans. I would find this out a day later, full on Red Robin's french fries, contemplating a daylit evening walk with a few others. Wyatt took his gun everywhere.

We ought to be praying for peace for everyone, the man told Wyatt, jabbing his finger in the direction of Wyatt's chest, but instead we're praying for our own safety.

Wyatt was a Christian first and then a soldier, and not one inclined to second-guess war. The man was jabbing his dirty finger at Wyatt's very essence. I sensed a certain deadliness in the flex of this interaction—two unhinged men playing bloody knuckles. But in a way I was captivated: here was a microcosmic performance of the liberal-conservative debate. Two sides showcasing their inflexible points of view, so consumed with anger at the other's stupidity that they're unable to hear what their opponent has to say.

If Alice, Carter, and I had not been there to persuade Wyatt, he would not have removed himself from the standoff.

As we walked away, I noticed a regal-postured woman padded in a psychedelic array of colorful scarves and sweaters perched on a nearby bench, where she rummaged through her plastic bags. She was in her forties with teased hair and a pretty, crepe-skin face. Purple eyeshadow darkened one eyelid, red the other.

Suddenly she rose and approached Alice, asking if we were Christians. Yes, Alice told her. Christians from Virginia in Alaska on a mission trip. Was the woman herself a Christian?

"Oh yes," she said. "I've been a Christian for many years." She began to pick her way through an intricate soliloquy on her personal theology, an original Frankenstein monster of superstition, Protestant Christianity, New Age spirituality, and gibberish. Alice interviewed her on the relevant questions.

She believed in God and the Bible, but was not born again. Still, she knew she was going to heaven because her spirit and her works granted her passage.

Alice gently protruded her lower lip. "Uh-huh," she said. "But so, you consider yourself a Christian."

"I'm a Christian, yes," the woman said, holding Alice's gaze. She lifted her hand and traced her finger along an edge of Alice's pink Bible. Alice flinched. "Is this your Bible?" the woman asked. It was. "May I?"

Alice thought for a moment. "Of course," she said, passing the woman her Bible and folding her arms.

The woman opened the Bible delicately and smoothed her hand over the pages. "I taught my children that the most important part of the Bible is the verse on spiritual gifts. I Corinthians 12." She found her verse with ease. "There are different kinds of gifts, but the same Spirit," she read aloud. "To one there is given through the Spirit the message of wisdom, to another the message of knowledge by means of the same Spirit, to another faith by the same Spirit, to another gifts of healing by that one Spirit, to another miraculous powers, to another prophecy, to another distinguishing between spirits, and still to another speaking in different kinds of tongues, and to still another the interpretation of tongues. All these are the work of one and the same Spirit, and he gives them to each one, just as he determines."

Nodding, her face a perfect pop of surprise, Alice accepted her Bible back from the woman.

"That passage," the woman said quietly, "is the most important in the Bible."

We walked 5th Street. I was disoriented, stumbling off curbs, as if I'd had my pupils dilated. Wyatt was still grumbling over his confrontation, but Alice excitedly replayed our encounters. She couldn't believe that Anna and Wagner believed in the Bible but had never been saved. She realized how true it was what Ray had said: so many people were out there who believed everything they needed to believe but had simply never prayed for salvation.

Alice admitted she'd been nervous and worried she'd done an incomplete job. It seemed a smaller effort than getting someone to accept a pizzeria coupon on the street.

"Now I'm thinking of all these things I should have said." She didn't follow the trifold, really, didn't reveal the whole argument, or tell the story of Christ's sacrifice before leading Anna and Wagner to God. I could tell she was wondering if they were really saved, although she never would have admitted it.

I told her I thought she'd performed admirably. I meant it, although my exhilaration was deeply freaking me out. In the moment with Anna and Wagner, it felt as if there was the tiniest flicker of vulnerability, and had Alice been too long-winded or elaborate, the flicker might have winked out. I imagined it was not unlike hunting. When an animal rustled the bushes, the hunter had to be efficient or else—poof, gone. Even though the man in the sport coat had simply been looking for a fight, hadn't shown the flicker, it was clear that Wyatt lacked that basic quality that made Alice a natural soul-winner: gentleness.

And the spiritual gifts woman? "She just turned right to that passage,"

Alice said, shaking her head. What was to be done with someone who had read the Bible but missed its meaning? The spiritual gifts woman read the Bible and saw possibility and variety, eye-bending layers and layers of tangled colored filaments. Our group read the Bible and saw one line.

"That was crazy," Carter said. "When she reached for your Bible, I was like, *Oh no . . .*"

Installed just off the sidewalk beside a fire station we found a sculpture called *The Save*. It was a tower of polished black stone in which the strong cast-iron hand of a firefighter extended down to the outstretched hand of a child. We all stood blinking at the sculpture in silence.

"That's you, Alice," I blurted finally, stupidly, pointing to the firefighter's paw, suddenly desperate to make light of everything, to diminish my vertigo by lowering the altitude at which we were cruising. I didn't want to be amazed.

Cars trundled by. Carter tightened his lips and Alice began to walk away. Inside I felt strings ribbon down into a pile. Wrong. *Not I, but Christ.*

Down alleyways and behind dumpsters, we ferreted out a few more contenders, and the frothy anticipation of fresh souls buried my error. We snared our last prospective on our way back to the Econo Inn. He was a middle-aged Asian man in mirrored sunglasses and a button-down flannel shirt stiff with street crud. He greeted us cheerfully, though I cringed as Wyatt asked if he had heard the good news. He hadn't, or was confused by the question, and so Wyatt delivered it.

Bristling visibly, the man said, "Dude, don't tell *me* about Jesus." He scoffed, staggered back, and released a peaty belch of whiskey. "Man, I'm out here every day. I could be hit by a goddamn *train*. If God loves everybody so much, why don't he stop people from getting kilt all the damn time? I could be run over by a goddamn car just minding my business, crossing this goddamn street."

Wyatt had no words. Alice stepped in, sinews rippling in her voice. "So could I. Anybody could. But when I die, I believe I'm going to be in heaven with Jesus." No tenderness. No flicker of opportunity.

The man roared with laughter. The collar of his shirt shifted and I saw a white chain around his neck. "Yeah, yeah," he said, straps of bitterness suddenly cinching in his voice. "Anybody could die." In the placket of his shirt I saw that a crucifix dangled below his throat: a rosary. "You tell me where God is when people are dyin' in the streets. A dude got kilt the other day. How'm I supposed to believe in Him when He don't care about me?"

Alice began to explain her beliefs about free will, but it was like explaining the electoral college to a music video on TV. The conversation was over.

IN THE AFTERNOON, we went east in two vans to Portage Glacier. To our right, a row of snow-drizzled mountains stood beyond the shining mercury slice of the Turnagain Arm. To our left, white Dall sheep—which Ray called billy goats—shinnied up the cliffs. As we curved along the road, Ray told hunting stories and pointed out blue slivers of valley glaciers—walkie-talkieing the rear van whenever he spotted them. Clementine batted her lashes and said, "They're billions and trillions of years old," and everyone laughed at the naivete of scientists, except for me.

Moments like these brought on brief, violent spells of disorientation, as I realized I was no friend to my friends at all.

Everyone traded evangelism stories. Ray and Clementine said that the man we'd seen on crutches was already a Christian, but needed help. They brought him to a camping store and bought him a sleeping bag.

We stopped frequently for photo ops, puny us posing in front of dizzying Alaskan panoramas. Everyone needed a picture. All the women posed and all the men stood opposite us in a clump, snapping their cameras, and then the women's cameras. I started calling the men "the Paparazzi," which became a popular joke.

Even after the brief rupture of Clementine's mountain joke, I felt cozy and exhausted in the van, lullabied, and I listened to some Christian music on Alice's iPod. It deepened my sense of ease.

"Don't you miss church music?" she asked.

I really did. I missed the way it sent starbursts through my chest and contracted my scalp. I missed sensing the moment in a song when hands were going to go up, and then seeing them lift. I missed it the way you miss hugging someone you love. Which was weird, since when I began going to church I thought the music was hysterically bad. Like luau music bad.

A few in our van had fallen asleep. Ray looked out at the Turnagain Arm and muttered, "Low tide the water goes all the way out. See that mud, Gina?" I did: brown mud flats snaked along the shore. "That mud's like quicksand. You step in, you can't step back out. People get stuck and drown when the tide comes in. They warn the tourists, but the tourists don't never listen."

Later I read that the Turnagain Arm has the highest tides in the country. Ray said when the tide goes out, it goes out so that the silt looks like a wide beach. The tide rolls in and out quickly, in a six-foot bore wave. People walk out to fish or appreciate the landscape, and boom.

One year, when Ray and Clementine were living up in North Pole, a woman walked out alone and her legs sank down into the silt, trapping her. She called for help, and emergency workers came and tried to free her, but they couldn't get to her in time. The tide rolled back in, and she drowned.

I stared out at the Turnagain Arm—the ultra-blue sky and the mountains carving into it, the metal sheet of water. The whole scene was a kind of tractor beam of majesty, the same kind that had pulled Misty Bernall, mother of the Columbine victim, back into faith at Breckenridge.

That drowned woman—I imagined she just pulled off the road, not intending to step out on the flats. Maybe once she was out of her car she felt drawn onto the mud by awe, just to get a little closer to the beauty, as if maybe by getting closer she might understand it better, get a richer taste.

I pictured the drowned woman, feet buried in silt, blue-white arms floating overhead. I asked Ray if her body was still out there.

"No," he said. "They went and got her come low tide."

Piling out of the vans at Portage Glacier, shrinking back at the frosted air, we all hurried down to the stone walk along the lake, where the pure ice water lapped over the edge and onto our feet. The glacier itself was totally hidden behind a dense wall of fog. We took pictures in front of the fog anyway. Alice wanted to take some of me standing alone, so I walked down to the edge of the lake, ice water washing over my flip-flops, zapping my toes. When I turned around to smile, I saw Mitchell lumbering toward me. He threw his arm over my shoulder and smiled at the camera. Everyone laughed.

We went to the Portage Glacier gift shop and cafeteria to eat a bite. There was a fireplace where Ethan warmed his thin hands, as he wasn't eating anything. The rest of us tucked into soups and sandwiches, a stuffed wolverine snarling down at us from a shelf high on the wall. Mounted antlers spiked out from the wall here and there. Ray said he saw Wyatt slap Bethany on the butt, and Wyatt turned purple and, seemingly unable to laugh at himself, said something like, "If only I had my .45 right now . . ."

Full on my sandwich, I went to look at the postcards in the gift shop. There were pictures of eagles, moose, mountains, and several postcards with side-by-side comparisons of early and more current photographs of Portage Glacier. It had receded dramatically. In older pictures, the glacier was a broad highway of ice, spilling down between mountains and spreading wide at their base. Now Portage Glacier was a vertical white dash punctuated by the slate gray dot of the cold lake grown fat on its runoff. I took one of these postcards off the rack and showed it to Carter.

"Look how much it's melted," I said.

He glanced at the postcard, pursed his lips, and went to look at T-shirts.

RACE WITH THE DEVIL

BY THE TIME WE PULLED INTO THE PARKING LOT AT THE RESCUE Mission to serve up beef stroganoff with a double helping of the Gospel, my sense of ease had dried up and displeasure was tightening across my back. The day had been emotional and I was tired.

Even our silly car ride laughs had stressed me out; the moment I admitted to myself I was having fun, bonding, I felt turbulent undercurrents of anxiety. Casting my mind forward, I tried to picture my friends' faces when they found out who I really was. They would think back on this time, remember me laughing with them, sharing gum, developing a catalog of mildly perverted inside jokes. The smiles would drop off their faces. They were going to hate me.

And then there were moments when I became suspicious of my own feelings. Perhaps some release valve had been activated, and I was only enjoying myself because what other alternative was there—perpetual crisis?

At the mission, the women had already eaten and the cafeteria was filled with men hunched over their dinner trays. I isolated myself in the kitchen pantry and sorted spices. I didn't want to talk, listen, or smile. I didn't even want to stand up. I wanted a glass of wine, a private room with a locking door, hours of numbing silence. I went to the bathroom to find a few minutes of peace, but a woman was having a violent coughing fit in one of the stalls. When she came out, I saw it was the spiritual gifts woman from the street. She didn't recognize me.

I went back to the spices. Baking spices lined one shelf. Cooking spices another. Flours and sugars were on a tall shelf near the floor. The mindless sorting was helping me relax, and I reassured myself that this small task was still a contribution: it would help the cooks prepare dinner more efficiently. I settled into the task with relief, as if I had decided to set my backpack down on the floor.

Freddy, the programmer, poked his head into the pantry and saw me organizing. He curled a calloused hand around the doorjamb and leveled a pitying gaze on me. "You fix that now, it's going to be a mess again in an hour."

In the chapel, sad-faced men with blurred tattoos packed the pews, hardened women filled the safe seats along the wall, and Ray directed the church ladies to line up along the altar as eye candy again. Lyle pounded out "Nothing But the Blood of Jesus" on the little piano. He sat straight-backed on the bench, and behind his glasses his full brown eyes were lifted heavenward. I watched him there in his flannel shirt, leading the chapel of missionaries and needy folk as we all sang:

> *Oh! Precious is the flow*
> *That makes me white as snow;*
> *No other fount I know,*
> *Nothing but the blood of Jesus.*

Everyone was belting it out, and I swore I felt the chapel rock. In that windowless, wood-walled room with the low ceiling and the rows of shouting men in their matted coats, I suddenly pictured us down in the steerage of some creaky ship, the seas mercilessly rough outside. At the sight of all those human faces carved with the scars of hardship lit up with the flush of hope, tears were melting in my eyes. We all held our hymnals in our hands, brushing against each other as we swayed to the music. I felt I was being hugged so tightly I might stop breathing.

Ray took the pulpit. Tonight he would give us his testimony, something he didn't do often. He knew he looked like a lucky duck, with his group of missionaries and his pretty wife. It wasn't always so. And well, he wouldn't say he'd had it the hardest, but he certainly hadn't had an easy go, either.

Ray's childhood story was a compound tale of abandonment. His father left the family when Ray was a little boy, and then his mother left, too, taking Ray's two sisters but choosing to leave her son behind. Ray was raised an only child by his grandmother. All this background—entirely new and heartbreaking to me—was delivered quickly and without much emotion.

In high school, Ray spread his wings, and they were black leather. He drank, he smoked pot, he tried other drugs, he fornicated. He had known Clementine since junior high school, but finally came around to asking her out. And even though Clementine was a pious Christian and Ray was nothing of the sort, she agreed to go steady. He was a cutup, irresistible even then, I was sure. But he was a terrible boyfriend. Ray once took Clementine to a party and kissed another girl.

Clementine's youth pastor put tremendous pressure on her to dump Ray. "He isn't a Christian," the pastor told her, "and he never will be."

But Clementine believed Ray was redeemable, and she prayed for him every week at church. She prayed and she prayed. She brought him to church some Sundays, dragging him out of bed in the morning, enduring his cynicism. But as much as she prayed, Ray simply would not clean up, would not fall to his knees.

One night, Ray took Clementine on a double date to the drive-in. Before the movie, Ray and his buddy got stoned without telling their dates. The movie was *Race with the Devil*, a cheesy horror flick starring Peter Fonda. In the movie, Peter Fonda, his buddy, and their wives set off in an RV on a road trip to Colorado. Having pitched camp along the highway, the road trippers accidentally witness a satanic ritual and sacrifice. For the remainder of the movie, they are pursued by a bloodthirsty cult of Satan worshippers. In every place they look for refuge the inscrutability on the faces of strangers appears to be malice. The cult seems to be everywhere.

Sitting in a diner after the movie, Ray was freaking out, pouring sweat and ill with fear. Two old women stared at him from a nearby table. He turned his face away, but he could still feel them staring. With the intensity of their focus he began to believe they were devil-possessed. He couldn't eat his hamburger, starting to think there might be devil-possessed people everywhere, watching him.

Even saying good night to Clementine, even home under the covers at night, he couldn't shake the feeling he was being watched—*pursued*—by the Devil. Sleep didn't come.

In the morning, he smoked more pot. It didn't serve to quell his fear. Petrified, he telephoned Clementine and told her he wanted to come to church as soon as possible.

The next Sunday—seeking protection from the Devil—Ray said the sinner's prayer at Clementine's church and got saved.

Now, he invited the pews of men and women in the little chapel to do the same. Ray couldn't begin to describe how his life had changed since becoming a Christian. "I ain't saying you'll get everything you want," he said. "Even I didn't get everything I prayed for."

When Ray asked who had prayed the prayer with him, hands lifted all across the chapel.

SEVERAL MONTHS LATER, back on my crepe myrtle–sheltered front porch in Virginia, on the phone with my mother in California, I told her about how we'd gone about keeping track of the people we saved in Alaska. She asked me the question my stepfather had asked her. How can you know if you've saved someone if there's never follow-up, never counseling, never a progress report? How can you be sure the person hasn't instantly reverted to his old ways? In other words, aren't you simply counting the people who prayed the prayer in that instant rather than counting new Christians?

"Well," I replied, "if you're a Christian you believe all it takes is that instant, as long as you're sincere. Once you've prayed the sinner's prayer, you're good to go. God is supposed to abide in you and guide you, but really your 'ways' don't matter. Your name is written forever in the Lamb's Book of Life."

The noise on the phone was like the bristled air on a tape recording of silence. "Uh-huh," she said.

I knew what was behind that dismissal: to her, it seemed evident that Evangelicals were padding their rosters.

OUT IN THE VANS after the Rescue Mission around 9 p.m. it was light as noon. I buckled myself in. My earlier feeling of suffocation had subsided for now, replaced by open-wound hunger. Ray backed out of his parking space and a row of homeless people smoking smiled and waved good-bye. We all waved back.

"Look at that," Ray said, his blinker ticking to turn onto Tudor Road. "Those people are happy and we complain."

*   *   *

BLACK BALLOONS HUNG in the air above us; before us, the mangled remains of burger platters and french fry baskets congealed. A black *Over the Hill!* banner sagged along the restaurant wall over the banquette. Ray had opened the birthday presents we gave him: adult diapers, denture cleanser, and herbal Viagra. Carter put a diaper on his head and Ray popped one of the black Viagra pills in his mouth, pulling a long drink from his soda straw, a devilish glimmer in his eye.

Clementine guffawed and slapped his shoulder. "*Ray!*" she gasped. "You didn't," she said softly. "Tell me you didn't."

Wiggling his eyebrows, Ray pulled a balloon down from overhead and held it over his crotch as if to hide his boner. The whole group was in embarrassed hysterics. Though she was still giggling, Clementine was beginning to look genuinely unnerved, so Ray spat the black pill into his hand and stuck the balloon under his fleece jacket.

Giddy chattering and camera flash flurries were making me light-headed, and I found myself unable to keep a toehold in the conversation I had been having with Amy about how she met her fiancé. I grew quiet.

Down the table from us, several people were loudly cajoling Mitchell and Lyle to sip from the same milkshake. Lyle didn't care; he didn't get gay jokes. Mitchell was reluctant, embarrassed, but also seemed to enjoy the sudden deluge of attention. Finally, they leaned in and sipped together. An explosion of screaming laughter, another hail of flash photography. The focus turned to Ursula and Carter: *Feed each other cake!*

I drained another huge cup of iced tea. Across the table, Ray—with his small rectangular reading glasses and the balloon stuffed under his velvety blue TRBC fleece—looked like a suburban Santa.

Ingrid said she couldn't believe all Clementine had put up with waiting for Ray to come around. Clementine cast a look of love at Ray, fingering one of the striped bows on the cuff of her shirt.

"I exaggerated some of that stuff," Ray said, his hands spread over his swollen belly. "I wasn't all that bad."

Our waitress, small-boned, bespectacled, dropped our checks. She had been good-natured and game the whole dinner, and she had separated our bills for us. Ray thanked her, and told her we were going to leave a big tip.

When I waited tables I always hated this declaration—it seemed to beg some kind of obsequious bow. The waitress thanked Ray quietly, wished him a happy birthday, and continued to distribute our checks.

"We're all Christians," Ray said, leaning back, slit-eyed with pleasure. "We're going to have to repent a lot."

"What happens in Alaska, stays in Alaska!" Carter chimed in.

The waitress smiled, taking cash from Wyatt. I remembered what guest pastor Floyd had said on the first meeting of Ray's 100% Effective Evangelism class about waiters loathing Christians for their cheapness. Knowing how waiters feel about Christians, Floyd had told us he always makes the following promise to his waiter before sitting down for a meal: "I'm going to give you a good tip. I'm going to give you twenty-five, thirty percent no matter what you do. If you forget to fill up my tea, if you mess up my food order, I'm still going to give you a good tip. All I ask is that you let me pray for you."

Waiters in Lynchburg opened up to Floyd about abuse, divorce, suicide attempts—you name it. They rarely turned down the offer of prayer. Once a nineteen-year-old African-American waitress asked Floyd to pray that she come to know Jesus. He shared the good news, and she knelt down right there at the table, her back to her other customers, and got saved, tears spilling down her cheeks.

Now, Ray was looking at our waitress, a thin smile on his face. "Are you married?" he asked.

"I am," she said, not looking at him, counting change from her apron for Pamela. I felt a sudden rash of heat. Yes, I knew what it felt like to be this waitress. As if she was a firefly caught in his cupped hands.

"Y'all go to church?"

The table was silent, as if we'd suddenly all plunged underwater. Sweat was breaking on my forehead and my clothes felt itchy.

"We don't," the waitress said.

"*You don't?*" Ray cried in ersatz disbelief.

Concentrating on collecting her checks, the waitress's smile guttered out.

"Well, honey," Ray said, still casual, "do you believe in God and the Bible?"

Down the table, no one seemed eager to watch this girl get saved. Everyone was turned away a bit, looking in purses and wallets. Proselytizing now seemed . . . inappropriate. Why? What was the difference? Perhaps Ray was trying to make a point: we shouldn't compartmentalize. But his pursuit of the waitress seemed lazy, reflexive. As if he were doodling idly. A master artist showing off.

The waitress was freezing him out, accepting a bill from Mitchell. "You need change?" she asked politely.

"Nah," Mitchell said, flapping his hand.

"Thank you," the waitress replied, moving down the table.

"Well," Ray said, pushing back in his chair, "God loves you, honey."

THAT NIGHT, CARTER, PAMELA, and Ursula came over for pillow talk. Carter sat on Alice's bed, but the girls declined my offer to sit on mine and sat on the floor instead. After we gossiped a bit, Alice asked to hear about the man Pamela led to the Lord. Pamela told the story—the man had recently had a stroke—and she blinked dreamily with a euphoric smile on her face. She had two distinct modes. When talking about church stuff, she was always this way: twinkle-eyed, gentle-voiced, vaguely romantic. About anything else—people she didn't like, plans going awry, food, travel, whatever—the romance vaporized and she was just as miserable and low-energy as a fourteen-year-old on a field trip to the city mint.

Alice asked Pamela if the words had come naturally.

Without hesitation, Pamela said she had felt as though she wasn't speaking at all, like the Holy Spirit was speaking through her. "I felt like a vessel."

"Uh-huh," Alice said, nodding slowly. "See, I felt like I had to really be on my toes."

Carter told the girls they'd both done a great job. Pamela screwed her smile tight and pointed her long index finger upward. *Not I.* Somehow, Pamela made *Not I* seem distinctly like *I*. I turned over in bed and tried to slam the shutters on my mind closed.

SOUL WINNING

———

T HE NEXT MORNING OUR GROUP GATHERED IN THE GRAND Ballroom, armored for rain. Ray was on the balls of his feet watching us struggle in, his hands clasped behind his back. His eyes were flat as a wild animal's. Ethan distributed candy bars, our new gimmick to entice the interest of street people. I ate the cap off a giant muffin and had a cup of pink juice.

When we were all present and stocked with candy, Ray reminded us of his suggested method of approach—"Can I pray with you?" Usually he was playful with us, especially the girls, and this helped me get in the mood for the day, helped me whack back the twisting vines of anxiety. But the plain expression on his face, his flat eyes, revealed he was worried about making the soul quota, and he was in no mood to flirt.

Our team set out with less alacrity than we had the day before, bowing our heads and pulling on our hoods. I followed Alice's example, tucking my Bible under my sweatshirt. It was drizzling and downtown Anchorage was dim gray and very cold.

Wyatt, carrying an enormous umbrella and wearing his aerodynamic sunglasses in spite of the low light, appeared to be conducting some kind of social norms experiment on me. His chivalry was at performance art proportions: he held his umbrella over me so devotedly he reminded me of a boom mike operator; he offered three times to hold my Bible in the zip pouch of his raincoat; he kept pace with my walking so precisely that when I stopped to tie my sneaker, he stopped, turned around and stood exactly where I was kneeling. I felt like flicking him in the shin. He even held his arm out in front of me at curbs. When I'd break free of him, he'd do the same for Alice. I was rolling my eyes so fiercely I thought they might rip free of their sockets.

Up and down the streets, into all the puddle-scarred alleys between the buildings, down near the train tracks, we looked in doorways, behind dumpsters. Carter observed that the homeless probably know where to hide when it rains. Wyatt wondered if they were hiding in parking garages. Several times we stopped at corners, cars hissing past us on the wet street, and looked in all directions. It seemed clear that we weren't going to find anyone.

We detoured behind a hotel and languished beneath a vent pouring out hot air. We wandered into a cemetery, much to Carter's dismay. He was visibly spooked and wanted to walk around it. We went in anyway, and once we were inside the gates the rain let up and Carter calmed down.

"This ain't so scary," he said.

The cemetery was peaceful and well manicured, and we walked around it in near silence, admiring the marble headstones and the granite angels, little flecks in them sparking in the sunlight. I thought it was strange that Carter had been so afraid of cemeteries, bodies just being bodies abandoned by ascended or descended souls, but I guess some fears are just animal and hard-wired, in a way similar to beliefs. You can't really decide to fear or believe something—something happens to you and you just *do*. And boy, thinking your way out of something like that, something that seems viscerally scary or true?

Outside the cemetery, we ran into Ray and Clementine. Clementine's pink lipstick was still as perfect and bright as a fresh tulip and Ray looked much more relaxed than he had that morning in the Grand Ballroom. He threw an arm over my shoulders and jostled me a little.

"Y'all get anybody?" he asked, as if we were on a scavenger hunt.

"No," Alice said. "Robocop over here is scaring 'em away."

Wyatt staggered back a few steps. His face hardened. "*Excuse* me," he said, too angry to say anything else.

"You'll find 'em," Ray said. "They're just like cockroaches. You stand in one place, you're sure to have some come by you." Ray and Clementine had saved a man and a woman already, and talked to a bunch more.

"Tell them what that one fella said," Clementine said, twirling her umbrella.

Talking to an Athabaskan man he wound up saving, Ray asked him if he believed he was a sinner. "Oh yes," the man said. "I'm a bad-ass sinner."

There wasn't much time left before we had to be back at the hotel, so Ray sent us off to try harder. "When you find somebody, you just go"— he pinched the wrapper of a Twix bar, dangling it in the air—"*How bad you wanna get saved?*"

Just before we needed to return, we intercepted a lanky old fellow making his way to the soup kitchen. He was happily a Christian already, he told us, but he was eager to chat anyway. He had served in Vietnam, and one of his sons was now in the military. He wanted us to pray for his daughter.

"She's dating a Buddha," he said.

Alice obliged, and we all bowed our heads. When she was finished, she gave him a candy bar and we said good-bye.

Heading back to the Econo Inn our team was quiet with disappointment.

AFTER LUNCH AT THE MALL, Alice drew the curtain in our room and we lay down to rest. In the corner, our clothes hung from the same rack. We were beginning to know each other's little private habits. I knew the angle at which Alice leaned over to iron her hair flat. The way she'd tilt her pedometer out from her waistband to check on the number of steps she'd taken that day. We laughed at precisely the same things—often, gently, at the expense of our fellow missionaries. The intimacy I once sought to avoid with Alice was turning out to be inevitable now that we were rooming together. We had started to overlap.

I turned on the television to check the weather. A map of the northwestern part of the continent appeared. Alaska's remote location came as a shock. Somehow, I had pictured us just up the road from California, just level with Canada's western edge. Imagining myself at the end of a vertical tether attached to friends and family down in the Bay Area had made me feel secure, like talk radio on the highway at night. But this weather-map Alaska, a white silhouette gazing out at the Bering Sea, snipped my tether. The distance between Alaska and familiar land was almost too much to face. I flipped to the news and turned the sound off.

"I had no idea how far away we were," I said.

"Me neither," said Alice.

Sometimes it seemed like we were each other's only real friend in this weird place. But I was a stranger to her.

We rested quietly for a while. And then, just as I knew she eventually would, Alice asked me how I became a Christian.

It occurred to me to unstop the dam of my lies. Alice was so smart she probably knew I was up to something anyway. And if she knew, she certainly didn't seem to care.

But in reality, she didn't know. And I couldn't tell her. So, reluctantly, I gave her a testimony that approximated the truth as closely as possible. I told her about my secular upbringing, about coming to Virginia, about my aimlessness after graduate school.

"So who brought you down to Thomas Road?"

A name flashed in my brain and I spoke it without hesitation. "Catherine Mason."

"*Cathy Mason?*" Alice said, sitting up in bed. My stomach dropped down a cold slide. "Cathy Mason with two little daughters?"

"I don't think so. She's my age." My voice sounded far away. "A friend from graduate school. She's moved to Philadelphia."

"Oh," Alice said. She lay back down in bed and stared emptily at the television.

My heart pounded and pounded and then grew quieter, as if it were shrinking. When I could breathe normally, I asked Alice for her testimony. She'd been just the opposite—a Christian since she could remember, a student at Liberty University, a member at Thomas Road for many years. Being a Christian was in her blood.

"But lately," she said, "I've been feeling a little jaded." She told me that her life as a Christian was beginning to feel routine, less satisfying, that she wasn't growing spiritually. She said that she, Donny, and Kelly had talked about striking out together to start a new church. She said she'd thought about starting a new career as a counselor.

I knew it was patronizing, but I couldn't help feeling that Alice was selling herself short by spending all her energy on church. Unlike so many Evangelicals, she was happy to engage with the secular world. She knew songs from Top 40 radio. She told me about hanging out with her secular coworkers, the fun they had. To be sure, there didn't seem to be any air pockets in her devotion to God, but in her face I saw a hint of sadness about the limits of her universe.

It was time to get ready to go to the mission. I turned up the volume on the news, and rummaged through my purse for a stick of gum.

On television, Barack Obama was on a stage somewhere, a microphone nestled in one long-fingered hand. His handsomeness was tweaked with concern. Obama wouldn't catch fire as a candidate until that fall, but even in July the aura of his campaign reminded me of the new climate at Thomas Road, and eventually I would recognize that he was tapping in to the same zeitgeist as Jonathan Falwell: the average American's desire to participate directly in change, to do more than sign a check or cast a vote. On his website Obama made it plain: "I'm asking you to believe. Not just in my ability to bring about real change in Washington. I'm asking you to believe in yours."

And now, on television, looking out into the crowd he said, "We've got to be as careful getting out as we were careless getting in."

"Psssh," Alice said, rolling her eyes, rolling out of bed, firing up her hair dryer, and drowning out the TV.

AT THE RESCUE MISSION, another church group was already helping in the kitchen. We weren't needed, so one of the programmers took us on a tour of the facility instead. There was a computer room and a weight room, a game area with a pool table, television rooms and spacious quarters for the programmers. We saw the men's dorm, a long hall lined with bunk beds and foot lockers. It looked like an army barracks. The women's dorm was locked with a keypad and alarm system to prevent rape. It was a nice shelter, orderly and clean, and people smiled at us wherever we saw them.

If I had been touring the mission before I'd grown close to Christians, if I had seen the crucifixes and scripture plaques ubiquitous as light switches, heard about the mandatory chapel attendance and the strict rules about permissible DVDs and books, I probably would have groaned about the tyranny of Evangelicals, wondering why they had to dose the broth of charity with religious toxins. But now I saw the religious touches as a comfort for those staying at the mission: the Christian calculus of sin, salvation, and eternal love was the opposite of street anarchy and desolation. I could imagine someone getting his life under control in an environment like this. I understood how the structure of religion could correct personal chaos. Did it matter that the message was a placebo if its curative properties were real?

Tempered by these thoughts, I was able to relax a little in the chapel before Ray's sermon. It was going to be a heartwarming night. We had taken up a small collection for Olive, a whisper-thin mission resident who was turning eighty that day. Olive told Ray she had recently been robbed and evicted from her apartment, and Ray had appealed to us to think of such a thing happening to our grandmothers. We all chipped in to give Olive a bit of pocket money and Ray and Clementine had ordered a birthday cake. The pocket money had been a controversial choice, since several of our group worried Olive could just be robbed again, but we didn't know what else to give her.

As it turned out, I wouldn't be there to see Olive blow out her candles. The director of ABT's Children's Church called Ray and told him he was coming by to collect five from our team to help out at Vacation Bible School in an Anchorage outpost called Mountain View. Ethan, Ingrid, and Pamela wanted to go and Alice and I decided it would be good to do something different.

Zooming down the road on our way to VBS, the director had to yell over the truck radio, which was roaring with great torrents of Christian rock. Alice and I were wedged into the front seat next to him, and Ethan, Ingrid, and Pamela sat in the back.

"We had lots of kids come forward for the invitation last night and only two counselors," the director said. He was wearing a white polo shirt with the words *One Child at a Time* embroidered in rainbow thread over the heart. "It'll be so awesome to have you guys tonight."

Brand-new superstores and espresso huts slid by; apartment complexes and car dealerships; motels, hotels, and strip malls; concrete lots disfigured by fissure lines and crabgrass. After a time we came to an area notable for its many pawn shops and liquor stores, where the only white faces were those inside the director's truck. On the distant horizon, the Chugach Mountains rose into the sky like nuclear bomb blasts.

We pulled into the parking lot of the Mountain View Community Center, a charmless single-story building with a few unsmiling teenagers languishing outside. We piled out.

"I wouldn't leave anything in the truck," the director said.

Inside, the Community Center could have been a grim city setting from my own childhood: the clinical fluorescent light, the dusty white linoleum crisscrossed with black scuffs, the posters peeling from the walls, the buzz of drinking fountains, and the swampy aroma of sweat long dried.

The director introduced us to our host, Eileen, a woman with a white shock of hair and the close-set, beady features of a hen. Eileen thrust name tags into our hands and made no attempt to disguise from us her exasperation.

"I don't need five counselors," she said. "Three of you can help with the third through sixth graders, one of you can help with the younger kids, and one of you can be a counselor. I only need one counselor." Clearly Eileen had not been copied on the memo about Christian good cheer.

Ethan was the most eager to counsel, so Alice, Ingrid, and I said we'd go with the older kids and Pamela took the younger ones.

At the moment, the kids were all grouped together in a large classroom off to our left. They were watching Marvin Jubb, a Christian magician. Jubb was to give an invitation after his act, and the kids who came forward would be carted off for counseling while all the others proceeded to activity time. The older ones did crafts in an adjacent classroom and the younger children played kickball in the gym. After half an hour, they would switch activities. Finally, all the children would come together for snack and special prizes for the most obedient. Eileen told us to single out the good kids and give them yellow slips of paper to accrue for the obedience prize. She gave us each a stack. They read: *Faith Coupon. Be A Winner With Jesus.* I slid them into my Bible.

Inside the classroom, about forty children sat on the floor. There were squirmy little ones near the front, slumping tired children with puffy eyes, children in huge white tank tops sitting on their knees, children with perfectly braided cornrows and puff ponytails. Several older children sat in chairs on one side of the room, their faces dead with boredom. Two proctors with unusual beard configurations, hungry jowls, and high-slung jeans stalked the perimeter of the group, their eyes scanning for misconduct.

A thin, plum-colored curtain hung against the front wall. Magician Marvin Jubb, standing with a little shell-eared boy, was in the middle of a trick. He told the boy to concentrate very hard on a certain letter, and the children in the audience were supposed to read the boy's mind to determine the letter. But for his clownish manner, Jubb could have been any cubicle drone: he was dressed corporate-casual, in black slacks and an orange button-down, a few pens in his chest pocket, and his gray hair was neatly side-parted.

He slid Coke-bottle gag glasses onto the boy's face, howling with fake laughter and slapping his knee. He then held up a hand mirror for the boy to see himself. On the reverse side of the mirror was a large, black letter *H*. Jubb bent down to peer into one of the boy's ears and waggled the mirror above the boy's head, signaling the audience to note the letter *H*.

"I can see your letter in there!" he giggled into the boy's ear.

I sat on the floor at the back of the room, my skin prickling with heat. Magicians, clowns, The Wiggles: adults performing for children straight up give me the willies. There seems to be a grotesque disjunction between the goofy act and the grave, adult reality of the person behind the shenanigans. It's cliché—the boozy dressing room, fits of rage, motel mirror despair. In a way, my feeling about a performer like Marvin Jubb paralleled the feeling many people have about Christians: suspicion that the beatific grins are designed to conceal a darker understanding of the world.

Jubb asked the children to shout out the boy's letter.

"*H*," they all shouted. The boy's mouth dropped open in delighted awe.

"Very good," Jubb said, jumping into the air. "And *H* is the first letter of two very important words: heaven . . . and hell! *Heaven* is where you get to spend eternity with God and his son Jesus Christ. *Hell* is the terrible, terrible place where you suffer forever and ever," he said, making a silly sad face. "Now. Who wants to go to heaven?" The children all raised their hands urgently. "All you have to do to go to heaven is accept the Lord Jesus Christ as your personal savior." Jubb thanked the little boy for his assistance and gave him "one of my special hundred dollar bills"—a giant, orange replica with Jubb's grinning face in the place of Benjamin Franklin's.

For his next trick, Jubb held up a piece of cardboard divided into quadrants numbered 1 through 4. Each number corresponded to a colored can, which Jubb lined up on a little shelf. He and his three child volunteers—who fidgeted in a line at the front of the room—must choose a number to open a can.

"One can has something nobody wants and the others have something that everybody wants," Jubb said several times.

As each child popped open their chosen can, Jubb plugged his ears as if bracing for an explosion. Restlessness moved through the audience during this trick, and one of the proctors, crossing the room in three long steps, descended on a cluster of rowdy boys and separated them roughly, like bales of hay.

At the front of the room, a little girl opened a can and extracted a piece of paper. Jubb read it aloud for her: "You get Eternal life with Jesus Christ in heaven!" A lanky boy got a slip of paper promising "Peace and assurance through salvation by Jesus Christ!" A girl with a white barrette clipped on top of her head got "Eternal joy through salvation by our Lord Jesus Christ!"

The children accepted their special hundred dollar bills and returned to the audience. One can remained on the shelf. Jubb eyed it nervously. He picked up colored balls and began to juggle, but the children would not be diverted.

"Open it! Open it!" they cried.

Jubb picked up the can and held it in a trembling hand. "One can has something that nobody wants," he whispered.

The children were rapt, leaning forward with their hands on the floor. Screwing his eyes shut, Jubb peeled the lid off the can and fished out its contents. It was a black cloth. Gently he set the can down. Pinching the corners and averting his gaze, Jubb unfurled a shiny black flag. A white death's head was printed in the center.

He peered down at it. "Uh. Maybe it's a pirate ship?"

"It's death!" the children shouted. "Death!"

"Maybe it's poison?"

"Death!" they shouted happily. "Death!"

"Ah," Jubb said, lowering the flag, seeming depressed. "You're right. It's death. Death and sentencing to hell is punishment for our sins, which can only be washed away by our Lord Jesus Christ."

The children showed no sign of comprehension or bewilderment, no change at all, except perhaps enthusiasm for Jubb's sad fate. Their faces were sweet and smooth, their guilelessness perfectly captured in their open-mouthed stares and unconscious nose-picking, their ruffled hair.

So they had heard this doctrine before and it was banal, or if they hadn't, it was not penetrating. Their indifference was making me more and more disquieted at the back of the room. I shifted into a squat and thought about going into the hall for air. These children were being ambushed. Certainly the parents approved, having some notion of what kind of after-school programming their children received at the club. Surely many of the children heard the gospel at church anyway. And hadn't I watched kids come forward at Children's Church and Thomas Road without feeling nauseated?

Well, this was a different landscape altogether. For one thing, the power dynamic in the room was heartbreakingly reactionary: white middle-class authority figures and poor children of color. There was also the misleadingly secular setting, the aggressive bearing of the workers, the Trojan Horse delivery of the gospel message. But most of all, I was unnerved by Jubb's focus on death and judgment. Even though I knew many adult Christians who had converted as children because they were afraid of going to hell, I had never witnessed evangelical eschatology delivered so directly to children, let alone by a stranger wearing a toothy smile. The message we had used at Children's Church was ultimately one that children could understand: everyone does bad things, and everyone can be loved and forgiven. In fact, I liked that message. But here was Jubb, dangling the bludgeon of death and the flail of hell.

There were a few more tricks—juggling, a shell game, and a trick with white and red feathers meant to illustrate how Christ's blood washes our sins clean. Then Jubb led the room in a prayer. He asked whoever wanted to get saved tonight to silently repeat the sinner's prayer with him. When he was finished, he asked those who had said the prayer for the first time to raise their hands. About ten hands lifted across the room. Those children were instructed to meet up with Bruce and Ethan at a door to the hall in the back of the room.

The other children were on their feet, hurrying to activity locations. In their bright T-shirts they looked like intersecting schools of tropical fish. The ten who had raised their hands after the prayer fell in with the others, obviously not wanting to be left behind. Eileen, who had been standing at the back of the room, hands on hips, charged into the crowd of children and pulled out those who had raised their hands, taking them to Bruce and Ethan.

"It's good she's doing that," Ingrid said. Alice nodded. Pamela went with the little kids and I began to unthinkingly follow Alice and Ingrid with the older ones.

Suddenly, Ethan was leaning in from the hall, urgency on his face. "Ingrid? Gina? We need more people." Confused, I followed Ingrid out into the hall, abandoning the line funneling into the adjacent classroom.

In the hall, the light was dim and shadowless. Off to my left was a large room with a scattering of plastic chairs and a long conference table pushed against the far wall. Ethan was ushering a boy inside, and Bruce was arranging chairs in circles with two kids. Down the hall to my right, Pamela and a stream of chattering children filtered into the gym for kickball. And in front of me a boy and a girl stood all alone, draped with the lead weights of shame as if they were apprehended trespassers. The boy stared down at his shoes as if he pitied them for having to be on his feet all the time and the little girl's eyes darted all around. She wiped her palms on her jeans.

Standing there with these children, with the silt of dread drifting down into my stomach, I realized too late what I had been called to do.

Ingrid introduced herself to the boy and I bent down to the little girl. Her wild black hair was pulled back off her face in a long ponytail. Her skin was golden and glowed as if there were candlelight nearby. I offered her my hand. "I'm Gina," I said.

She swallowed her reply, but a name tag stuck to her bright pink shirt read *Clara*. Her hand was a small, hot sparrow in mine. We turned and walked down the hall together.

"How old are you, Clara?" I asked.

"Nine," she said.

I pulled up two chairs against the far wall, buying time by moving slowly, trying to tune the static in my mind. I gave Clara the one that faced the room so that she could see everything going on and I sat across from her, our knees touching. In my ears the overlapping voices of Bruce, Ethan, and Ingrid rose and fell, becoming one, scrambled like a Pentecostal babbling in tongues. Beadlets of sweat shone on Clara's forehead and she was looking past me.

Looking at the fear on her face, knowing she probably didn't have family here at the center, that maybe she didn't even have a friend, I realized I had been thrust into the unsupported role of surrogate, a position for which I could not have been less qualified.

Back at Thomas Road when a child came forward during the invitation, their parents walked down the aisle with them, maybe a step behind them, resting a hand on the child's shoulder, gliding past familiar faces smiling from the theater chairs. Even at ABT Children's Church the kids knew one another and their parents were worshipping just down the hall. But here—at this dismal little center with its sketchy parking lot and un-smiling workers, with a program that oddly ran during dinner hours, with its out-of-towner magician and strange Virginians appearing with no in-troduction, poor Clara must have felt terrified. And the onus was on me to make her feel better.

"Did you raise your hand after the magic show?" I asked her softly. Her eyes pinned me briefly and then slipped away, scanning the room as she nodded.

"Do you know what it meant to raise your hand?"

Clara nodded again.

"Can you tell me?" I asked.

She looked at me with miserable wet eyes. Bubbles of affection rose in my heart. I tried putting my hand on hers for reassurance, but my hand suddenly felt as large and awkward as a broken umbrella.

"Do you think you understand the gospel?" I asked. She didn't reply. The continuing distance in her eyes made me instantly regret my choice of words. I was trying to prove to her that she didn't understand. And for whose benefit? Revealing her lack of comprehension would be vindi-cation for me alone.

Suddenly I felt as if I had been swimming deep underwater and had lost track of the direction of the surface. I couldn't remember what I had been looking for here in Alaska, how my interaction with this poor little girl figured into any of it. I could simply leave. I could find a pay phone to call a taxi. I knew the name of our hotel. I had enough money in the bank to buy a ticket back to Virginia. But looking at Clara, at her delicate fea-tures and her glistening eyes, I realized that leaving would do more harm to her than staying. And it would just mean that someone else would save her tonight. I decided I had to follow the script, editing to diminish the negative impact.

Moments earlier I had noticed Bruce pulling a few tracts off the con-ference table and I followed suit. The salvation tract was a little cartoon booklet called *God Loves You!* I pulled my chair next to Clara's so that we could read it side-by-side. I followed the words with my finger and read aloud as if I were telling her *Goodnight, Moon*.

"Did you know that God loves you?" I began.

The pamphlet explained that out of love for the world, God gave his son so that we could have life everlasting. God wanted everyone to enjoy that gift, but our sins—"the bad things you do"—prevented us from doing so. Being holy, God had no choice but to punish us. However, the pamphlet continued cheerfully, "if you will receive Jesus as your savior, he will take away your sins and you will be God's child forever!"

Declaiming these words to an actual child sickened me, but Clara seemed comfortable, and wanted a pen to write her name into blanks in the sinner's prayer printed on the last page. She was filling it in (*For God so loved* Clara *that He gave His only begotten Son that if* Clara *will believe in Him . . .*) when a hand on my shoulder yanked me back hard. I jerked around in my seat, a glint of anger in my chest. Behind me was Eileen, her face even sharper than before. Her lips were a wrinkled pucker.

"What are you doing here?" she snapped. I had no answer. "What are you doing out here?" she repeated. Her words pelted me like gravel. I was afraid to turn around to see if Ethan or Ingrid had noticed. Clara was looking at me helplessly. "I told you to go to craft. We need you at craft. We don't need you out here."

Orienting myself, deciding that a penetrating mind was not foremost among Eileen's strengths, I stared into her angry little dot eyes and said in a low voice, "I was called to help out here. We are almost finished and then I will help out at craft."

Eileen glared down at Clara. "Did she fill out a card?"

She had not.

"Well, hurry up and get her to fill this in and then get to craft." She handed me a large index card with blanks for Clara's personal details, and then she was gone again.

Clara filled out her first and last names, her age, her school, and her phone number. She didn't know her parents' first names or her street address.

When we had finished with the card, we rose and I hugged Clara. She melted into my arms for a moment. Then we walked together into the action of the craft room and she disappeared from my side.

Even though Eileen's demeanor seemed outrageous, I could see why she wanted me at craft. Squirming at the four tables running the length of the room were about thirty children, applying themselves to their work with uneven success. The project was a yarn-bound notebook. After assembling the book, the kids were to cut shapes out of sticky-backed foam sheets, and there were also pages with the pre-cut letters of the alphabet. Each child was supposed to spell their first name on the book with the pre-cut letters.

"First names *only!*" Eileen stressed.

Some children were struggling to tie the yarn binding according to instructions, some were finished and roaming around the room, many more were eagerly grabbing for the craft supplies piled along the tables. Alice, Eileen, and another dour-faced woman were in helping poses around the room: bent over, leaning down.

I sat at an unsupervised table where the kids seemed stalled. Passing letters and scissors, I felt blurred and stunned, as if I'd just looked up from staring at a light bulb.

Two tables away Eileen grabbed a book back from a little boy and re-did the knot on his binding. "Tie it *over*, not under," she said, putting the book on the table and moving to the next child.

Clara was a fuchsia blur with a long black ponytail in my peripheral vision. I could feel her looking at me but I didn't look back. Each passing second separating me from the encounter made it harder to recall precisely why I had made the choices I made. I wished I could wave my hands and make Clara magically forget me. In an hour I'd be gone.

But even though I was absent from the work, lazily showing a girl how to cut along a folded edge to make a symmetrical shape, I noticed a nice thing begin to happen: children who had finished their projects were choosing to help others still working. One little girl called me over, needing help collecting letters to spell two names on her cover page: Deanna and Jesus. A couple of other children assisted us, passing down flimsy pages with most of the letters stamped out.

When we had the two names on her cover, she began to cut out a heart to stick on and I assisted a little boy making a star.

Suddenly, Eileen was bending over Deanna's work, pursing her dry lips. She jabbed a rigid finger at the girl's book. "First names only!" she said. She looked at me, her eyes sparking with disbelief. "Did you help her with this?" I had. "Each child is only supposed to do their first name—there aren't enough letters!"

I moved away, cleaning up peeled-off sticker paper and foam shreds.

At kickball, screams and babbles multiplied in the ample airspace of the wood-floored gym. There were too many players for the teams to look like teams. The at-bat line stretched down the wall and the outfielders were a mob. The bearded proctors patrolled the gym as if the children were prisoners in the yard.

Some kids bunted, others sent the ball soaring. One boy's foot whiffed across the top of the ball. Bases were loaded and stolen, outs tagged too hard; balls caught, thrown, missed; little hands grazing them as they cannoned overhead. A girl in tight braids punched a bucktoothed boy in the eye and a proctor angrily exiled her to the bleachers. Her friends gathered around her as she leaned her elbows on her knees, glaring into the stale gym air.

Ethan snapped pictures from the sidelines and Alice was engaged in the game, egging on kickers, cheering, running alongside them. Her goodness seemed to give her endless energy.

And where was I?—at a random coordinate in the outer outfield, clapping when others clapped, watching the ball streak across the wood floor, stepping aside when children tumbled in my direction. I felt like a kid lost at a crowded amusement park: what should have been fun and thrilling was revealed as dangerously chaotic. Sounds were too loud, aromas too rich, and the disorienting rush of bodies passing made me want to sit on the ground, to confirm that at least down was still down.

The ball was pitched, kicked, and a kid was tagged—three outs. Kickers ran to outfield, outfield to kick. I was surprised to see Clara purposefully walking toward me, her gaze leveled on my face. I smiled a smile stripped of meaning and depth, not wanting to confirm that there was any connective tissue between us. She stood next to me anyway, close. I could hear her wispy breathing underneath all the noise of the game. We watched the game together, staring straight ahead for a while. I began to feel she wanted me to say something to her, so I did.

"Did you have fun making your book?" I asked.

"Yeah," she said. Her posture was straight and there was a sapling confidence about her I hadn't noticed before.

"What are you going to do with it?" I asked.

She thought for a moment, webbing her fingers together. Over at home plate, a little girl thumped a foul ball back into her team's line. Children howled with laughter and the little girl's face darkened. This was one of the reasons I always felt uncomfortable around children: you see formative traumas unfold in real time.

Clara turned to me, twisting her interwoven hands as if working to break them apart. "I'm going to write about God," she said, "and I'm also going to draw a picture of you."

I was more than a little speechless, flattered in a warped way, as if I'd just been complimented on a quality I disliked in others. I thanked her stiffly and gave her a pathetic little pat on the shoulder.

The teams switched again and Clara lined up to kick. And over the next couple of innings, as I watched the kids play, I found myself drawn into the infield, feeling less alien. Maybe I was being too analytical. Kickball was plainly just kickball and maybe craft was just craft. And maybe exposing kids to all the death and damnation stuff through a magic show wasn't as sinister as I'd made it out to be. The plain fact of their attendance at this camp meant the children were probably hearing the rhetoric at home anyway. And as anti-intellectual as it was, I began to think that the content didn't matter—Christian eschatology was too sophisticated for children to understand. The only imperative for me seemed to be making the kids feel safe and loved: the very feeling evangelical doctrine was packaged to produce.

Lightening up, I joked around with a group of boys and even helped out with a play. Alice was having a look at the boy who'd been punched. He was rubbing his eye. "Do you want some ice?" I asked. He shook his head, smiling a little.

One of the tough girl's friends stalked over from the bleachers, hands in her pockets. "She wants to know how come you didn't hit her back," the girl said.

The boy shrugged. "It's against the law to hit girls."

Parents began to filter in to pick up their sons and daughters and kickball ended without ceremony. Unclaimed children lined up along the wall to return to the magic room. I saw Clara with them and, without really thinking about it, I approached her and knelt down, clumsily unknotting the bracelet I'd made at Children's Church.

"I want to give this to you," I said. She held out her arm so I could tie the bracelet for her. Her wrist was tiny, overwhelmed by the clacking row of colored beads. She didn't ask what they meant and I didn't tell her.

Finishing the knot, I said, "So you can remember today." I meant to be ambiguous. It seemed best for Clara to determine the importance of our encounter on her own. But as she hugged me I was speared by the hope that the bracelet would serve as a memento not of Christ's sacrifice but of human bonds.

"HOSTELS ARE BAAAAAD, man," Ethan said, shaking his head and lowering his enormous hamburger. We were at Red Robin again, deep into uncounted cycles of refillable french-fry baskets, and Ethan was finally off his fast. He was uncharacteristically cheerful and talkative, rejuvenated not only by the food but also, it was clear, by the knowledge that he'd just secured a place in heaven for two little boys. Pamela had been exhausted by the day and the Children's Church director had dropped her off at the Econo Inn.

For some reason no one wanted to talk much about Mountain View. I was immensely relieved that I didn't have to shellac and peddle my Clara story as if I were some perky public relations intern. Instead we had been talking about accommodations, joking about the Econo Inn and the Grand Ballroom, trading stories about unpleasant places we'd stayed in the past. But Ethan was displaying a smug authority on everything in the universe that was officially getting under my skin. I mentioned, rather irritably, that my sister and I had stayed in several hostels while traveling together and we'd never had a problem.

"Well, I've never stayed in one," Ethan said, lifting his eyebrows, seemingly amused at my guff, "but I know that girls stay with boys at hostels, and when girls stay with boys, bad things happen." He shook his head again and chuckled to himself, tucking into his burger, seeming to imply that we singles wouldn't have a clue what he meant.

Later, when none of us could even entertain the notion of another french fry, we asked for the check and leaned back from the table. A contented silence settled over us like a light blanket of snow. After a time, Alice said, "Did y'all hear about the Michael Vick thing?" Vick, quarterback for the Atlanta Falcons and former star player at Virginia Tech, had just been charged for his involvement in a dog-fighting ring. "They killed the dogs if they didn't win! Isn't that awful?"

Ingrid and I nodded, clucking our tongues. It *was* awful. It was simply unthinkable.

Ethan smirked and shook his head. "See, what's crazy to me is people get so upset about those dogs but millions of unborn children are killed and no one says a thing."

Heavy plates clattered off in the kitchen and Sheryl Crow moaned from invisible speakers overheard, and behind my lips my teeth were clenched so tightly I thought I might grind them into dust.

"I never thought about it that way," Alice said.

The light outside was weak tea, watery and dim, and the four of us began to cross the wide, wide parking lot toward the gray cluster of buildings we recognized as our neighborhood. Since we all felt fat and underexercised, we'd decided to strike off for the Econo Inn on foot rather than wait for Clementine to arrive with the van.

This is when I learned about Wyatt's gun. Ingrid had seen it when we stopped on the way to Portage Glacier. When the men were climbing on top of a large rock to pose for pictures a breeze lifted Wyatt's T-shirt and Ingrid spied the gun tucked into his waistband.

I stopped walking. "He's carrying a *gun*?"

"You haven't seen it?" Alice asked me casually, as if I had just learned some old scrap of celebrity gossip. "It's always bulging under his shirt."

"Why is he carrying a *gun*?" I asked.

I'm unusually squeamish about guns. And we were in Alaska, so theoretically we could have been confronted by a rampaging bear or caribou, or maybe we could have gotten lost on the road and Wyatt would have had to shoot our dinner. But there was much about the fact of the gun that unsettled me: the impropriety of its presence on a sightseeing trip spent in the car, the instability and machismo of the person packing, my own secret, which had the potential to inspire violence.

Still, I was not honestly afraid that Wyatt would murder me or that the gun would accidentally fire during a photo op. I was mainly disturbed by what the gun signified: hostility toward the unknown and the suspicion that the farther one traveled from home, the more imperiled one became. Ignorant paranoia—the poison well from which so many Evangelicals draw bad conclusions.

I wanted to know if Wyatt had carried the gun to the Rescue Mission and to Children's Church. No one knew for sure.

"Well," Ethan said, smirking, "I brought a gun, too. But we haven't done anything yet where I've had to bring it."

Clementine drove up in the van before we made it across the parking lot, and just as I needed to take a seat. How disoriented I was, bouncing home to the Econo Inn, stuffed to nausea with fries, suddenly aware of the guns (were there more?), unable to call or write anyone from my other life to share my disturbances.

And Alice, my dear friend Alice sitting up front, smiling at me over her shoulder, feeling bonded to me and I to her, as if we had been and would be friends forever. Alice, unaware that inside the perfect fruit of our friendship was black rot. I had done that. Maybe I was a bad person, or maybe I was just exhausted from a single day that seemed to begin ages ago. And how had it started? . . . I felt around for the end of the thread, but in my fingers it became a loop.

With all this roiling in my head, I was only half listening on our way back to the Econo Inn as Alice compared notes with Clementine. But I did hear Clementine say that the Rescue Mission had yielded seven more souls, to put our mission total at 97.

"Oh my word," Alice said. "Clem, we got three at VBS. Oh my word."

A sharp chill zipped through the van and I became as alert as a startled deer. That day was our last in Anchorage, and with the evangelism duties of our trip officially behind us, we had met the soul-winning quota with unnerving precision. We'd been taking souls as they came—four here, seven there—with as much control as a fisherman dropping his line. And somehow, we ended right on the mark.

"Well that's just spooky, ain't it?" Clementine laughed. "I mean it's just spooky! Look at this—the hairs on my arm are standing up!"

At the Econo Inn Ray and Carter approached our van before we could pull in to park. Ray was wearing his royal blue TRBC fleece and shorts. His bald head was gleaming in the weak midnight sun and there were little crescent puffs under his glinting eyes. With the van still idling, stopped at an odd angle to the other spaces, Ray leaned into Clementine's window, and gripping the lip of the door asked hopefully, "Y'all get anybody?" Carter was peeking past his shoulder as if to read the answer on our faces.

"Did you?" Ethan asked, prolonging Ray's suspense.

"We got seven raised their hands after the sermon," Carter said.

"Which puts us at 97 altogether," Ray added.

"Ray," Clementine said, smiling up at her husband, her eyes twinkling prettily, "they got three kids at VBS."

Ray released the door and leaned back. "Holy Shi-ite," he said, his blue eyes perfect coins of surprise.

Everyone in the van laughed a little nuttily. I was getting chills over and over.

"Exactly a hundred!" Ethan barked, leaning forward from the back-seat, gnawing at the bones of his disbelief.

"Well, y'all," Ray said, shaking his head and chuckling, "that ain't good. That's some hoodoo or I don't *know* what! I can't go back and tell Jonathan we got exactly a hundred. He'll either think we're pulling his leg or we're cursed or we could've had more and stopped when we hit our number!"

My wonder at this strange coincidence was like a column of bright light, and I was a little surprised to see that others felt the same way. I would have expected them to nod contentedly: *Ask and ye shall receive, duh!* But we were all riding the same current, spooked, going over how strange it was, how unbelievable it was, just letting the waves of it crash over us. When something even weirder happened.

As Clementine reassured Ray that the trip wasn't over yet and that we'd have plenty more opportunities for soul-winning in North Pole and Valdez, a diminutive Athabaskan man in a baseball cap, his shoulders tense and his hands jammed into the center pocket of his hooded sweatshirt, suddenly appeared by Ray's side and whispered something in his ear. Ray put his hand on the man's shoulder and leaned down to listen. A silencing glance shot between all of us in the van. When the man had finished speaking, Ray gave him a gentle clap on the shoulder and with a tenderness in his eyes and voice said, "Sure, buddy, I'll pray with you."

Clementine put the van in drive and quietly pulled away. Once parked, we all watched on tenterhooks as if from a stakeout car. Ray, with Carter standing at his back sober as a butler, scrunched his eyes closed and bowed his head with the man, his lips moving rapidly. In a few short minutes, the man in the sweatshirt was smearing tears from his cheeks, and everyone in the van turned away, not wanting to gawk.

"I didn't even see him walk up," Alice whispered.

Ingrid had the happy, open smile of a baby. "He must have seen *Anchorage Baptist Temple* written on the side of the van," she said.

Clementine was turned around in her seat, smiling warmly. Her beauty was something I was only beginning to understand. When I first met her, I saw only garishly painted lips and nails, overtanned skin and heavy mascara. Now when I looked at her I saw the richness in her blue eyes as they looked at me, the powerful affection in her white smile. And

I was even starting to like her style: her tennis bracelet made of gold hearts, her playful orange capri pants. She just seemed the picture of happiness. She shook her head in wonder, her golden hair glinting. "Isn't the Lord amazing?"

When Ray and the man finally hugged and parted, we piled out of the van and caught up with him on the way in to the hotel.

"A hundred and one," Ray said, rubbing hand sanitizer into his palms.

If we were fishermen, this last soul was like a silvery salmon that flopped its way up the riverbank and into our basket, catching itself.

CURIOUS CREATURES

—

W E DROPPED BY THE HOSPITAL IN THE MORNING TO PICK UP Joey—who'd spent several nights laid up with a kidney stone— and then departed Anchorage late morning in two rented vans. We drove along Route 1 headed for North Pole, the town near Fairbanks where Ray and Clementine had lived while Ray was stationed at Eielson Air Force Base. For lunch we stopped in a wildflower-encircled lodge in Wasilla with a view of craggy mountains so crisp and light-blasted you could feel your chest cavity cracking open.

Alice and I sat by the picture window with Lyle. He lived alone and had a job washing dishes at a nursing home and he usually took his meals there. He told us which meals were served on which days of the week, practically breaking my heart with the repetition of his life. He told us he dreamed of going back to school. "I want to learn most of all about the psychology of the white male," he told us, sticking a finger in the air for emphasis.

"Is that so?" Alice said. I looked out the window at the throbbing white mountain peaks, the burnt-black slopes below.

Lyle also began telling us what he looked for in a mate. He seemed to be flirting with Alice (he kept calling her Jennifer) and at one point he looked at her legs under the table.

"My daddy taught me to play around before marriage," he said, "but I don't believe in having babies before the wedding."

Back on the road, the Alaskan vistas were so beautiful I felt as if my troubles were lifting off and away like dandelion spores. Great canvases of vegetation stretched off to the east and west, the surfaces bruising with blues and greens, light filtering through the clouds in magical beams. Trees resembling spires from a child's crystal garden stippled the plains, and straight ahead the gold-tinted base of McKinley was visible. McKinley's peaks were obscured by a fuzzy gray stratum of clouds, but the breadth of the visible base was grandeur enough. Somehow it was brighter up ahead where the mountains were, giving the appearance that a second sun was shedding light.

Our van was silenced by the beauty well into Denali National Park, where we all began to scan the scrub-grass valleys and slopes for animal activity. We didn't have time to take a bus ride into the park's interior, but Ray reckoned we could see a bear or two on the road open to private vehicles.

Which we might have, had our other van not broken down. It was engine trouble or something equally damning, and as Ray kept his cool over the phone with the Anchorage rental company, the rest of us stood off in the wildflowers by the side of the road, gazing quietly into the sweep of big-sky country. The landscape still dazzled—Elysian fields! twinkling mercury rivers! furry streaks of pastel bushes!—but I was suddenly unimpressed. We were stuck, and still had hours and hours left to drive. My ability to appreciate majesty, it seemed, was heavily contingent upon the suspension of reality.

The rental company promised to meet us with another car in North Pole the next morning. We abandoned the broken-down van in the park and the seventeen of us sardined into the other 15-seater, Xander perching on the wheel well with his portable DVD player. The remainder of the drive was a giant drag—the van air ripening with personal odors, the insectile buzzing of several sets of earphones, and several of the perkier among us lobbying to stop every thirty miles for photographs and souvenir shopping.

Wyatt had contributed a large, homemade-looking device to play iPods through the car stereo, and after several rounds of Christian music on others' iPods, he turned to me.

"Do you have anything?" he asked. "Anything . . . appropriate?"

I quickly scrolled through my iPod library. David Bowie, Elliott Smith, The Halo Benders, My Bloody Valentine, the New Pornographers, 50 Cent. A band called Bad Veins. The thing was so loaded with un-Christian music it might as well have been in the shape of a little pentagram. I did have one Christian song—"Something Happens"—which had produced Feeling X in me once at Thomas Road. The version I had found on iTunes was done by a black gospel choir.

"Oh, well . . ." I said, affecting a casual iPod scroll, "I'm not sure."

A chorus of titillated "ooooohs!" filled the van, but they were good-natured.

We arrived in Fairbanks around eight and, after a meal at Ray and Clementine's favorite Chinese restaurant, where Lyle read aloud a love poem he'd written for Alice—("*You'll wear fishnet stockings, because a woman shouldn't show her legs before marriage*")—we finally made it to our North Pole accommodations, the Beaver Lake Resort Hotel.

The hotel was made up of several three-story log cabins lining the shore of a handsome lake. Our rooms were large and luxurious compared to the offerings at the Econo Inn. We had a kitchenette, couches, and plenty of space to spread out our luggage. Alice and I had a room adjoining Pamela and Ursula's, but by this point in the trip Alice and I had had our fill of Pamela's piety and Ursula's icy silence.

The group gathered at the edge of Beaver Lake a little after ten. It was evening light and had been that way for a while; it didn't seem to be getting any darker.

Ray, who had one foot perched on the picnic table bench, said we should feel free to walk around the property, but cautioned us against going off into the woods or even walking all the way around the lake. "There are wild animals around here," he said. "And you do not want to come face to face with a grizzly, I guarantee you that."

Still wearing his aerodynamic sunglasses in the dim light, Wyatt patted the bulge under his T-shirt. "As long as I have time to draw."

Ray ignored him and told us about an orientation video he'd seen when first stationed at Eielson Air Force Base. In the video was a story about a tragic incident that took place at a lake near where we were. Two men met a grizzly bear and, faced with what they were sure would be a horrible, painful death by mauling, chose to drown themselves in the lake.

I felt myself blanching, looking out at silvery Beaver Lake. Stories of people electing to die a particular way, of a gruesome death being so imminent that suicide seemed a preferable option, were beyond the feelers of my comprehension.

"You may see a moose," Ray continued. "Do not approach a moose either, okay? They may look cute and friendly, but a moose can rear up and come down on your head with both of his hooves, and you do not want that."

MOST OF OUR GROUP wanted to go to North Pole's Santa Claus House the following day. Clementine needed replacement parts for her Eskimo nativity scene and some were hoping for pictures with Santa and the Missus, as well as several reindeer kept in a chain-link pen outside. Ingrid wanted to look for a children's book someone had recommended to her about how Santa felt guilty for taking attention away from Jesus on Christmas.

The sportier among us opted for a salmon-fishing trip with Ray, and after a group breakfast at McDonald's we all said good-bye and parted ways.

"You're all my children," Ray said as the fishing group loaded into the van. "I should be able to write you off on my tax return."

We stopped at Eielson so Ray could arrange for a boat and some poles. Checking in at the hut outside the main gates, I noticed a group of black enamel plaques mounted on one wall under an enormous rack of caribou antlers. Ray's name and rank were engraved on one plaque with the title *Caribou Hunt of Denial*.

I pointed it out to him.

"No, it's *Caribou Hunt of Denali*," he said.

I knew that, I told him, but it was a funny misspelling.

"Well, Gina, I don't know," he said irritably.

None of our group was allowed inside the base gates, so we hung out near the hut while Ray drove in for supplies. We were standing next to a wide airstrip, and shortly after Ray drove off through the gates an F-15 came roaring in our direction, and then with the orange blast of its afterburner and a spine-vibrating boom it became a dot in the sky, and then nothing at all. I readied my camera, my heart beating fast in anticipation of another jet.

Being in Alaska was jabbing at something atavistic in me. I had always been turned off by anything related to the sporting section of the hardware store. Macho gear-chatter made me zone out, military history sent my eyes rolling, and I dismissed hunting as perverse bloodlust. I'd never had the patience to watch through to the end of *Top Gun*.

But having opened myself up to evangelical thought and culture, I was welcoming other things I had historically eschewed. Everywhere we went there were dead posed bears and wall-mounted antlers, and I was beginning to develop a childlike fascination with them. I wondered who shot and gutted and dragged them out of the wilderness, who stuffed them and how. I wanted to feel a giant salmon thrashing at the end of a fishing line, see its large flat eye tilting toward the light. Ray had guaranteed I wouldn't be able to pull one in on my own, but I wanted to try. And now I found myself in delighted awe of these fighter planes, how fast they shot by, the science-fiction sounds they made. Watching them was like sticking my finger into the cage of a dangerous animal.

I was learning not to overthink, to just soak it up like everyone else. Everywhere we went I said, *Wow*. Ray ribbed me for it: "Ooooh, oh wow," he said, giggling. "Like, *wow*." I bet him I wouldn't say it for a whole day and I lost the bet within an hour.

At a hardware store near the base our group lined up along a firearms display case to purchase shiny lures, bug spray, and fishing licenses. Ethan was there with a full camping backpack, and Xander, Pamela, and Alice.

High on the wall behind the counter large rifles were mounted beside a snarling wolverine and several caribou heads wearing placid expressions, as if they were sitting for portrait artists. The man behind the counter—head-to-toe camouflage, sandbag gut, beady eyes, a kind of anti-Santa with his full white beard—looked at me askance as I gaped at the guns, and then visibly stiffened when I passed him my California driver's license. At this point I'd been made fun of so much for being from California that it didn't faze me, and it hadn't prevented anybody from accepting I was one of them.

On the pebbly banks of the Salcha River we tied our salmon lures and waited for our boat to arrive. A bald eagle soared overhead. Word around Eielson was that we'd missed the salmon run by just a week; no one else was on the water.

"When they're running you can see 'em jumping like this across the whole surface," Ray said, bumping and swerving his hand like a swimming fish. "When they're running, this whole river is filled with boats."

We decided to eat our sandwiches. Ray leaned on Xander to give the prayer, and he did so reluctantly—under his breath, and in a hurry.

Xander was just a kid, twenty-one and a new Christian. He had two modes: aloof and interrogative. If he wasn't mutely stalking off into the woods to take photographs of flowers, he was asking naive questions.

Can I take the train to North Pole instead of driving with you guys? Are we going to get to walk out on any glaciers? When can we see a bear up close? Once, when Ray told us that sometimes on the drive to Portage Glacier white beluga whales come right up where you can see them, Xander asked, "Can I go swim with them?"

"Yeah, buddy," Ray had said, "you do that."

Now, Xander was blinking down at his sandwich. "What makes ham have these shiny parts?" he asked.

Ray rolled his eyes. "By gummy worm, Xander, I don't *know*. Why is grass green? Because God made it so."

After lunch I practiced casting a line at the water's edge for a long time, enjoying the solitude, the plunk of the lure in the water.

When our boat finally arrived, Ray shuttled us three at a time around the bend to a rocky little beach. It was exhilarating, motoring up the river, wind-blasted, the tang of gas filling my nose. When we got to the beach Ray told us he'd take two of us out at a time. He kept checking the sky: gray thunderheads were visible in the distance and a hot wind blew.

The river was fishless, a uniform brown-green. The salmon run had ended. But I didn't care. I loved it all: bobbing the pole as Ray ran the motor against the current just enough to keep the boat in one place, the lure murmuring on the surface of the water, the lap-lap of the river and the deep green trees all around. While others were out in the boat I walked along the river's edge, picking up black rocks glittering with minerals. I gave a particularly silvery one to Alice. I was so happy just being near the water, I could have stayed there all day and come back the next.

But suddenly Ray was steering the boat back to shore and hopping onto the beach. "Xander, buddy, we'd better get this baptism done because the storm's comin' in," he said, removing his sneakers. This came as a surprise; I hadn't known they were planning a baptism. I watched Ray wade out into the river in his shiny athletic shorts, his T-shirt tucked into the elastic waistband, wraparound sunglasses just visible under the brim of his white baseball cap.

The clouds were leadening and pressing toward us; wind hissed in the leaves.

Ethan drew a handgun from the back of his jeans and stowed it in the camper's backpack he had propped against a rock. "Let me put this away first," he said.

Xander popped off his shirt and, wearing only board shorts printed with a black and gray thorn pattern, sloshed out to join Ray in the river. "Whoa, buddy!" Ray said. We hadn't pulled any fish from the river that day, but here we were, about to pull out a new Christian.

We lined up along the shore to watch as they stood side-by-side in the shallows, river water lapping brownish yellow around their knees. Xander was small and olive-skinned, a trickle of hair running down his middle. The sun beat down on his head and his scalp was shiny and visible under his spiked hair. Large, pink Ray took Xander's left hand in his own and wrapped his right around the back of Xander's neck, as if picking up a kitten by its scruff.

Xander offered to kneel, to make the tipping easier, but Ray thought he could dip him back far enough.

"All right, let's have a word of prayer," Ray said, dropping Xander's hand momentarily to remove his sunglasses and slide them onto the brim of his cap. "Let's pray. Father, we do love you, thank you that you love us. Thank you for Xander and his profession of faith in you and his obedience to your command to be baptized." Xander had a goofy grin on his face. I wondered what thoughts were tickling him, wondered if he was just loopy on the excitement of being baptized in a river in Alaska.

Ray went on, "We pray that you would bless this moment, and use Xander for your honor and your glory." And in a brighter voice, "Xander?"

His eyes blinked open as if he were surprised awake. "Yeah?"

"Have you accepted Jesus Christ as your Lord and your savior?"

"Yes, sir," he said.

Ray lifted his hand from Xander's neck and raised it above his head in swearing position. "Then because of your profession of faith I baptize you my brother in the name of the Father, the Son, and of the Holy Ghost. Buried in the likeness of his death"—and here Ray grabbed both Xander's wrists, dipped him down and under, and as he yanked him back up, Xander spat a great plume of river water and Ray's laughter ate holes in the rest of his words. Xander yanked his board shorts from crawling up his legs and lunged to stagger away, his grin as toothy as a skull's.

Ray braced himself on Xander's shoulder, chuckling. "Hey, would you like to say something?" he joked. "Yeah," he answered himself, and then mimicked Xander spewing breathlessly.

Motoring back down the Salcha to the boat launch and parking lot,

Ray twisted around from his post at the stern, peering back toward the little beach.

"The Lord would be happy with all the work we've done serving him," he said. And then under his breath, as he turned around to the front, "But I'm glad we didn't get just a hundred."

RAY SOMEHOW MANAGED to get the entire group on base for dinner, and after we stuffed ourselves to the gills at the pasta bar and traded river stories for stories from the Santa Claus house, he took us on a tour. It was a grim place—vast concrete slabs and dormitory blocks dropped on the flat land like mailed packages, airstrips slashing past, greenery in between trimmed as neatly as a regulation haircut. We drove by a field where men were playing soccer. Ray rolled down his window. "We got women in here need men!" he shouted at them.

We came around to the officers' subdivision, an area so suburban it looked like a set crafted for military exercises: cul-de-sacs with rounded curbs, two-story beige townhomes. Ray and Clementine decided to surprise a couple they had been best friends with when they lived on base. They disappeared inside the couple's home for a while; when they came out to meet our group, the wife visited the other van and the husband, Martin, poked his head into ours.

Martin, zipped into his flyboy jumpsuit, was a fresh breeze. He had the bronzed good looks of an action hero and a wry, funny charm. He was a Gatling gunner for the Air Force and, at Ray's prompting, he brought out an A10 bullet shell to show us. Ray said that Gatling guns fire sixty-five A10 bullets per second. I simply couldn't visualize this. I had prodded Ray to describe how it was possible, but he told me Martin would be a better person to ask.

Martin passed me the gold shell, which was heavy and cold and about the size of a popsicle. I weighed it in my hand as he described for me the spinning ring of barrels, each one spraying these bullets. This explanation left me both awed and saddened, thinking about what was on the receiving end of such a weapon, but Martin's charisma made it easier not to overthink. We talked some more, and he and his wife sent us off with a huge ziplock bag of home-smoked salmon.

We drove out of the subdivision and past dozens of blank brown buildings, stopping briefly to take photographs at a memorial site featuring a mothballed fleet of retired war planes. And then we took off to the edges of the base to find moose. Ray told us to look carefully whenever we passed a body of water. "I guarantee we'll see at least one moose," he said.

At the edges of the base the road passed into stands of bushy trees and tall grasses, swamp water glimmering here and there. As we drove, I told Ray and Clementine how much I had enjoyed meeting Martin.

"He's a great buddy," Ray said, driving slowly and scanning the woods for moose. "But you know, Martin's one of those who *thinks* he's a Christian. Now his *wife* is a good Christian—a good, Bible-believing Christian. And Martin, he volunteered at AWANA, did things for the church. Ever who needs something, Martin's right there to give it. One of the best guys you'd ever want to meet." Ray's voice became soft now. "But he just won't pray the prayer, and so unfortunately he'll be one of those saying, *Lord, Lord . . .*"

Clementine cast a sad gaze at Ray, shook her head. They felt sorry for Martin.

We had been driving for around twenty minutes and were passing an elephant-gray wall of rock scarred with thousands of small black holes. The walkie-talkie crackled to life. It was Wyatt in the rear van. "Hey, Colonel, what are those holes in the rock?" Wyatt managed to sound smug asking for the information, as if he knew the answer would be wrong.

Ray sighed. Wyatt had been jockeying for authority all evening, seemingly threatened by Ray's more visible stature as a military man. "Why don't you stick your hand in and find out?"

Driving on, Ray entertained us with funny stories from his days on base. Just past a grassy firing range, he pointed out a serpentine stretch of the Alaska pipeline. Silvery and shiny enough to reflect the clouds in the sky, it rose up out of the ground and then ran through the grass before disappearing into a dark thicket of trees.

Wyatt came on the walkie-talkie again, his smirk audible, and asked, "Hey, Colonel, how come the pipeline is so close to the firing range?"

Ray lobbed back: "Because unlike Navy boys, Air Force men know how to shoot straight." Our van fell all over ourselves laughing. Ray replaced the receiver in the center console. "Watch. You watch," Ray said. "You can hear him working to come up with something. You can hear his little computer going *wheee . . .*"

Static finally crackled again. "Or maybe it's because whoever built this place knows Air Force boys are too lazy to ever come out to the range for practice."

"See," Ray said, "what'd I tell you?" And then in a small voice: "Dickhead."

THE MOOSE CALL Ray taught us was a nasal groan followed by a series of grunts. It was a pretty vulgar sound and the van was in hysterics over it. Our group was comfortable enough now that we were making sex jokes with increasing regularity. Alice and I popped the windows open and called to the moose all along the road.

Deep into the backwoods on the edges of the base, we finally found two moose drinking in a swamp: a mother and a baby. Everyone piled out of the vans and tiptoed into the tall grass beside the road, aiming cameras.

Neither moose had antlers. Their fur was brown velvet and their bodies were awkward: humped shoulders, knobby legs. The mother's head was bowed to drink and the baby stood behind her.

"Call her, Gina!" Alice whispered. "Do the call!"

My heart was beating so fast I could feel it in my temples. I did a long, loud call that brought tears to my eyes. The mother lifted her anvil head from the swamp water and looked right at me, shooting a bolt into my chest. Feeling X: connection without comprehension. I had captured her alive. It lasted for a few seconds and then she lowered her head to drink and it was gone, leaving behind a smoldering burn mark.

After a while, we all loaded back into the vans and drove away. Taps played over loudspeakers somewhere in the distance. Sunk down in my seat, I asked Ray if they played taps every night on base.

"Only during wartime," he said, "in memory of those who have died."

It was ten, dim, as if a net had been thrown over the day. For a little while, silence held down the wings of our conversation.

Finally, Ray told us that the overthrow of Saddam hadn't taken long. "But what we didn't plan for was that no one was like, 'Yeehaw! We're free!' They picked up guns and started shooting us, shooting each other, and . . ." Ray looked out his window at a plain of concrete. "New chapel was supposed to be over here, but the war sucked up all the money."

Clementine scanned Ray's face and then flopped around in her seat to look at all of us. "Did y'all know that Ray gave the opening prayer for the war?" Over his shoulder, I saw Ray's hands knead the steering wheel.

"He was in Qatar when the first planes went to bomb Iraq and they asked him to give the prayer."

Everyone in the van expressed variations of muted surprise and interest.

Ray muttered, "Now, Clem, they don't want to hear about that."

Sitting back in her seat, Clementine exchanged a long, encoded look with Ray. "Sure they do, Ray." She turned to us again. "Don't take it personal," she said. "He doesn't like to talk about it. His own daughters don't know what his Bronze Star is for."

Ray was uncharacteristically silent, navigating the streets of the base.

"Ray was on the team that saved Jessica Lynch, right, honey?" There was nothing in her voice but the simplest beacon of pride, but Ray kept at a shadowed remove, watching the road. "Tell them about Jessie Lynch," Clementine said.

Ray spoke quietly: "They aren't interested, Clem."

"They're interested! Right, girls?"

We all chimed in, but with tempered enthusiasm. Whether it was because the Jessica Lynch narrative had been revealed as a fairy tale; or because the war had become an unremitting, unequivocal fiasco; or because he considered his military service confidential; or because he was a modest man, Ray was clearly serious about not wanting to discuss it.

He inhaled deeply. "Well of course they're saying they're interested now. What are they gonna say?"

Clementine sank back into her seat and regarded Ray with some complicated version of pity. We were all quiet and uncomfortable, as if compromising pictures of Ray had just slipped out of Clementine's pocketbook.

The checkpoint and exit gate were directly ahead. "I don't want to talk about it," Ray said, liveliness rushing back into his voice. "I'll get the Agent Orange flashbacks." He flinched and crouched down. "Oh my gosh, what's that?"

Laughter flushed out the toxic air. We were alright now. Ray exchanged a few words with the gate attendant and we were back on the road to Beaver Lake.

And suddenly, a lone moose was galloping through the trees to our right, running at around thirty miles per hour. Sometimes she was a brown blur visible in flashes behind a thick line of foliage, sometimes starkly clear and close to the van. With her outsized head and weird, jaunty body, she looked like a mutant horse or an extinct creature from another age.

The van was alight with a sweet sensation of joy. Ray kept pace with her and she with him, and as we traveled on parallel tracks it seemed as if she wanted to run with us. I allowed myself to enter this perspective for a time: a moose running with us for pleasure. You can see anything you want if you've already decided what you're looking at.

But squinting through the trees as they flew past, I saw that beyond the running moose was a chain-link fence preventing her from getting away from us. By driving alongside her, we were creating a second fence, propelling her forward, forcing her to seem game. And eventually the moose found what she needed: a break in the fence to her right, through which she disappeared.

LITTLE SWITZERLAND

———

MIDWAY DOWN THE DAZZLING RICHARDSON HIGHWAY, WHICH
runs 368 miles from Fairbanks to Valdez, our group was crowded
along the railing of a deck built over a roadside stream. Fat salmon slid
around the bend in the stream, past eddies clogged with gray trout. The
salmon were nearing the end of their lives. Their bodies were blood red
and their heads silver. There was a path leading to the stream's edge, and
we joked about walking down to snatch fish right out of the water.

"These are the last of the run," Ray said. "They're gonna lay their
eggs and go off to die."

"Wow," I said. Ray cut up laughing.

Up the road, Pamela was sitting on a bench with her back to us, facing a muscular parade of snow-crowned mountains. I wandered off from
the group and watched her for a while, wondering if she was crying. She
had been quiet in the backseat of the van all day and now she was just
sitting there by herself—unusual behavior for this crowd.

I consulted with Alice and Clementine, who had also noticed Pamela's
self-segregation.

"She's had a hard life," Clementine said diplomatically. We all agreed
that Pamela could be a bit of a buzzkill, a bit overserious, but we re-
solved to make more of an effort to be kind.

Soon Pamela rose from the bench and came back our way. It was
evident she had not been crying.

"You okay, honeybun?" Clementine asked, rubbing a pink-nailed
hand across Pamela's shoulders.

Pamela lifted her eyebrows, seeming amused by the question. "I'm fine!"

"What were you thinking about over there by yourself?"

"I was just praying," Pamela said. Her voiced was iced with her awful superiority, as if to say, *I was praying, unlike some people.* "I just wanted to take some time to thank God for his beautiful creation."

Well, fair enough—it was hard to know *what* to do with the beauty all around. High virgin clouds above enormous postcard mountains, white glaciers pouring down their crevices like melted marshmallow; fiber-optic wildflowers blazing across grasses; molten metal lakes and streams glinting in the sun. Even the oil pipeline, the stupid pipeline, inspired wonder. We had stopped beside the Richardson Highway to look at it up close. It ran back along the road and up and up to Prudhoe Bay, and then, going south, it became a silver fairy-tale serpent, striking off into the wild green plain, dipping down into a valley and over a hill and out of sight. Amy climbed on and straddled it, whipping her hand as if riding a rodeo bull.

The scale of Alaska's beauty left me feeling feeble in my wonder: I wanted to plunge into it or be perpetually electrocuted by its mysteries. But trying to appreciate Alaska was like trying to French-kiss the open ocean: there was something fundamentally too small about the human capacity. Pamela, presumably facing the same feeling, triangulated: thanks to God, for wonders beyond comprehension.

"Well, Pamela," Clementine said sweetly, "you're just the cream of wheat."

Back on the highway, Alice, Carter, Ray, and I were mucking around in the pigpen of our usual innuendo-inflected banter. After a particularly naughty streak, Ray turned to Clementine and muttered so only she, and Alice and I in the seat behind, could hear: "Pamela is going to turn us in when we get back home, boy."

"What was that?" Pamela called, leaning forward from way in back. "Did I hear my name?"

Ray looked into the rearview mirror and raised his voice. "I was just saying what a godly woman you are, Pam!"

Clementine was shaking her head now, arms folded, looking out the window.

THE RICHARDSON HIGHWAY PLUMMETED straight down, down past white lace waterfalls and blue blankets of glacier, to the placid edge of the Valdez Narrows, a limp finger trailing off Prince William Sound.

Valdez is a dead-flat bay town surrounded by sharp-edged, towering mountains. Depending on the light, the peaks can look like killer whales, black with snowy markings or like the lush green hills of a tropical forest. Even though Valdez's physical template earned it the nickname Little Switzerland, something about it reminded me of Lynchburg: the way the buildings huddled in the grasp of the mountains, the way—standing in town—you could imagine there was nothing at all beyond the peaks.

Most famous for the 1989 Exxon oil spill and images of blackened seabirds, Valdez was ravaged by a less-publicized calamity in the 1960s. The Good Friday earthquake of 1964 was, at 8.4 on the Richter scale, the most powerful in North American history. The earthquake caused destruction over much of coastal Alaska, and its force resulted in a 30-foot tsunami that came roaring out of Prince William Sound to crash down on the town, wiping out many of its buildings and killing thirty-two people. The town relocated four miles to the west on more solid ground. And still Valdez had a feeling of impermanence, as if no one was willing to place a sizable bet on the town's survival. Ray told us it was a seasonal place—people came here to fish when the fishing was good; when it wasn't, the town was nearly empty. Many of the buildings were corrugated aluminum portables and piles of gravel stood in empty lots like nightmare anthills. At the edge of the Narrows stood a trailer park, which appeared to be the liveliest spot in town.

It was our last night in Alaska. We were all a little irritable after a long day in the car, our charms squashed flat as if we had been sitting on them since North Pole.

After checking in to a crummy motel and eating a salmon dinner under the glass-eyed watch of another lunging stuffed bear at the Totem Inn, some of us went for a walk along the water and then a drive to the Eagle Food grocery for dessert. Alice and I split up—she wanted to go to the motel to prepare for the trip to Virginia the following day.

At Eagle Food, Carter and Clementine ran in to find ice-cream bars while Pamela and I waited in the van with Ray. Through the bug-speckled windshield we watched a man with slicked-back hair and a windbreaker dialing on a pay phone. A woman in a giant T-shirt and burnt-orange sweatpants leaned against the wall beside him, a stillness in her posture that suggested she might have been there for hours.

Ray was staring at them in an unfocused way, his eyes as far away as the stuffed bear's at the Totem Inn. "It's so sad to think all these people have an eternal soul and they don't even know it," he said, shaking his head almost imperceptibly. The man in the windbreaker hung up the pay phone, held the receiver a moment, and then picked it up and dialed again. "Some of them don't even care."

CARTER WAS IN OUR ROOM for the last night of pillow talk, but neither Alice nor I were really talking. Hair conditioner had squirted everywhere in my bag. Alice was refolding the contents of her luggage. Carter roamed the room uncomfortably, chattering, his hands in his pockets. His restlessness was making me nervous, as if I too would never be able to get to sleep.

Finally, I said, "Carter, sit down for God's sake."

A stillness fell over Alice and Carter and the voice of the weatherman on television was suddenly as shrill as a seabird's. They were blinking at me. It was as if I had taken my eye off the road to check the time and, in an instant, crashed off a cliff. Here we were—I was revealed. I glopped up hair conditioner with a wad of paper towels held in a trembling hand. I braced myself for a barrage of questions, or worse: more silence.

Alice said, "Yeah, Carter," mocking—*something*; "sit down for God's sake."

I don't know. She may have been on to me. But whatever was on her mind, she was proving herself to be one of the most accepting people I had ever known.

AGAINST EVERYONE'S WISHES, I ran alone early the next morning. Maybe it was unsafe, maybe I was vulnerable, but I was looking down the barrel of a long drive back to Anchorage, a long flight to Chicago, then Roanoke, then a drive to Lynchburg, and finally I'd be back alone in my car and headed to Charlottesville. Two full days of travel. I considered my jog a final gulp of air before going under.

I ran the docks along the Narrows as far as I could, passing anchored boats and seabirds rocking in the harbor, whose waters were tinted a milky blue from glacial runoff.

The night before we had walked into the waterside trailer park to stand on boulders piled along the edge of the Narrows. I had marveled at the way the rocky peninsula manipulated the sunlight coming through.

The sun was so low and had such a small passage that its light had been focused like a projector beam. Where the beam fell, the mountains looked green and inviting, as if edible plants grew there.

Now, on my run, in the even, dim light of morning, the mountains were green and brown in the plainest way, like mountains anywhere.

Once I came to the end of the docks, I crossed town in the other direction, running past all the motels and restaurants, the T-shirt and fishing shops, past gravel piles and radio towers. I passed signs informing me that I was going the wrong way along the tsunami evacuation route. I ran on, crossing a bridge over a gushing river, passing quiet subdivisions. Signs informed me that I had entered a tsunami hazard zone, and that I should seek high ground in the event of an earthquake. On the sign, a little white figure leapt up a hill, giant waves curling at its back.

The road ended at an empty parking lot for a trailhead leading to Gold Creek and Shoup Bay. I had the urge to run farther. The trail was shaded by the low branches of dense trees and I could only see ahead fifty feet or so. Looking at the map on the trailhead sign, I saw I certainly wasn't going to be able to make it all the way out to Shoup: it was five miles away. But maybe I could get to high ground and see down to the water, get the lay of the land. Maybe catch a glimpse of Shoup Glacier, picture what it would have been like for that tsunami to roll in. After all, I would probably never in my life be back in this place.

As I considered running the trail, I noticed a laminated sign tacked next to the trail map. It was an information sheet about the types of bears inhabiting the area around the trail, how to differentiate among them, and what to do if you found yourself in a close encounter. Identify yourself. Don't run. If the bear is brown, lie down. If the bear is black, fight back.

I considered this information, turning the volume way down on my iPod and wandering down the trail. I peered into the woods, looking for a flash of fur, feeling for a rumble in the ground, something to confirm or allay my fears. But in the end, I was either too sensible or too chicken to face the wilderness head-on, and I ran back to the motel.

ONE VAN GOT A HEAD START back up the Richardson so they could spend more time taking photographs of the glaciers and waterfalls. Alice and I joined Pamela, Carter, and Amy in sticking with Ray and Clementine, who wanted to buy salmon to take back to Macel Falwell.

While Ray was finding a good deal on vacuum-packed salmon, the rest of us got coffee and browsed a row of souvenir shops.

"How *is* Mrs. F?" Amy finally asked Clementine.

Clementine pressed her lips together and looked out at the Narrows, a crack of worry breaking into her expression. "Every day is different," she said. We all nodded. "But she started flying places on airplanes, and she never did do that before."

OUR VAN ZOOMED ALONG a ridge carved high on a mountainside. Far below us a valley spilled out and away, mountain peaks repeating far into the distance. We were driving back to Anchorage, and Clementine spent a few hours "peeling our onions," asking us personal questions that seemed designed to figure out why we were all still single. In spite of nearly having a heart attack fielding her probing into my life and history, I provided no great revelations, and we moved on to share our favorite moments from the trip. Every person in the van named a salvation episode as a favorite experience, including myself. I nominated Alice's early encounter on that Anchorage side street as my favorite.

"I had been praying for y'all to lead people to the Lord," Ray said, lifting his voice. "Most people think they can't evangelize or they're too shy to try. They don't realize the Lord does it. And once you realize you're doing work for the Lord, the shame and embarrassment disappear."

Alice was sunk down in her seat, scrolling through pictures on her digital camera. "Why are there no women in leadership in the church?" she asked.

"Well, it's because the Bible says women shouldn't have authority over men." Ray paused for a moment. "I'm not personally opposed to it. But in the Air Force I told people I thought they should allow women chaplains and I almost got shot for it."

Clementine kicked her flip-flopped feet up on the dashboard. "Well, I think the way things are is the right way," she said.

We rode for a time in a blank silence.

After a while, Clementine tapped her fingernail on her window. "Can you imagine what it would be like to be sitting here during a big earthquake and have that mountain come down on you?" she said. She turned around in her seat to address the van. "That's what they're going to be wishing for in the tribulation—for the mountains to come down on them."

"Well thank you, Clem, for that biblical knowledge," Ray said.

Clementine folded her arms across her chest. "Somebody's got to be spiritual in this car."

She was kidding a little, but I sensed that she felt chagrined that much of our trip had been relatively secular, that she hadn't done enough to push against the avalanche of our teasing and naughty jokes, and Ray had been the rumble that started it.

After another spell of silence, she nuzzled into her headrest and asked Ray, "Do you think there'll be mountains in heaven?"

"I don't know, Clem," he said. "But we're not going to be in heaven for long. The Bible says the earth'll be destroyed and we'll come to live on a new earth. The new earth'll come from heaven. But I can't say whether or not there'll be mountains. Only He knows." Ray stole glances out the driver's side window. Creamy blue glaciers pooled on the valley floor below, encircled by wide halos of brown dirt. "Y'all see those brown parts around the glaciers?" Ray asked us. "Everything that's brown there is the area that glacier used to cover."

I held my breath. Outside Valdez we had stopped for a time at Worthington Glacier, which came pouring down the mountainside like a roaring river frozen solid. Except that when several of us walked down from the observation deck to see the glacier up close, it wasn't frozen solid at all. Up close the glacier was a slab of ice that appeared to have blue lights embedded somewhere deep inside. The ice looked so soft I felt I could karate-chop a big piece of it off. Water was coursing off the edges in sheets, shushing and tinkling on the black rocks below.

Xander and I had walked around it a bit together, and I tried to talk to him about what we were seeing—even if it was natural glacial runoff, you couldn't help but be reminded of rapid melting. But Xander was too enraptured about getting close enough to touch a glacier and by the grizzly we spied lumbering across the mountain high above us.

Al Gore and the Intergovernmental Panel on Climate Change wouldn't be awarded the Nobel Prize until that fall, and in February, eighty-six evangelical leaders had signed the Evangelical Climate Initiative, but many Evangelicals stubbornly clung to the position that there was no scientific consensus on global warming. This conclusion seemed designed to guard against wind on a fragile house of cards: the evangelical belief that Earth is only a few thousand years old. Because of this belief, many Evangelicals are unable to entertain one of Gore's more persuasive pieces of evidence in *An Inconvenient Truth*: warming trends of the past hundred years are exponentially more intense than any warming trend during the past several billion.

But now, as we all gazed down on the shrinking glaciers in the valley below us, looking more like meager snow left over from last winter than ancient masses of ice, as Ray contemplated how much larger the glaciers were when he and Clementine had lived in Alaska, I wondered whether he was getting ready to concede that the whole global warming thing might be more than liberal propaganda. Without prompting, Ray fanned out his views on the matter.

"I personally don't believe in global warming," he said. "Sure, it's a little warmer, but I honestly believe this is one of the natural processes of the earth." He spoke as if he assumed we would disagree, even though Dr. Falwell had preached a sermon on the Myth of Global Warming and I had never once seen a member of Thomas Road think twice about fueling up an SUV or dumping a soda can in the garbage. "After the flood, when these glaciers formed, I honestly believe it took a thousand or two thousand years for them to melt enough for us to notice it." He pointed to a strip of ice on the valley floor. "That glacier'll be gone in ten years."

Clementine frowned. "It's sad."

"No, it isn't."

"They're beautiful!" she cried. "What do you mean it isn't sad?"

"Because, honey," Ray said, kneading Clementine's shoulder, "the end is better than the beginning."

LYLE GOT HELD UP at security in the Anchorage airport because of a large jar of fruit preserves he had purchased for his mother and packed in his carry-on. After examining the jar, a bag screener told Lyle he'd have to check it in his luggage or throw it away. All our bags had already been checked and Lyle was growing agitated; he didn't understand the gels and liquids restriction. After a few tense moments of Lyle trying to make the bag screener understand why he had the preserves, the screener sighed and passed the jar to Alice.

"How many ounces of jelly are in that jar?" he asked.

Alice looked at the jar. "Three," she lied.

"Okay then, son," the screener said, "you can keep it."

Lyle thanked the screener and slid the jar back into his carry-on. Suddenly, he had his Bible out and was holding it up. "Sir, this is a Bible." Everyone in our group froze. Lyle didn't make the distinctions everyone else made about when and where to evangelize. Most in our group knew to limit their efforts to scheduled evangelism activities and maybe a few forced encounters at the shopping mall. Only experts like Ray evangelized to people going about their jobs. But Lyle seemed immune to the constraints of social norms. And so while the group agreed that the unsaved were all around us, only Lyle felt unilaterally emboldened to approach. At Denali, he had targeted a coffee barista, leaning across the counter and barking "*Stop!* Do you want to go to heaven?"

Now, Lyle waggled his Bible. "Do you believe in this book?"

The bag screener sighed impatiently. He told Lyle he did.

"Well—have you accepted Jesus Christ as your personal savior?"

Blood darkened the man's face and his eyes became hard as gems. "Son, I'm fifty-five years old and I served in Vietnam. If I didn't believe in Jesus, I'd be in a whole lot of trouble."

At the gate, our group laughed a little uneasily about the whole episode.

Ray chuckled. "We created an evangelism monster!"

Our flight to Chicago was overbooked. Alice wanted to see if she and I could arrange to sit together, so we waited in the long line at the gate desk. Ray was waiting in line, too, hoping to get an exit row so he and Clementine could stretch out. Behind us, a Wall Street–type paced in front of a stuffed Kodiak bear reared up on its hindquarters. The man was shouting into his cell phone, apparently at a United Airlines customer service representative. " 'Scheduling changes' is not an answer!" he screamed. "And I've got a whole line of people staring at me now, so why don't you tell me the real answer so I can tell them!"

Ray laughed and shook his head. "Whoa, buddy, don't give yourself a heart attack," he said. Two women near us in line laughed when they heard Ray and shifted toward him, commenting on the spectacle behind us. We chatted with them a while, talking about Denali Park, fishing, wildlife. Eventually, one of the women asked what our group was doing in Alaska.

"We came here on a missions trip," Ray said proudly. "We're from Lynchburg, Virginia—Jerry Falwell's church. Our goal was to get a hundred people saved, and we ended up with a hundred and one."

One of the women grabbed Ray's wrist happily and said, "Well, hal-lelujah!" The other smiled wanly, checked her watch, and shifted away. If Ray or Alice noticed, they didn't let on.

At the desk, Ray tried to massage the gate attendant with his charms. Sweat was beading her lip and her hair was frizzing wirily out of a bun. "I'm not doing any seat assignments right now," she said, eyes fixed down at her computer screen. "Some people don't even have seats!"

Ray pushed back from the counter. After a moment, he asked softly, "Can I pray for you?"

The woman coughed up a bitter little thistle of a laugh, averting her eyes. He was kidding, it seemed clear.

But then Ray extended his hand, his gold wristwatch glinting under the fluorescent lights, and held the woman's forearm. He bowed his head and squinched his eyes closed, and said rapidly, "Dear Heavenly Father, please help this woman. In Jesus' name, Amen."

I still wasn't sure if Ray was joking, although I should have known better: Ray didn't joke about prayer. And to my utter shock, the woman didn't seem at all perturbed. "I need a prayer *and* a blessing," she said, shaking her head.

Our group settled into a couple of rows of chairs to wait for boarding. Carter gave me a Valium for the flight. The man who had been shouting into the cell phone was sitting some seats away from us, his head tipped back, his hand over his eyes as if he were holding an ice pack there.

Twenty minutes later, Ray was shouting my name from the gate podium. I looked over—he was beckoning urgently to me and Alice. "Get Carter, too!" he shouted.

At the podium, he told us the gate attendant had called him over and arranged an exit row for him and Clementine, and that she was going to not only put Alice and me together, but she could put Carter with us, too. The three of us were also getting an exit row.

When the gate attendant finished reissuing our boarding passes, she looked up brightly. "Is there anyone else in your party I can help?"

Walking back to the waiting area, Ray clapped a big paw on my shoulder. "See?" he said quietly. "Power of prayer."

PHANTOM LIMB

———

OUTSIDE THE BAGGAGE CLAIM IN ROANOKE, IDLING IN THE belch-breath air of Virginia summer, our bus was waiting—cargo hatches open, AC roaring, stereo speakers atomizing Jonathan Falwell's whispering voice into the bus like fine perfume. We had arrived on a Sunday morning, just as the TRBC eleven o'clock service was drawing to a close. Jonathan was still on his sermon series about building the church—consulting the blueprints before putting up the walls. He was talking about why the Leaning Tower of Pisa was leaning, that it had been built without blueprints. We were chattering as we boarded, but once we heard what Jonathan was saying we were silenced one after another.

"Do you want to change the world? Do you want to reach people for Jesus Christ?" he whispered. "Do you want to live that kind of life of victory? That kind of life of success? That kind of life of excitement? Then we have to follow the blueprints. We have to follow the plan. We have to follow the design."

As the bus accelerated out of the airport, everyone was sitting up straight in their seats, invigorated by coincidence, proud that we seemed to be living the lives he was talking about.

Jonathan began to steer his sermon toward the invitation. "My friends, I know there are people in this room today, right here, right now, not following the designs that God has laid out. And it might be you. It might be you. You might be sitting here with all the greatest intentions. You may be sitting here with your heart ready and willing."

It was me. "We" weren't living those victorious lives, I remembered. "They" were. I was the subject of this other part.

"You are not using the blueprint that God has given to you! You are not building up your faith, and you are not studying His word, and you're not obeying His word. You're not doing it! So you have the greatest intentions, but in the end, you build something of no value."

THE BUS PULLED OVER in Ray and Clementine's little suburb in Lynchburg. They hugged and kissed us and told us they loved us, that we were their children. And as the bus pulled back on the road and the pastor and his wife slid out of view, I felt shocked and bereft, as if I'd lost them in a hard gust of wind.

Back in the lower lot at Thomas Road, siblings and parents and friends were waiting near our abandoned vehicles. Seeing them instantly shut off the ties I'd felt connecting us all. They helped transfer suitcases from the bus hold to individual trunks and backseats. It was like the last day of summer camp. The soft-shelled friendships we had developed in Alaska were about to be speared by the through lines of our lives. I waved goodbye, carrying my own bags.

And then poof—nearly two days after we left Anchorage, I was alone, unlocking my front door in Charlottesville, entering the stillness of my front hall, setting down my suitcase, which had lost a wheel in cargo and promptly toppled over.

Getting home was hardly a relief. *The greatest intentions*, I kept thinking, *but no value*.

IN THE WEEK AFTER my return from Alaska, I was taut, in a grim mood. I stood paralyzed at the foot of a few emails and bills. My cats, apparently deranged by my absence, had stained the bathtub by using it as a litterbox. On the way to pick up some eggs and bread from the grocery store, I got road rage so violent that I scared myself. My face broke out in pimples so painful they felt rooted to my brain. I was exhausted by the realization that I was going to have to brush my teeth twice a day for the rest of my life. And when I sat down to digest my notes from Alaska, straining to decipher my own handwriting, I thought each word looked more like a scribble to get the pen's ink moving than anything legible.

This should have all been banal, returning-from-a-trip type of stuff, but somehow every little plan and errand tensed me up into a whole body cramp that felt as if it could kill me if I let it.

On my drive back to Charlottesville I had decided I was going to leave the church, decided as easily as if I'd been ordered to stop going. In a way, I felt that Jonathan's sermon had constituted that order—I wasn't following their design, and I wasn't going to respond to their invitation so it was time for me to leave them alone.

I wasn't exactly thrilled about leaving, which meant no more church music, no more group therapy in the guise of sermon, no more community I could always count on to be happy to see me. It meant leaving my church friends, probably forever. My weeks would be stripped of the chemical bonds holding them together—my trips to Lynchburg. No more structure, nothing to look forward to.

Leaving also meant having to confront all of the ethically dubious stuff I'd done: I had proselytized to a little girl, helped lock her into something I didn't believe in. I had been saved and baptized without believing. I had prayed and been prayed for. I had eaten little symbols of the body of Christ while mostly contemplating my own hunger. I had cultivated intimate friendships—with Alice, with Ray and Clementine, with Carter, with Ingrid and the rest—on a foundation of lies. That was what I felt worst about: deceiving people I couldn't help but consider true friends.

I didn't have the stomach for meals and I didn't want to see anyone at all. When I slept, I had unspeakable nightmares. I felt fluish with self-loathing.

"What's happened is you realized these people are human," my mother told me.

I wasn't sure she was wrong, but I knew that wasn't the whole story.

A writer friend told me not to worry about the deception. "No one loves the one writing about them," he said. Even if they'd known from the start I was writing a book, he said, they would probably still hate me in the end. I would be absolved by my fellow poachers. As Joan Didion put it, "writers are always selling somebody out."

None of that made me feel better. When I started at Thomas Road I expected to go in as a sort of anthropologist. I expected to discover the sociological underpinnings for evangelical wackiness. I never imagined that I would feel a kind of belonging. Because beyond basically appreciating my friends as fellow human beings, I finally understood what it felt like to believe you knew something that had the power to improve the lives of others. You felt compelled to share it. And whose fault was their ignorance? It was hard to blame them entirely.

There were idle moments, taking a long shower or lying awake at night, when I imagined getting rid of this self-loathing by staying undercover forever. Could I be a Christian woman to a Christian man? Could I hold his hand and my zipper-bagged Bible as we hurried into church together? Could I look at him across a basket of bottomless fries and be content knowing he considered it part of his Christian duty to treat me well? Could I consider it part of my duty to have his children? Maybe I could be like Ray, living on having prayed the prayer, but secretly not really believing it until one day the truth opened and washed over my real life, like a black-and-white movie blooming into Technicolor. And then, could I be satisfied living on the reassurance that God was on my side?

I couldn't. I couldn't work back from who I was or what I believed, and in truth, I didn't want to. I preferred analysis, reason, and the satisfying realism of hard truths. I didn't mind leaving some corners of the universe cast in the shadow of ambiguity. Moral structure might have been the key to happiness, but maybe happiness wasn't the only thing worth unlocking.

WHEN I RETURNED the next Sunday morning for EPIC and church, everyone smiled to see me. Ray and I hugged, and I hugged Clementine, who looked a little overdone, prettier in her natural Alaska look, with messy hair and no rouge. She laughed as she told me about a picture Carter had taken of me, making a fish mouth and bulging out my eyes.

Before EPIC sermon, Ray asked that members of the Salt and Light group get up and share an impression from Alaska with everyone. As Pamela spoke about God's greatness, as Ingrid spoke about the evangelism possibilities in Lynchburg, as Alice described the elevation she'd felt leading the homeless woman to the Lord, as Ray said how proud he was seeing us all reach our potential as evangelizers I decided I really didn't want to lie. That would be my challenge for myself: never to lie to them again.

When it was my turn, I spoke about Alice's evangelizing to the homeless woman in Anchorage without invoking God. I said how much it moved me to take part in an effort to reach out to people who were desperately in need (of *blank*), how inspired I'd been by the commitment of my fellow missionaries. When I sat down, I felt a little cleaner.

Donny's father was visiting and gave a guest sermon on meeting his current wife after Donny's mother's death. He and his wife took turns telling the story: Donny's stepmother had dated men on and off all her life, and had prayed all the while for God to send her a husband. When she finally met Donny's father seventeen years after she began to pray, she knew her prayer had finally been answered. She and her husband both saw their eventual meeting as a sort of longwave miracle, arranged by God. And I thought, Who's to say it wasn't?

On our way down the hall to church, my girlfriends shared their own prayers for finding a man. Britney told us she had stopped praying to meet someone, and started praying instead to know the man God had already prepared for her. Laura and Alice both liked that notion—it somehow removed desperation from the equation, because it assumed a happy ending.

Alice told us that right after we got back from Alaska she'd gone on two dates with an incredible guy: funny, handsome, educated, successful. But he wasn't a Christian. When she had asked him about religion, he had said something nebulous about hoping he would meet someone right for him and his daughter, and that life would continue after this one for all of them.

On their second date, when he asked her what non-negotiables there were in her life, she said God.

"Wow," he said. "Most people say friends and family."

When she asked him the same question, he told her he'd never let anyone come between him and his daughter.

Alice looked at us meaningfully, and I understood how her look was finishing his sentence: *not even Jesus.* She didn't want to, but she knew she had to let him go. She searched our eyes as if she wanted us to tell her different.

Laura gave her a pitying look, as if she were a child learning a hard truth. "He's not a Christian, Alice."

No, and neither was I, and the sad way Alice shrugged I feared that distance would always be between us. But when church started in the gloriously bright vault of the sanctuary and we rose from our seats, I was amazed at how great I felt to have that worship music exploding around me again. That feeling of glitter dust sparkling down all around drew my eyes heavenward, and, singing barrel-chested, I had the sensation that silken veils were slipping just beneath my skin.

Jonathan was preaching about the vision of building the church, standing onstage next to a little chapel made of cardboard bricks, as if it had been constructed for a school pageant. Blueprints curled on the floor at his feet, a big white cross staked nearby. Forty-five people had joined the church the Sunday before, the Sunday we returned from Alaska. They hadn't come for miracles, he told us, they came looking for the miracle worker. "As you look at all the religions of our world, you'll notice that all the leaders of those religions are dead. Mohammed? Dead. Buddha? Dead. L. Ron Hubbard? Dead. Mary Baker Glover Patterson Eddy?"—the founder of Christian Science—"Dead. Jesus Christ is alive. He is *alive*. And it's incredible to think that we know, without a shadow of a doubt, that Jesus Christ is God. We must build our lives and our church on that foundational truth that Jesus Christ is God. You ask me how I know he lives? He lives within my heart. We know it."

Each wall of the cardboard church symbolized a "load-bearing truth" that would make the building last. Jesus is God. Jesus paid it all. Jesus is risen. Jesus secures our future. And there was a fifth—running through the middle of the house—Jesus is coming back. These were the truths we would need moving forward. "It is through those truths that we find—victory."

I didn't stay for Sunday night services. Jonathan Falwell, proud of our soul-haul from Alaska, had asked that the Salt and Light group go up in front of the congregation to present our slideshow, including video I'd taken of Xander's baptism. The thought of someone passing me a microphone so that I could give my testimonial to hundreds of listening Christians sickened me as physically as if I'd tried to fill up on candy.

A FANCY DESK CHAIR arrived on my porch in Charlottesville the next day. It was a gift from my mother. I thought she was trying to send me a message: *Sit your butt down and stay home.* And I was going to—except that I wanted to see everyone's Alaska pictures. Because they were important for this book? Or because I wanted to soak in nostalgia? I wasn't sure. Wyatt had everyone's pictures collected for the slideshow I'd missed, and in an email he offered to save them to a disc for me. The files were too large to send. It seemed as if I had to go back.

I decided to go and try to talk as little as possible, leave as soon as

EPIC concluded. Someday I'd have to tell them about this whole thing, and I looked forward to it with a peculiar combination of impatience and bone terror.

Back in Lynchburg that Wednesday, Ray met me at the bottom of the wheelchair ramp, and hugged his arm around me. I felt safe and strong under there. He told me he'd brought a bachelor for my consideration, and pointed to a blond boy wearing a polo shirt and a big gold watch, talking to Alice with his hands on his hips. We were all going out to Macado's for dinner afterward.

I said, thanks, Ray, but I couldn't.

"Well, I'm doing my job," he said irritably.

Alice called me over to join her at the "hot girls" table in the front of the room, but I saw the weird doctor sitting there, grinning and giving me romance eyes. I went to sit at a table off to the side with Clementine, Amy, her fiancé, and Lyle.

Over the next several weeks Ray would be "peeling our onions" on Wednesday nights. Tonight we would talk about being single, and next week Ray was going to start a series on finding our purpose in life. Some people were going to be mad at him, he said, because he was going to show them that the thing they'd thought was their purpose was all wrong. We were going to be revealed. "The thing about singles is, you only know what they want to show you. There's a lot they hide."

Definitely time for me to duck out, I thought.

But when we watched the Salt and Light slideshow, loving tears warmed my eyes. Carter in his brown Zacchaeus robe, Pamela with her hand clamped on the boy's wrist in Children's Church, Alice and I in the motorboat, gazing up at Ray as he steered us up the Salcha River.

"Like, wow," Ray said.

After the slideshow, we submitted our prayer requests, and I asked for prayers for my stepfather, who was dealing with a whole tangle of family issues. And when Clementine sent up my request and added a prayer for his salvation, I found I wasn't bothered a whit.

On a projection screen hung low over the stage, the words of Psalm 139 glowed. Ray read it aloud.

> *O LORD, you have searched me*
> *and you know me.*
> *You know when I sit and when I rise;*

you perceive my thoughts from afar.
You discern my going out and my lying down;
you are familiar with all my ways.
Before a word is on my tongue
you know it completely, O LORD.
You hem me in—behind and before;
you have laid your hand upon me.
Such knowledge is too wonderful for me,
too lofty for me to attain.
Where can I go from your Spirit?
Where can I flee from your presence?
If I go up to the heavens, you are there;
if I make my bed in the depths, you are there.
If I rise on the wings of the dawn,
if I settle on the far side of the sea,
even there your hand will guide me,
your right hand will hold me fast.
If I say, "Surely the darkness will hide me
and the light become night around me,"
even the darkness will not be dark to you;
the night will shine like the day,
for darkness is as light to you.
For you created my inmost being;
you knit me together in my mother's womb.
I praise you because I am fearfully and wonderfully made;
your works are wonderful,
I know that full well.
My frame was not hidden from you
when I was made in the secret place.

"The secret place is, you know," Ray clarified, "when a man and a woman get together and do the natural thing."

When I was woven together in the depths of the earth,
your eyes saw my unformed body.
All the days ordained for me
were written in your book
before one of them came to be.

How precious to me are your thoughts, O God!
  How vast is the sum of them!
Were I to count them,
  they would outnumber the grains of sand.
When I awake,
  I am still with you.
If only you would slay the wicked, O God!
  Away from me, you bloodthirsty men!
They speak of you with evil intent;
  your adversaries misuse your name.
Do I not hate those who hate you, O LORD,
  and abhor those who rise up against you?
I have nothing but hatred for them;
  I count them my enemies.
Search me, O God, and know my heart;
  test me and know my anxious thoughts.
See if there is any offensive way in me,
  and lead me in the way everlasting.

The beauty of this psalm unfurled in me like great spools of ribbon. God-love—I felt I finally saw it. Human love was this awkward thing, like the most delicious fish you could ever hope to eat but you had to eat it alive. Sometimes it made you feel desperate and crazed, as though you'd have to become the person to ever have enough of them. But God-love, the love in the psalm, the love in *Jesus loves you*—that was Mobius strip love, love with no beginning or end, love that was both calm and complete, unflinching in the face of anything you could reveal about yourself. Who wouldn't want that? I certainly did, especially in that moment—knowing the secrets in my own heart, knowing that soon they'd be revealed.

But wanting it still didn't make me believe it.

Ray put some questions up on the screen, and asked that each table come up with some answers:

1. What's a good thing about being single?
2. What's a tough thing about being single?
3. What do people assume about you because you're single?
4. What age should people get married by?
5. What's one thing I never expected about being single?

As each table began to rumble in discussion, Clementine leaned over and whispered, "Jerry Jr.'s assistant's assistant is single, twenty-nine, and asked if my daughters had any friends. I gave him three names: Ursula, Gina, and Alice."

Jerry Jr.'s assistant's assistant? This was a high compliment, I knew, an invitation to draw closer to the church. I thanked her.

She snapped up in her chair as if I'd said something insulting. "But you've got your date! Did you go on your date?"

At the Beaver Creek Lodge in North Pole, I had checked email on Wyatt's computer and received a message from a friend of a friend, asking if I'd like to go out with him. The guy was a Mennonite, which honestly would have turned me off in an instant before I'd started at Thomas Road. How could I date someone who would name his religion as one of the most important elements of his identity? The God thing was too weird. But now I really didn't care. What was the difference? At least I knew he felt accountable to *somebody*. Alice had been there when I got the email. I told her about the date, of course, and then in the van on our way down to Valdez Alice told Ray and Clementine. Ray ribbed me all the way down the Hutchinson: "You're gonna have to wear one'a them homemade dresses to your own wedding."

Now I smiled at Clementine. "We're going out next week," I said.

Lyle, sitting next to me, was confused. "You're getting married?"

"It's just a date," I said.

Clementine leaned in and her warm smile fell across me in beams. "Ray doesn't want you going on that date," she said, her eyes searching mine to add meaning to her words. "He's not happy about it."

I looked at her pretty face and wished there was some way we could have become friends without my having to be Christian. "Because he's a Mennonite?" I asked.

"Yeah," she said, and a little laugh budded between us.

When each table had answers ready, we discussed them together. People liked being single for the free time, for the ability to live as an individual. "I'm not broke," one guy said. More time for friends and family, I said. Other people said you can do what you want, when you want, with whoever you want. Ray gave us a skeptical look, said, "I don't know about *that*," and sent the whole room into titillated hysterics.

Hearing the difficult things plucked feathers off my sinking heart. No one to listen to your ideas. Hard to make big purchases alone. Going to functions by yourself. People think you're weird, desperate. "I'm afraid I won't be able to share my ideas of what a marriage should be like with another person," Lyle said. People think you're difficult, I added. People think you're incomplete. People think something is physically wrong with you. Loneliness, everyone said, *loneliness*. Most people never expected they would be single for so long.

I was just as alone as everyone else, and yet I felt pain for them in a way I didn't feel for myself. Somehow their loneliness seemed tragic. These people tried so hard to be good, served their God and prayed their modest prayers, and still—God had yielded nobody.

Only one girl had an age by which a person should be married. "Thirty or thirty-three," she said. Now everyone was insulted, and side conversations started up in a chorus of disagreement.

"Whenever you're mature enough," someone said.

"It's case by case," Alice said.

"Whenever God sends you someone."

Ray contemplated our answers, nodding. "You know, a lot of singles *choose* to be single." He set the heavy parcel of his gaze down on me. "You don't realize it, but the choices you're making are making you single. If you'd just make different choices, you might not be single!" His eyes surfed the room. "But some of you are going to be single for the rest of your lives, and that's okay. God has chosen some people to be celibate. Not very many people. But if it's God's plan for you that you're going to be single for the rest of your life then you need to accept that. The Apostle Paul was a single, and let's not forget Jesus. But if God wants you to be married, if you make the right choices and pray about it, I guarantee you you'll be married."

What were these choices? Did he mean *standards*?

After class, Ethan, Ingrid, and Alice came over to say hello. We were catching up in a superficial way—how hard the time change was, feeling tired all the time—when Ray came over and hugged Alice and me as if he were going to try carrying us away. "How come y'all weren't sittin' together?" he asked. "Y'all get a divorce?"

Alice smiled at me, and I said something about not wanting to sit right in front. Clementine called me over to speak to her and another woman before I had to say anything more. "Ray says we've got to get you down to Lynchburg," she said. The woman—Ms. Nancy—had an apartment she could rent to me. I could move as soon as I wanted.

I told Clementine I'd think about it, and started backing up the wheelchair ramp, saying good-bye, good-bye. Alice and Ingrid called out their good-byes, Carter, too, and Wyatt and Mitchell waved from the back of the room. "You sure you don't want to come to Macado's?" Ray called. "Last chance."

"Next time," I said.

HEADING OUT OF LYNCHBURG, the sun floating down over the grassy hills to the west, I had a rawness in the back of my chest as if I were being ripped away from something to which I'd been grafted. As I crossed the bridge over the James I winced at the river's beauty—its waters lit up silver, reflecting the last light off into the distance.

AFTER MISSING ONLY TWO days of church—a Sunday and a Wednesday—phone calls began to dribble in. I let them go to voice mail. Ray left a message saying, "We love you and we miss you." He told me he had talked again to the man in charge of adjuncts at Liberty, who said I just needed to send my application in and I would be all set up to teach. Alice called and said she was thinking of me. Carter phoned again and again.

In Charlottesville, I was freaking out. I had nightmares every night. During the day, I was lethargic. I couldn't write or read. I was often tempted to throw out my Alaska notes in disgust.

Instead of writing I dragged my laptop into bed and watched old TRBC services on my computer, horrifying myself by singing along to the songs I knew, even feeling a smidge transported by the sound of "Days of Elijah" piping through my laptop speakers.

A friend asked me if I thought I was depressed. Not really, I said, but that was a lie.

I felt awful if I slept late on Sundays, couldn't figure out how to organize my day, couldn't relax. I missed hearing Ray preach. I really missed my friends. I missed the warmth, the easy smiles people offered me when I walked into the room. I missed singing at the top of my lungs in church. I wanted to be able to go back without having to talk to anyone.

My stepfather suggested I revisit a book he had sent me called *Cults in Our Midst,* in particular the section on leaving a cult.

I got all kinds of suggestions from friends about how to remove myself from church: "Say you're having a crisis of faith!" "Say you moved out of the state!" "Say you're going to church in Charlottesville!"

I was sick from lying. I had a sour stomach all the time.

Bad things began to happen, and I superstitiously aligned them with leaving church. My cat died, a friend betrayed me, men rejected me. Things had seemed so easy and lucky when I had been going to church. Jobs had fallen into my lap, compliments were forthcoming. I had always had somewhere to go, people looking forward to seeing me. Now, it seemed, I was alone.

My homespun life philosophy suddenly seemed unbearably flaky. *Positive out, positive in*. Oh, as if I was just in a negative-out, negative-in rut? I felt punished for my absence at church. Punished, maybe, by God.

I went around as if draped with a heavy net. Was it just a mind net? Could it be a God net?

ONE NIGHT ON THE PHONE my mother asked me what advice I might give to someone in my situation. As I thought about this question, another call beeped in. It was Carter. "Mom," I said, pressing Ignore, "I can't even think to answer that question right now."

My stepfather's advice on leaving church was simple and seemed to neatly fuse together the fragments troubling me. He suggested I tell people at church that I was going through some personal issues and I needed some time and space to resolve them. This was close to the truth, he said, and would constitute a specific request for the contact to end.

"Don't be surprised if they try even harder," my stepfather warned. "And if they do, you know you're dealing with a cult situation. But eventually the calls *will* peter out."

I did it. I sent emails to Ray, Alice, and Carter, saying essentially what my stepfather had suggested I say: I was wrestling with some personal matters, and would be staying in Charlottesville indefinitely, trying to work out my problems. I missed them, missed church, appreciated the phone calls, but needed some time alone.

Ray didn't respond to my email—I presumed he merely didn't check it—but the emails I got back from Alice and Carter were respectful, affectionate, personal, and agonizing to read.

ON A THURSDAY a few weeks later, the calls and emails started up again. The fact that they all came on the same day led me to suspect there had been a conversation about me at Wednesday Community Interest Group the night before, a group resolution to reach out to me.

"Remember, I've got three children your age," Ray said in his voice mail. "Whatever you're going through, you can bet I've been through it, too."

I pictured those I had betrayed most: Alice submitting a prayer request for me during Prayer 911 on Wednesday night, her pink Bible on her knees as she lifted me up to God, later puzzling over my absence as she locked the refreshment closet for the night; Carter at his parents' house, praying in darkness at his bedside with his forehead pressed against clasped hands; Ray and Clementine on their back patio in the colorless evening light, saying worried prayers for me before forking into lasagna and strawberry cake.

Together, I felt certain, they were showering me with prayers. But they weren't going to do any good, for anybody.

I had recurring nightmares about church. In one, I am in a small sanctuary with the Thomas Road congregation. I have come to sing in a crowd and get Feeling X again, and I'm hoping to leave before the end of the sermon, before anyone recognizes me. But church people, people I don't even know, recognize me and call my name, and I have to run away.

In another, I park in the church parking lot to visit a public library, and by the time I get back to my car, other cars are rolling into the lot for church services. A girl is sitting in an attendant booth at the parking lot gates. She won't let me out of the gate because I don't have a church pass in my car.

"What's your name?" she asks, smiling.

I tell her. I say it quietly, afraid to call attention to myself. She makes me repeat it a few times.

"Why you talk like that?"

"I'm from California," I said.

"Where's that?" she asks with disgust.

In another dream Ray asks me to come before EPIC, to tell them why I went undercover. In the Communication Training Center, Ray is pacing behind me, muttering angry comments. I'm trying to explain why I did it—why I went undercover, why it was so important to see Evangelicals up close—but the EPIC singles are so upset they begin to puke. One and then another, and soon *everyone* is puking on their own feet. A man I've never seen, a man with a soothing, untroubled expression, puts his hand on my shoulder. "Don't worry," he says. "It's not you. There's something in the water."

The worst dreams are about Alice. Waiting for an elevator to take me up to the offices of a fashion magazine that wants to take my picture, I find myself next to a hospital bed set up next to the elevator banks. Alice lies on the bed, unconscious, and her mother cries at her bedside. They don't see me, and I have to decide whether I can live with myself if I don't pay my respects.

In Alice's living room I sit on her couch as she moves around her kitchen, aware of me but not looking at me.

In another dream I have a manila envelope full of time sheets I'm supposed to submit to a mail room at church, which, in the dream, is right next to where EPIC meets. I get to the mail room minutes after they've shuttered the windows and cannot submit the time sheets. I hear voices in the EPIC room next door—Ingrid's, Britney's. Suddenly, I hear Alice's cheerful voice coming closer. I turn to run outside. Will she recognize my hair and winter coat as I run away? Of course. She calls my name and runs after me. Outside, I realize how running looks. I stop and come back to her, masking my terror with wild tears.

"Gina, are you okay?"

I am intentionally incomprehensible, stammering. I am crying because I'm scared, but I am pretending to cry because I'm in crisis.

"Is there anything I can do for you?" Alice asks.

I whine louder and louder and wake up.

In all these nightmares, I'm the furtive stranger. I'm the terrible thing.

Am I as terrible as my dreams suggest? Are the revelations I've gathered about Evangelicals eclipsed by the methods I've used to gather them? I don't think so. I give a lot of thought to what Ray once said: that if I don't love you—and you—and you, God's not going to give me anyone else to love. I feel a version of this about our country. If we don't love Evangelicals, if we don't make an effort to understand and accept them, to eat the fish even as it wriggles in our hands, we'll always be each other's nemeses. We'll always be trying to drown each other out.

Threaten them, ridicule them, celebrate their humiliation, and you create a toxic dump, fertile ground for a ferocious adversary to rise, again and again. But listen to them, include them in the public conversation, understand the sentiments behind their convictions, and you invent the possibility of kinship.

ONE NIGHT, sometime in the middle of my year with EPIC Alice and I were going to Campus Church after Wednesday night class and we ran into Britney. She was skipping church to get dinner with a friend.

"While you go get fed at Panera we're going to go get spiritually fed at church," Alice said, all faux sassy.

We watched Liberty students get dunked through the square hole in the baptistry, and as the pastor introduced each student by name, dorm, and hometown, friends sitting with us in the sanctuary cheered and hollered.

The sanctuary lights dimmed and a smoke machine released tufted lamb's wool clouds into the air as the entire sanctuary rose to its feet, hands skyward, belting out the songs a Christian rock band played from the altar.

The preaching pastor that night was Johnnie Moore, the cute young pastor, wearing a red track jacket and distressed jeans. He was the guy I'd heard about at the roller rink, the one who would lead Britney's mission trip to India.

"He's cute!" I told Alice.

"He's single," she whispered, "but short."

Pulpitless, Johnnie perched on a wooden stool and told us a story. Recently he'd found himself famished in nearby Amherst, late at night, where the only place open was a McDonald's. Johnnie tried to get a meal there, but their credit card machine was down. "I'm a postmodern twenty-something," he told the sanctuary. "I don't use cash. I have my debit card and some pennies."

Aggravated and starving, he went to a nearby grocery to get some food, and found himself in a self-checkout line behind an old woman who was rubbing her packages on the scanner, not looking for the barcode. The packages wouldn't scan, so she began to bang them fruitlessly against the scanner. Rage began to boil in Johnnie—senseless, wild rage.

Now, Johnnie pointed us to a passage in Matthew, where Peter asks Jesus how many times he should be expected to forgive a brother who sins against him. "Don't forgive them seven times, but seventy-seven times," Jesus told him.

"We have to think that's our equivalent of seven trillion times," Johnnie said. "It's not in our nature to be as forgiving as Jesus, but you have to choose to forgive. You can do that because you have Christ to help you. And you're never more like Christ than when you're forgiving the unforgivable."

As Alice and I walked out to the parking lot after church that night, she was talking about how much she loved one of the songs we sang, "Holy, Holy Is God Almighty," but I was distracted: Johnnie Moore's sermon had been strikingly similar to a commencement address David Foster Wallace gave at Kenyon College in 2005, one I'd read and reread online for its wisdom on living at peace with others. After describing a similarly aggravating grocery store scenario, Wallace gave this advice: ". . . if you really learn how to pay attention . . . it will actually be within your power to experience a crowded, hot, slow, consumer hell–type situation as not only meaningful, but sacred, on fire with the same force that made the stars: love, fellowship, the mystical oneness of all things deep down. Not that that mystical stuff is necessarily true. The only thing that's capital-T True is that you get to decide how you're gonna try to see it."

So this—this became the basis of my love for Evangelicals: I was going to choose to see the mystical oneness. And once I started to see it that way, loving them wasn't very hard to do.

In some sense, these days I'm just as I always was: godless and churchless, sure that when we die, we're dead. There is no part of me that's me forever.

And yet everyone who knows me says I'm different. I think it's because in the part of me that's me for now, there *is* something new, an invisible socket, a phantom limb extending from it: the friends I had and lost who forever enlarged my view of the world. I can sense them even now.

EPILOGUE

———

DURING THE TIME I SPENT SINKING INTO LIFE AT THOMAS Road, and during the two subsequent years of climbing back out, I often pictured what it would be like returning to Lynchburg to reveal myself. But whenever someone asked me about going back there, I'd say, "I don't even want to think about it."

But I was thinking about it. Before Jerry Falwell died, I imagined myself someday perching on a wingback chair in his sunny office, a corona of light tracing his white hair as he listened to my story. He'd smile as if he'd already heard everything I'd come to say. When I finished, he'd tip back in his chair and reshuffle my narrative to imply the probable outcome that I'd become a believer.

"You know, Gina," he'd say, hands on his armrests glowing white, "no man was born a believer. The Lord is every bit as much yours as he is mine, and it's never too late to come on home to Him."

I didn't think Falwell would focus on what I had done, and I didn't think he'd be angry. He'd been scrutinized for so long and he didn't seem to think he had anything to hide. Besides, by infiltrating his church and lying about my identity it would seem that I had done him the favor of confirming his every assertion about godless liberals. Now all he'd see in me, I felt sure, was my potential to become another amazing footnote in the great book of Thomas Road conversion stories.

But Jerry Falwell was dead, and the church I walked into on a sunny Wednesday in May 2009 wasn't his anymore. I had no idea whether the people who knew me, the people to whom the church belonged, would be so philosophical about it. Picturing my return to Lynchburg I had a vague plan to gather everyone around a table at TGIFriday's to tell them about my book. When it did come time to actually go back, I realized how foolish it would be to make a group announcement like that. It would seem callous, generalizing, as if I thought of all the people I'd known as a single body, a body I was coming to put on alert.

Once I decided that I was just going to talk to Alice and Ray in turn, I felt fine. In fact, I felt better than I had in years. Since I'd left Thomas Road I'd experienced occasional spells of fear that I was a bad person, so bad that I didn't even know the depths of my badness. I had become a writing teacher, and one of the things I always said to my students was, "First, tell the truth."

How could I be this person, the one who saw honesty as both the first moral rule and the precondition for anything of value, but also the one who had lied to dozens of people? How could I be a person who respects the reverence of others, who wouldn't dare to lie about what I believe, and also the one who plunged unworthily into a baptismal pool and helped guide a little girl into the arms of a God I thought was fictional?

Knowing I was going to finally tell the truth was enough to make me feel a bit freer from all that angst. Of course, I wanted forgiveness, but if no one wanted to give it that would be the punishment I'd suffer for the things I'd done. That seemed fair.

I emailed Alice and Ray and asked them each to meet with me. I told them I couldn't begin to say how sorry I was for disappearing without an explanation.

"You don't have to give me any explanation," Alice wrote in her reply, "but I would so love to catch up with you!"

Ray seemed a bit more circumspect. "Great to hear from you. I figured you were a CIA person and had a task to accomplish," he wrote. "Just kidding."

Ray's spy joke came as a little capsule of relief. In some sense I figured that meant he was somewhat prepared. But Alice—there was only tenderness in her response, and that made me very nervous.

WHEN I DROVE DOWN 29 to Lynchburg it was a perfect spring morning, and green trees cheered along the highway like boosters at a race. Alice called to say Ray had asked if he could meet with me first; he had to go to North Carolina that afternoon with Jonathan Falwell. I called Ray to arrange details.

"Do you want to meet on Main Street or in my office?" he asked.

I pictured trying to find my way to downtown Lynchburg, and then I pictured Main Street—all those empty storefronts along the James. Why would Ray want to meet there anyway?

"I'll just come to church," I said.

He was silent for a moment, and I realized so much time had passed that I'd forgotten there was a second Main Street at Thomas Road.

I added, "To your office, I mean."

Soon I was gliding across Main Street's dark marble expanse, smiling at everyone I passed. I stopped to consider the empty, inviting swoop of sanctuary seats, to buy water at the Lion and Lamb Café, to peer into the darkened EPIC room. I felt serene and comfortable. I'd missed this place. And now I was able to come back as myself, for a single, clean purpose.

Even though I'd never been to Ray's office I had a sense where to find it: I knew where Jerry Falwell's parking space had been, and Ray once said he missed the sound of Falwell blowing the train horn in his GMC truck as he pulled into his spot below the window.

Clicking down the hall I knew would lead me to Ray, I heard his voice several yards before I'd cleared his doorway: "Hey, girl!"

When I heard the delight in that voice I clenched up, realizing just how badly this could go, just how precipitous the drop between who Ray thought I was and who I really was. I turned into his office and he was already up from his desk to hug me.

"You knew it was me?" I asked.

"I heard somebody," he said.

Ray looked different. He was now completely hairless—he'd always been Bic-bald on top, but now his goatee was gone too. He looked softer, heavier. Tired. Outside the temperature was in the 70s, but Ray wore a thick Coogi sweater and corduroy pants. His smile seemed to weaken as he noticed my frigidity. We settled into chairs on either side of his desk, on which a Big Gulp soda cup sat in a puddle of its own condensation. Framed photographs lined the top of a high bookshelf against the wall. A soft-focus 8 × 10 portrait of Clementine smiled down benevolently. Ray slapped his hands on his desk and smiled afresh. "So what's going on, girl?"

"I've got a lot to tell you," I said, "and if you don't mind, I'd like to get it right out of the way." For a chilling instant, his face was perfectly neutral, and I realized it was the last moment he would think of me as this other girl—as a member of the flock. But as I tipped into the new moment, I felt my stiffness melt off mercifully: it was the end of lying.

"I haven't been honest with you about who I am," I said in a big exhale. "I'm not a Christian, and I never have been." I told him about growing up in Berkeley, thinking I was born an atheist the way some people are born Italian. I told him about coming to Virginia for graduate school, about meeting Christians and discovering an intolerance I hadn't known was in me. "I had an idea for a book," I said. A lot of books were coming out about evangelical Christians by people like me that were very divisive and judgmental. I wanted to try to write something more sensitive and intimate. I wanted to try to relate to evangelical Christians myself, but I didn't know how to do that, given that my background was so different. I thought the best way to figure out what it was like in churches was to go undercover. So I started coming to Thomas Road in 2005, and in 2006, I sold a book to write about my experience pretending to be a Christian.

As I spoke, I gripped him with the kind of eye contact I hoped would let him know I was ready to tell him everything. And the character of his gaze began to shift. Warmth left his eyes, as if some facet of his vision had stopped working. His mouth set.

I had misgivings all along about being dishonest, I told him. "There were times I thought I could've written just as good a book if I hadn't pretended at all. But I still pursued the project." When we went to Alaska, I was destabilized by how close I felt to everyone. So when we came back I decided I couldn't lie anymore. I started to confront how wrong it was for me to feign belief in something that other people considered the most serious thing in the universe.

For a while I thought I wasn't going to be able to write the book. I came around on the other side of that time thinking that I still had the opportunity to do what I initially set out to do, which was write something that would promote tolerance. To write something that would help people like me feel less nervous about evangelical Christians. To show them how I came to terms with believers.

"So that's what the book is," I said. "It's not a love letter. But it's certainly not an exposé. It's the story of me learning to relate to Christians."

Ray was looking at me coldly.

"I'm not coming here to ask you for forgiveness," I said, "because I don't think that's a reasonable thing for me to ask. I'm here because my book is about learning to respect you. And in keeping with that motive, I need to be the one to tell you about it, and I need to be available for whatever questions you have."

In saying this, in speaking to Ray so professionally, I realized I was exerting a kind of power over him. I was presenting myself as a serious adult when he'd only ever thought of me as one of his goofy children. This knocked him off balance. He nodded and looked around the room a bit. Then he chuckled and said, "You really did have some people going."

I shook my head. I feared he'd missed the point.

"You won that evangelism contest, didn't you?" He sucked his cheeks. "I'm running my mind back over the things I said. Is there going to be stuff in there that's embarrassing to people? I mean, in Alaska . . ."

The book wasn't like that, I said. I tried to tell the truth about what I saw, leaving out information that seemed too personal.

He nodded. "When you left, we were real worried about you."

"I can only imagine," I said. "I'm very sorry."

"When you left, you were getting ready to go out on a date with a guy you'd only met once. You were up there all alone, without your parents or nobody. We thought he might've hurt you, killed you."

Hearing this made me feel sick. I hadn't thought they would worry like that.

"Clementine felt sure you'd got pregnant. I thought maybe he raped you and you got pregnant and didn't want to tell nobody because you were ashamed."

"Oh no," I said. I should have known they would think along these lines; when they thought of what might make a woman feel unable to show her face, this narrative would come to mind.

"We thought about coming up there to look for you, but we decided that might make it worse. I remember we'd sit around thinking, What are we going to do about it?"

I spilled over with apologies. "I didn't know how to tell you I was okay without having to lie about anything else. I'm so sorry I worried you. If I could do it over . . . well, I still don't know what I'd do differently."

"When you first started at EPIC me and Clem felt sorry for you," Ray said. "You were all alone and didn't have anyone up in Charlottesville."

He was telling me this in part to make me feel guilty; it was designed to make me see the extent to which I'd taken advantage of them. This wasn't something he needed to do. I felt it already.

Ray took a long pull from the giant soda cup on his desk and set it down. "Well, I ain't mad at you. I can tell you there are going to be some people who are disappointed. But I'm not. I don't have any hard feelings."

He'd run into Alice that morning at church, and they had been jumping for joy that they were both going to see me. I told him I thought at the very least he'd had some inkling of what I was coming to say, given his email.

"Not a clue," he said, and thought for a minute. "Did you have all of your 'wows' in there from Alaska?"

I did.

"Did you tell all about how amazing our trip was?"

"In my way," I said. "I think I experienced everything differently since I'm not a believer."

"Well," Ray said, "now I've got something to pray about." He reached across his desk and picked up his thick, soft Bible. "What I'll tell you is you get alone with this book"—he held it up at me the way he'd held it up at the Rescue Mission in Alaska—"and you say, 'All right, God. If you're real, show me.'" He set his Bible down and chuckled to himself. "And boy, watch out."

We caught up a little. I had moved to Washington, D.C., I told him, and was teaching writing at a university. He couldn't believe I still wasn't married.

"Mitchell got married, you know. Clem said, 'I never thought I'd say it about Mitchell, but she ain't good enough for him.'"

Ray wasn't the EPIC pastor anymore. Last year he'd gone to the doctor to see about a kidney stone. The doctor found a lump the size of a pinhead in his prostate, and it was cancerous. He and Clementine went up to Johns Hopkins and Ray had his prostate removed. Just this week he'd gone through his thirty-eighth round of radiation. He'd gained twenty-five pounds. "It's my own fault," he said mournfully. "I wasn't watching what I was eating."

So last year was full of trials for Ray. Each of his children had run into problems. "I said, 'Lord, how much can one man take?'" He sighed. "I don't mean to feel sorry for myself. Bad things happen to good and bad people and everything in between."

But prospects were looking up. When Ray came back to Thomas Road they offered him a counseling position. So now he counsels singles, couples, not all of them affiliated with church. "Sometimes people just call the church and say, 'I hear y'all offer counseling.'"

It was time to go. I had to meet Alice, and Ray had to get a plane.

He regarded me evenly. "I hope you'll come and see us whenever you want to, and you'll know whenever you have dark times, that there's a man and a woman who love you, me and Clem, and we're here to talk whenever you need us. We don't have to talk about Jesus and the apostles or nothing. Just—whenever you need us."

I was overcome with a kind of misty appreciation for this gesture, and not because I was in the least surprised that Ray was capable of such generosity. Ray's swift, dignified readiness to weather any type of news and still emerge a giver was stunning to behold, and a powerful blessing to receive. This unusual largesse was what I loved most about him. I thanked him, and said I genuinely hoped we'd stay in touch.

"Girl, I wanna be the redneck preacher at your wedding," he said. "Just don't make it too long, or I may not be around."

"Not sure I have much control over it," I said. I drank in his face and felt the full gravitational force of how much I cared for him. I searched for something to say to communicate the depth of that feeling. "I just really hope you stay in good health."

Ray smiled. "Well, the worst thing that'll happen is I get to go to heaven. But I've got a family I'm not quite ready to leave behind."

I nodded.

"I'd like to say a prayer with you," Ray said.

"Of course," I said.

He stretched an arm across his desk and bowed his head. I bowed mine. "Dear Father, we do love you; thank you that you love us." He thanked God for for bringing me there and for my honesty. "You know her heart. Guide her and reveal yourself to her, protect her and watch over her in Washington."

We hugged good-bye. "Clem'll be sad she missed you," he said. "Come back and see us soon."

I didn't answer him. Whether or not I came back largely hinged on how Alice took the news.

ALICE WAS WAITING for me at Panera. I tried not to smile upon seeing her, but the sight of my long-lost friend lifted my heart.

"Well, you still look like Gina," she said, eyeing me a little warily.

We ordered our sandwiches without saying much. She was waiting for me to speak, but I could barely look at her directly until we sat down. And then I told her everything, mostly the way I'd told Ray. I leaned across the table and talked quietly and intently. Two people I recognized from EPIC walked by our booth and said hello to her, and stared at me as if they couldn't quite place me. The pager the clerk had given us to announce when our order was ready started clattering on the table. I picked it up so I could finish speaking. She began to cry, and I cried, too. When I was done, we searched each other's eyes.

"Let's go get our food," she said. "I need a second."

When we sat back down, we ignored our sandwiches.

"Did you get my phone calls?" she asked. "And the cards I sent?"

I did. I told her I didn't know what to tell her to reassure her without lying anymore, but I wasn't free to talk about my book.

"I felt abandoned," she said. "I thought we were friends."

"We were," I said. "I genuinely cared, and care for you, which was in large part what got me to the point where I decided I had to leave church."

She told me she thought I'd gotten pregnant and was too embarrassed to tell her. "I thought you were going to show up with a baby," she said.

For a long time, she told me, she thought she might have done something to make me think she wouldn't be a supportive friend, that she might judge me. She'd imagined me getting her call, looking at the Caller ID, and snapping my phone shut. Eventually she came to know she hadn't done anything, and she was only left with questions and the scraped-out pain of abandonment.

"I'm sorry I hurt you," I said.

Alice scanned my face thoughtfully. "Did you come up with the idea? Did you pick Jerry Falwell?" I did. "Why him? What was the point—to expose him?"

I told her I had wanted to go undercover in a church where the believers were as different from me as possible, where the challenge of relating to them would be the greatest.

"Why did you spend so much money going to Alaska?" she asked. "To find out if we were being real? If we were who we said we were?"

Not really, I told her. I told her about not understanding evangelism, and wanting to experience it firsthand to get a better grip on it.

"Did you go to Yale?" she asked. We'd become friends on Facebook the day before, and she must have seen that on my page.

When I started at church, I told her, I'd mentioned to Woody that I'd gone to Yale and he seemed suspicious of it. I was afraid to tell anybody after that.

"I probably wouldn't have thought anything," Alice said. "I just would've been like, 'She's the smartest person I know.'"

Did I really have any of the jobs I told her I'd had? Was that really my mother who came to visit? Was my name really Gina Welch?

"I want to tell you I lied about as little as possible to mitigate the effects of lying," I said. "But that doesn't matter because . . ." I searched for the words.

"Because you lied about the most important stuff," Alice said.

"Yes," I said. "Sometimes I thought I shouldn't have lied about anything. That if I'd just presented myself truthfully, and if I'd been more patient and understanding, I would have gotten the same story."

Alice shook her head. "But you wouldn't have known if we were being real with you."

I was surprised to hear her say that.

"Is it fiction or nonfiction?" she asked.

"Nonfiction," I said.

"That means it's true, right?"

It did.

She pursed her lips. "Am I in the book?"

She was, in a major way. "I changed your name to Alice," I said.

"Alice?" she said with digust. "I hate that name!"

We laughed.

She took a deep breath. "I don't feel mad. I know you said I don't have to forgive you, but I don't feel mad at you. I just still feel abandoned. And I'm glad to know you're all right."

I felt sure her feelings would change as she absorbed the news, and I told her that if she became angry later that was okay. I wanted to be available to her for whatever questions or thoughts she had.

She wanted to tell me what had happened to everybody from our Alaska trip. Ingrid and Ethan had a baby, and Connie and Joey, too.

Wyatt and Bethany dated for eight months and then split; he left EPIC for the college-age ministry, the Fellowship.

Pamela and Ursula didn't come anymore.

Carter had bought a town house, though it took him a few months to move out of his parents' place. "For a while he was saying it was because the town house didn't have cable yet," Alice said.

A new member in EPIC had given Lyle a makeover. A soul patch had replaced Lyle's mustache and he was now wearing contacts. He had a fashionable haircut, pants that fit, shoes that went with everything. He went on a mission trip to the Bahamas last year with EPIC, and Alice saw there how much he had to give. "If you gave Lyle a nail gun and told him to stand there for eight hours with that nail gun, he'd do it. The rest of us would complain, but he's a great servant."

Alice had quit her job and was taking some time off. She started riding her bicycle a lot, and began doing triathlons. She had been thinking about happiness and realized that it didn't come from a professional title or money.

I told her I remembered her struggles with her job, and that was actually something I'd included in the book.

"I was going through a lot of change around then," she said. "I still have those notes." She said she was glad I'd put that in.

We chatted for a long time, just the way we used to, sharing ideas and funny stories.

"Even though I'm not mad, I don't know how I'm going to feel in a few days, let alone after I see the book. I might feel violated." She thought about it some more. "But you know, it might be good for me to look back and see what I was going through then. And it just shows you that you should be one way with everybody because you never know who's watching."

She struck me as someone who didn't need to worry about that, because she always seemed to be herself. I told her how much I admired her and again how sorry I was to have lied to her.

"Everything happens for a reason," she said. "You came into my life for a reason, and someday I'll know why."

We promised to keep in touch, and she said she'd like to visit me in Washington.

"You know, we're the same, just on opposite sides of the spectrum," she said. I felt exhilarated to hear it. "You couldn't imagine being a Christian, I can't imagine what it would be like to go six months without going to church. When I go to Virginia Beach to visit my sister, I have to be back for church on Sunday morning. I need that accountability, that time for reflection."

Church had changed me, I said. I loved having that sense of community and also that serious, regular self-inquiry. Our relationship had changed me; feeling so happy in our friendship had made me think differently about Christians. But just like her, I couldn't imagine ever believing anything other than what I believed. I had no choice in that.

"Well, I pray that one day you'll see it is a choice, and He is real," she said.

I thanked her for lunch and for her understanding.

"Is this going to be in the book?" she asked.

"Maybe," I said. "Probably."

She smiled. "You probably didn't think you'd meet someone like me, someone you could be such good friends with. But now you see it doesn't matter if you're Christian or not."

THE POSSIBILITY THAT Ray's amazing forgiveness was an act of prudence, that as he drank from that Big Gulp he was also swallowing back any ugly feelings he might have, knowing now he was on the record—this was not lost on me. Nevertheless, I admired it as a great feat of strength, one that showed the incredible character I knew him to be.

But there didn't seem to be any additional motive behind Alice's forgiveness: it was simply an extraordinary act of understanding. She really wasn't mad, and we've remained close. She came to meet me for an afternoon stroll and dinner in Charlottesville in June, and I showed her around all the places she'd never been before, introduced her to some people I ran into on the street. She didn't blink when I ordered wine with dinner. We got into a discussion about evangelizing to children, disagreed, and moved on. It all felt perfectly natural, as it does with friends.

ACKNOWLEDGMENTS

———

Everything good in this book is the result of support I've received from a network of endlessly generous individuals.

Above all, I want to thank the members of Thomas Road Baptist Church, in particular everyone on the Salt and Light mission to Alaska. You each accepted me with such kindness and grace, and the privilege of participating in your lives truly altered the way I live mine. I only hope that when you read this book you're able to detect the gratitude and admiration I feel for every one of you. Thanks, too, to Jerry Falwell for building the house I made my home for almost two years.

My debt to my family is lifelong and multifaceted. I don't think I can manage appreciation commensurate with my mother's wisdom and all she has given to support my writing. More than anything, I'm lucky to have in her someone who unwaveringly believes in me, but won't hesitate to tell me when I'm wrong. My stepfather, Scott Adams, has provided me with steadfast encouragement and good cheer in the grimmest moments. I have a best friend and a sharp editor in my sister, Shannon Welch. She read early and late drafts, provided me with insight and comfort every week in between, and generated the title for this book when I'd all but given up trying myself. My stepbrothers, Tyler and Caleb Adams, cheered me along.

At Metropolitan my wise, exacting editor, Sara Bershtel, turned rookie drafts into something structured and meaningful. She set bars that seemed beyond reach and then taught me how to get to them. Riva Hocherman's elegant, patient edits make me seem like a better writer in every way. Not only was she able to capture and inhabit the spirit of the book in her direction, but she helped me get control over it myself. I hardly deserve either of these women as editors, and I feel so fortunate to have somehow tricked them into working with me. Megan Quirk was always sweetly available to manage my questions and despair. I also want to thank Nicole Dewey, Melanie DeNardo, and Amanda Schoonmaker for their enthusiastic work. Thanks to Ellis Levine for combing the manuscript.

My agent, Susan Golomb, took me on when I had very little proof that I could do what I had planned, and her faith that I was a good writer made me a better one. Casey Panell provided critical, unswerving support beyond the call of his duties, and Terra Chalberg helped immensely with the logistics.

My brilliant friend Emma Rathbone has been a critical reader, voice of reason, and an inspiring wit. I feel certain this book couldn't exist without her sustaining presence. David Sarno and Rocco DeBonis also generously dedicated their time and intelligence to drafts and gave me encouragement and smart advice. Justin Bailey read my very first pages, showed me just how much I didn't know about Christians, and provided seamless support during the tempestuous glimmer-in-the-eye stage. For assuaging my doubts, resisting my sloppy thinking, and lending the kind of patient ear I probably should have had to pay for, thank you Katey Shirey, Reid Collier, Heather Tanton, Brian Weinberg, Ryan Leone, Erin Brown, Eleanor Henderson, Ashlee Ferlito, Jeffrey Engelhardt, and Sandy Han. I'm grateful to Pamela and Dale Hetherington, who housed me in their nursery on my early trips to Lynchburg. My colleagues in the English Department at George Washington University have doled out generous helpings of advice and support.

I owe a great debt to Robert Stone, who took my writing seriously before I had the courage to do so myself. Conversations with some truly great intellects shaped my thinking and elevated me to new plateaus of understanding: John Casey, Deborah Eisenberg, Chris Tilghman, Ann Beattie, Wallace Shawn, Jamie Ross, Lisa Russ Spaar, Sydney Blair, Boyd Zenner, and Kevin and Gail Buckley. Thank you all.

For their scholarship on evangelical Christians, I'm grateful for the work of William Martin, Mel White, Christian Smith, Jeffrey L. Sheler, Frances FitzGerald, Jim Wallis, Hanna Rosin, Frank Schaeffer, Lauren Sandler, Michelle Goldberg, and Chris Hedges.

All mistakes and shortcomings in this book are my own.

INDEX

ABOUT THE AUTHOR

———

GINA WELCH, a graduate of Yale University, teaches English at George Washington University. Her writing has previously appeared in *Meridian*, *Time Out New York*, and *Playboy*. *In the Land of Believers* is her first book.